The PSALMS
St. Joseph
NEW CATHOLIC VERSION

The PSALMS

St. Joseph

NEW CATHOLIC VERSION

WITH HELPFUL APPENDIX
An Index of Sunday Responsorial Psalms
and a Table of the Four-Week Psalter
for Morning and Evening Prayer

CATHOLIC BOOK PUBLISHING CO.
New Jersey

IMPRIMATUR:

✠ Most Reverend Joseph A. Fiorenza

President, United States Conference of Catholic Bishops

August 16, 2001

RESCRIPT

In accord with canon 825, §1 of the Code of Canon Law, the United States Conference of Catholic Bishops hereby approves for publication *The Psalms, New Catholic Version,* published by the Catholic Book Publishing Company. This translation of the Psalms is intended for private use and study only and may never be used for liturgical purposes.

(T-665)

CONTENTS

ABBREVIATIONS OF BOOKS OF THE BIBLE

Acts—Acts of the Apostles
Am—Amos
Bar—Baruch
1 Chr—1 Chronicles
2 Chr—2 Chronicles
Col—Colossians
1 Cor—1 Corinthians
2 Cor—2 Corinthians
Dan—Daniel
Deut—Deuteronomy
Eccl—Ecclesiastes
Eph—Ephesians
Est—Esther
Ex—Exodus
Ezek—Ezekiel
Ezr—Ezra
Gal—Galatians
Gen—Genesis
Hab—Habakkuk
Hag—Haggai
Heb—Hebrews
Hos—Hosea
Isa—Isaiah
Jas—James

Jdg—Judges
Jer—Jeremiah
Jn—John
1 Jn—1 John
2 Jn—2 John
3 Jn—3 John
Job—Job
Joel—Joel
Jon—Jonah
Jos—Joshua
Jud—Judith
Jude—Jude
1 Ki—1 Kings
2 Ki—2 Kings
Lam—Lamentations
Lev—Leviticus
Lk—Luke
1 Mac—1 Maccabees
2 Mac—2 Maccabees
Mal—Malachi
Mic—Micah
Mk—Mark
Mt—Matthew
Nah—Nahum
Neh—Nehemiah

Num—Numbers
Ob—Obadiah
1 Pet—1 Peter
2 Pet—2 Peter
Phil—Philippians
Philem—Philemon
Prov—Proverbs
Ps(s)—Psalms
Rev—Revelation
Rom—Romans
Ru—Ruth
1 Sam—1 Samuel
2 Sam—2 Samuel
Sir—Sirach
Song—Song of Songs
1 Thes—1 Thessalonians
2 Thes—2 Thessalonians
1 Tim—1 Timothy
2 Tim—2 Timothy
Tit—Titus
Tob—Tobit
Wis—Wisdom
Zec—Zechariah
Zep—Zephaniah

NOTE: For greater clarity and convenience, the footnotes and cross-references are printed at the bottom of each page and cross-indexed in the text itself. An *asterisk* (*) in the text indicates that there is a *footnote* to the text in question. Each footnote is in turn clearly marked with the number of the chapter and verse to which it pertains. Similarly, a *superior letter* (ᵃ) in the text indicates that there is a *cross-reference* to a particular verse. The reference itself is also clearly marked with the same letter. Hence, the reader is always aware of a footnote or cross-reference simply by *reading the text.*

[ ] Indicates a gloss   Par = Parallel passages
/ = Divides verse
a, b, c, d, e, f   Identify the lines of any verse in successive order.

SIMPLE KEY TO REFERENCES

Gen 1:1 refers to the Book of Genesis, chapter 1, verse 1.
Gen 1:1f refers to the Book of Genesis, chapter 1, verse 1, and the following verse (2).
Gen 1:1-10 refers to the Book of Genesis, chapter 1, verses 1 to 10 inclusive.
Gen 1:1-10, 14 refers to the Book of Genesis, chapter 1, verses 1 to 10 inclusive and verse 14.
Gen 1:1—2:3 refers to the Book of Genesis, chapter 1, verse 1, to chapter 2, verse 3 inclusive.
Gen 1:1; 2:3 refers to the Book of Genesis, chapter 1, verse 1, and chapter 2, verse 3.

PREFACE

In the life of Christians, there can never be too many translations of the Psalter. The Psalms are the prayer of God's assembly, the public prayer par excellence of the People of God. No prayer of Israel is comparable to the Psalter because of its universal character. The idea of the unity of the chosen people's prayer guided its elaboration as well as its adoption by the Church.

The Psalms may be looked upon as the prayer-book of the Holy Spirit. Over the long centuries of Israel's existence, the Spirit of God inspired the psalmists (typified by King David) to compose magnificent prayers and hymns for every religious desire and need, mood and feeling. Thus, the Psalms have great power to raise minds to God, to inspire devotion, to evoke gratitude in favorable times, and to bring consolation and strength in times of trial.

Furthermore, in giving us the Psalter, which sums up the major aspects of our relationship to our Creator and Redeemer, God puts into our mouths the words he wishes to hear, and indicates to us the dimensions of prayer:

"The Psalms call to mind the truths revealed by God to the chosen people, which were at one time frightening and at another filled with wonderful tenderness; they keep repeating and fostering the hope of the promised Redeemer, which in ancient times was kept alive with song, either around the hearth or in the stately temple; they show forth in splendid light the prophesied glory of Jesus Christ: first, his supreme and eternal power, then his lowly coming to this earthly exile, his kingly dignity and priestly power, and finally his beneficent labors, and the shedding of his blood for our redemption.

"In a similar way they express the joy, the bitterness, the hope and fear of our hearts and our desire of loving God and hoping in him alone, and our mystic ascent to divine tabernacles" (Pope Pius XII, *Mediator Dei*, no. 148).

In short, the Psalms constitute an inexhaustible treasury of prayers for every occasion and mood in a format that is true to the whole tradition of the history of salvation.

Jesus and the Psalms

Jesus often prayed the Psalms. At the age of twelve, as a pilgrim on the way to the temple in Jerusalem, he sang the Psalms meant for this journey: "I rejoiced when they said to me, 'Let us go to the house of the LORD.' And finally our feet are standing at your gates, O Jerusalem" (Ps 122:1f).

The Gospels tell us that Jesus frequented the synagogue of Nazareth on the Sabbath and that consequently he took part in the reading of the Scriptures and the recitation of the Psalms.

Again, Jesus took part in the singing of the great Alleluia Psalm with its refrain, "His love endures forever" (Ps 136).

If we read carefully the account of the Passion of Jesus, we glimpse citations from many Psalms; finally, his last words on the Cross were supplied by the Psalms: "My God, my God, why have you forsaken me?" (Ps 22:1) and "Into your hands I commend my spirit" (Ps 31:6)

Under the guidance of the Holy Spirit, the first Christian community made the Psalms its own, applying to the Lord and to itself what was said in the Psalms about the People of God, Jerusalem, the king, the temple, the promised land, the kingdom, and the Covenant.

Jewish prayers become the prayers of the Church; the dead and risen Lord is the new

Passover; the Eucharist is the everlasting Covenant.

Thus, Christians who pray the Psalms should be aware of their total meaning, especially their Messianic meaning, which was the reason for the Church's introduction of the Psalter into her prayer. This Messianic meaning was fully revealed in the New Testament and indeed was publicly acknowledged by Christ the Lord when he said to his apostles: "Everything written about me in the Law of Moses, the Prophets, and the Psalms must be fulfilled" (Lk 24:44). The best known example of this Messianic meaning is the dialogue in Matthew's Gospel on the Messiah as Son of David and David's Lord (22:44ff): there Psalm 110 is interpreted as Messianic.

Following this line of thought, the Fathers of the Church saw the whole Psalter as a prophecy of Christ and the Church and explained it in this sense; for the same reason the Psalms have been chosen for use in the sacred Liturgy.

Prayer Book of the Church

Some may wonder why the Church makes use of Psalms from ancient times in order to pray in our day? Isn't she capable of creating new prayers? In truth, the creativity of the Church is evidenced in many other ways. However, she knows that there is no need for new Psalms since these were the work of the Holy Spirit. They are *inspired prayers*, appropriate for all times.

The Church knows and teaches that there is only one economy of salvation and it includes both the Old and the New Covenant. The Psalter is *the* prayer book for this entire history—containing both thanksgiving for the wonders that God has already accomplished and expectation for the promises of the Kingdom.

Naturally, then, she invites us to pray the Psalms with understanding. This means reading all the historical or prophetic accounts to which they allude. Such a study certainly is in accord with the Biblical study of them made by Jesus with the disciples on the way to Emmaus (Lk 24:44-45).

Perhaps no one used the Psalms in this sense more than St. Augustine. He pored over the Psalms till he practically knew them by heart. His all-around knowledge of them led him to use the Psalms as his own.

The opening words of his classic *Confessions* are woven out of the Psalms: "Great are you, O Lord, and worthy of praise; great is your power and incalculable is your wisdom." Cardinal Michael Pellegrino pointed out that these words are formed from a combination of four Psalms (47:1; 95:4; 144:5; 146:5).

This use of the Psalms shows that St. Augustine found in them the most fitting words to express his religious feeling at those moments when it was most intense. The Italian Scripture scholar Gianfranco Ravasi has noted that out of 60,000 Biblical quotations used by St. Augustine in his works 25,000 came from the Old Testament and of those *11,500 were from the Psalms.*

We should follow the example of the Bishop of Hippo and be suffused with the Psalms so that the Bible becomes our history. We enter anew into the Biblical tradition to relive the experience of the Exodus, of the departure into Exile, and of the Return.

We rediscover in our own history the actualization of the history of God with human beings. God always says the same thing. It is up to us to discover this unique Word beneath the everyday events.

This is how our praying of the Psalms can become concrete and can lead us to a surer unraveling of the ways God acts in the world.

Praying with the Psalms in the Name of Christ

Christ made his own the prayer of the Psalms. He made his own the cries, the suffering, and the despair of the Psalms. He purified, transfigured, and fulfilled the cry of his people and the prayer of the poor.

The Word incarnate assumed the human condition of sinful human beings with its trials and infirmities (except sin). He experienced moments of exultation in the presence of God, human beings, and creation.

At the same time, he also experienced the anguish brought on by the apparent absence or indifference of God and the wrath of enemies. He experienced physical trials (fatigue, suffering, and death) with the moral trials that accompany them.

He experienced all the feelings of those who prayed the Psalms and all the situations underlying their prayers. He had no need of inventing formulas to pray in these diverse situations, for the Holy Spirit had prepared for him human formulas patterned after his celestial chant.

Jesus used the Psalms for his prayer from the first instant of his life until his death on the Cross. He had recourse to the Psalms for the liturgy of his supreme offering. And he used a verse from the Psalms as his last word: "Into your hands I commend my spirit" (Psalm 31:6; Luke 23:46).

Jesus placed himself on high, drawing all people with and after him. He became part of sacred history and made its prayer his own. He inhabited the Psalms.

Since he has effectively expressed his piety in the Psalms, Jesus invites us to see in them the faithful mirror of the sentiments and motions of his soul, the mirror that permits us to grasp his spiritual life. The Psalms enable us to complete and make precise the spiritual portrait that the Gospels give us of Christ.

Thus, the entire Psalter presents Christ to us—his voice, his history, from his birth to his Resurrection. All the Psalms refer to him. By praying them, we receive a kind of *Fifth Gospel: the Gospel of the Holy Spirit.*

As mentioned above, the Fathers of the Church believed that every Psalm speaks to us of Christ. On this point, too, we can call upon St. Augustine as their spokesperson:

"To announce Christ, the Scriptures make use of figures; this veil that hid the truths contained in the ancient books was to be removed when the Truth in person appeared on earth. Hence, when we read the Psalms, the Prophets, and the Law, written before the coming of our Lord Jesus Christ, our sole concern should be to *discern Christ and to know Christ*" (*Commentary on Psalm 98*).

Praying with the Psalms in the Name of the Church

The Church has made her own the prayer of the Psalms. She makes use of the Psalms in the Liturgy of the Hours and in the Sacraments, especially the Eucharist. This is altogether appropriate since the Church is the Body of Christ.

As St. Augustine indicated, praying with the Psalms is a case of praying in two voices: that of Christ and that of the Church, the Head and the Body. "Sometimes, the Head alone speaks; at other times he speaks in the name of his Body, the Church, spread out through the whole earth" (*Commentary on Psalm 37:6*).

We should strive to pray with the Psalms in the name of the Church. If we do so, difficulties disappear when we notice in prayer that the feelings of our hearts are different from the emotions expressed in the Psalm—for example, when a Psalm of joy finds us sad and overcome with grief or a Psalm of sorrow finds us full of joy.

If we pray in this way, we can always find a reason for joy or sadness, for the saying of the Apostles applies in this case too: "Rejoice with those who rejoice; weep with those who weep" (Rom 12:15). In this way, our human frailty, wounded by self-love, is healed in that degree of love in which our mind and voice are in harmony.

In the Psalms we recognize the voice of the Church, the Apostles and the Martyrs. The whole Church, throughout her history, presents herself before God like a single supplicant, immense and perpetual.

In the Church, Christ continues his Passion, just as he continues his prayer. There is the passion of the Martyrs, the passion of human distress, the passion of the poor, overwhelmed with the universal suffering that causes the Psalmist to cry out: "[They] . . . seek my life" (Psalm 63:10).

Praying with the Psalms in Our Own Name

A third way of praying with the Psalms is in our own name. By bringing our own experience of life to the praying of the Psalms we make these ancient prayers our own. Because our life is constantly changing, we bring something fresh to the Psalms every time we pray them.

In praying the Psalms this way, we must realize that God not only speaks to us but also inspires our response. In the words of St. Augustine, "the Psalter is the voice of the Spirit of God—if he did not inspire these words in us, we would not say them. . . . In the final analysis, they are our words, for they express our wretchedness, and at the same time they are not since they are a gift of the Spirit" (*Commentary on Psalm 26, 1*).

Thus, praying with the Psalms also entails a *listening*. We pray them with wisdom, that is, we discern clearly in them what we must say or sing. If we do, we will pray them with understanding, and our words will be a true prayer.

We must approach the Psalms as being human words, the utterances of very incarnate human beings confronted with the risks of human life. Through them we rediscover our whole humanity with its struggles, rebellions, anguish, and even salvation and joy—life and death. We come to understand that everything is a way to God.

If we enter into the Psalter, it will become an opportunity to rediscover our own humanity: its anguish, its rebellion, its violence, and its reconciliation as well.

In the Psalms, people have a body: a mouth to cry out, a heart to love, arms to stretch out, and legs to dance. The Psalms allow us to use our bodies as expressions of ourselves: of our cry, our fear, our death, and doubtless our resurrection. They restore to us the primary instrument of prayer that God has given us. They teach us to pray with our bodies as well as with our words.

Thus, in the final analysis, we hope to draw from the Psalms spiritual food for faith, hope, and love. On this point, St. Augustine is once more on the mark:

"Every page of Scripture recommends to us faithful patience in present evils, firm hope in future goals, and ardent love for the One whom we do not see so that we may hold fast to him when we do see him" (*Commentary on Psalm 91*).

A St. Joseph Edition

It is a well known fact that different translations of the Psalms (like different translations of any subject) bring different meanings for each one of us. The Bible and especially the Psalms are so full of meaning that we can rightly say no single edition will do them full justice.

Hence, it has become customary for Christians to make use of many translations of the sacred books in order to get to know the Bible and pray with its text.

Therefore, we have thought it worthwhile to make available a Catholic Version of the Psalms in the renowned and exclusive format of our St. Joseph Editions of Bibles and Missals. The St. Joseph Edition is an editorial system developed over a span of fifty years. It consists in a series of features intended to ensure that a text (particularly a biblical or liturgical text) is user friendly, leading to greater readability and easier understanding.

The textual features or format in the present case are a large readable typeface, additional headings or titles, and a full measure extension for long lines of poetry that clearly indicates when a line has a runover. It also includes a general introduction to the Psalter, Psalm introductions, copious cross-references, and pastoral notes. For greater clarity and convenience, the footnotes and cross-references are printed at the bottom of each page and cross-indexed in the text itself.

An asterisk (*) in the text indicates that there is a footnote to the text in question. Each footnote is in turn clearly marked with the number of the Psalm and the verse to which it pertains. Similarly, a superior letter (ᵃ) in the text indicates that there is a cross-reference to a particular verse. The reference itself is also clearly marked with the same letter. Hence, the reader is always aware of a helpful footnote or cross-reference, simply by reading the text.

Variations in Numbering

The Psalter contains 150 Psalms in the Hebrew and the Latin Vulgate. Their numbering, however, is slightly different since the Vulgate joins Pss 9 and 10 of the Hebrew into a single psalm, and again 114 and 115 of the Hebrew into a single psalm, while dividing 116 and 147 of the Hebrew into two psalms. The numbering is as follows:

Hebrew		Vulgate
1—8	=	1—8
9	=	9:1-21
10	=	9:22-39
11—113	=	10—112
114	=	113:1-8
115	=	113:9-26
116:1-9	=	114
116:10-19	=	115
117—146	=	116—145
147:1-11	=	146
147:12-20	=	147
148—150	=	148—150

Most Catholic translations after 1943 (in accord with the recommendation of Pope Pius XII in his ground-breaking encyclical *Divino Afflante Spiritu* to translate from the original languages—Hebrew, Aramaic, and Greek—instead of the Latin Vulgate) make use of the Hebrew numbering of the Psalms. Those completed before 1943 usually have the Vulgate numbering. This fact is important especially when Catholics desire to locate the Psalms used in the Liturgy.

Liturgical English texts sometimes follow the Latin Vulgate since they are a translation from the Latin liturgical books. Hence, to find the text of the Responsorial Psalm for any Sunday Mass, one must be guided by the above chart to get the number correct.

However, there is also a second difference in numbering—the enumeration of the verses. All but

35 of the Psalms begin with "superscriptions" (sometimes called "titles"). These contain the name of the supposed author of the psalm, the circumstances of its composition, a note about its liturgical use, and obscure phrases about its melody or its musical accompaniment. Most Catholic Bibles have traditionally assigned a verse number to these superscriptions. In some, however, these superscriptions are not assigned a number.

This means that, in most cases, the numbers that give the references for psalm verses used in the Liturgy are at least one digit higher than the corresponding verses in versions that do not number the superscriptions. For the convenience of our readers, one part of the Appendix lists the correct verse numbers for the Responsorial Psalm for every Sunday celebration. Another part of the Appendix lists the psalms in the four-week Psalter for Morning and Evening Prayer of the Liturgy of the Hours.

We trust this new edition of the Psalms will lead many into a better understanding of the Psalms and a fuller knowledge of Jesus Christ the incarnate Word, of whom the Psalms so faithfully testify.

INTRODUCTION

A Liturgical Anthology

Many prayers and liturgical chants are scattered throughout the Bible, but the most substantial part of Israel's praise and petition is to be found in the one hundred and fifty poetical compositions called "Psalms" after their Greek name, with "Psalter" designating the entire collection (*psaltêrion,* the stringed instrument that accompanied the singing of the psalms). In Hebrew, on the other hand, the hymns, which form the most considerable part, have given the entire collection the name *Sefer Tehillim* (Books of Praises). The Psalter, in more or less its present form, was already available to the liturgical authorities in Jerusalem during the period of the second temple (third century B.C.).

By analogy with the five Books of the Pentateuch (the Torah), the Psalter was divided, quite arbitrarily, into five books; this division seems to go back to the third century B.C. On the other hand, three main sections can be distinguished according to the name used for God ("the LORD," *Yahweh,* in the first and third sections; "God," *Elohim,* in the second); the three sections are Psalms 1—41, 42—89, and 90—150.

There are also psalms that are part of less important pre-existing collections belonging to groups of cantors, such as those of Asaph (73—83) or Korah (42—50; 84—88), who had been charged with organizing the liturgical functions. In addition, the Psalter includes other distinguishable collections: the pilgrim psalms (120—134), songs of the kingdom (93—100), the canticles of Zion and the Alleluia hymns (113—119, 135—136, and 146—150).

More than one psalm already had a history and life of its own before being given its definitive text and definitive place in the Psalter as we now have it. In fact, some very ancient psalms were used and reread from century to century, adapted to new circumstances, and often revised (e.g., Pss 2 and 110).

At the beginning of each psalm the Hebrew text provides some introductory notes that are still rather mysterious to us. These are the "superscriptions" or "titles." They indicate the presumed author of the psalm, the historical circumstances that supposedly inspired it, some instructions on the musical instruments to be used, and so on. Some critics think that these superscriptions are ancient, perhaps composed before the Exile; others think that they are much later additions, inserted when the collection had already been completed. In any case, rather than giving the objective meaning of the psalm, the superscription shows how it was understood and sung at a time far removed from its origin.

Many superscriptions attribute a given psalm to David (all those of the first book, except for 32; and others). There is no doubt that the royal musician and poet who danced before the Ark and organized Israel's worship gave a decisive impulse to the liturgy and sacred songs, and that some of his compositions have been preserved (see 2 Sam 1:19-27; 23:1-7).

Moreover, as head of Israel, David represented the entire people. Once the monarchy disappeared, he became, after the Exile, the model for believers and the type of the future Messiah, of the Jesus who would speak in the name of all the people and even of all humankind. For this reason, even if David did not himself compose any of the hundred and fifty psalms, at least in their present form (as some believe), the memory of him certainly inspired the cantors, who put his name over their own liturgical compositions.

Various Attitudes toward God

It is difficult to discern any particular order in the present sequence of the Psalter. Prayers of entreaty stand side by side with the most enthusiastic thanksgivings, just as in real life. The most that can be stated is that the burden of misfortune weighs more heavily in the first half of the Book, while praise becomes more sustained toward the end of it. In the commentary that follows we try unobtrusively to suggest this rhythm.

Each psalm will therefore be viewed in itself without trying to establish any relationship of continuity.* This does not mean that the Psalms cannot be grouped into some typical categories, depending on the ideas and emotions they express, on the liturgical needs they meet, and even on their rhythm and structure. Identification of the category to which a psalm belongs can contribute greatly to understanding it.

The Hebrew name for the Psalter is "Book of Praises," and in fact there are many hymns of praise. The Alleluia psalms for the most part belong to this category. Another homogeneous group of psalms acclaim the Lord as King of the people and of the universe; these are the psalms of the kingdom, the Messianic hymns (47; 93; 96; 97; 98; 99; 145). Still another group voices the love of the people for Jerusalem, the mountain on which God dwells and on which the dynasty of its Messianic King is perpetuated; we call these the canticles of Zion (24; 46; 48; 78; 84; 87; 122).

The songs of thanksgiving expressed wonder and gratitude. Petitions, complaints, and prayers of repentance and sorrow are perhaps the most frequent subjects of the Psalms. Some songs by unhappy singers became psalms of trust and gratitude (e.g., 13; 16; 22; 23; 31; 32; etc.).

The sapiential psalms are somewhat didactic in tone. The wise men in question endeavor to penetrate the riddle of life and unveil its meaning.

•The dating of the psalms given in this volume is approximate. Most scholars agree that dating them is very difficult and open to a great deal of discussion.

Finally, there are the royal psalms: songs and prayers that focus on the king and were perhaps used, at least initially, for the festival of consecration or the anniversary of enthronement. Like the psalms of the kingdom, in the course of time these were reread in a Messianic perspective.

We should also note that some psalms turn the history of Israel into a prophecy in which the lessons of the past are solemnly proclaimed on the occasion of some great feast (78; 105; 106).

Hebrew Poetry

Verses in Hebrew poetry are composed of two (sometimes three or more) parts, which are called "stichs," the second of them being in some way symmetrical with the first. This is the characteristic element in all Hebrew poetry and is called "parallelism." Parallelism can take any of three forms. One is *synonymy*, which is the most common form; here the same idea is repeated in different words (e.g., Ps 114:4: "The mountains skipped like rams,/the hills like lambs of the flock"; Ps 49:2: "Hear this, all you peoples;/listen carefully, all you inhabitants of the world").

A second is *antithesis*, with the contrast putting the same idea into relief (e.g., "A wise son brings joy to his father,/but a foolish son is a mother's grief"—Prov 10:1); this is, consequently, the form most used in sententious sayings.

A third form, which lends itself to great variety, is a *parallelism in a broad sense*, when the second stich simply completes the first (e.g., Ps 3:5: "Whenever I cry aloud to the LORD,/he answers me from his holy mountain"). In this third form, then, each of the two stichs often presents part of the idea, so that the entire thought is given by the two together. Thus in the example given from Proverbs the point is not that the good son gives joy to the father alone, while the bad son gives pain to the mother alone, but rather that each of the two sons obviously brings joy or sorrow to the "parents." So too, in Psalm 92:3, "to proclaim your kindness in the morning/and your faithfulness during the night" means to extol the divine goodness all day long, or "night and day."

Although verses composed of two stichs are by far the most common, there are, as was said above, verses containing three or more stichs. In fact, the Psalter begins with a three-membered verse: "Blessed is the man who does not walk in the counsel of the wicked/or stand in the way of sinners/or sit in the company of scoffers." If we look closely, it seems clear that since "scoffers" is parallel to "wicked" and "sinners," it is a synonym for these, "scoffing" being a form of wickedness and sin.

Generally speaking, attention to parallelism is a great help for grasping the precise meaning of a passage. When we read: "O God, endow the king with your judgment,/the son of kings with your righteousness" (Ps 72:1), we will not think of two different persons for whom two different favors are being asked, but that the king in question belongs to a royal dynasty.

As can be readily inferred from what has been said, there is no question of having a set number of syllables, as in our own classical meters. Meter is indeed not lacking, but it is meter after the fashion of modern poetry, which is concerned with rhythm alone. That is, a verse must have a certain number of accented syllables, but there is no other requirement. The number of such syllables can vary from two to five; in this last case, the rhythm is usually 3 + 2, that is, the second half is shorter (elegiac rhythm). Between two accented syllables there are ordinarily one, two, or three unaccented syllables.

The conclusions reached on this subject by modern scholars do not permit us to restore the origi-

nal rhythmic beauty of Biblical poetic compositions by accurately dividing the stichs or even the
verses, which not infrequently have been wrongly
divided in the traditional Masoretic Text.

Scholars have not yet reached unanimity in regard to strophes or stanzas; it is generally admitted
that they exist, but in practice it is not easy to dis-
tinguish them.

The External Form

Some psalms are acrostic or alphabetical; that is,
their verses (or strophes) start with a word that
begins with one of the twenty-two letters of the Hebrew alphabet (in alphabetical order). This device,
like others common in poetry (rhyme, strophes,
etc.), has for its purpose to heighten merit, but it
can also result in embarrassment from the viewpoint of artistic inspiration and literary perfection.

Hope Stimulated by Remembrance of the Past

The history of the Psalms is ongoing. It is true, of
course, that the Psalter reflects the spiritual adventure of the ancient People of God, with its lights
and shadows. But the Jewish tradition began at a
quite early date to regard this Book as the herald
of a unique religious experience that looked to the
Messiah as witness and privileged beneficiary of
the divine work of salvation. Thus the entire
Psalter, which is a synthesis of the Old Testament
in the form of poetry and prayer, becomes a Messianic prayer. The Christian tradition has therefore
legitimately regarded it as also a prophecy and
prefiguration of Jesus, who suffers before entering
into his glory (Ps 22:19 and Jn 19:24; Ps 2:1-2 and
Acts 4:25-27; etc.).

Because they had been used by Jesus and were
fervently recited with new understanding by the first
Christian community, which had emerged from Judaism, the Psalms automatically became the prayer

of the Church, as they had been that of Israel; from that time on, they have been continually prayed by the Church. The new and spiritual Jerusalem sees partially realized in itself the glory of Zion, which the chosen people saw as still in the future.

There is no feast or celebration or reading of the Word of God for which the Liturgy cannot find appropriate expressions or at least allusions in the Psalms. In praying the Psalms, the children of the Church express through these imperfect but irreplaceable songs from another age the human and supernatural experience of sorrow and joy that they, the new People of God, also have as they travel toward the radiant goal of the history of the Church and humanity: "Zion, perfect in beauty," where "God shines forth" (Ps 50:2 and Rev 21:2).

Calls for Vengeance?

At the same time, however, many of these songs are filled with curses and calls for vengeance, sometimes expressing a cruelty that is truly disconcerting (5:11; 31:18; 54:7; 83:14; 109:6f; 139:19f). We are dismayed to read: "Happy will he be who seizes your babies and smashes them against a rock!" (137:9). But we ought not be astonished by such language. The Psalms date from a time when the Gospel was not yet known; when placed on the lips of those being persecuted, they voice an urgent appeal for divine justice. (See note on Ps 5:11 and introduction to Ps 35.)

On the other hand, these vengeance psalms have a deeper meaning: at one time, they struck out against the enemies of the chosen people, the "heathen," that is, the enemies of God; today they give voice to a different hatred, that which Christians ought to have for the evil that Jesus intended to destroy by his death and against which Paul the apostle exhorts us to fight (Eph 6:11-13).

PROLOGUE — PSALMS 1–2*

PSALM 1*

True Happiness

¹ Blessed is the man
　　who does not walk in the counsel of the
　　　　wicked,
　　nor stand in the way of sinners,
　　　　nor sit in the company of scoffers.*ᵃ

---

a Pss 10:2-11; 26:4-5, 9; 40:5; 51:15; 89:16; 128:4; Gen 49:6; Deut 33:29; Job 21:16; Prov 1:22; 4:18-19; Isa 28:14; Jer 15:17; Hos 7:5; Mt 7:13-14.

Pss 1—2 These first two psalms are regarded as a preface to the entire Psalter. Collections of psalms that were originally different were gradually re-grouped to comprise the Psalter as we have it; the psalms attributed to David (3—41 and 51—72), the songs of Ascents (120—134), and the chants of the Hallel (105—107, 111—118, 135—150) constitute the most remarkable of these primary collections. But as presently arranged in our Bible, the Book of Psalms is divided like the Pentateuch (the first five Books of the Bible that are called the Law) into five unequal parts, each of which ends with a formula of acclamation.

Ps 1 At the entrance to the collection of the Psalms, we are immediately placed before a life-choice: God or nothingness. This option imposes itself on us throughout all the pages of the Bible. In the historical accounts, law codes, prophecies, prayers, and meditative texts, a line of division is set forth. It distinguishes between righteousness and impiety, self-reliance and faith, good and evil, wickedness and love. The words are varied and the experiences are numerous in order to bear witness to this rupture.

They mark a division between peoples, between individuals, and between the acts and projects of our lives. Appearances may produce change and daily contradict the faithful's overly naive dreams about prosperity; however, one fact remains: a life of righteousness and truth is a path of happiness, a path to God, whereas those who deaden their conscience for their own ends have no other future but ruin.

Every time a reader prays a psalm, he or she is forced to choose between the "two ways" (see Deut 30:15; Prov 4:18f; Jer 21:8), the difference between which is underscored by Jesus (see Mt 7:13; 25). The righteous are blessed for they are separated from sin, Bible-centered, and prosperous. Unlike them are the wicked who are doomed to judgment.

1:1 The Psalter begins by declaring the blessedness of the righteous (v. 1) and concludes by summoning all creation to praise God in heaven and on earth (Ps 150). Human beings are made for happiness, and the revealed moral law is oriented toward that happiness. *Blessed:* the happy state of life in fellowship with God, revering him and obeying his laws (see Pss 94:12; 112:1; 119:1f; 128:1; Prov 29:18). *Scoffers:* those who reject God and his law (see Prov 1:10-19).

² Rather, his delight is in the law of the Lord,*
and on that law he meditates day and
night.*b*

³ He is like a tree planted near streams of
water,*c*
which bears fruit in its season,
and whose leaves never wither.*
In the same way,
everything he does will prosper.

⁴ This is not true of the wicked,
for they are like chaff that the wind blows
away.*d*

⁵ Therefore, the wicked will not stand firm at
the judgment,*
nor sinners in the assembly of the righteous.*e*

⁶ For the Lord watches over* the way of the
righteous,
but the way of the wicked will perish.*f*

---

b Pss 112:1; 119:16, 35; Jos 1:8; Sir 39:1; Ezek 11:20; Rom 7:22.—c Pss
52:10; 92:13-15; Jer 17:8; Ezek 47:12.—d Pss 35:5; 83:14-16; Job 21:18;
Isa 40:24; Jer 13:24.—e Pss 5:5; 35:18; 82:1; 111:1.—f Pss 37:18; 112:10;
121:5; Nah 1:7.

1:2 *The law of the Lord:* either the first five Books of the Bible, known as the
Torah (law), or divine instruction. *Meditates:* literally, "murmurs," i.e., assimi-
lates the law of life that incarnates the presence of God and teaches the believer
how to attain joyous intimacy with the Lord. Indeed, the law is a judgment of God
and a happiness for human beings.

1:3 *Like a tree . . . never wither:* the righteous are able to withstand the rigors
of life. Like a tree planted on fertile ground, they are able to enhance their spiritual life.

1:4 *Like chaff . . . blows away:* the wicked are completely powerless spiritually,
for they are like chaff that is easily borne away, even by the slightest breeze.

1:5 At the judgment—either God's judgment of the wicked during life (see Pss
76:7f; 130:3; Ezr 9:15) or his judgment of them at the end of time (see Mal 3:2;
Mt 25:31-46; Rev 6:17)—the wicked will bear the brunt of their misdeeds. *Righteous:* a name for the faithful People of God, i.e., those who reverence God and
diligently strive to carry out his laws in every phase of their lives.

1:6 *Watches over:* the Lord takes an avid interest in their conduct (see Pss
31:7f; 37:18; Gen 18:19; Am 3:2; Nah 1:7). *The way of the wicked will perish:* a
similar fate is set forth for the wicked in Ps 112:10: "the desires of the wicked
will be fruitless." The theme of the two ways has already been found in Deut
30:15f and Jer 21:8; it will be taken up again in Prov 4:18f and Mt 7:13.

PSALM 2*

Universal Reign of the Messiah

1 Why do the nations rage
    and the peoples devise futile plots?g
2 The kings of the earth rise up,
    and the princes conspire together
  against the LORD
    and against his Anointed One:*h
3 "Let us finally break their shackles
    and cast away their chains from us."i

4 The one who is enthroned in heaven laughs;
    the LORD mocks their plans.j
5 Then he rebukes them in his anger
    and terrifies them in his wrath, sayingk

---

g Ps 21:12; Prov 24:2; Acts 4:25-28; Rev 11:18.—h Pss 48:5; 83:6; Acts 4:25-26; Rev 19:19.—i Ps 149:8; 2 Sam 3:34; Job 36:8.—j Pss 37:13; 59:9; Prov 1:26; Wis 4:18; Isa 37:16; 40:15-17; 66:1.—k Pss 6:2; 21:10; 27:9; 38:1; 79:6; 90:7; 110:5.

Ps 2 Although the surrounding peoples are rising up, the People of God are enthroning a new king; empowered by God's assistance, he shatters the coalition of their foes. This is the drama evoked in the present psalm, and it recurs more than once in the history of Israel. Thus, this poem found its place in a liturgy for royal consecration, for each king was a "messiah," that is, a man anointed with the sacred unction in the name of God. But the Prophets and the New Testament enlarged these perspectives. Hence, this ancient text evokes the whole drama of the world. It proclaims the sovereignty of God in the midst of the tumult of peoples and our human rebellions.

Behind the king of v. 6 can be glimpsed the Messiah (the Christ), a descendant of David and the Son of God, who will save his people (see Isa 9:5-6; Acts 4:25; 13:33; Heb 1:5). There is a premonition of the struggle that will take place at the end of time (see Ezek 38—39; Dan 12), a struggle already begun in the Passion of Jesus and in the persecutions of the Church (see Acts 4:25-28). But the psalm also expresses the hope of a final conversion of all the nations as they at last acknowledge the Lord (see Isa 45; Rev 19:15). God's plan will be achieved in the glory of the Messianic Kingdom.

2:2 *Anointed One:* in Hebrew, *Mashiah* (whence the word "Messiah"), which in the Greek translation is *Christos;* it referred originally to the Davidic King but ultimately to Jesus Christ. This phrase has given rise to two titles of Jesus: "Messiah" from the Hebrew and "Christ" from the Greek. In Israel the power of office was bestowed by anointing both on kings (see Jdg 9:8; 1 Sam 9:16; 16:12f) and on high priests (see Lev 8:12; Num 3:3).

6 "I myself have anointed my king[l]
on Zion, my holy mountain."*

7 I will proclaim the decree* of the LORD:
He said to me, "You are my son;
this day I have begotten you."[m]
8 Simply make the request of me,
and I will give you the nations as your inheritance,[n]
and the ends of the earth as your possession.*
9 You will rule them with an iron scepter;
you will shatter them like a potter's vessel.*[o]

10 Therefore, O kings, pay heed;
take warning, O rulers of the earth.[p]
11 Serve the LORD with fear, and rejoice before him;
with trembling 12 bow down in homage*[q]
lest he become angry
and you perish from the way,
for his wrath can flare up in an instant.

Blessed* are all those
who take refuge in him.[r]

l Pss 10:16; 24:10; 110:2.—m Pss 89:27f; 110:2-3; Isa 49:1; Lk 3:22; Heb 1:5; 6:5.—n Ps 22:28; Mt 21:38; Rev 2:26.—o Ps 110:5-6; Job 34:24; Jer 19:10; Rev 2:27; 12:5; 19:15.—p Ps 141:6; Prov 27:11; Wis 6:1.—q Pss 9:3; 34:10; 103:11.—r Pss 84:12; 146:5; Prov 16:20; Rev 6:16.

2:6 *Holy mountain:* reference to the site of the temple (see 2 Chr 3:4; 15:1; 33:15). Pss 43:3 and 46:5 have "holy mountain" and "holy place" respectively. Ps 48:3 has "holy mountain" and Ps 87:1 has "holy mountains."

2:7 *Decree:* this is nothing less than the prophecy of Nathan (see 2 Sam 7:14) applied to the Messiah by 1 Chr 17:13 (see Ps 89:27). Here the Messiah speaks after the rebels (v. 3) and after God who in an oracle (v. 6) has just enthroned him as King of Israel. He has also declared him his Son according to a formula familiar to the ancient Orient.

2:8 The Messiah's reign will be coextensive with that of God (see Isa 49:6; Dan 7:14). This verse is applied by Heb 1:5 (see Heb 5:5), then by tradition and the Liturgy, to the eternal generation of the Word.

2:9 The Book of Revelation applies this verse to Christ's triumphant reign (see Rev 12:5; 19:15).

2:12 *Bow down in homage:* another possible translation is: "honor the Son." *Blessed:* see note on Ps 1:1.

BOOK I—PSALMS 3–41*

PSALM 3*

Trust in God in Time of Danger

¹ A psalm of David. When he was fleeing from his son Absalom.ˢ

² O LORD, how great is the number of my enemies,
  how many are those who rise up against me.
³ How numerous are the ones who say of me,
  "He will not receive salvation from God."ᵗ
        *Selah**

⁴ But you, O LORD, are a shield to protect me;
  you are my glory and the one who raises
  my head high.*ᵘ
⁵ Whenever I cry aloud to the LORD,
  he answers me from his holy mountain.*ᵛ
        Selah

⁶ I lie down and sleep;ʷ
  I awaken again, for the LORD sustains me.*

---

s 2 Sam 15:13ff.—t Pss 22:8; 71:11; Isa 36:15; 37:20.—u Pss 7:11; 18:3; 62:7-8; Gen 15:1; Deut 33:29; Isa 60:19.—v Ps 2:6.—w Pss 4:9; 17:15; Lev 26:6; Prov 3:24.

Pss 3—41 At the beginning of the Book we find a collection of psalms attributed to David. His life, replete with difficulties and brimming with confidence, was presented as an example: it inspired poems that David did not himself compose. One theme dominates the diversity of psalms that make up this first part: the innocent find themselves in the grip of the wicked. Hope is ceaselessly renewed as is torment: "My God, my God, why have you forsaken me?" (Ps 22:1). It is the trial of darkness; still one certitude remains: "You will fill me with joy in your presence" (Ps 16:11). Is not this the dialogue that takes place in the life of believers!

Ps 3 In time of great danger and anguish, the psalmist finds refuge in God as his shield (protector) and the one who fills him with courage. God answers his prayer and bestows peace and deliverance.

3:3 *Selah:* a word whose meaning is uncertain; possibly a musical term.

3:4 God will preserve the psalmist from dishonor and humiliation by means of his grace (see Pss 18:3; 27:5; 62:8; 110:5; Deut 33:29; Sir 11:12f).

3:5 *Holy Mountain:* see note on Ps 2:6..

3:6 This passage (see Prov 3:24) is applied by the Fathers of the Church to the dead and risen Christ.

7 Thus, I will not fear the multitudes
  who have surrounded me on every side.ˣ

8 Rise up, O LORD!
   Rescue me, O my God!
  You will strike all my enemies across the
     face*
   and break the teeth of the wicked.ʸ

9 Salvation comes from the LORD.
   May your blessing be upon your people.ᶻ
                                    Selah

PSALM 4*

Joyful Confidence in God

1 For the director.* With stringed instruments. A psalm
of David.

2 When I call upon you, answer me, O God,
   you who uphold my rights.
  When I was in distress, you set me free;
   have pity on me and listen to my prayer.ᵃ

3 How long* will you people turn my glory into
     shame,
   cherishing what is worthless and pursuing
     what is false?ᵇ   *Selah*

---

x Pss 23:4; 118:11; Job 11:15.—y Pss 6:5; 7:2; 58:7; Isa 25:9; Jer
42:11.—z Pss 27:1; 28:9; Isa 43:3; Jon 2:9; Rev 7:10.—a Pss 13:4; 27:7;
30:11; 118:5.—b Ps 62:4; Ex 16:7; 2 Ki 19:26; Jer 13:25.

3:8 God treats the wicked like ferocious beasts whose jaws are shattered
(see Pss 22:14f; 35:16; 58:7; Job 29:17; Ezek 22:25). The initial appeal reminds
one of Jer 2:27. See note on Ps 5:10 and introduction to Ps 35.
   Ps 4 Those who are well established in life delude themselves by seeking happiness in riches and worldly vanities. The psalmist, rich in divine trust and joy,
invites them to discover the price of God's friendship: "the light of [God's] face."
This is an evening prayer (see vv. 5 and 9), filled with desire for God; Christians
move beyond its earthly perspectives. Prayer brings openness of heart, assurance
of God's help, faith, divine approval, joy, and peace.
   4:1 *For the director:* these words are thought to be a musical or liturgical notation.
   4:3 *How long . . . ?:* see note on Ps 6:4.

4 Remember that the LORD wonderfully favors
   those who are faithful,*
   and the LORD listens when I call out to
   him.*c*

5 When you are angry, be careful not to sin;
   reflect in silence *
   as you lie upon your beds.*d*   *Selah*
6 Offer worthy sacrifices
   and place your trust in the LORD.*e*

7 Many exclaim, "Who will show us better
   times!
   Let the light of your face shine on* us, O
   LORD!"*f*
8 You have granted my heart* greater joy
   than others experience when grain and
   wine abound.*g*
9 In peace I lie down and sleep,
   for only with your help, O LORD,
   can I rest secure.*h*

---

c Ps 12:2; 1 Tim 4:7; 2 Pet 3:11.—d Ps 63:7; Dan 2:28; Eph 4:26.—e Pss
31:7; 51:21; Isa 26:4; Jn 14:1.—f Ps 31:17; 44:4; 67:2; 80:4; Num 6:25;
Job 13:24; Dan 9:17.—g Isa 9:3; Acts 14:17.—h Ps 3:6; Lev 26:6.

4:4 *Those who are faithful:* one of several words (sometimes translated as
"saints") for the People of God, who should be faithful to him (see Pss 12:2;
31:24; 32:6; 34:10). See also notes on Pss 16:3 and 34:10.
4:5-6 One must fear to offend God but rather pray to him in the calm and silence of adoration. *When you are angry be careful not to sin:* these words are
cited by Paul in Eph 4:26 with the sense that if anger takes hold of you, let it not
lead you to act evilly—for there is such a thing as righteous anger (see Mk 3:5).
Beds: can refer to the spot where one prostrated oneself to pray (see Ps 95:6; Sir
50:17), which is also suggested by the presence of the term *Selah* or pause.
4:7 *Face shine on:* this image of benevolence and contentment (see Num 6:25;
Prov 16:15; Dan 9:17) occurs frequently in the Psalter (see Pss 31:17; 67:2;
119:135; and especially note on Ps 13:2). The reading in the Septuagint and Vulgate is: "The light of your countenance, O LORD, is signed [or: imprinted] on us."
It was interpreted as referring to the soul created in the image of God and regen-
erated by the baptismal character that makes a Christian a child of light (see Lk
16:8; Jn 12:36; 1 Thes 5:5; Eph 5:8).
4:8 *Heart:* the biblical center of the human spirit, which harbors a person's
thoughts and emotions and gives rise to action.

PSALM 5*

Morning Prayer for Divine Help

[1] For the director.* With flutes. A psalm of David.

[2] Listen to my words, O LORD;
   pay heed to my sighs.[i]

[3] Hear my cry for help,
   my King and my God;
   for to you I pray.[j]

[4] O LORD, at daybreak* you hear my voice;
   at daybreak I bring my petition before you
   and await your reply.[k]

[5] For you are not a God who delights in wicked-
      ness;
   evil cannot remain in your presence.[l]

[6] The arrogant shrink before your gaze;
   you hate all who do evil.[m]

[7] You destroy all who tell lies;
   the LORD detests the violent and the deceit-
      ful.[n]

[8] But I will enter your house
   because of your great kindness,*

---

i Pss 17:1; 40:2; 86:6; 130:1-2; Isa 35:10.—j Pss 44:5; 84:4.—k Wis 16:28; Isa 28:19; Ezek 46:13; Rom 8:19.—l Ps 1:5; Prov 2:22.—m Ps 73:3; 2 Ki 19:32; Prov 8:13.—n Ps 101:7; Prov 6:17-19; Wis 14:9; Hab 1:13; Acts 5:3; Rev 21:8.

Ps 5 This is a morning prayer (see v. 4) in which the psalmist prays for the Lord to hear his prayer and grant a sense of God's goodness and justice, bestow guidance, punish enemies, and bless the righteous. Broken by tribulation, the persecuted man appeals for the justice of God against his own enemies. Christians must spiritualize the call for vengeance, hating evil rather than those who do evil. To love God is to choose the cause of justice and bear the witness of a purified joy.

5:1 *For the director:* these words are thought to be a musical or liturgical notation.

5:4 The morning is the privileged moment for divine favors (see Pss 17:14f; 30:6; 46:6; 59:17). *I bring my petition:* other possible translations are: "I offer my vows" and "I prepare my offering."

5:8 *Kindness:* Hebrew *hesed*; this word denotes the sentiments that flow from a natural community, family, clan, or society (benevolence, favor). It is also the love of the Covenant between the Lord and the community of Israel, regarded as his spouse and child. Finally, it includes the sentiments that are found in each of its members (grace and love on the part of the Lord, and piety on the part of the faithful). See also note on Ps 6:5.

and I will bow down in your holy temple,
  filled with awe of you.[o]
9 Lead me in your ways of righteousness, O
    LORD,
    for I am surrounded by enemies;
    make your path straight before me.[*][p]

10 For there is nothing trustworthy in their
    mouth;[q]
    their heart devises treacherous schemes.
  Their throat is a wide open grave;
    with their tongue they utter flattery.[*]
11 Punish them, O God;
    may their intrigues result in their downfall.[r]
  Cast them out because of their many trans-
    gressions,
    for they have rebelled against you.[*]

12 But may all who take refuge in you rejoice;
    may they shout for joy forever.[s]
  Grant them your protection
    so that those who love your name[*] may re-
    joice in you.
13 Truly, you bless the righteous, O LORD;
    you surround them with your goodwill as
    with a shield.[t]

---

o Ps 138:2; 1 Ki 8:44; Dan 6:10; Jon 2:4.—p Ps 23:3; Prov 4:11; Isa 26:7;
Jn 1:23.—q Ps 12:3; Prov 15:4; Jer 5:16; Rom 3:13.—r Pss 78:40; 141:10;
Lam 1:5.—s Pss 33:1; 64:11; Rev 7:15-16.—t Pss 32:7; 35:2; 103:4; 112:3.

5:9 *Make your path straight before me:* the Greek reads: "Make straight my
way before you."

5:10 With mouth, heart, throat, and tongue they spread harm around. *Their
throat is a wide open grave:* their words bring death to their hearers (see Jer
5:16)—a theme cited in Rom 3:13. *Heart:* see note on Ps 4:8.

5:11 This verse reminds us that the so-called imprecatory (or cursing) psalms
(see introduction to Ps 35) have been a problem for Christians from the beginning of the use of the Psalter. Christ instructed Christians to pray for enemies
(see Mt 5:44) and gave an example of this on the cross (see Lk 23:34). Yet the
psalmists at times call for punishment (even of the most drastic kind) on enemies. Christians may look upon these statements as appeals for strict redress of
evil in accord with the divine justice or direct them toward the enemies of their
souls, the devil and his minions who are implacable foes of God.

5:12 *Your name:* a name usually designates the person, hence the Lord himself. See also note on Ps 8:2, 10.

PSALM 6*

Evening Prayer for God's Mercy

1 For the director.* With stringed instruments. "Upon the eighth." A psalm of David.

2 O LORD, do not rebuke me in your anger
   or punish me in your wrath.u

3 Have mercy on me, O LORD, for I am tottering;
   help me, O LORD, for my body* is in agony.v

4 My soul* is also filled with anguish.
   But you, O LORD—how long?w

5 Turn, O LORD, and deliver my soul;
   save me because of your kindness.*

6 For among the dead who remembers you?x
   In the netherworld who sings your praises?*

7 I am exhausted from my sighing;
   every night I flood my bed with my tears,
   and I soak my couch with my weeping.

---

u Ps 38:2; Jer 10:24.—v Ps 61:3; Jer 17:14-15.—w Pss 13:2-3; 74:10; 79:5; 89:47.—x Pss 30:10; 88:11-13; 115:17; Eccl 9:10; Isa 38:18.

Ps 6 This is the first of the so-called Penitential Psalms (6; 32; 38; 51; 102; 130; 143), a designation for psalms suitable for expressing repentance that goes back to the sixth century A.D. In affliction, the psalmist invokes the divine mercy, begs to be saved from death, confesses his wretchedness, and expresses faith in his own deliverance and his enemies' total abasement.

6:1 *For the director:* these words are thought to be a musical or liturgical notation. *Upon the eighth:* probably a musical term referring to an eight-stringed instrument.

6:3 *Body is in agony:* literally, "bones are shaken."

6:4 *Soul:* the Hebrew word *nephesh* usually means a person's life-giving breath, which disappears at death. It is thus applied to a person's very self as a living, conscious being ("my soul" equals "myself"). *How long?:* elliptical formula used in psalms of lamentation both in Babylonia and in Israel (see Ps 74:10; 80:5; 90:13; 94:3) to express anxiety over the divine aid that is late in coming.

6:5 *Kindness:* Hebrew *hesed,* which may also be translated as "mercy" and refers to all that God promised to give to his people (see Deut 7:9, 12) through the Davidic dynasty (see Ps 89:25, 29, 34; 2 Sam 7:15; Isa 55:3). See also note on Ps 5:8.

6:6 The psalmist offers a motive for God to save him from death: it is the living who praise him. The netherworld was viewed as the place where the souls of the dead had a kind of shadowy existence, with no activity or lofty emotion. Just what that existence entailed at any given Old Testament period is difficult to gauge until the second century B.C. It is then that the sacred Books begin to speak more clearly about life after death (see Wis 3; Dan 12:1-3).

⁸ My eyes grow dim because of my grief;
　　they are worn out* because of all my foes.ʸ

⁹ Depart from me, all you evildoers,*
　　for the Lord has heard the sound of my
　　　weeping.ᶻ
¹⁰ The Lord has listened to my pleas;
　　the Lord has accepted my prayer.
¹¹ All my enemies will be shamed and terrified;
　　they will flee in utter confusion.*ᵃ

PSALM 7*

Appeal to the Divine Judge

¹ A plaintive song of David, which he sang to the Lord
concerning Cush,* a Benjaminite.

² O Lord, my God, I take refuge in you;
　　keep me safe from all my pursuers and de-
　　　liver me,ᵇ
³ lest like a lion they tear me to pieces
　　and carry me off, with no one to rescue me.

⁴ O Lord, my God, if I have done this,
　　if my hands are stained with guilt,

---

y Pss 31:10; 38:11; 40:13; 69:4; Job 16:78f; Isa 38:14.—z Pss 5:6; 119:115; 139:19; Mt 7:23; Lk 13:27.—a Pss 35:4, 26; 40:15; 71:13; 2 Ki 19:26.—b Pss 2:12; 3:8; 6:5; 11:1; 22:21; 31:2, 16; 119:86, 157, 161.

6:8 *Eyes grow dim . . . worn out:* a sign of failing strength (see Ps 38:11; 1 Sam 14:27, 29; Jer 14:6) or sorrow in affliction (see Pss 31:10; 88:10; Job 17:7; Lam 2:11) or dashed hopes (see Pss 69:4; 119:82, 123; Deut 28:32; Isa 38:14).

6:9 This apostrophe (taken up in Mt 7:23) has been prepared for by the end of v. 8. The enemies of the sick person, like the friends of Job, see in his trials a heavenly chastisement for hidden faults; they insult him and accuse him unjustly—a theme that is more developed elsewhere (see Pss 31; 35; 38; 69).

6:11 See note on Ps 5:11 and introduction to Ps 35.

Ps 7 Falsely accused, the psalmist implores the divine assistance, affirms his innocence, invokes God's just judgment, and expresses limitless confidence in the punishment of his enemy as well as his own salvation, concluding with praise for God's righteousness.

7:1 *Cush* is not otherwise known, but as a Benjaminite he was probably a supporter of Saul. Hence, the psalm is associated with Saul's determined attempts on David's life.

5 if I have repaid a friend with treachery—
     I who spared the lives of those who with-
          out cause were my enemies—*
6 then let my foe pursue and overtake me;
     let him trample my life into the ground
     and leave my honor in the dust.^c   *Selah*

7 Rise up, O LORD, in your indignation;
     rise against the fury of my enemies.
   Rouse yourself for me,
     and fulfill the judgment you have decreed.^d
8 Let the peoples assemble in your presence
     as you sit above them enthroned on high.
9   The LORD is the judge of the nations.

   Therefore, pass judgment on me, O LORD, ac-
          cording to my righteousness,
     according to my innocence, O Most High.
10 Put an end to the malice of the wicked
     but continue to sustain the righteous,
   O God of justice,
     you who search minds and hearts.*^e

11 God is a shield to me;
     he saves those who are upright of heart.^f
12 God is a just judge,
     a God who expresses his indignation every
          day.

13 When a sinner refuses to repent,
     God sharpens his sword,
     and he bends and aims his bow.^g
14 He has prepared deadly weapons for him
     and made his arrows into fiery shafts.^h

---

c Ps 143:3; Isa 10:6.—d Pss 9:5; 138:7.—e Pss 17:3; 26:2; 35:24; 43:1;
139:23; Wis 1:6; Jer 11:20; 17:10; 20:12; Rev 2:23.—f Ps 3:3; Job 33:3.—g
Ps 11:2; Ezek 3:19.—h Ps 18:15; Isa 50:11.

7:5 *I who . . . enemies:* an alternative translation is: "and without cause have
despoiled an enemy."
7:10 *Minds and hearts:* literally, "hearts and kidneys." These words were used as
virtual synonyms (but "heart" most often) to refer to the innermost center of human
life. To "search mind and heart" was a conventional expression for God's examination of a person's hidden character and motives (see Jer 11:20; 17:10; 20:12).

15 Behold, he who conceives iniquity*
    and is pregnant with mischief
     will give birth to lies.*i*
16 He digs a pit and makes it deep,
    but he will fall into the trap he has made.*j*
17 His wickedness will recoil upon his own head,
    and his violence will fall back on his own
     crown.

18 I will offer thanks to the LORD because of his
    righteousness,
     and I will sing hymns of praise* to the
     name of the LORD Most High.*k*

PSALM 8*

The Majesty of God and the Dignity of Human Beings

1 For the director.* "Upon the *gittith*." A psalm of David.

2 O LORD, our LORD,
    how glorious is your name* in all the earth!
    You have exalted your majesty above the
     heavens.

---

i Job 15:35; Isa 59:4; Jas 1:15.—j Pss 9:16; 35:8; 57:7; 94:13; Prov 26:27; Eccl 10:8; Sir 27:26.—k Pss 18:50; 30:5; 135:3; 146:2; Rom 15:11.

7:15-17 See note on Ps 5:11 and introduction to Ps 35.

7:18 *I will offer thanks . . . and I will sing hymns of praise:* a vow to praise the Lord in keeping with the Israelite belief that praise must follow deliverance. The praise involved thank offerings and celebrating God's saving deed in the presence of others in the temple (see Ps 50:14f, 23). See also note on Ps 9:2. *Name:* see notes on Pss 5:12 and 8:2, below.

Ps 8 In the midst of disconsolate supplications, here is a hymn that chants the splendor of God. But is not the best reflection of the divine majesty the grandeur of the human being? For the Lord has made this tiny being lost in the immensity of the world the crown of all creation. In the man "crowned with glory" Paul and the author of the Letter to the Hebrews see the glorified and risen Christ, who, while on earth, was for a time made lower than the heavenly creatures (see 1 Cor 15:25-27; Eph 1:22; Heb 2:5-9).

8:1 *For the director:* these words are thought to be a musical or liturgical notation. *Gittith:* possibly a musical instrument from the Philistine city of Gath, or else a song for the harvest and the winepress.

8:2, 10 *Name:* according to Semitic usage, this word designates the person with all its essential qualities. See also note on Ps 5:12.

3 Out of the mouths of newborn babes and
    infants*
        you have brought forth praise
    as a bulwark against your foes,
        to silence the enemy and the avenger.[l]

4 When I look up at your heavens
        that have been formed by your fingers,
    the moon and the stars
        that you set in place,
5 what is man that you are mindful of him,[m]
        the son of man* that you care for him?[n]

6 You have made him a little less than the
    angels*
        and crowned him with glory and honor.

7 You have given him dominion over the works
        of your hands[o]
        and placed everything under his feet:
8 all sheep and oxen
        as well as the beasts of the field,
9 the birds of the air, the fish of the sea,
        and whatever swims in the paths of the sea.

10 O LORD, our LORD,
        how glorious is your name in all the earth!

---

l Ps 143:12; Wis 10:21; Mt 21:16.—m Ps 144:3; Job 7:17.—n 1 Chr
29:14; Heb 2:6ff.—o Ps 19:2; Gen 1:26, 28; Wis 9:2; 1 Cor 15:27; Eph 1:22.

8:3 *Out of the mouths of newborn babes and infants:* Jesus cites this passage
with reference to the children who acclaim him on the day of his triumphal entry
into Jerusalem (see Mt 21:16).

8:5 *Son of man:* a phrase used here and elsewhere as a synonym for human
(see Ps 80:18; Ezek 2) and a sign of humility. Later it became a Messianic title in
Daniel (7:13f) and Jewish apocryphal tradition (see 1 Enoch, 2 Esdras, and 2
Baruch). Eventually, Jesus made use of it to express his twofold destiny of suffering (see Mk 8:31; 9:13, 31; 10:33; 14:21) and of glory (see Mk 8:38; 12:36; 14:62).

8:6 *A little less than the angels:* that is, a little lower than the beings who comprise the heavenly court. The text for heavenly beings is *elohim,* that is, "God"; in
effect, God created human beings in his own image and likeness. Some translate:
"a little less than godlike"; and in Heb 2:9 this passage is said to be eminently fulfilled in Jesus Christ, the God-man. See also 1 Cor 15:27 and Eph 1:22, where Paul
applies to Christ the words "you have . . . placed everything under his feet" (v. 7).

PSALM 9—10*

PSALM 9*

Thanksgiving for the Triumph of Justice

¹ For the director.* According to *Muth Labben*. A psalm of David.

² I will offer praise to you, O LORD,
　　with my whole heart;
　　I will recount all your wondrous deeds.*
³ I will rejoice and exult in you;
　　I will sing praise to your name,* O Most
　　High.

⁴ For my enemies have turned back;
　　in your presence they stumble and perish.
⁵ But you have upheld my just cause,
　　you who are seated on your throne as a
　　righteous judge.

⁶ You have rebuked the nations and destroyed
　　the wicked,
　　erasing their name forever and ever.ᵖ
⁷ The enemies have suffered endless ruin;
　　their cities have been utterly destroyed,
　　and not even their memory remains.

---

p Pss 37:10; 59:6; 105:14; Job 18:17; Isa 26:14.

Ps 9—10 In this psalm we are perhaps in the period of the return from the Exile, toward the end of the sixth century; the foreign occupiers and the people who had remained in Palestine regarded returning deportees as intruders and they mistreated them. This is the first alphabetical psalm; in the Masoretic Text it is divided into two psalms, while in the Greek Septuagint and Latin Vulgate Psalms 9 and 10 constitute one psalm. This accounts for the difference in the numbering of the psalms in these versions (see Preface, p. 15).

Ps 9 is predominantly praise of God for his royal blessings and glories, including deliverance from hostile nations, concluding with a short prayer for God's continuing righteous judgments (see v. 5) on the nations.

9:1 *For the director:* these words are thought to be a musical or liturgical notation. *According to Muth Labben:* nothing is known about these words.

9:2 The praise rendered to the Lord by the psalmists in the Psalter is customarily public praise for his goodness and glory as well as the saving acts he has performed on behalf of his people. Some have described such praise as the forerunner of the Gospel preaching in the New Testament. See also note on Ps 7:18.

9:3, 6, 11 *Name:* see note on Ps 5:12.

8 The LORD is enthroned forever;
    he has established his throne for judgment.
9 He governs the world in righteousness
    and judges the peoples with equity.^q
10 The LORD is a refuge for the oppressed,
    a refuge in times of distress.^r
11 Those who revere your name place their trust
        in you,
        for you never abandon those who seek
        you, O LORD.

12 Sing praise to the LORD enthroned in Zion;*
    proclaim to the nations his wondrous deeds.
13 For the avenger of blood remembers them;
    he does not ignore the cry of the afflicted.^s

14 Have mercy on me, O LORD;
    behold how my enemies afflict me,
    you who save me from the gates of death.^t
15 Then I will recount all your praises
    and rejoice in your salvation
    at the gates of the Daughter of Zion.*

16 The nations have fallen into the pit they made;
        their feet have been caught in the snare
        they laid.*
17 The LORD has made himself known and ren-
        dered judgment;
        the wicked are ensnared in the work of their
        own hands.^u   *Higgaion,* Selah*

---

q Pss 7:12; 96:10; 98:9.—r Pss 10:18; 37:39; Isa 25:4.—s Ps 10:17; Job 16:18.—t Num 10:9; Wis 16:13.—u Prov 5:22; Sir 27:26.

9:12 *Enthroned in Zion:* the Lord is enthroned not only in heaven (see Pss 2:4; 113:5) but also on earth—in the temple of Jerusalem from which he rules the world (see note on Ps 2:6; see also Ps 132:13).

9:15 *Daughter of Zion:* a personification of Jerusalem and its inhabitants in accord with ancient Near Eastern practice (see Pss 45:12; 137:8).

9:16-19 Under the Lord's just rule and in accord with the law of talion (see Ex 21:23-25; Lev 24:19f; Deut 19:21), the wicked who attack others are punished by the very actions they perform (see Ps 7:16). But the "needy" (v. 19), those who are attacked, will be saved by their trust in the Lord. Thus, God's honor and glory are vindicated when he judges and punishes the wicked.

9:17 *Higgaion:* probably a musical notation.

¹⁸ The wicked will depart into the netherworld,
 all the nations that turned away from God.
¹⁹ But the needy will not be forgotten forever,
 nor will the hope of the afflicted ever come
 to naught.^v

²⁰ Rise up, O L<small>ORD</small>! Do not let man triumph;
 let the nations be judged before you.
²¹ Strike them with fear, O L<small>ORD</small>;
 let the nations know that they are mere
 mortals.   *Selah*

PSALM 10*

Prayer for Help against Oppressors

¹ Why, O L<small>ORD</small>, do you stand far off?
 Why do you remain hidden in times of
 trouble?
² In his arrogance the wicked hunts down the
 poor;
 let him be ensnared by the schemes he has
 devised.^w

³ The wicked boasts of his wicked desires;
 he upholds the greedy and renounces the
 L<small>ORD</small>.^x
⁴ Filled with arrogance, he does not seek God,
 but thinks, "God does not exist."*^y
⁵ The wicked always seems to prosper;
 your judgments are far from his mind,
 and he scoffs at all those who oppose him.
⁶ He says in his heart,* "I will not be swayed;
 I will never experience misfortune."

---

v Ps 25:3; Prov 23:18.—w Job 20:19; Isa 32:7.—x Pss 36:2; 49:7; 94:4;
Jer 14:8.—y Pss 14:1b; 36:2; Job 22:13; Isa 29:15; Jer 5:12; Zep 1:12.

Ps 10 A prayer of one in trouble and seeking to be rescued, it explores the
ways and motives of the wicked and calls on God the King to arise and defend
the oppressed.
 10:4 In denying the action of Providence the wicked in effect denies God (see
Pss 10:13; 14:1b; 36:2f; Zep 1:12), who is some far-off personage (v. 5).
 10:6, 10, 11, 13 *Heart:* see note on Ps 4:8.

7 His mouth is filled with curses, deceit, and
    threats;*
    his tongue breeds evil and malice.*z*

8 He lies in wait near the villages,
    and from ambush he slays the innocent;
    his eyes are on the watch for the helpless.*a*

9 He lies in wait like a lurking lion,
    ready to strike the helpless;
he snares his victims,
    seizing them in his net.*b*

10 He crouches and lies low,
    and the poor are overwhelmed by his
    might.

11 He thinks in his heart,
    "God has forgotten;
    he hides his face and will never see what is
    happening."*c*

12 Arise, O Lᴏʀᴅ! Lift up your hand, O God!
    Do not forget the afflicted.

13 Why should the wicked reject God
    and say in his heart,
    "He will not call me to account"?

14 But you note our troubles and our grief
    so that you may resolve our difficulties.*d*
The helpless entrusts himself to you;
    you are the recourse of the fatherless.*e*

15 Break the arms of the sinner and the evildoer;
    seek out the wicked
    until no more endure.*

---

z Ps 73:8; Isa 32:7; Rom 3:14.—a Pss 11:2; 17:12; Job 24:14; Jer 5:26;
Hos 6:9; Hab 3:14.—b Ps 17:12; Job 18:8; Prov 1:11; Jer 5:26.—c Pss
44:24; 64:5; 73:11; 94:7; Job 22:13; Ezek 9:9.—d Pss 22:12; 31:8; 56:9; 2
Ki 20:5; Isa 25:8; Rev 7:17.—e Pss 68:6; 82:3; 146:9; Ex 22:21-22; Deut
10:18; 33:29.

10:7 *Curses, deceit, and threats:* this text, which contains the three most common weapons of the tongue in Israel's experience, is cited in Rom 3:14. *Curses*
were believed to have real power over those upon whom they were leveled; *deceit*
referred to slander and false testimony for evil purposes (see 1 Ki 21:8-15).

10:15 See note on Ps 5:11 and introduction to Ps 35.

¹⁶ The LORD is King forever and ever;*
     the heathen will disappear from his land.*f*
¹⁷ You listen, O LORD, to the longings of the poor;
     you strengthen their courage and heed
        their prayers.
¹⁸ You ensure justice for the fatherless and the
        oppressed
     so that no one on earth may fill them with
        terror.*g*

PSALM 11*

Unshakable Confidence in God

¹ For the director.* Of David.

In the LORD I take refuge.*
     How can you say to me,
     "Flee like a bird to your mountains!*h*
² For behold, the wicked are bending their bows*
     as they fit their arrows to the string
     so that from the shadows
        they can shoot at those who are upright.*i*

---

f Ps 145:13; Ex 15:18; Jer 10:10.—g Ps 146:9; Deut 10:18.—h Pss 7:2;
55:7; 91:3.—i Pss 7:14; 10:8; 37:14; 64:5; 2 Sam 22:35.

10:16-18 The Lord is the hope of the righteous ("the poor") in a just world, for
he is "King forever." Because he is faithful to his Covenant, he will defeat "the
heathen" for he listens to the "longings of the poor" and establishes justice for
them. Hence, "no one on earth" is to be feared.
     Ps 11 This is a confession of confident trust in the Lord's righteous rule at a
time when one's wicked adversaries seem to have the upper hand. Friends counsel flight to a mountain refuge to escape trouble, but the innocent psalmist
stands fast, for the Lord protects those who seek asylum in his temple.
     In praying this psalm, we should be mindful that although we can rely on God,
we are never sure of ourselves. The Spirit of God is quick to help, but the "flesh,"
human nature, is weak—so much so that we must ask not to be put to the test
(see Mt 26:41) and must flee from it if this is possible and permitted (see Mt
10:23).
     11:1a *For the director:* these words are thought to be a musical or liturgical
notation.
     11:1b-3 The psalmist remains confident in the Lord even though he is under
attack by the wicked and receives counsel from his advisers to flee.
     11:2 The wicked are likened to archers setting traps; they are treacherous,
furtive, and bent on maligning the upright and making them fall (see Pss 10:7-
10; 37:14). *Those who are upright:* i.e., the righteous who know and love the Lord
(see Pss 7:10; 36:11; 73:1).

3 If the foundations are destroyed,
    what can be done by those who are righ-
      teous?"*

4 The LORD is in his holy temple;*
    the LORD, whose throne is in heaven.
His eyes are fixed on the world;
    his gaze examines everyone.*j*

5 The LORD tests the upright and the wicked;
    he detests the lover of violence.
6 Upon the wicked he will rain down
    fiery coals and brimstone;*
    a scorching wind will be their allotted por-
      tion.*k*

7 For the LORD is just
    and he loves righteous deeds;
    the upright will behold his face.*

---

j Pss 14:2; 18:7; 27:4; 102:20; Deut 26:15; 1 Ki 8:48; Isa 66:1; Jon 2:8; Mic 1:2; Hab 2:20; Mt 5:34; 23:22.—k Pss 120:4; 140:11; Gen 19:24; 41:23, 27; Job 15:2; Prov 16:27; Isa 11:15; Ezek 10:2; 38:22; Rev 8:5; 20:10.

11:3 The psalmist's advisers are concerned about the collapse of the "foundations" (i.e., the order of society; see Ps 75:4; 82:5; Ezek 30:4). This order has been established by the Lord at creation and is being maintained by him.

11:4-7 The psalmist relies on God, who is seated on his heavenly throne—a symbol of his royal rule and authority to judge (see Pss 9:8; 47:9)—and totally against those who love violence. At the right time, he will mete out to the wicked the judgment they deserve, and he will deliver the upright and grant them access to himself.

11:6 *Fiery coals and brimstone:* an image of judgment taken from the destruction of Sodom and Gomorrah (see Gen 19:24; Deut 29:23; Ezek 38:22). *Scorching wind:* another image of judgment taken from the hot desert winds that blow over the Middle East and devastate the vegetation (see Isa 21:1; 40:7f; Jer 4:11). *Their allotted portion:* literally, "the portion of their cup." The cup that God gives people to drink is a symbol for their destiny (see Ps 16:5; Mt 20:22; 26:39; Rev 14:10).

11:7 *Behold his face:* an expression usually denoting access, especially to the king. Here the expression indicates access to the heavenly King, with reference to his presence at the temple (God's royal house on earth). It is legitimate for us to see in this text an allusion to ultimate access to the heavenly temple (see Pss 16:11; 17:15; 23:6; 140:14).

PSALM 12*

Prayer against the Arrogance of Sinners

¹ For the director.* "Upon the eighth." A psalm of David.

² Help, O LORD, for there are no godly left;
    the faithful have vanished from the human
    race.*l*

³ Neighbors utter lies to each other;
    they speak with flattering lips and deceitful
    hearts.**m*

⁴ May the LORD destroy all flattering lips
    and every boastful tongue,
⁵ those who say, "We will prevail by our
    tongues;
    with our lips as our ally,
    who can lord it over us?"*n*

⁶ "The poor have been oppressed,
    and those who are needy groan.
  Therefore, I will rise up now," says the LORD;
    "I will grant them the safety
    for which they long."*o*

⁷ And the promises of the LORD are certain;
    they are like silver refined in a furnace
    and purified seven times.**p*

---

l Pss 14:3; 116:11; Isa 57:1; 59:15; Mic 7:2.—m Pss 28:3; 35:14; 55:22; Isa 59:3-4; Jer 9:8.—n Ps 31:19; Prov 18:21; Sir 5:3; Jas 3:6.—o Pss 34:7; 44:24f; Isa 33:10.—p Pss 18:31; 19:8; 2 Sam 22:31; Prov 30:5.

Ps 12 The psalmist, surrounded by the treachery and arrogance of sinners (see Mic 7:1-7), calls for help and is certain that God will judge them as their iniquity reaches its zenith. The words of the Lord can be fully relied on, whereas the boastful words of the adversaries are completely futile.

We Christians can make this supplication our own, for we feel deeply every disorder in the social realm. Eager for justice, we are outraged by every injustice, every disloyalty and fraud in social relations.

12:1 *For the director:* these words are thought to be a musical or liturgical notation. *Upon the eighth:* see note on Ps 6:1.

12:3 *Hearts:* see note on Ps 4:8.

12:7 *Purified seven times:* the number seven signified fullness or complete-ness; hence the phrase means "refined through and through." The words of the Lord are absolutely pure and true (see Ps 18:31; 19:8; Prov 30:5).

8 You, O LORD, will watch over us*
and preserve us from this generation forever.
9 For the wicked prowl on every side,
and what is vile is exalted by mankind.

PSALM 13*

Prayer of One in Sorrow

1 For the director.* A psalm of David.

2 How long,* O LORD—will you forget me forever?
How long will you hide your face from me?[q]
3 How long must I suffer anguish in my soul
and sorrow in my heart* day and night?
How long will my enemy lord it over me?

4 Look upon me, O LORD, my God, and answer
me;
enlighten my eyes, lest I sleep in death,
5 lest my enemy say, "I have defeated him,"
and my foes exult in my collapse.[r]

6 As for me, I trust in your kindness;*
my heart rejoices in your salvation.
7 I will sing to the LORD[s]
because he has been good to me.*

q Pss 6:4; 22:25; 42:10; 44:25; 77:8; 79:5; 89:47; 94:3; Deut 31:17; Isa 8:17; Lam 5:20.—r Pss 25:2; 38:17; 71:2.—s Pss 7:18; 116:7.

12:8-9 The psalmist voices his confidence that, although the wicked are at present lording it over the righteous, God will take care of the latter.

Ps 13 The suffering psalmist cries out to God in despair over his impending death and the triumph of his enemies. Suddenly (perhaps after a religious experience of some kind), his tone changes; he speaks from a heart brimming with complete trust in God and voices his joy and gratitude.

In praying this psalm, we can think of Christ in his abandonment on the cross and provisional defeat by death, in the face of his enemies' ephemeral success. We too experience the critical trial of God's silence and apparent absence. Far from weakening our confidence in God, this eventuality should strengthen it.

13:1 *For the director:* most likely a musical or liturgical notation.

13:2 *How long:* see note on Ps 6:4. *Hide your face:* when God hides his face, the righteous become concerned (see Pss 30:8; 104:29), for when God's face shines on people it brings deliverance and blessings (see Pss 31:17; 67:2; 80:4; 119:135).

13:3, 6 *Heart:* see note on Ps 4:8.

13:6 *Kindness:* see note on Ps 6:5.

13:7 The Septuagint and Vulgate add another line: "I will sing to the name of the LORD most high."

PSALM 14*
Corruption and Punishment of the Godless

¹ For the director.* Of David.

The fool says in his heart,
  "There is no God."
People are depraved and their deeds are vile;
  there is no one who does what is right.*ᵗ

² The LORD* looks down from heaven
  upon the entire human race,ᵘ
to see if there are any who act with wisdom,ᵛ
  if even a single one seeks God.

³ But they have all left the right path;
  all alike are corrupt.
There is no one who does what is right,
  not even one.*ʷ

⁴ Have all these evildoers no understanding?
  They devour my people as they eat bread,ˣ
  and they never call upon the LORD.*ʸ

---

t Pss 10:4; 36:2; Isa 32:6; Jer 5:12; Mic 7:2; Zep 1:12.—u Pss 11:4;
102:20; Job 41:34.—v 2b-4: Rom 3:10-12.—w Ps 12:2; 1 Sam 8:3.—x Pss
27:2; 53:5; Isa 9:11.—y Ps 79:6; Isa 65:1; Jer 10:25; Hos 7:7.

Ps 14 The psalmist envisions the world divided into "the fools" (also termed
"evildoers") and "the company of the righteous" (also termed "the poor" and "my
people"). Although the fools act as though there is no God and persecute the
righteous, the psalmist is confident that God will eventually punish evildoers and
reward the righteous. Ps 53 is a somewhat revised duplicate of this psalm.

When Paul rereads this psalm, he will see in it a description of our sinful condition. No one is just in God's sight; we all need to be saved by Jesus Christ (Rom
3:10-25).

14:1a *For the director:* these words are thought to be a musical or liturgical
notation.

14:1b Elsewhere the psalmists included themselves among those who are not
righteous in God's eyes (see Pss 130:3; 143:2; see also 1 Ki 8:39; Job 9:2; Eccl
7:20). *Heart:* see note on Ps 4:8.

14:2 *The LORD:* in contrast with what "the fool" (v. 1b) thinks, the Lord is very
much in evidence and has his eyes on the whole earth. *Seeks God:* see Ps 15 for a
description of those who truly seek God.

14:3 After this verse, many Greek and Latin manuscripts add the Old Testament citations that were first combined in Rom 3:13-18.

14:4 Evildoers live by the violence of their own doing rather than by reliance on
the Lord (see Ps 10:2-4).

5 But later they will be filled with terror,
    for God is on the side of the righteous.*
6 They sought to crush the hopes of the poor,*
    but the LORD is their refuge.

7 Who will accomplish the salvation of Israel
    that is to come out of Zion?
When the LORD restores the fortunes of his
    people,
    Jacob will rejoice and Israel will exult.*z

PSALM 15*
The Righteous: Guests of God

1 A psalm of David.

O LORD, who may dwell in your sanctuary?a
Who may abide on your holy mountain?*

2 The one who leads a blameless life*
    and does what is right,
who speaks the truth from the heartb
3   and does not slander anyone,

---

z Pss 85:2; 126:1.—a Ps 24:3-6; Isa 56:7; Mic 6:6-8.—b Ps 119:1; Eph 1:4.

14:5 God is on the side of the righteous and, anytime he wishes, strikes sudden terror in the hearts of the wicked (see Deut 28:67; 1 Sam 14:15; 2 Chr 14:13; Job 3:25). *Righteous:* see note on Ps 1:5.

14:6 *Poor:* see note on Ps 22:27.

14:7 The righteous poor are identified with God's people. *Who will . . . Zion:* another possible translation is: "Oh, if only salvation for Israel / will come forth from Zion."

Ps 15 The psalmist presents a summary of moral conduct in the form of an instruction to those who have access to God at his temple (see Ps 24:3-6; Isa 33:14-16; Mic 6:6-8). He indicates that sanctity of life is necessary for those who wish to approach God and emphasizes the social virtues of justice and charity.

In praying this psalm, Christians keep in mind that by becoming man the Word has pitched his tent among us (see Jn 1:14), and in his body dwells the fullness of the divinity. In close contact and in profound communion with the Body of Jesus, of whom she is the visible extension on earth, the Church constitutes the dwelling of God in the world (see 1 Cor 3:16f).

15:1 *Holy mountain:* an ancient designation for the temple, the place where God dwells upon the earth (see Pss 2:6; 3:5; 43:3; 48:2).

15:2-5 It is not sacrifices or ritual purity but moral righteousness that gives access to the Lord (see the basic covenantal law: Ex 20:1-17; see also Isa 1:10-17; 33:14-16; 58:6-10; Jer 7:2-7; Ezek 18:5-9; Hos 6:6; Am 5:14f, 21-24; Mic 6:6-8; Zec 7:9f; 8:16f). *Heart:* see note on Ps 4:8. *Those who fear the LORD:* a frequent expression in the Psalter (see, e.g., Ps 115:11), it refers to those who fear God and live in accordance with his will because of their reverence for him. Later it

who does not harm a friend
and does not scorn a neighbor,
4 who looks with disdain on the wicked
but honors those who fear the LORD,
who abides by his oath,
no matter what the cost,
5 who does not charge interest on a loan
and refuses to accept a bribe against the
innocent.*c*

Whoever does these things
will never fall.

PSALM 16*

God the Supreme Good

1 A *miktam** of David.

Protect me, O God,
for in you I take refuge.*d*

2 I say to the LORD, "You are my Lord;
I have no good apart from you."
3 As for the saints who are in the land,
they are the noble ones,
and in them there is all my delight.*

---

c Ex 22:24; 23:8; 1 Sam 8:3.—d Pss 2:12; 12:8; 25:20; 2 Pet 1:10.

will take on a technical sense and refer to proselytes to Judaism not yet circumcised (see Acts 2:11; 10:2). *Interest on a loan:* laws dealing with interest on loans are found in Ex 22:24-27; Lev 25:35-37; Deut 15:7-11; 23:19f). In general, interest for profit was not to be charged to Israelites. Jesus went even further (see Lk 6:34f).

Ps 16 A prayer for safekeeping, pleading for the Lord's protection against the threat of death. It could also be called a psalm of trust. This psalm prepares the way for belief in an everlasting life with God. And it is easy to see how early Christian preachers could understand the final verses as a detailed prophecy of the Resurrection of Christ (Acts 2:24-28; 13:25).

This psalm is in a special way the prayer of those who have "chosen God" in one or other form of consecrated life. Rarely has the joy of a life lived in the presence of God been expressed with such enthusiasm. The wonder felt penetrates to the innermost being of the believer (that is, the "heart," which for the ancients was the seat of one's thoughts as well as desires and affections).

16:1 *Miktam:* its meaning is unknown. Some translate it as "song" or "poem"; others suggest that it means "in a low voice."

16:3 Another possible translation is: "As for the gods who are in the land / and the lofty ones, / I take no delight in them." *Saints:* i.e., the godly who live on earth as opposed to the angelic beings who are heavenly. See notes on Pss 4:4 and 34:10.

4 Those who chase after other gods
   only multiply their sorrows.
  Never will I pour out libations of blood to them,
   nor will I take up their names* on my lips.

5 O LORD, you are my allotted portion and my
   cup;*
   you have made my lot secure.[e]

6 The boundary lines have established a pleasant site for me;
   I have truly received a wonderful inheritance.

7 I bless the LORD who offers me counsel;
   even during the night my heart instructs me.

8 I keep the LORD always before me,
   for with him at my right hand
   I will never fall.[f]

9 Therefore, my heart is glad*
   and my soul rejoices;
   my body too is filled with confidence.

10 For you will not abandon me to the netherworld
   or allow your Holy One* to suffer corruption.[g]

---

e Pss 23:5; 73:26; Num 18:20; Deut 10:9; Sir 45:20-22; Lam 3:24.—f Pss
15:5; 73:23; 121:5; Acts 2:25-28.—g Pss 28:1; 30:4; 49:16; 86:13; Num
16:30; 2 Ki 19:22; Job 17:14; Hos 13:14; Jon 2:6; Acts 13:35.

16:4 *Take up their names:* that is, appeal to or worship them (see Jos 23:7).
 16:5 *Cup:* a metaphor referring to what the host offers his guests to drink. To
the righteous the Lord offers a cup of blessings (see Ps 23:5) or salvation (see Ps
116:13), but he makes the wicked drink from a cup of wrath (see Jer 25:15; Rev
14:10; 16:19).
 16:9-11 The Lord, in whom the psalmist takes refuge, wills life for him (hence
he has made known to him the path of life, v. 11) and will not abandon him to the
grave, even though "heart and . . . flesh fail" (Ps 73:26). But implicit in these
words of assurance (if not actually explicit) is the confidence that, with the Lord
as his refuge, even the grave cannot rob him of life (see Pss 17:15; 73:24). If this
could be said of David, how much more of David's promised Son! So Peter quotes
vv. 8-11 and declares that with these words David prophesied of Christ and his
Resurrection (Acts 2:25-28; see Paul's similar use of v. 10b in Acts 13:35). *Heart:*
see note on Ps 4:8.
 16:10 *Holy One:* the reference is first of all to David, but the psalm is ultimately fulfilled in Christ.

11 You will show me the path to life;
you will fill me with joy in your presence
and everlasting delights at your right hand.

PSALM 17*
Prayer in Time of Persecution

1 A prayer of David.

Hear, O LORD, my call for justice;
give heed to my cry.
Listen to the prayer of my lips,
for they are free of deceit.
2 Let my vindication issue forth from you;
let your eyes discern what is right.

3 You have probed my heart*
and examined me throughout the night.
You have tested me
and found no malice in me,
for I have not sinned with my mouth.[h]

4 Despite what other people do,
I have been guided by the word of your lips*
and refrained from their acts of violence.
5 My steps have held fast to your paths;
my feet have not wavered.[i]

6 I call upon you, O God, for you will answer me.
Incline your ear to me and listen to my
plea.

---

h Pss 26:2; 139:23; Job 7:18; 23:10.—i Pss 18:37; 44:19; Job 23:11-12.

Ps 17 Here again we have a picture of smug and pitiless people whose heart is closed to the word of God as well as to the cry of the poor. The psalmist who endures their unjust accusations begs God to show forth his innocence and to punish his evil accusers. He is willing to leave earthly goods to them (v. 14) as long as he can rejoice in God's presence. Perhaps we can see in this desire for awakening enlightened by God's face (v. 15) the burgeoning hope of the resurrection.

In praying this psalm, we should recall that in the Church (his Mystical Body) and in each Christian (as in a part of that Body), Jesus relives the mystery of his undeserved Passion and glorious Resurrection (see Acts 9:4f).

17:3 *Heart:* see note on Ps 4:8.

17:4 *Word of your lips:* God's revelation by which he made known the "paths" his faithful are to follow. *And refrained . . . violence:* an alternative translation is: "and kept the words of your law."

7 Show how wonderful is your kindness,*
  you who save those who seek protection
  by taking refuge at your right hand.

8 Guard me as the apple of your eye;[j]
  hide me in the shadow of your wings*
9 from the wicked who treat me with violence,
  from deadly enemies who surround me.[k]

10 There is no compassion in their hearts,*
   and arrogance issues from their mouths.
11 They track me down and begin to close in,
   watching for the chance to strike me down,
12 like a lion primed to attack its prey,
   like a young lion lurking in hiding.

13 Rise up, O LORD, confront them, and cast them
     down;*
   deliver me from the wicked by your sword.
14 With your hand, O LORD, snatch me from such
     people,
   from the worldly whose reward is in this
     life.*

  You satisfy the hunger of those you cherish;
    their children have all they desire
    and leave their wealth to their little ones.
15 But in my righteousness I will see your face;*
   when I awaken, I will be blessed by be-
     holding you.[l]

---

j 8-9: Pss 36:8; 57:2; 61:5; 63:8; 91:4; Deut 32:10; Ru 2:12; Prov 7:2; Zec
2:12; Mt 23:37.—k 9b-12: Pss 10:9; 22:13, 21; 35:17; 57:5; 58:7; Job 4:10-
11.—l Pss 4:7; 31:17; 67:2; 73:25-26; 80:4; Num 6:25; Dan 9:17; Rev 22:4.

17:7 *Kindness:* see note on Ps 6:5.
17:8 *Apple of your eye . . . shadow of your wings:* conventional Hebrew
metaphors for protection (see Deut 32:10; Prov 7:2; Isa 49:2).
17:10 *Hearts:* see note on Ps 4:8. *Arrogance . . . mouths:* see notes on Pss 5:11
and 10:7.
17:13 *Cast them down:* see note on Ps 5:11 and introduction to Ps 35.
17:14 *From the worldly . . . life:* or: "from mortals whose part in life is transitory." *You satisfy . . . little ones:* or: "With your treasures you fill their bellies; /
their sons are enriched / and bequeath their abundance to their little ones."
17:15 *See your face:* see note on Ps 11:7. *When I awaken:* from the night of
death; however, inasmuch as death is often compared to sleep (see Ps 76:6; Dan
12:1f), it may refer to a new awakening after death.

PSALM 18*

Thanksgiving for God's Help

¹ For the director.* Of David, the servant of the LORD.
He sang to the LORD the words of this song after the LORD
had rescued him from the clutches of all his enemies and
from the hand of Saul.ᵐ ² He said:

I love you, O LORD, my strength,
³   O LORD, my rock,* my fortress, my deliverer.
My God is my rock in whom I take refuge,
    my shield and the horn of my salvation,
    my stronghold.ⁿ
⁴ I call upon the LORD, who is worthy of all
        praise;
    and I am saved from my enemies.

⁵ The cords of death encompassed me,
    and the torrents of destruction assailed
        me.
⁶ The cords of the netherworld ensnared me,
    and the snares of death* rose up before me.ᵒ

---

m 1-51: 2 Sam 22:1-51.—n Pss 3:4; 28:8; 31:2-4; 42:10; Gen 49:24; Deut
32:4; 1 Sam 2:1-2.—o Pss 88:8; 93:3-4; 116:3-4; Num 16:33f; Prov 13:14.

Ps 18 This song of David occurs also in 2 Sam 22 with minor variations. It is
composed of an introduction (vv. 1-4), a conclusion (vv. 47-51), and three major
divisions: (1) the Lord's deliverance of David from mortal enemies (vv. 5-20); (2)
the moral grounds for the Lord's help (vv. 21-30); and (3) the Lord's help recounted (vv. 31-46).

Already emerging in this splendid psalm, which is both a song of thanksgiving
and a song of victory, is the image of the King-Messiah, Jesus, born of the house
of David and beloved Son of the Father; he will conquer the forces of evil. This
poem is a festal song expressing wonder and thanksgiving and glorifying God.

To the extent that we can allow ourselves to be identified with Christ and become
kings in him (see Ps 2), we can use this psalm to praise God the Father for the wonders that Paul celebrates in the hymn of the Letter to the Ephesians (1:3-15).

18:1 *For the director:* these words are thought to be a musical or liturgical
notation.

18:3 *Rock:* a common symbol for God indicating his strength as a refuge or as
a deliverer (see Pss 19:15; 31:3f; 42:10; 62:3, 8; 71:3; 73:26; 78:35; 89:27;
92:16; 94:22; 95:1; 144:1; Deut 32:15; Isa 17:10). See Jesus' use of the word in
Mt 16:18. *Horn:* a symbol of strength (see Deut 33:17; Jer 48:25); it often had
Messianic overtones (see Ps 132:17; Ezek 29:21).

18:6 *Cords of the netherworld . . . snares of death:* the psalmist had been in
the grip of death and a prisoner of the grave (see Ps 116:3; Job 36:8).

7 In my anguish I cried out to the LORD
    and called to my God for help.
  From his temple* he heard my voice,
    and my cry to him reached his ears.^{p}

8 The earth swayed and rocked;*
    the foundations of the mountains shook,^{q}
    rocking because of his blazing anger.
9 Smoke poured forth from his nostrils,
    while a scorching fire blazed out of his mouth
    and kindled coals into flame.

10 He parted the heavens and came down;
    dark clouds lay under his feet.^{r}
11 He rode upon a cherub,*
    soaring swiftly on the wings of the wind.

12 He used the darkness as his covering,
    and dense thunderclouds as his canopy.
13 From the radiance before him thick clouds
        emerged,
    spewing hail and flashes of fire.^{s}

14 The LORD thundered from the heavens,
    and the Most High let his voice be heard.^{t}
15 He shot his arrows* and scattered them,
    hurled his lightning bolts and routed them.^{u}
16 Then the depths of the sea were exposed,
    and the earth's foundations were laid bare,

---

p Ps 30:3; Jon 2:2.—q Pss 97:3-4; 99:1; Jdg 5:4-5; Isa 64:1; Jer 10:10; Hab 3:9-11.—r Pss 50:3; 104:3; 144:5; Isa 63:19.—s Ps 104:3; Ex 13:21; 19:16; Deut 4:11.—t Pss 29; 77:19; Ex 19:19; 1 Sam 2:10; Job 36:29-30; 37:3-4.—u Ps 144:6; Deut 32:23; Wis 5:21; Rev 4:5.

18:7 *Temple:* God's heavenly dwelling where he is enthroned (see Pss 11:4; 113:5; Isa 6:1; 40:22).
18:8-16 In these powerful images the ancients sang of the presence and glory of God in creation and in events (see Pss 68:9f; 97:2-5; Ex 19:15-18; Jdg 5:4f; Job 36:29f; Isa 30:27f; Hab 3:3-15). The description gives a presentiment of the struggle at the end of time in which God triumphs.
18:11 *Cherub:* a winged being, represented at the entrance of Mesopotamian temples. Two cherubim stood on the Ark of the Covenant (see Ex 25:18; 1 Ki 6:23-28). God was regarded as enthroned on them (see Pss 80:2; 99:1) and riding upon the storm clouds (see Ps 104:3) or upon the cherubim.
18:15 *Arrows:* shafts of lightning (see Ps 77:18; 144:6; Hab 3:11).

at the rebuke of the L<small>ORD</small>,*
    at the blast of wind from his nostrils.*v*

17 He reached down from on high and snatched
    me up;
    he drew me out of the watery depths.**w*

18 He delivered me from my powerful enemy,
    and from my foes, who were too strong for
    me.

19 They assailed me in the day of my misfortune,
    but the L<small>ORD</small> came forward to uphold me.

20 He led me forth into the open field;
    he set me free because he was pleased with
    me.

21 The L<small>ORD</small> has dealt with me according to my
    righteousness;*
    because my hands were pure, he has re-
    warded me.*x*

22 For I have kept the ways of the L<small>ORD</small>*
    and refused to turn away from my God.

23 His laws are clearly known to me,
    and I have not failed to observe his decrees.

24 I was blameless in his sight,
    and I kept myself free of sin.

25 Therefore, the L<small>ORD</small> has rewarded me ac-
    cording to my righteousness,
    because of the cleanness of my hands in
    his eyes.

26 To the loyal, you show yourself to be loyal;
    to the blameless, you show yourself to be
    blameless;*y*

---

v Ps 77:17; Ex 15:8; Isa 50:2; Zec 9:14.—w Ps 144:7; Ex 15:5; Prov
20:5.—x Ps 26:1; 1 Sam 26:23; 2 Chr 15:7; Job 22:30.—y Pss 31:24; 89:25;
125:4.

18:16 The psalmist may be referring to the wondrous deed God accomplished
at the Red Sea during the Exodus (see Ex 14:15-22).
    18:17 *Watery depths:* symbols of great danger (see Ps 32:6; 40:3; 42:8; 66:12;
69:3, 15; 88:18; 130:1; Job 22:11; Isa 30:28; Jon 2:5f).
    18:21 *Righteousness:* see note on Ps 1:5.
    18:22 *Ways of the L<small>ORD</small>:* see note on Ps 25:10.

27 to the pure, you show yourself to be pure;
   but to the perverse, you show yourself to
   be shrewd.*
28 For you save the humble,
   but you bring down the haughty.z

29 You, O Lord, are light for my lamp;*
   O my God, you make my darkness turn to
   light.a
30 With your help I can storm a rampart;
   with my God to aid me, I can scale any wall.
31 The way of God is blameless,
   and the Lord's promise proves true;
  he is a shield to all
   who flee to him for safety.b

32 Indeed, who is God except the Lord?
   Who is the Rock besides our God?c
33 It is God who clothes me with strength
   and makes my way blameless.
34 He gives me the swift feet of a deer
   and places me securely on the heights.d
35 He trains my hands for ware
   and my arms to bend a bow of bronze.*

36 You have given me the shield of your salvation;
   your right hand sustains me,
   and your goodness makes me great.
37 You broadened the path beneath me
   so that my feet have never stumbled.f

38 I went after my enemies and overtook them;
   I did not turn back until they were defeated.

---

z Job 22:29; Prov 3:34; Mt 23:12.—a Pss 27:1; 36:10; 43:3; 119:105;
132:17; Job 29:3; Mic 7:8.—b Pss 12:7; 77:14; Deut 32:4; Prov 30:5.—c Ps
35:10; Isa 44:8; 45:21.—d Deut 32:13; Isa 58:14; Hab 3:19.—e Ps 144:1; 2
Sam 22:35.—f Pss 17:5; 31:9; 66:9; Job 18:7.

18:27 God treats people the way they treat him and others. *The perverse:* those
who stray from the straight way of the Lord. *Show yourself to be shrewd:* the Lord
counters the evil acts of the wicked, one against the other.

18:29 *Light for my lamp:* a figure of life and happiness (see 1 Ki 11:36). *Light:*
see note on Ps 27:1.

18:35 *Bow of bronze:* a bow difficult to bend that would shoot arrows with
greater force.

39 When I knocked them down, they were
      unable to rise;
    they fell down at my feet.

40 You clothed me with strength for the battle
    and cast down my adversaries beneath me.
41 You made my enemies retreat before me,
    so that I could scatter those who hated me.

42 They called for help, but there was no one to
      deliver them;
    they called to the LORD, but no answer
      came.
43 I crushed them like fine dust before the wind;
    I trod on them like mud in the streets.

44 You delivered me from a people in rebellion,
    and you placed me in charge of the nations;
    people I did not know have become my
      subjects.
45 As soon as they heard me, they obeyed;
    foreigners groveled before me.
46 Then they became disheartened
    and came forth trembling from their strong-
      holds.*g*

47 The LORD lives! Blessed* be my Rock!
    Exalted be God, my Savior!*h*
48 O God, you obtained vindication for me,
    subjected nations under me,*i*
49   and freed me from my enemies.
  You exalted me over my adversaries
    and delivered me from the violent.

50 For this, O LORD, I will praise you among the
      nations
    and sing praise to your name.**j*

---

g Mic 7:17; Heb 12:3.—h Pss 21:14; 144:1.—i Pss 20:7; 144:2.—j Pss
7:18; 9:12; 30:5; 57:10; 101:1; 108:2; 135:3; 146:2; Rom 15:9.

18:47 *Blessed:* i.e., adored, praised, and thanked.
18:50 This text is cited by Paul (Rom 15:9) as a prediction of the conversion of
the Gentiles. *Name:* see note on Ps 5:12.

51 You have bestowed great victories on your
king,
and you have shown kindness to your
anointed,*
to David and his descendants forever.*k*

PSALM 19*
God's Glory in Creation

1 For the director.* A psalm of David.

2 The heavens proclaim the glory of God;*
the firmament shows forth the work of his
hands.*l*

3 One day imparts that message to the next,
and night conveys that knowledge to night.

4 All this occurs without speech or utterance;
no voice can be heard.

5 Yet their message goes forth throughout the
earth,
and their words to the ends of the world.*

---

k Pss 89:5, 29-38; 144:10; 1 Sam 2:10; 2 Sam 23:1.—l Pss 8:1; 50:6;
89:6; 97:6; 147:4-5; 148:3-4; Gen 1:1-8; Isa 40:22; Rom 1:19-20.

18:51 *You have shown kindness to your anointed:* the Lord is mindful of his
covenant with his anointed king and never ceases bestowing blessings upon him.
This is even more true of the King and Anointed par excellence, Jesus Christ.
Kindness: see note on Ps 6:5.

Ps 19 The universe is a hymn to the glory of the Lord, but this is even more true
of the Mosaic Law. The silent revelation of creation is offered to all human beings,
but the Law, privilege of Israel, reveals to the hearts of believers God's perfection,
justice, truth, and goodness and challenges them to imitate the divine life.

The ode to the sun in this psalm (vv. 5b-7) seems to be an imitation of a frag-
mentary Assyrian text in which the sun-god rises from the ocean and passes
through the gates of the east to meet the goddess. The Christmas Liturgy uses
this image to recall, in poetic language, the coming to earth of the Son of God.

By its splendor and vastness, the star-studded heavens teach us the glory, the
splendor and infinite power, the prodigious artistry of the Father, the Son, and the
Holy Spirit who work together in its continuous creation. The Law, perfect as far
as its epoch and its place in the divine economy of salvation are concerned, was
brought to its absolute perfection by Christ (see Mt 5:17).

19:1 *For the director:* these words are thought to be a musical or liturgical
notation.

19:2-5b The heavens show forth the glory of their Creator to all peoples (see
Ps 148:3).

19:5ab Paul interprets this proclamation of the heavens as referring also to
the proclamation of the Gospel (see Rom 10:18).

In the heavens he has placed a tent for the sun,*
6   which comes forth like a bridegroom from
      his wedding chamber,
   rejoicing like an athlete who runs his course.
7 It rises from one end of the heavens,
      and its circuit is completed at the other;
   nothing can be hidden from its heat.

8 The law of the LORD is perfect,
      affording refreshment to the soul.
   The decree of the LORD is worthy of trust,
      imparting wisdom to the simple.*[m]
9 The precepts of the LORD are right,
      causing the heart* to rejoice.
   The commands of the LORD are clear,
      giving light to the eyes.

10 The fear of the LORD* is pure,
      destined to endure forever.
   The ordinances of the LORD are true,
      and all of them are just.
11 They are even more precious than gold,
      than an abundance of the purest gold;
   they are also sweeter than honey[n]
      that drips from the comb.*

---

m Pss 12:7; 93:5; 111:7; 119:130, 138, 144; Deut 4:6.—n Ps 119:72, 103, 127; 1 Sam 14:27; Job 22:24-25; Prov 8:10; Song 4:11; Sir 24:19; Ezek 3:3.

19:5c-7 The heavens are the divinely pitched tent for the lordly sun—widely worshiped in the ancient Near East (see Deut 4:19; 17:3; 2 Ki 23:5, 11; Jer 8:2; Ezek 8:16), but here a mere creature of God (as in Gen 1:16; Ps 136:8f). Of the created realm, the sun is the supreme metaphor of the glory of God (see Ps 84:12; Isa 60:19f), as it makes its daily triumphant sweep across the whole extent of the heavens and pours out its heat (felt presence) on every creature. The literature of the time applied to the sun the six synonyms for God's revelation in vv.8-11.
19:8 *The simple:* those who are inexperienced and hence childlike (see Pss 119:98-100; Prov 1:4); the New Testament shows that heavenly wisdom is a gift to "children," hidden from the worldly-wise (see Lk 10:21; 1 Cor 1:18ff; 2:8-10; 2 Tim 3:15).
19:9 *Heart:* see note on Ps 4:8.
19:10 *Fear of the LORD:* see note on Ps 15:2-5. In this case, some exegetes believe that the term "fear" should really be "word."
19:11 See Ps 119:103, 127. This entire hymn to the Law is closely connected to the long Psalm 119.

¹² By these your servant is instructed;*
    obedience in following them will ensure a
      great reward.
¹³ But who can fully recognize his shortcom-
    ings?
    Cleanse me of my hidden faults.

¹⁴ From willful sins preserve your servant;
    never let them gain power over me.
  Then I will be blameless
    and innocent of serious sin.

¹⁵ Let the words of my mouth and the thoughts
    of my heart
    find favor in your sight,
    O LORD, my Rock and my Redeemer.*

PSALM 20*
Prayer in Praise of the Messiah King

¹ For the director.* A psalm of David.

² May the LORD answer you in times of trouble;
    may the name* of the God of Jacob protect
      you.

19:12-14 The psalmist knows that God's commandments lead to life (see Deut 5:33). Yet he is also aware that like all human beings he is weak and imperfect. He may err unknowingly and need to seek forgiveness of "hidden faults" (v. 13; see Lev 5:2-4). However, "willful sins" (v. 14) are another matter; they cut one off from God and his people (see Num 15:30f). He prays to be preserved from them.

19:15 This meditation is presented to the Lord as a praise offering (see notes on Pss 7:18 and 9:2; see also Pss 50:14; 104:33). *Heart:* see note on Ps 4:8. *Rock:* see note on Ps 18:3.

Ps 20 During a liturgy of prayer for the king just before he engages in battle with a powerful foe (2 Chr 20:6), the people (perhaps the assembled soldiers) pray for their king: is he not a "messiah," that is, an "anointed one" of the Lord (v. 7) and the head of the chosen people of the God of Jacob (v. 3)? A choir chants the petition (vv. 3-6) and a soloist (perhaps a Levite: see 2 Chr 20:14) responds (vv. 7-9); he announces assurance that the prayer will be heard, for Israel does not rely on the force of arms as its pagan neighbors do but on its God and Savior. Thus, the people already celebrate the coming triumph of the Lord.

In praying this psalm, we can ask the Father to grant the integral victory of Christ in his mystical members, just as he gained it in and for himself (see 1 Cor 15:22f). For the Father is the accomplisher of all things (see Rom 11:36).

20:1 *For the director:* these words are thought to be a musical or liturgical notation.

20:2, 6, 8 *Name:* see notes on Pss 5:12 and 8:2. *Protect you:* literally, "raise you to a high, safe place."

3 May he send you help from the sanctuary
and grant you support from Zion.*[o]
4 May he remember* all your sacrifices
and accept all your burnt offerings. *Selah*

5 May he give you your heart's desire*
and grant you success in all your plans.
6 May we shout with joy over your victory
and lift up our banners in the name of our God.*
May the Lord grant your every request.

7 Now I know that the LORD will grant victory to his anointed;*
he will answer him from his holy heaven,
granting mighty victories with his right hand.[p]

8 Some trust in chariots, and some in horses,[q]
but we trust in the name of the LORD, our God. *
9 They will collapse and fall,
but we will rise up and stand firm.[r]

10 O LORD, save the king,
and answer us when we call upon you.

---

o Pss 30:10; 128:5; 134:3.—p Pss 18:51; 28:8; 144:10; 1 Sam 2:10; Job 40:14; Hab 3:13.—q Ps 147:10-11; 1 Sam 17:45; 2 Chr 14:10; Prov 21:31; Isa 31:1; 36:9; 40:30-31; Hos 1:7.—r Ps 27:2; Isa 40:30; Jer 46:6.

20:3 *Zion:* see note on Ps 9:12.

20:4 *Remember:* with God, remembering and acting go together (see Gen 8:1; Ex 2:24).

20:5 *Heart's desire:* see note on Ps 4:8.

20:6 *May we shout . . . name of our God:* see note on Ps 7:18. The Hebrew word "victory" could also be translated as "salvation."

20:7 *His anointed:* i.e., the king of Israel (see Pss 2:2; 132:10); the divine help is his as intrinsic to his kingship (see Ps 18:51). See note on Ps 2:2.

20:8-9 The force of arms is useless in the face of the divine power. The Prophets were always against the use of horses and chariots in Israel, in imitation of the neighboring pagans (see Deut 17:16; Isa 31:1; Hos 1:7; Mic 5:10; Zec 12:4). The same affirmation occurs in Pss 33:16f; 147:10; Prov 21:31. A similar expression of confidence in the Lord rather than in human weaponry is made by David when facing Goliath (1 Sam 17:45-47).

20:10 The psalm ends in the same way as it began—with fervent prayers that the Lord will come to the aid of the king.

PSALM 21*

Thanksgiving for Messianic Blessings

¹ For the director.* A psalm of David.

² O Lᴏʀᴅ, the king rejoices in your strength;
   your victories fill him with great joy.ˢ
³ You have granted him the desire of his heart*
   and not withheld from him the request of
      his lips.   *Selah*

⁴ You welcomed him with choice blessings*
      and placed a crown of pure gold upon his
      head.
⁵ He asked you for life, and you gave it to him,
   length of days forever and ever.ᵗ

⁶ He has achieved great glory through your
      victory;
   you have bestowed upon him splendor and
      majesty.*

---

s Ps 63:12; 1 Sam 2:10; 2 Sam 22:51.—t Pss 10:16; 45:18; 48:15; 133:3;
1 Ki 3:14; 2 Ki 20:1-7; Isa 38:1-20.

Ps 21 One would have a poor understanding of feasts if one did not allow
chants to intermingle desires and reality. On a feast, the king appears to share
the privileges of God: authority, long rule, and majesty, for the Lord has blessed
and established him to save his people from their foes. The history of Israel will
more than once give the lie to this ideal figure of the monarch. The Church sees
therein the traits of Jesus Christ, King and Savior of the People of God; in him resides the blessing for the whole world. The psalm continued to be sung in Israel
even when the kingship ended after the sixth century A.D.—but this time concerning a future Messianic King.

By a very simple spiritual transposition, this psalm enables us to sing of the
divine blessings granted to Christ, especially his Resurrection, and to hope for
his complete and decisive triumph over his enemies (the devil, sin, and death).

21:1 *For the director:* these words are thought to be a musical or liturgical
notation.

21:3 *Heart:* see note on Ps 4:8.

21:4 *You welcomed him with choice blessings:* as you once welcomed Abraham (see Gen 12:2) and Joseph (see Gen 48:20). *Placed a crown . . . upon his
head:* alludes either to his own crown reinforcing his kingship after his victory or
to the crown of the king that he had defeated (see 2 Sam 12:30). This verse is
eminently applied to the Messiah (see Pss 45:4; 72:17; 2 Sam 7:29; 1 Chr 17:27).

21:6 *Glory . . . splendor and majesty:* like those of the heavenly King (see Ps
96:3).

⁷ You have conferred everlasting blessings* on
    him;
    you gladdened him with the joy of your
        presence.
⁸ For the king places his trust in the LORD;
    through the kindness* of the Most High he
        will not fall.

⁹ Your hand will lay hold of all your enemies;*
    your right hand will overcome all your foes.
¹⁰ On the day when you appear,*
    you will cast them into a fiery furnace.
  The LORD's anger will engulf them,
    and fire will consume them.
¹¹ You will blot out their descendants from the
        earth
    and rid the human race of their posterity.*

¹² They have devised wicked schemes against
        you,
    but, plot though they may, they will not
        succeed.
¹³ For you will force them to retreat
    when you aim your bows at them.

¹⁴ Be exalted, O LORD, in your strength;*
    we will sing and praise your power.ᵘ

---

u Pss 18:2, 47; 144:1; Num 10:35.

21:7 *Everlasting blessings:* this phrase may refer to blessings of enduring
value or an unending number of blessings. *Your presence:* God's favor, which is
the greatest cause of joy inasmuch as it is the supreme blessing, leading to all
others.
21:8 *Kindness:* see note on Ps 6:5.
21:9-13 The king's future victories are described as certain because of the
Lord's action.
21:10 The expression *on the day when you appear,* literally, "on the day of your
face [judgment]" (see Ps 34:17; Lam 4:16) and the mention of the fire are eschatological themes (see Ps 2:12; 2 Sam 23:7; Isa 30:33; Hos 7:7; Mal 3:19).
21:11 The foes of the king will have no descendants to make war on him.
21:14 The word "strength" in the concluding verse connects the theme with
the opening verse: "O LORD, the king rejoices in your strength" (v. 2), and we will
offer you our praise.

PSALM 22*

Suffering and Triumph of the Messiah

¹ For the director.* According to "The Deer of the Dawn."
A psalm of David.

² My God, my God, why have you forsaken me?*
    Why have you paid no heed to my call for
      help,
    to my cries of anguish?ᵛ
³ O my God, I cry by day, but you do not an-
    swer,
    by night, but I am afforded no relief.*ʷ

⁴ Yet you are enthroned as the Holy One;
    you are the praise of Israel.ˣ
⁵ Our ancestors placed their trust in you;
    they trusted, and you gave them deliverance.
⁶ They cried out to you and were saved,
    they trusted in you and were not put to
      shame.ʸ

---

v Ps 10:1; Job 3:24; Isa 49:14; 54:7; Mt 27:46; Mk 15:34.—w Ps 42:4;
Sir 2:10.—x Ps 71:22; Isa 6:3.—y Ps 25:3; Isa 49:23; Dan 3:39f; Rom 9:33.

Ps 22 This psalm draws its inspiration from the "Songs of the Suffering Righteous Man (*or* Servant)" (Isa 52:13—53:12) and from the "Confessions of
Jeremiah" (Jer 15:15; 17:15; 20:7); it ends, as they do, with the proclamation that
the sufferings of the righteous man will restore life to humanity. Such a text
seems planned, as it were, to become the prayer of Christ (Mk 15:34), and the
Gospels have also singled out details from it that describe in advance the Passion of Jesus (e.g., Mt 27:35, 39, 43; Jn 19:23f, 28). The author of Hebrews even
placed the words of v. 23 on the lips of Jesus (Heb 2:12). Indeed, no other psalm
is so often quoted in the New Testament.

In praying this psalm, we can keep in mind that Christ continues to pray it
through the Church and Christians, since he continues the mystery of his abandonment in his Mystical Body.

22:1 *For the director:* these words are thought to be a musical or liturgical
notation. *According to "The Deer of the Dawn":* nothing is known about these
words.

22:2-12 Why? The question erupts from the heart of a righteous man. Yesterday he was still enjoying God's favor as a son, but now he feels abandoned for no
reason and afflicted with atrocious sufferings and made the laughingstock of
free-thinkers. Has God changed?

22:3 *But I am afforded no relief:* the Hebrew text is obscure here. Some translate: "by night, and am not silent."

7 But I am a worm and not human,*
  scorned by people and despised by my
    kinsmen.ᶻ
8 All who see me jeer at me;
  they sneer in mockery and toss their
    heads:*ᵃ
9 "He relied on the LORD;ᵇ
  let the LORD set him free.
Let the LORD deliver him,
  if he loves him."*

10 Yet you brought me out of the womb
  and made me feel secure
  upon my mother's breast.
11 I was entrusted to your care at my birth;*
  from my mother's womb, you have been
    my God.ᶜ
12 Do not remain aloof from me,
  for trouble is near
  and no one can help me.ᵈ

13 * Many bulls* are encircling me;
  fierce bulls of Bashan are closing in on me.
14 They open wide their mouths against me
  like ravening and roaring lions.ᵉ

---

z Ps 31:12; Isa 53:3.—a Pss 35:16; 109:25; Mt 27:39; Mk 15:29; Lk 23:36.—b Pss 71:11; 91:14; Wis 2:18-20; Mt 27:43.—c Ps 71:6; Gen 50:23; Isa 44:2; 46:3.—d Pss 35:22; 38:21; 40:14; 71:12; 2 Ki 14:26; Isa 41:28.—e Ps 17:12; Job 4:10; Ezek 22:25; Zep 3:3; 1 Pet 5:8.

22:7 *I am a worm and not human:* this passage clearly depicts the psalmist's sense of isolation (see Job 25:6; Isa 41:14).
22:8 *They sneer in mockery and toss their heads:* words and gestures of scorn, also indulged in by Christ's foes on Calvary (see Mt 27:39; Mk 15:29). See also note on Ps 5:10.
22:9 Cited in Mt 27:43. *If he loves him:* may be taken as "if God loves the sufferer" or "if the sufferer loves God."
22:11 *I was entrusted to your care at my birth:* the father customarily acknowledged the newborn by taking it upon his knees (see Gen 50:23; Job 3:12).
22:13-22 Around the beleaguered man there arises a wave of hostility; he experiences in his flesh the whole of human sorrow. The images are delusive, and the cries become pathetic. Here is a man whose life is being taken away.
22:13f, 17 *Bulls . . . lions. . . . dogs:* these are metaphors for the enemies. *Bashan:* a land east of the Jordan that was noted for its good pasturage and the size and quality of its animals (see Deut 32:14; Ezek 39:18; Am 4:1).

¹⁵ My strength is trickling away like water,
     and all my bones are dislocated.
My heart* has turned to wax
     and melts within me.
¹⁶ My mouth is as dry as clayware,
     and my tongue sticks to my jaw;*
     you have laid me down in the dust of death.

¹⁷ A pack of dogs surrounds me;
     a band of evildoers is closing in on me.
They have pierced my hands and my feet;*
¹⁸   I can count all my bones.*^f
They stare at me and gloat;
¹⁹   they divide my garments among them,
     and for my clothing they cast lots.*^g

²⁰ But you, O LORD, do not remain aloof from me.
O my Strength, come quickly to my aid.*
²¹ Deliver my soul from the sword,
     my precious life from the grasp of the dogs.
²² Save me* from the lion's mouth
     and from the horns of wild oxen.^h

---

f Ps 109:24; Mic 7:8.—g Lev 16:8; Mt 27:35; Mk 15:24; Lk 23:34; Jn 19:24.—h Pss 7:2-3; 17:12; 35:17; 57:5; 58:7; Job 4:10; 2 Tim 4:17.

22:15 *Bones . . . heart:* his combination of "bones" and "heart" (see note on Ps 4:8) was used to refer to the whole person (body and spirit) (see Ps 102:4; Prov 14:30; 15:30; Isa 66:14).

22:16 *My mouth . . . jaw:* see Jn 19:28 ("I thirst"). *The dust of death:* the netherworld, domain of the dead; the author is using the language of his day, as in Mesopotamian descriptions of the netherworld (see Job 7:9, 21).

22:17 *Pierced my hands and my feet:* his limbs are wounded by the dogs as he seeks to fend off their attacks (see also Isa 53:5; Zec 12:10; Jn 19:34). Although the phrase finds its complete fulfillment in Christ's crucifixion, it is not expressly used by the Evangelists in the Passion account.

22:18 *I can count all my bones:* this could also be translated as "I must display all my bones." The meaning is that one is attacked and stripped of his garments (see v. 19).

22:19 Explicitly cited in Jn 19:24 as a prophecy fulfilled in the action of the soldiers who divided Christ's garments among them on Calvary.

22:20-22 The scene shifts as the beleaguered psalmist is led to confront the God of the Covenant. He thus recalls God's promises to be near his people and to protect them from all adversity. He throws himself on the Lord's mercy and is comforted.

22:22 *Save me:* an alternative translation is: "You have heard me." The psalmist knows he has been heard and will be delivered from death.

²³ I will proclaim your name to my family;*
    in the midst of the assembly I will praise
        you:ⁱ
²⁴ "You who fear the LORD, praise him.
    All you descendants of Jacob, give him glory.
    Revere him, all you descendants of Israel.
²⁵ For he has not scorned or disregarded
    the wretched man in his suffering;
  he has not hidden his face* from him
    but has heeded his call for help."

²⁶ I will offer my praise to you in the great
        assembly;
    in the presence of those who fear him, I
        will fulfill my vows.
²⁷ The poor* will eat and be filled;
    those who seek the LORD will praise him:
    "May your hearts live forever."ʲ

²⁸ All the ends of the earth
    will remember and turn to the LORD.
  All the families of the nations
    will bow low before him.ᵏ
²⁹ For kingly power belongs to the LORD;
    he is the ruler of all the nations.ˡ

---

i Pss 26:12; 35:18; 40:11; 68:27; 109:30; 149:1; 2 Sam 22:50; Heb 2:12.—j Pss 23:5; 69:34; 107:9.—k Pss 86:9; 102:23; Job 13:11; Isa 45:22; 52:10; Zec 14:16.—l Pss 47:8; 103:19; Ob 21; Zec 14:9.

22:23-32 God reverses the righteous man's condition; his hope returns. In the temple, he celebrates his deliverance and offers a sacrifice of communion amidst the poor who love God. Then the perspective is enlarged even more. The whole earth gives thanks to God who rules the world and dispenses justice. The poor are called to the table of God, and the line of the righteous shall never be extinguished from the midst of human beings. Indeed, the passion of the righteous man has changed something in the human world. *Name:* see note on Ps 5:12.

22:25 *Not hidden his face:* a metaphor for God withdrawing from someone (see Pss 13:2; 27:9; 69:18; 88:15; 102:3; 143:7; Isa 8:17; Mic 3:4).

22:27-32 In an allusion to the Messianic Banquet (see Ps 23:5; Prov 9:1f; Isa 25:6; 55:1; 65:13), the psalmist describes a worldwide company of people from every state in life who will ultimately take up God's praise from age to age. It constitutes one of the grandest visions of the scope of the worshipers who will come to praise the saving acts of the Lord.

22:27 *The poor:* the *anawim,* originally the poor who depended on God for their livelihood; later, the humble, pious, and devout—those who hoped in God alone.

³⁰ All those who prosper on the earth will bow
    down before him;
    all those who lie in the grave will kneel in
      homage.
But I will live for the LORD,
³¹   and my descendants will serve him.
Future generations will be told about the Lord
³²   so that they may proclaim to a people yet
     unborn
    the deliverance he has accomplished.*[m]

PSALM 23*

Prayer to the Good Shepherd

¹ A psalm of David.

The LORD is my shepherd;
    there is nothing I shall lack.[n]
² He makes me lie down in green pastures;*
    he leads me to tranquil streams.

---

m Pss 40:11; 48:14-15; 71:18; 78:6; 102:19; Isa 53:10; Lk 18:31; Eph
2:7.—n Pss 80:2; 95:7; 100:3; Gen 48:15; Deut 2:7; Ezek 34:2; Jn 10:11.

22:30c-32 *But I will live for the LORD . . . he has accomplished:* this is the
more common translation (and the one found in the new Vulgate). An alternative
translation is: "and those who cannot keep themselves alive. / Posterity will serve
him; / future generations will be told about the LORD. / They will proclaim his
righteousness / to a people yet unborn— / for he has done it."

Ps 23 This psalm is a profession of joyful trust in the Lord as the good Shepherd-King that has become one of the world's greatest prayers. The image of God
in shepherd's garb has parallels in the Prophets (see Isa 40:11; Ezek 34:11-16)
and will be the best known of the allegories in which Jesus speaks of himself (see
Jn 10:11-18), so much so that the New Testament writers love to give him this
title (see Heb 13:20; 1 Pet 2:25; Rev 7:17). The water, oil, and cup of wine of
which the text speaks made Christians think of the Sacraments of initiation:
Baptism, Confirmation, and Eucharist. As a result, the psalm used to be sung
during the Easter Vigil by the newly baptized, who were filled with the joy of God.

In praying this psalm, we can dwell on the fact that the heavenly Father's love
embraces us from eternity, preparing for us in Christ all kinds of spiritual blessings: election, adoption, redemption, incorporation into Christ (see Eph 1:3-14).
He watches over us solicitously (see Mt 6:25-34) and follows us through the Good
Shepherd who seeks out the straying sheep until he finds it again (see Lk 15).

23:2 *Green pastures:* a symbol for everything that makes life flourish. *Tranquil
streams:* literally, "waters of resting places," waters that bring refreshment and
well-being (see Isa 49:10).

³ He restores my soul,*
  guiding me in paths of righteousness
  so that his name may be glorified.^o
⁴ Even though I wander
  through the valley of the shadow of death,*
  I will fear no evil,
    for you are at my side,
  with your rod and your staff
    that comfort me.^p

⁵ You spread a table* for me
  in the presence of my enemies.^q
You anoint my head with oil;
  my cup overflows.*^r
⁶ Only goodness and kindness* will follow me
  all the days of my life,
and I will dwell in the house of the LORD
  forever and ever.^s

---

o Ps 115:1; Prov 4:11.—p Ps 107:14; Job 10:21; Isa 50:10.—q Pss 22:27; 63:6; 92:11.—r Pss 16:5; 116:13; Lk 7:46.—s Pss 27:4; 61:5; Neh 9:25.

23:3 *Restores my soul:* the Lord revitalizes the psalmist's spirit (see Ps 19:8; Ru 4:15; Prov 25:13; Lam 1:16). *Paths of righteousness:* paths that conform to the will of the Lord, the "right way."

23:4 *Valley of the shadow of death:* another possible translation is: "through the darkest valley." It refers to any situation that is death-threatening.

23:5-6 What was only a comparison used by the psalmist to indicate the happiness of those who dwell in the house of the Lord has become a wonderful reality in the New Covenant. God sets the table for all who as members of his Church seek rest and protection in the house of God during their pilgrimage. He gives them the Bread of Heaven and the cup of his love and the riches of his grace—Christ's Precious Blood and the anointing of the Spirit with his sevenfold gifts.

23:5 In the ancient Near East, covenants were frequently made at a meal (see Ps 41:10; Gen 31:54; Ob 7). *Anoint my head with oil:* reception customarily accorded to an honored guest at a banquet (see Lk 7:46; see also 2 Sam 12:20; Eccl 9:8; Dan 10:3). *Cup:* the same image is found in Pss 16:5; 75:9; 116:13. This verse indicates that the Messianic Banquet (see Ps 22:27) is reserved for the righteous; the wicked are excluded from it (see Isa 65:13f).

23:6 *Goodness and kindness:* the terms often refer to blessings of God's Covenant with Israel; here they are personified (see Pss 25:21; 43:3; 79:8; 89:14). *Days of my life:* see Pss 27:4; 128:5. *Forever:* this word could mean "throughout the years." However, since even the pagan people surrounding Israel believed that human life continued after death in some kind of shadowy existence in the netherworld (see notes on Pss 11:7; 16:9-11), the word "forever" legitimately can be taken in its true sense.

PSALM 24*

The Lord's Solemn Entry into Jerusalem

[1] A psalm of David.

The earth is the LORD's and everything in it,[t]
   the world and all who live in it.*
[2] For he founded it on the seas
   and established* it on the rivers.[u]

[3] Who may ascend the mountain of the LORD?
   Who may stand in his holy place?[v]
[4] One who has clean hands and a pure heart,*
   who does not turn his mind to vanities
   or swear an oath in order to deceive.

[5] He will receive a blessing from the LORD
   and vindication from God, his Savior.
[6] This is the generation of those who seek him,
   who seek the face of the God of Jacob.
                                   Selah

---

t Pss 50:12; 89:12; Ex 9:29; Deut 10:14; Isa 66:1-2; 1 Cor 10:26.—u Pss 75:4; 136:6; Gen 1:6; Isa 42:5.—v Pss 2:6; 15:1; 65:5.

Ps 24 A procession wends its way toward the temple; perhaps it bears the Ark of the Covenant to the holy place. Chants are expressed. They acclaim the Creator and thus recall the conditions for a true participation in worship: "clean hands and a pure heart" (vv. 3-6). At the entrance to the sanctuary, the cortege comes to a halt as the participants take time to meditate wonderingly about the presence of God. They must needs celebrate God the Vanquisher who takes possession of his holy dwelling; the titles given him (vv. 8-10) evoke the time when, represented by the ark, the Lord would take his place at the head of the armies of Israel and lead them to victory (Num 10:35; Jos 6).

This psalm is well adapted to celebrating feasts of the Lord and to calling for the coming of his kingdom. It is also a psalm that makes demands, since it tells us of the conditions required for receiving the kingdom of God. The Church has always used this psalm in celebrating Christ's Ascension into the heavenly Jerusalem and into the sanctuary on high.

24:1-2 The Lord is proclaimed as the Creator, Sustainer, and Owner of the entire world. Therefore, he is worthy of the title "King of glory" (vv. 7-10). See Pss 29; 33:6-11; 89:6-19; 95:3-5; 104).

24:1 See Ps 89:12; Deut 10:14. This text is cited in 1 Cor 10:26.

24:2 *Founded . . . established:* a metaphor taken from the founding of a city. Extra-Biblical records indicate that temples were regarded as microcosms of the created world; hence language applicable to temples was also applicable to the earth.

24:4 *Clean hands . . . pure heart:* those who do no evil and think no evil. Jesus said that the "pure of heart . . . will see God" (Mt 5:8).

7 Lift up your arches, O gates;*
    rise up, you ancient portals, *
    so that the King of glory may come in.ʷ
8 Who is this King of glory?
    The Lᴏʀᴅ, strong and mighty,
    the Lᴏʀᴅ, valiant in battle.

9 Lift up your arches, O gates,
    rise up, you ancient portals,
    so that the King of glory may come in.
10 Who is this King of glory?
    The Lᴏʀᴅ of hosts:*
    he is the King of glory.   *Selah*

PSALM 25*
Prayer for Guidance and Help

1 Of David.

To you, O Lᴏʀᴅ, I lift up my soul;*ˣ
2   in you, O my God, I trust.ʸ

---

w Ps 118:19-20; Ezek 44:2; Mal 3:1.—x Pss 86:4; 143:8.—y Ps 71:1.

24:7-10 These verses speak of the arrival of the Lord, the King of glory, at his sanctuary in Zion after his victorious journey from Egypt. "The Lᴏʀᴅ of hosts" (v. 10), "the Lᴏʀᴅ, valiant in battle" (v. 8; see Ex 15:1-18), has routed his enemies and now comes in triumph to his own city (see Pss 46; 48; 76; 87).

24:7, 9 *Lift up your arches, O gates . . . you ancient portals:* the gates and doors are personified in accord with extra-Biblical parallels.

24:10 *The Lᴏʀᴅ of hosts:* in Hebrew, *Yahweh Sabaoth,* sometimes translated as "the Lord of armies." The expression suggests, first of all, the God who leads the Israelite army, therefore the Almighty who is surrounded by angels and stars and who controls the cosmic forces; then the expression becomes simply a way of emphasizing the greatness and power of God. See also note on Ps 59:6.

Ps 25 One admires the inner quality of the righteous man who addresses himself to God in this alphabetical psalm (see p. 23). He does not believe that he is totally innocent. He takes false steps and deserves his wretchedness and his isolation because of his sins. His confession testifies to much uprightness and honesty. It is the attitude of a humble person who knows he is loved by God and trusts in him; he hopes to receive pardon, counsel, and assistance from the Lord. The theme of this beautiful prayer is given in the cry of hope in vv. 1-2, which the Liturgy puts on the lips of Christians at the beginning of Advent.

In praying this psalm, we can dwell on the fact that in his unfailing love God is pleased to lead us back to the right path when we go astray and to keep us on it. Christ gives us salvation through the remission of sins (see Lk 1:77-79).

25:1-3 Prayer for relief from distress and the ensuing slander from one's foes.

Do not let me be put to shame,
    or permit my enemies to gloat over me.
3 No one who places his hope in you
    will ever be put to shame,
but shame will be the lot of all
    who break faith without justification.z

4 Make your ways known to me, O LORD;*
    teach me your paths.a
5 Guide me in your truth and instruct me,
    for you are God, my Savior,
    and in you I hope all the day long.

6 Be mindful, O LORD, that mercy and kindness*
    have been yours from of old.b
7 Remember not the sins of my youth
    or my many transgressions,
but remember me in your kindness,
    for the sake of your goodness, O LORD.c

8 Good and upright is the LORD;*
    therefore, he instructs sinners in his ways.
9 He guides the humble in what is right
    and teaches them the path to follow.
10 The ways of the LORD* are kindness and truth
    for those who keep his covenant and his
        decrees.
11 For the sake of your name,* O LORD,
    pardon my iniquity, great though it be.

12 Who, then, is the man that fears the LORD?d
    He will be shown the path he should choose.*

---

z Ps 22:6; Isa 24:16; 49:23; Dan 3:40; 2 Tim 3:4-5.—a Pss 27:11; 86:11;
119:12, 35; 143:8, 10; Ex 33:13; Jn 14:6.—b Ps 98:3; Sir 51:8; Isa 63:7.—c
Ps 106:4; Job 13:26; Isa 64:8.—d Ps 128:1; Job 1:8; Prov 19:23.

25:4-7 Prayer for guidance and pardon. *Your ways:* that is, "your commandments" (see Pss 27:11; 86:11; 128:1; 143:8). *Kindness:* see note on Ps 6:5.
    25:8-15 Trust in the Lord's Covenant blessings.
    25:10 *Ways of the LORD:* God's manner of dealing kindly with those who remain
faithful to the Covenant (see Pss 103:7; 138:5). See also Ps 85:10; Gen 32:10;
Deut 33:9; and Paul's magnificent summary in Rom 8:28: "We know that God
makes all things work together for good for those who love him."
    25:11 *Name:* see note on Ps 5:12.
    25:12 *The path he should choose:* or "the path chosen for him."

¹³ He will enjoy lasting prosperity,*e*
   and his descendants will inherit the land.*

¹⁴ The LORD manifests himself to those who
    fear him,*
   and he makes his covenant known to them.
¹⁵ My eyes are ever upon the LORD,
   for he alone can free my feet from the
    snare.*f*

¹⁶ Turn to me and have mercy on me,*
   for I am alone and afflicted.*g*
¹⁷ Relieve the anguish of my heart*
   and free me from my distress.
¹⁸ Look upon my affliction and suffering,
   and forgive all my sins.

¹⁹ Consider how numerous are my enemies,
   and how fierce is their hatred of me.
²⁰ Preserve my life and deliver me;
   do not let me be put to shame,
   for I seek refuge in you.
²¹ Let integrity and virtue preserve me,
   for in you I place my hope.

²² Redeem Israel, O God,
   from all its troubles.*

---

e Ps 37:9, 29; Isa 57:13; Mt 5:5.—f Pss 123:2; 141:8; 2 Chr 20:12; Heb 12:2.—g Pss 6:5; 86:16; 119:132; Num 6:25.

25:13 *Inherit the land:* according to the teaching of the sages, God rewards the righteous here below by bestowing on them earthly goods that he withholds from the wicked (see Ps 37:9, 29; Prov 19:23). To this is added the returned exiles' hope for the enjoyment of the land of their ancestors (see Isa 57:13; 60:21; 65:9).

25:14 *The LORD manifests himself to those who fear him:* some translations have "The LORD manifests *his secret* to those who fear him," which is to be understood as divine intimacy and friendship (see Ps 73:28; Ex 33:11; Job 29:4; Prov 3:32; Jn 15:5) united with the understanding of divine things (see Jer 16:21; 31:34; Hos 6:6).

25:16-21 Renewed prayer for relief from distress and foes.

25:17 *Heart:* see note on Ps 4:8.

25:22 Concluding prayer on behalf of all God's people. *Redeem:* i.e., "deliver."

PSALM 26*
Prayer for the Righteous

¹ Of David.

O LORD, come to my defense,
    for I have lived a blameless life.
I have placed my trust in the LORD,
    and never have I wavered in that regard.^h

² Test me, O LORD, and try me;
    probe my heart and my mind.ⁱ
³ For your kindness* is before my eyes,
    and I am constantly guided by your truth.^j

⁴ I do not sit in the company of deceivers,
    nor do I associate with hypocrites.
⁵ I abhor the assembly of the wicked,
    and I refuse to associate with evildoers.

⁶ I wash my hands in innocence*
    and join the procession around your altar,
    O LORD,^k

---

h Pss 15:2; 59:3; Heb 10:23.—i Pss 7:10; 17:3; 139:23; Jer 20:12.—j Pss 43:3; 86:11; 119:30.—k Ps 73:13; Deut 21:6-7; Mal 3:14; Mt 27:4.

Ps 26 This psalm is a prayer for God's discerning mercies to spare his faithful servant from the death that overtakes the wicked. In the psalms of supplication, we often hear this protestation from those accused who call upon God to bear witness to their innocence. The prayer that we now read is perhaps that of a Levite, but certainly of a man who loves the life of the temple. He is very sure of his rectitude in the face of others' accusations. Possibly he is also quite conscious of the faults that everyone has in his life.

He teaches us a great certainty: it is better to throw ourselves upon the judgment of God than to let ourselves be crushed by the judgment of others. This believer, who is at ease to praise the Lord in the temple, loves a clear and decided fidelity. Who would fail to be attracted by such a desire for uprightness and sincerity before God!

In praying this psalm, we can recall that since we share by faith and Baptism in the mystery of Christ dead and risen, our old self has been crucified with Christ so that the sinful body might be destroyed and we might cease to be enslaved by sin. Divested of our old nature and invested with the new nature of Christ who becomes all in all (see Col 3:9-11), we share in his holiness and irreproachable innocence before God, being purified from all injustice (see Rom 8:1; 1 Jn 1:9).

26:3 *Kindness:* see note on Ps 6:5.

26:6 *Wash my hands in innocence:* a liturgical action (see Ex 30:19, 21; 40:31f), which symbolized both inner and outer cleanliness (see Isa 1:16). Those who come to God must have "clean hands and a pure heart" (Ps 24:4). *Around your altar:* celebrating God's saving acts beside his altar was regarded as a public act of devotion in which assembled worshipers could be invited to participate (see Ps 43:5).

7 giving voice to your praises
and proclaiming all your wondrous deeds.*

8 I love the house where you dwell, O LORD,[l]
the place where your glory resides.*

9 Do not sweep my soul away with sinners,
nor my life with those who thirst for
blood,*[m]

10 whose hands carry out evil schemes,
and whose right hands are full of bribes.

11 Rather, I choose to walk in innocence;[n]
redeem me and be merciful to me.[o]

12 My feet stand on level ground;*
in the full assembly I will bless the LORD.[p]

PSALM 27*

Trust in God, Our Light and Salvation

1 Of David.

The LORD is my light* and my salvation;
whom should I fear?

---

l Pss 29:9; 63:3; 96:6; Ex 24:16; 25:8: 2 Chr 7;1; Isa 66:10.—m Pss 5:6; 28:3; 139:19.—n Pss 73:13; 101:6.—o Pss 25:16; 31:6; 69:19; Jn 1:16.—p Pss 22:23; 35:18; 40:10; 52:11; 143:10; 149:1.

26:7 *Proclaiming . . . wondrous deeds:* see note on Ps 9:2.
26:8 *Where your glory resides:* the presence of God's glory meant the presence of God himself (see Ex 24:16; 33:22). His glory dwelt in the tabernacle (see Ex 40:35) and later in the temple (see 1 Ki 8:11). Jn 1:14 places that same presence in the Word made flesh who "dwelt among us."
26:9 A premature death was a divine chastisement (see Pss 5:7; 28:4; 55:24).
26:12 *Level ground:* where there is safety and no danger of falling. *Assembly:* worshiping at the sanctuary (as in Pss 1:5; 22:26; 35:18; 40:10f; 111:1; 149:1).
Ps 27 Although enemies or the difficulties of existence may be multiplied, the believer finds a sure refuge in God—such is the cry of trust that opens this psalm. Then the movement of the prayer deepens, becoming the search and avid desire for God. It is in the temple that one discovers the presence of the Lord in the sacrifice, chant, supplication, and the Law. If such a search becomes necessary for life, will not God be present to his most forsaken and pressured servant?
In praying this psalm, we can place a similar confidence in God and the Lord Jesus, one capable of enabling us to overcome all adversity and death itself.
27:1 *The LORD is my light:* "light" often symbolizes happiness and well-being (see Pss 18:29; 36:10; 43:3; 97:11) or life and salvation (see Isa 9:2; 49:6; 58:8; Jer 13:16; Am 5:18-20), whose source is the Lord (see Isa 10:17; Mic 7:8f).

The LORD is the stronghold of my life;
   of whom should I be afraid?*q*

2 When evildoers close in on me
   to devour my flesh,*
it is they, my adversaries and enemies,
   who stumble and fall.*r*
3 Even if an army encamps against me,
   my heart will not succumb to fear;
even if war breaks out against me,
   I will not have my trust shaken.*

4 There is only one thing I ask of the LORD,
   just one thing I seek:
to dwell in the house of the LORD
   all the days of my life,*s*
so that I may enjoy the beauty of the LORD
   and gaze on his temple.*

5 For he will hide me in his shelter
   in times of trouble.
He will conceal me under the cover of his tent*
   and place me high upon a rock.*t*
6 Even now my head is raised high
   above my enemies who surround me.
In his tent I will offer sacrifices* with joyous
   shouts;
   I will sing and chant praise to the LORD.

---

q Pss 9:10; 18:29; 36:10; 43:3; 56:5; Ex 15:2; 2 Sam 22:29; Isa 10:17; Mic 7:8.—r Pss 9:4; 14:4; Job 19:22; Rom 11:11.—s Pss 23:6; 42:3; 61:5; Lk 10:42.—t Pss 12:8; 17:8; 31:21; 40:3; Rev 7:15-16.

27:2 *To devour my flesh:* the psalmist's enemies are like rapacious beasts (see Pss 7:3; 17:12; 22:13f, 17); in the figurative sense, this refers to calumny (see Dan 3:8).
27:3 With the Lord as his stronghold and helper, the psalmist fears nothing—not even an army arrayed against him. So long as this strong union with God remains unbroken, the psalmist is secure. *Heart:* see note on Ps 4:8.
27:4 Tarrying in the house of the Lord is an expression and sign of spiritual union with God and intimacy with him. *Beauty of the LORD:* i.e., his goodness (see Ps 90:17).
27:5 *Shelter . . . tent:* references to the sanctuary of Jerusalem (see Rev 7:15f). See also Pss 31:21; 32:7; 61:5; 91:1.
27:6 *I will offer sacrifices:* see note on Ps 7:18.

7 O LORD, hear my voice when I cry out;
  be merciful to me and answer me.
8 My heart* says of you,
  "Seek his face."

It is your face, O LORD, that I seek;[u]
9   do not hide your face from me.
Do not turn away your servant in anger,
  you who have been my help.

Do not reject or forsake me,
  O God, my Savior.
10 Even if my father and mother abandon me,[v]
  the LORD will gather me up.*

11 Teach me your way, O LORD,
  and lead me along a level path
  because of my enemies.[w]
12 Do not abandon me to the will of my adver-
    saries,
  for lying witnesses have risen against me,
  breathing forth violence in their malice.

13 I am confident that I will behold the goodness
    of the LORD*
  in the land of the living.[x]
14 Place your hope in the LORD:
  be strong and courageous in your heart,
  and place your hope in the LORD.

---

u Pss 24:6; 105:4; Hos 5:15.—v Isa 49:15; Jer 31:20; Hos 11:8.—w Pss 5:9; 25:4; 72:4; 86:11.—x Pss 31:19; 116:9; 142:6; 145:6; Isa 38:11.

27:8 *Heart* (also v. 14): see note on Ps 4:8. *Seek his face:* an idiom meaning to commune with the Lord, originating in the custom of pilgrimages to sacred places (see Pss 24:6; 105:4; 2 Sam 21:1; Hos 5:15). It then took on the general sense of seeking to know the Lord, anticipate his desires, and live in his presence. In a word, to seek the Lord is to serve him faithfully (Deut 4:29-31).

27:10 Union with God gives confidence in prayer; and prayer is something that even the most devout person must do. Sirach says: "Pray in [the LORD'S] presence" (17:20) and "Let nothing hinder you from promptly discharging your vows [i.e., your prayer]" (18:22).

27:13 *Goodness of the LORD:* the good things promised in the Covenant with David (see 2 Sam 7:28). *Land of the living:* reference to this life or to the temple (see Pss 52:7; 116:9; Isa 38:11), where the God of life is present; the psalmist is speaking of the world of the living as opposed to the world of the dead.

PSALM 28*

Thanksgiving for Supplications Heard

1 Of David.

To you I call out, O LORD, my Rock;*
  do not turn a deaf ear to my cry.*y*
For if you remain silent,
  I will be like those who go down to the pit.*z*
2 Hear my voice in supplication
  as I plead for your help,
as I lift up my hands*
  toward your Most Holy Place.*a*

3 Do not snatch me away with the wicked,*b*
  with those whose deeds are evil,*
who talk of peace to their neighbors
  while treachery is in their hearts.*c*

---

y Ps 18:3; Prov 28:9.—z Pss 30:4; 88:5; 143:7; Deut 1:45; Prov 1:12; Jon 2:7.—a Pss 5:8; 134:2; 141:2; 1 Ki 8:48.—b Pss 26:9; 55:24; 139:19.—c Pss 12:3; 55:22; 62:5; Prov 26:24-28; Isa 1:15; 59:3-4; Jer 9:7.

Ps 28 The psalmist calls upon God and curses his persecutors; such vehemence indicates that he is close to the end of his strength. Deaf for a time, the Lord finally hears his servant; after anguish here is the thanksgiving. The concluding formula transforms the psalm into a prayer for Israel, the "anointed one," that is, the people consecrated (v. 8) to the service of God. Believers will one day refuse the sentiments of vengeance that spring up here from the experience of the oppressed psalmist; for God could not indistinctly combine honesty with wrongdoing.

In praying this psalm, we should keep in mind that in this life Christ does not normally answer our desire for escape or special privilege. He sends us out and immerses us in the world and its tribulations (see Jn 15:18—16:4; 17:18) after his election has drawn us out of it (see Jn 15:19). Yet we already foresee victory, for the same divine power that raised Christ from the dead will raise us also and lead our humanity into a state of glory (see Eph 1:17-20).

28:1 *Rock:* the Lord is the Rock, who gives strength and sustenance to his people and provides refuge for them (see Ps 18:3 and note). *Pit:* metaphor for the grave.

28:2 *Lift up my hands:* the usual posture for prayer (see Pss 63:5; 134:2; 141:2). *Most Holy Place:* the innermost part of the temple, the Holy of Holies, which contained the Ark of the Covenant and was looked upon as the place of God's presence on earth (see 1 Ki 6:16, 19-23; 8:6-8).

28:3 The psalmist prays that the Lord will deliver him from his adversities (see Ps 26:9-12) so that he will not be numbered with the wicked nor judged with them. *Hearts:* see note on Ps 4:8.

4 Repay them as their deeds deserve*
    in accordance with the evil they inflict;
repay them for the works of their hands
    and heap upon them what they justly
        deserve.*d*

5 Since they have paid no heed to the deeds of
        the LORD
    or to the works of his hands,
he will strike them down
    and refuse to restore them.*e*

6 Blessed be the LORD,
    for he has heard my cry of supplication.*

7 The LORD is my strength and my shield;
    my heart places its trust in him.
He has helped me, and I exult;
    then with my song I praise him.*

8 The LORD is the strength of his people,
    the refuge where his anointed one finds
        salvation.*

9 Save your people and bless your heritage;
    be their shepherd* and sustain them for-
        ever.

---

d 2 Sam 3:39; Isa 3:11; Jer 50:29; 2 Tim 4:14; Rev 18:6; 22:12.—e Isa 5:12; 52:5; Am 6:5f.

28:4-5 The wicked have not learned to respond to the Lord and his wondrous deeds in redemptive history ("the works of his hands"). Therefore, they will be judged according to "the works of their hands." Justice requires that evil be removed so that its power will be completely voided. See note on Ps 5:11 and introduction to Ps 35.

28:6 The psalmist gives praise to the Lord for having heard his prayer; this will result in righteous judgment and vindication. *Blessed:* see note on Ps 18:47.

28:7 No longer does the psalmist feel threatened to the point of despairing. He is overjoyed and jubilant because he knows that the Lord will come to his aid as his strength (see Ex 15:2) and his shield (see Ps 3:4). *Heart:* see note on Ps 4:8. *I will give thanks:* see note on Ps 7:18.

28:8 *Anointed one:* here the reference seems to be to the entire people of God, which is consecrated to his service (see Ps 105:15; Ex 19:6; Hab 3:13). See also note on Ps 2:2.

28:9 *Be their shepherd:* a theme found also in Ps 80:2; Isa 40:11; Jer 31:10; Ezek 34; Mic 5:4. The Lord answered this prayer by sending the Good Shepherd, Jesus Christ (Jn 10:11, 14), who died for his sheep.

PSALM 29*

God's Majesty in the Storm

¹ A psalm of David.

Ascribe to the LORD, O mighty ones,*
  ascribe to the LORD glory and might.
² Ascribe to the LORD the glory due to his name;*
  worship the LORD in the splendor of his
  holiness.ᶠ

³ The voice of the LORD* echoes over the waters;ᵍ
  the God of glory thunders,
  the LORD thunders over mighty waters.
⁴ The voice of the LORD is powerful;
  the voice of the LORD is filled with majesty.

⁵ The voice of the LORD shatters the cedars;
  the LORD shatters the cedars of Lebanon.*
⁶ He makes Lebanon skip like a calf,
  and Sirion* like a young wild ox.

---

f Pss 68:35; 96:7-9; Deut 7:21; 1 Chr 16:29.—g 3-4: Pss 18:14; 46:7; 68:33; 77:19-20; 104:7; Ex 15:10; Job 37:4; Isa 30:10; Ezek 10:5.

Ps 29 The psalmist sings a hymn of praise to the Lord, the King of creation, evoking his power and glory in the storm that terrifies the foes of Israel, while sparing the chosen people. He concludes by asking the Lord to give similar power to the king and to Israel.

We can pray this psalm in the knowledge that the voice of God has acquired a body in Christ Jesus, living Word of the Father. It calls upon all who are in heaven, on earth, and in the netherworld to attribute to Christ all glory and power, and to adore him alone.

29:1 *Mighty ones:* literally, "sons of God," which in the beginning probably referred to the pagan deities but later came to be understood as referring to the angels (see Pss 82:1; 89:7; Job 1:6). To eliminate the polytheistic meaning of the expression, the Septuagint and Vulgate added immediately after "mighty ones" the line "bring to the LORD the offspring of rams." This passage is sometimes applied to Israel, the son of God (see Ex 4:22; Deut 14:1; see Acts 17:28).

29:2 *Name:* see note on Ps 5:12.

29:3 *The voice of the LORD:* this phrase appears seven times in imitation of the sound of thunder and symbolizes the power of God, the Lord of history as well as the Master of the elements, whose voice no one can resist (see Job 37:4f; Ezek 10:5).

29:5 *The cedars of Lebanon:* i.e., the strongest of all trees (see Isa 2:13).

29:6 *Sirion:* a Phoenician name for Mount Hermon in northern Palestine. The mountains there were originally given the general name of Lebanon.

⁷ The voice of the LORD flashes forth
    with bolts of lightning.
⁸ The voice of the LORD shakes the wilderness;
    the LORD shakes the wilderness of Kadesh.*
⁹ The voice of the LORD batters the oaks
    and strips the forests bare,
    while in his temple all cry out, "Glory!"*

¹⁰ The LORD sits enthroned above the flood;*
    the LORD is enthroned as king forever.ʰ
¹¹ May the LORD grant strength to his people.
    May the LORD bless his people with peace.ⁱ

PSALM 30*

Thanksgiving for Deliverance from Death

¹ A psalm. A song for the dedication of the temple. Of
David.

² I will exalt you, O LORD,
    for you have raised me out of the depths*
    and have not let my enemies exult over me.

---

h Gen 6—9; Isa 54:9; Bar 3:3.—i Pss 18:2-3; 28:8; 68:36; Isa 40:29;
41:10; 50:2; Dan 7:27.

29:8 *The wilderness of Kadesh:* probably a border location in southern Palestine;
some believe it is a location north of Palestine near Lebanon and Mount Hermon.

29:9 The cry of "Glory!" takes place either in heaven (v. 2) or in the temple of
Jerusalem whose liturgy echoes the heavenly praises.

29:10 *Enthroned above the flood:* a reference to God's control of the unruly pri-
mordial waters (see Gen 1:2, 6-10) or to his sending of the flood (see Gen 6:17),
which was the first manifestation of the divine justice. Thus, the Lord will know how
to make the cause of his people triumph (see Job 20:28; 22:16; Isa 24:18; 59:9ff).

Ps 30 This is a psalm of thanksgiving arising out of the experience of someone
who was at death's door because of an illness, compounded by feelings of
haughtiness in time of prosperity and despair in times of humiliation. The Lord
listened to his cry and healed him; hence the psalmist calls for praise. This
psalm came to be applied to Israel itself, especially in its experience of the Exile,
and was chanted at the Feast of the Dedication of the Temple in commemoration
of the purification of the temple in 164 B.C. (see Ezr 6:16; 1 Mac 4:36ff).

    This psalm reminds us that while we await life eternal and union with Christ,
the present life with its adversities offers us the opportunity to receive from the
divine goodness a cure, various deliverances, and even spiritual resurrection.

30:2 *Out of the depths:* a common Old Testament phrase of extreme distress
(see Pss 69:3, 16; 71:20; 88:6; 130:1; Lam 3:55; Jon 2:2) usually connected with
the words "the grave" and "the pit."

3 O Lord, my God,
  I called to you and you healed me.*
4 O Lord, you lifted me up from the nether-
    world;*
  you saved me from sinking into the pit.*j*

5 Sing praise to the Lord, O you his saints;*
  give thanks to his holy name.
6 For his anger lasts for only a moment,
    while his goodwill endures for a lifetime.
  Weeping may last throughout the night,*
    but at daybreak there is rejoicing.

7 In time of good fortune, I said,
    "Nothing can ever sway me."*
8 O Lord, in your goodness
    you established me as an impregnable
      mountain;
  however, when you hid your face,
    I was filled with terror.*k*

9 To you, O Lord, I cried out,*
    and I implored my God for mercy:
10 "What advantage would my death provide
    if I descend into the pit?
  Can the dust praise you?
    Can it proclaim your faithfulness?
11 Listen, O Lord, and have mercy on me;
    O Lord, be my helper."

---

j Ps 28:1; Num 16:33; 1 Sam 2:6; Jon 2:7.—k Ps 104:29; Deut 31:17.

30:3 *You healed me:* other passages that proclaim God as a healer are: Pss 103:3; 107:20; Hos 6:1; 7:1; 11:3; 14:5.
30:4 *Netherworld:* symbol for a life-threatening experience (see Ps 18:6; Jon 2:2). *Pit:* metaphor for the grave.
30:5 *Saints:* see note on Ps 16:3. *Name:* see note on Ps 5:12.
30:6 *Last throughout the night:* literally, "come in at evening to lodge," like a guest seeking a night's rest.
30:7 *In time of good fortune, I said, "Nothing can ever sway me":* security brings forgetfulness of God (see Deut 8:8-10; Hos 13:6; Prov 30:9). The secure psalmist spoke similar words to those of the wicked in Ps 10:6 and so lost the blessing promised to the righteous (see Ps 15:5).
30:9-11 In the stillness and inactivity of the pit, no one gives praise to God; the psalmist prays to be delivered so that he may rejoin those who worship the Lord (see Pss 6:6; 88:11-13; 115:17; Isa 38:18).

12 You have turned my mourning into dancing;
    you have taken away my sackcloth*
    and clothed me with joy.[l]
13 My heart* will therefore sing
    in unceasing praise to you;
  O Lord, my God,
    I will praise you forever.

PSALM 31*
Prayer of Trust and Thanksgiving

1 For the director.* A psalm of David.

2 In you, O Lord, I have taken refuge;*
    let me never be put to shame;[m]
    in your righteousness deliver me.
3 Turn your ear to me,
    and act quickly to save me.
  Be to me a rock* of refuge,
    a strong fortress to save me.

4 You are truly my rock and my fortress;
      for the sake of your name,* lead and guide
      me.[n]
5 Deliver me from the snare that has been set
    for me,
    for you are my refuge.

---

l Ps 126:1-2; Est 9:22; Isa 61:3; Jer 31:13.—m 2-4: Pss 18:3; 71:1-2.—n
Pss 9:9; 18:3; 71:3.

30:12 *Sackcloth:* a symbol of mourning (see Ps 35:13; Gen 37:34).
30:13 *Heart:* see note on Ps 4:8.
Ps 31 Faith, distress, and gratitude alternate in this prayer, evoking the "confessions" of the prophet Jeremiah, his dolorous destiny, and his intimacy with the Lord (Jer 17:14-18; 20:7-18). At the moment of death on the cross, Jesus will use this psalm to express his trusting abandonment to the Father (see Lk 23:46).
We should be mindful that God will often place us in a situation in which we can unite our voice to that of Christ in reciting this psalm, especially by letting us share his sufferings and making us become like him in death so that we may rise with him from the dead (see Phil 3:10f).
31:1 *For the director:* these words are thought to be a musical or liturgical notation.
31:2-9 No matter what may be the conflict in which we are enmeshed, God remains the one certitude. The images of the rock and the fortress attest to a serene and unshakable trust in God.
31:3 *Rock:* see note on Ps 18:3.
31:4 *Name:* see note on Ps 5:12.

6 Into your hands I commend my spirit;*
you will redeem me, O LORD, God of truth.[o]

7 You hate those who cling to false idols,
but I put my trust in the LORD.
8 I will rejoice and exult in your kindness*
because you have witnessed my affliction
and have taken note of my anguish.[p]
9 You have not abandoned me into the power
of the enemy;
rather, you have set my feet in the open.

10 Have mercy on me, O LORD,*
for I am in trouble.
My weeping is laying waste to my eyes
as well as my soul* and my body.
11 My life is consumed with sorrow
and my years with sighing.
My strength ebbs because of my misery,
and my bones are wasting away.[q]

12 I am an object of scorn
to all my enemies,
a loathsome sight to my neighbors,
and an object of dread to my friends.
When people catch sight of me outside,
they quickly turn away.[r]

13 I have passed out of their minds
like someone who has died;
I have become like a broken vessel.*

o Isa 45:19; Lk 23:46; Acts 7:59.—p Pss 10:14; 13:4; Lk 22:44.—q Pss 6:3; 32:3; 38:11; 73:26.—r Pss 25:19; 38:12; Job 19:13-19.

31:6 *Into your hands I commend my spirit:* last word of Christ on the cross (see Lk 23:46) and St. Stephen (see Acts 7:59). *Spirit:* life itself.

31:8, 17, 22 *Kindness:* see note on Ps 6:5.

31:10-19 The prayer changes tone; after serenity comes a gasping cry. The stricken person is also one who is despised and rejected, an object of utter contempt by others. This is the despairing cry at times when we seem completely alone.

31:10 *Soul:* see note on Ps 6:5.

31:13 *Like a broken vessel:* a customary comparison for something that has been rendered useless (see Isa 30:14; Jer 19:11; 22:28).

14 I have heard the hissing of many:
  "There is terror on every side,"*
as they conspire together against me
  and plot to end my life.

15 But I place my trust in you, O LORD.
  I say, "You are my God."ˢ
16 My life is in your hands;*
  deliver me from the power of my enemies,
  from the clutches of those who pursue me.
17 Let your face shine* upon your servant;
  save me in your kindness.ᵗ

18 Do not let me be put to shame, O LORD,*
  for I have cried out to you.
Let the wicked be put to shame
  and lie silent in the netherworld.
19 Let their lying lips be struck dumb,
  lips that speak insolently against the righ-
    teous
  with pride and contempt.ᵘ

20 How great is your goodness, O LORD,*
  which you have stored up* for those who
    fear you
and which you bestow on those who take
    refuge in you,
  in the presence of all the people.

---

s Pss 4:6; 140:7; Isa 25:1.—t Pss 4:7; 67:2; Num 6:25.—u Pss 12:4; 120:2.

31:14 *There is terror on every side:* a cry used when danger lurks (see Jer 6:25; 20:10; 46:5; 49:29).

31:16 *My life is in your hands:* God is the ultimate master of every moment of everyone's life.

31:17 *Face shine:* see note on Ps 13:2.

31:18-19 See note on Ps 5:11 and introduction to Ps 35.

31:20-25 A moment arrives when the believer experiences anew the power of God's presence. This holds good despite the mockery and false accusations of enemies, that is, the war of words that constitutes one of the greatest trials of our human relationships. Certain of God, the believer does not let himself become enmeshed in conflicts.

31:20 *Stored up:* the psalmist relies on the Lord who has stored up his goodness (his Covenant promises) for his faithful ones.

²¹ You hide them in the safety of your presence
   from those who conspire against them;
   you keep them safe in your shelter,
      far away from contentious tongues.ᵛ

²² Blessed* be the LORD,
      for he has manifested his wondrous kind-
         ness to me
      when I was under siege.
²³ I had cried out in terror,ʷ
      "I have been cut off from your sight."
   But you heard my plea
      when I cried out to you for assistance.

²⁴ Love the LORD, all his saints.*
      The LORD protects his loyal servants,
      but the arrogant he repays beyond measure.
²⁵ Be strong and courageous in your hearts,
      all you who place your hope in the LORD.

PSALM 32*
The Joy of Being Forgiven

¹ Of David. A *maskil.**

Blessed is the one whose offense is forgiven,*
   whose sin is erased.ˣ

---

v Pss 27:5; 109:3; Rev 7:15.—w Ps 116:11; Jon 2:4.—x Ps 65:4; Prov
28:13; Isa 1:18; Hos 14:2; Rom 4:7-8.

31:22 *Blessed:* see note on Ps 18:47. *Kindness:* see note on Ps 4:8.
31:24 *Saints:* see notes on Pss 4:4; 16:3; and 34:10. *The arrogant:* often equal to
the wicked, for the arrogant act as if they have no need of God and are a law to themselves (see Pss 10:2-11; 73:6; 94:2-7; Deut 8:14; Isa 2:17; Ezek 28:2, 5; Hos 13:6).
Ps 32 This is the second of the seven Penitential Psalms (6; 32; 38; 51; 102;
130; 143), a joyous testimony of gratitude for God's gift of forgiveness for those
who confess their sins and follow the law of God. Instead of constantly pondering
their sins, believers acknowledge their wretchedness before God and accept forgiveness and reconciliation. Their torment ceases, and a new person is born,
overwhelmed by grace, confidence, and a sense of obedience.
   In praying this psalm, we can focus not only on the happiness resulting from the
forgiveness of particular sin but also on the more profound happiness obtained by
the complete victory given us by God in Christ over sin under all its forms.
32:1a *Maskil:* this term cannot be given a precise translation; perhaps it
means "teaching" or "training."
32:1b-2 Joyous declaration of the happiness of having one's sins forgiven by
God (see Pss 65:5; 85:2; Job 31:33). This text is cited by Paul in Rom 4:7-8.
Blessed: see note on Ps 1:1.

² Blessed is the one to whom the LORD charges
   no guilt
   and in whose spirit there is no guile.

³ As long as I remained silent,*
   my body wasted away
   as the result of my groaning throughout
   the day.*ʸ*
⁴ For day and night
   your hand was heavy upon me;*
   my strength withered steadily
   as though consumed by the summer heat.
                                                 Selah

⁵ Then I acknowledged my sin to you,
   and I made no attempt to conceal my guilt.
   I said, "I will confess my offenses* to the
   LORD,"
   and you removed the guilt of my sin.*ᶻ*
                                                 Selah

⁶ Therefore, let everyone who is faithful pray
   to you
   where you may be found.
   Even if great floods threaten,*ᵃ*
   they will never reach him.*
⁷ You are a place of refuge for me;
   you preserve me from trouble
   and surround me with songs of deliverance.*
                                                 Selah

---

y Pss 6:7; 31:11.—z Pss 38:19; 51:5; Job 31:33.—a Pss 18:5; 69:14.

32:3 *I remained silent:* did not confess the sin before God. *Body:* literally, "bones."

32:4 According to St. Augustine, even before penitents acknowledge their sin, God hears the cry of their heart and pardons it because of their true contrition (see 2 Sam 12:13).

32:5 *Sin . . . guilt . . . offenses:* these are the three most common Hebrew words for evil thoughts and actions (see Ps 51:3-4; Isa 59:12).

32:6 The psalmist encourages the godly to draw near to God; even in the greatest adversities, the Lord will protect them. *Where . . . found:* another version is "in time of distress." *Great floods:* symbol of grave danger (see note on Ps 18:17).

32:7 After receiving God's help, the psalmist will be surrounded by people celebrating this latest act of deliverance while he brings thank offerings.

⁸ I will instruct you
  and guide you in the way you should go;
I will counsel you
  and keep my eyes upon you.
⁹ Do not behave without understanding
  like a horse or a mule;
if its temper is not curbed with bit and bridle,
  it will not come near you.

¹⁰ The wicked has a multitude of troubles,
  but the man who trusts in the LORD
  is surrounded by kindness.*
¹¹ Be glad in the LORD and rejoice, you righteous;
  shout for joy, all you upright of heart.*ᵇ

PSALM 33*

Praise of God's Providence

¹ Rejoice in the LORD, you righteous;
  it is fitting for the upright to praise him.ᶜ
² Give thanks to the LORD on the harp;
  offer praise to him on the ten-stringed lyre.ᵈ
³ Sing to him a new song;*
  play skillfully on the strings with joyful
  shouts.

---

b Pss 33:1; 64:11; 92:2.—c Pss 5:12; 11:7; 32:11; 101:1; 147:1.—d 2-3: Pss 40:4; 92:4; 144:9; Rev 5:8.

32:10 *Kindness:* see note on Ps 6:5.
32:11 *Heart:* see note on Ps 4:8.
Ps 33 This psalm follows a classical pattern. First, the psalmist calls for praise to God. Then he proclaims praise for his great deeds: his word that created the three-tiered universe (vv. 4-9), his intervention in history when he chose his people from among the nations (vv. 10-12), and finally his powerful help for those who fear him (vv. 13-19). Thus, he contemplates God's work in creation, in the history of Israel, and in the lives of the righteous. The people acclaim Providence, whose wise plan is universal in its scope.
In Ephesians (1:9; 3:4f), Paul will explain this hidden plan of God that is carried to fulfillment in Christ's Passover in order that humankind may have life and the world may attain its goal.
33:3 *Sing to him a new song:* celebrate God's saving deed with a new song to make known his greatness to others and to give him praise (see Ps 7:18, and note; 40:4; 96:1; 98:1; 144:9; 149:1; Isa 42:10; Rev 5:9; 14:3).

⁴ For the word of the LORD is true,*
   and he is faithful in everything he does.
⁵ The LORD loves righteousness and justice;ᵉ
   the earth is filled with his kindness.

⁶ The heavens were made by the word of the
      LORD,ᶠ
   and all their host by the breath of his mouth.*
⁷ He gathers the waters of the sea as in a bowl;*
   he places the deep in storehouses.ᵍ

⁸ Let all the earth fear the LORD;*
   let all the inhabitants of the world revere
      him.
⁹ For he spoke, and it came to be;*
   he commanded, and it stood firm.ʰ

¹⁰ The LORD thwarts the plans of nations
   and frustrates the designs of peoples.
¹¹ But the plan of the LORD remains forever,
   the designs of his heart for all generations.ⁱ

---

e Pss 11:7; 119:64.—f Gen 2:1; Jn 1:1; Heb 11:3.—g Ps 78:13; Gen 1:9-10; Ex 15:8; Job 38:8.—h Ps 148:5; Gen 1:3f; Jud 16:14; Isa 48:13; Jn 1:3.—i Prov 19:21; Isa 40:8; 46:10.

33:4-5 The psalmist celebrates especially the perfections of the Lord. His nature and his self-revelation are in complete harmony; he is faithful ("true") in everything that he does. He also loves righteousness and justice, i.e., he carries out his plans by his verdicts, rule, and Covenant relationship with his people. Furthermore, his kindness is evident in his works on earth; he shows the same loyalty, constancy, and love toward the rest of creation that he shows to his people (v. 22). *Kindness:* see note on Ps 6:5.

33:6 The Fathers of the Church applied this verse to the Blessed Trinity: LORD = Father; word = Son; breath = Spirit. *All their host:* the stars of the sky were viewed as an army (see Neh 9:6; Isa 40:26; 45:12; Jer 33:22). See also note on Ps 24:10.

33:7 *He gathers the waters . . . as in a bowl:* God rules the dangerous waters so easily that it is like a person putting water into a bowl (see Ps 104:9; Gen 1:9f; Job 38:8-11; Prov 8:29; Jer 5:22).

33:8 The nations of the world feared many gods, each of whom reigned over the various heavenly bodies and over the land, sea, and sky. But the psalmist stresses that the Lord is the Creator-Ruler of the world and everything in it. Hence, he calls upon all nations and all peoples to fear the Lord because of his greatness and his goodness.

33:9-12 Whatever God spoke came into existence (see Heb 11:3). Everything reflects his wise rule. The nations are completely under his control (see Prov 19:21; 21:30; Isa 8:10; 19:17; 46:10f; Jer 29:11; Mic 4:12). God's providence works out his purposes. *Heart:* see note on Ps 4:8.

¹² Blessed is the nation whose God is the Lord,*
 the people whom he has chosen as his heritage.*ʲ

¹³ The Lord gazes down from heaven*
 and beholds the entire human race.ᵏ
¹⁴ From his royal throne
 he watches all who dwell on the earth.
¹⁵ He who has fashioned the hearts of them all
 observes everything they do.

¹⁶ A king is not saved by a large army,
 nor is a warrior delivered by great strength.
¹⁷ A horse offers false hope for victory;
 despite its power it cannot save.

¹⁸ But the eyes of the Lord are on those who
   fear him,*
 on those who trust in his kindness,
¹⁹ to deliver them from death
 and to preserve their lives in time of famine.

²⁰ Our soul waits in hope for the Lord;*
 he is our help and our shield.ˡ
²¹ Our hearts rejoice in him
 because we trust in his holy name.
²² O Lord, let your kindness rest upon us,
 for we have placed our hope in you.

---

j Ps 144:15; Ex 8:22; Deut 7:6.—k Ps 53:3; Job 34:21; Sir 15:19; Jer
16:17; 32:19.—l Pss 27:14; 28:7; 33:20; 115:9.

33:12-22 The psalmist now meditates on the election of God's people, after he
has stressed the Lord's power and steadfast carrying out of his plans.
33:12 The Lord freely chose his people as his heritage (see Pss 28:9; 74:2;
78:62, 71; 94:5, 14; 106:5, 40; Ex 19:5; Deut 4:20; 9:26, 29).
33:13-17 The Lord sees everything that happens on earth (vv. 13-15) and controls human destinies. *Hearts:* see note on Ps 4:8.
33:18-19 Success in any venture does not depend on earthly means but on God
alone, who watches over his faithful and delivers them from death and every danger.
Eyes of the Lord: a metaphor for the Lord's loving care. *Kindness:* see note on Ps 6:5.
33:20-22 The people respond by expressing a renewal of their Covenant commitment. The Lord is their help and shield (see Pss 3:4; 28:7), and they trust in
his holy name, with which they associate past acts of deliverance (see Ps 30:5).
They promise to be submissive and abandon themselves to him as he works out
his plans for the establishment of his kingdom and the renewal of the earth.
Soul: see note on Ps 6:4. *Hearts:* see note on Ps 4:8. *Name:* see note on Ps 5:12.
Kindness: see note on Ps 6:5.

PSALM 34*

Presence of God, Protector of the Righteous

¹ Of David. When he pretended to be mad before Abimelech, who forced him to depart.*

² I will bless the LORD at all times;*
    his praise will be continually on my lips.^m
³ My soul* will glory in the LORD;
    let the lowly hear and be glad.
⁴ Magnify the LORD with me;
    let us exalt his name together.

⁵ I sought the LORD, and he answered me;
    he set me free from all my fears.
⁶ Look to him and you will be radiant;
    your faces will never be covered with shame.
⁷ In my anguish* I cried out;
    the LORD heard my plea,
    and I was saved from all my troubles.

---

m Pss 71:6; 145:2; Eph 1:20; 1 Thes 5:18.

Ps 34 This alphabetical psalm (see p. 23) has two parts. The first voices thanksgiving for the solicitude with which God surrounds the righteous and the poor to deliver them from their anguish. Doubtless the psalmist has experienced this in life and gives his disciples the fruit of his experience. The second part takes the tone of an instruction (vv. 13-23): a sage invites the listeners to discover the path to happiness in the fear of the Lord.

The poorest of the poor and the wisest of the sages is Christ, and it is upon his lips that we can place this psalm after the example of John (19:36), numbering ourselves—in accord with the express indication of Peter (see 1 Pet 3:10-12)—among the children to whom he teaches the way of life and happiness. From the early days of Christianity this psalm served to teach those who were preparing for the Christian life and for Baptism (1 Pet 2:3).

34:1 The superscription refers to 1 Sam 21:11-15, but (probably as the result of a scribal error) erroneously substitutes Abimelech for Achish, King of Gath.

34:2-4 The praise of the Lord is continual, God-centered, and the response of a grateful heart—an offering that the Lord will never reject (see Ps 50:14-23; Hos 14:2; Heb 13:15). Its purpose is to acknowledge the Lord's greatness (see Pss 30:2; 69:31; 99:5; 107:32; 145:1). *Name:* see note on Ps 5:12.

34:3 *Soul:* see note on Ps 6:4.

34:7 *In my anguish:* literally, "this poor man." The word "poor" is usually applied to one who depends completely on God for his deliverance and his very life. See also note on Ps 22:27.

8 The angel of the LORD* encamps around
those who fear God,
and he delivers them.[n]
9 Taste and see that the LORD is good;
blessed is the man who takes refuge in
him.*[o]

10 Fear the LORD,* you his saints;
nothing is lacking for those who fear him.[p]
11 The powerful* suffer want and go hungry,
but those who seek the LORD want for no
good thing.

12 *Come, my children,* and listen to me;
I will teach you the fear of the LORD.[q]
13 Who among you delights in life[r]
and desires many years to enjoy prosperity?*
14 Then keep your tongue* from evil
and your lips from telling lies.
15 Shun evil and do good;
seek peace and pursue it.[s]

n Gen 16:7; Ex 14:19.—o Ps 2:12; 1 Pet 2:3.—p Deut 6:13; Prov 3:7.—q
Ps 66:16; Prov 1:8; 4:1.—r 13-17: 1 Pet 3:10-12.—s Ps 37:27; Mt 5:9; Heb
12:14.

34:8 *Angel of the LORD:* i.e., the Lord's protection or the presence of God. However, such protection, although promised by the Lord (see Ps 91:11; Gen 32:2; 2
Ki 6:17; Mt 4:5f), is not automatic; it depends on one's allegiance to the Covenant—the "fear of the LORD"—entailing the practices mentioned in vv. 12-15.
34:9 This verse is applied to the Holy Eucharist by the Fathers of the Church
and the Liturgy (see 1 Pet 2:3). *Blessed:* see note on Ps 1:1.
34:10 *Fear the LORD:* see note on Ps 15:2-5. *Saints:* that is, those consecrated
to God and sharing in his holiness (see Ex 19:6; Lev 19:2; Num 16:3; Isa 4:3; Dan
8:24). See also notes on Pss 4:4 and 16:3.
34:11 *Powerful:* literally, "lions"—fierce animals were symbols of people with
power.
34:12-15 To gain wisdom entails two things: fearing the Lord and doing his
will. The latter calls for integrity of language rather than deception (v. 14; see Jer
4:2), practicing good rather than evil (v. 15; see Ps 37:3, 27), and working for
rather than against peace (vv. 15, 16; see Ps 37:37; Mt 5:9; Rom 12:18; 14:19;
Heb 12:14).
34:12 *Children:* a term (also translated as "simple" or "sons") for students in
Wisdom literature (see Prov 1:22; 4:1; 8:32; Sir 3:1; 23:7).
34:13 This verse is found word for word in an Egyptian text of the 18th dynasty
(tomb of Ai) (see 1 Pet 3:10f).
34:14 *Tongue:* see note on Ps 5:10.

16 The eyes of the LORD are on the righteous,*
   and his ears are open to their cry.*t*

17 The face of the LORD is turned against those
      who do evil,
   to erase all memory of them from the earth.

18 The righteous call out, and the LORD hears
      them;*
   he rescues them from all their troubles.

19 The LORD remains close to the brokenhearted,
   and he saves those whose spirit is crushed.

20 The misfortunes of the righteous man are
      many,*
   but the LORD delivers him* from all of them.

21 He watches with care over all his bones;
   not a single one will be broken.*u*

22 Evil will bring death to the wicked,*
   and those who hate the righteous will be
      condemned.

23 The LORD redeems the lives of those who
      serve him;
   no one will be condemned who takes refuge
      in him.

---

t Ps 33:18; Mal 3:16.—u Jn 19:36.

34:16-17 The eyes and ears of the Lord are attuned to the righteous (see Ps 33:18), but the face of the Lord (see note on Ps 13:2) is against evildoers (see Lev 17:10; Jer 23:30; 1 Pet 3:10-12).

34:18-19 Compunction and humility are requirements for benefiting from the grace of salvation (see Ps 51:19; Mt 11:29f). The Lord hears the cry of the righteous (see Ps 145:19) and the brokenhearted (see Ps 147:3) and saves them from their afflictions.

34:20-21 No matter how many are the troubles of the righteous man, the Lord will deliver him (see Job 5:19; 2 Tim 3:11), protecting "all his bones," a phrase representative of his whole being. *Not a single one will be broken:* John applies this text to Jesus on the cross as the righteous man par excellence. Hence, this text is regarded as a prophecy about Christ when he was crucified. Although it was the custom of the Romans to break the legs of a person who was crucified so that death would come more quickly, it was not carried out in this case and not one of Christ's bones was broken.

34:20 *Delivers him:* God promises to be our source of power, courage, and wisdom to help us through our troubles; at times he even chooses to take them away from us.

34:22-23 The wicked will perish in their own evil and be condemned (see Ps 9:16), but the righteous will be saved by the Lord (see Ex 6:6; Lk 1:68; Rev 14:3).

PSALM 35*

Appeal for Help against Injustice

1 Of David.

Plead my cause, O LORD, with those who
strive against me;
fight against those who fight against me.
2 Grasp your shield and buckler
and spring to my aid.
3 Brandish your spear and battle-ax
against those who pursue me.
Say to my soul,*
"I am your salvation."

4 May those who seek my life
suffer shame and disgrace.
May those who plan my downfall
be forced to retreat in disgrace.v
5 May they be like chaff flying in the wind,*
with the angel of the LORD scattering
them.w

---

v Pss 38:13; 40:15; 69:7; 70:3; 71:13; 83:17; Isa 45:16; Mal 2:9.—w Pss
1:4; 34:8; 83:14; Job 21:18.

Ps 35 This is one of the so-called imprecatory (or cursing) psalms that call
upon God to mete out justice to enemies (see Pss 3:8; 5:11; 6:10; 17:14-16;
28:4f; 31:18f; 35:24-26; 37:2, 9-10, 15, 20, 35f; 40:15f; 54:7; 55:10, 16, 24;
58:8-12; 63:10-12; 64:8-10; 69:23-29; 71:13; 79:6, 12; 83:10-19; 129:5-8;
137:8-9; 139:19-22; 140:10-12; 141:10; 143:12). In their thirst for justice, the
authors of these psalms use hyperbole (or overstatement) in order to move others
to oppose sin and evil (see also note on Ps 5:11). In three successive waves, the
frantic and indignant cry of the persecuted righteous man rises toward God; and
three successive times the suppliant rediscovers hope. He is a man overwhelmed
by the underhanded wickedness, betrayal, and calumnies of friends as well as
the dark designs of adversaries. It reminds us once again of the evils suffered by
the prophet Jeremiah (Jer 20:10-13), and we cannot refrain from thinking of the
trial of Jesus before a tribunal bent on sending him to his death (Mt 26:57ff).

Christians are aware that the world continues to pursue Christ in the person of
his disciples (see Mt 5:11; 10:17f; Jn 15:18-25), unjustly directing accusations
and persecutions against them. Hence, the prayer formulated in this psalm must
spring forth from the lips and hearts of the disciples united with their Master.

35:3 *Soul:* see note on Ps 6:4.

35:5 *Like chaff flying in the wind:* i.e., easily carried away. *Angel of the LORD:*
see note on Ps 34:8.

⁶ May their way be shadowy and slippery,
    with the angel of the LORD in pursuit.

⁷ Without cause they laid a net to trap me;
    without cause they dug a pit to ensnare me.
⁸ May ruin come upon them unawares;
    may the net they laid entrap them;
    may they topple into the pit they dug.ˣ

⁹ Then my soul* will rejoice in the LORD
    and exult in his salvation.
¹⁰ My whole being* will say,
    "O LORD, who is there like you?
  You deliver those who are weak
    from those who are too strong for them,
  and you protect the poor and needy
    from those who seek to exploit them."ʸ

¹¹ False witnesses step forward
    and question me about things I do not know.
¹² They give me back evil in place of good
    and leave my soul in sorrow.ᶻ

¹³ Yet, when they were ill, I put on sackcloth*
    and afflicted myself with fasting,
    while I poured forth prayers from my heart.
¹⁴ I went about as though in grief,
    as though for a friend or brother.
  I bowed down in sorrow
    as though lamenting for a mother.

¹⁵ But when I stumbled, they rejoiced and came
      together;
    they came together and struck me unawares.
  They slandered me without letup.

---

x Pss 7:16; 9:16; 57:7; Prov 26:27; Eccl 10:8; Sir 27:26; Isa 47:11; 1 Thes 5:3; 1 Jn 5:3.—y Pss 18:12; 51:10; 86:8; 89:7, 9; Ex 9:14; 15:11.—z Pss 27:12; 38:21-22; 109:5; Prov 17:13; Jer 18:20.

35:9 *Soul:* see note on Ps 6:4.
35:10 *My whole being:* literally, "all my bones." *Poor and needy:* see notes on Pss 22:27 and 34:7.
35:13 *Sackcloth:* a symbol of mourning. *Fasting:* an act of mourning (see Ps 69:10). *Heart:* see note on Ps 4:8.

¹⁶ They mocked me with ever increasing fury
    as they gnashed their teeth at me.

¹⁷ How long,* O LORD, will you look on?
    Rescue me from these ravening beasts;
    preserve my precious life from these lions.ᵃ
¹⁸ I will offer you thanks in the great assembly;
    I will praise you amid the vast throng.ᵇ

¹⁹ Do not allow my treacherous enemies
    to gloat over me;
  do not permit those who hate me without rea-
    son*
    to wink their eyes at me.ᶜ
²⁰ For they do not speak words of peace,
    but they contrive deceitful words
    to lead astray the peaceful in the land.ᵈ
²¹ They open wide their mouths shouting, "Aha!
    Aha!
    We have seen it with our own eyes."ᵉ

²² You have seen, O LORD; do not be silent.
    O LORD, do not be far from me.ᶠ
²³ Awaken and be diligent in my defense;
    come to my aid, my God and my LORD.

²⁴ Defend me, O LORD, my God,*
    according to your righteousness,
    and do not let them gloat over me.
²⁵ Do not let them think,
    "Aha! This is just what we wanted."
  Do not let them say,
    "We have swallowed him up."

---

a Pss 6:4; 17:12; 22:22; 57:5; 58:7.—b Pss 22:23; 26:12; 40:11; 42:5; 149:1.—c Pss 9:14; 38:17; 69:5; Prov 6:13; Jn 15:25.—d Pss 38:13; 55:22; 120:6-7; Jer 9:7.—e Pss 40:16; 70:4; Lam 2:16; Ezek 25:3.—f Pss 10:1, 14; 22:12; 38:22; 109:1; Ex 3:7.

35:17 *How long. . .?:* see note on Ps 6:4. *Lions:* a metaphor for enemies.

35:19 *Treacherous enemies . . . those who hate me without reason:* cited in Jn 15:25, since this psalm as well as Ps 69 was regarded by the New Testament authors as foreshadowing the Passion of Christ.

35:24-26 See introduction above and note on Ps 5:11.

²⁶ Let all those who rejoice at my downfall
    be put to shame and dismayed.
  Let those who rise up arrogantly against me
    be covered with shame and dishonor.

²⁷ But let those who desire my vindication
    shout for joy and be glad.
  Let them cry out continually,
    "Exalted be the LORD
      who delights to see his servant in peace."
²⁸ Then my tongue shall proclaim your righteous-
    ness
    and sing your praise all the day long.ᵍ

PSALM 36*
Human Weakness and Divine Goodness

¹ For the director.* Of David the servant of the LORD.

² Sin speaks to the wicked man in his heart;*
    in his eyes there is no fear of God.ʰ
³ He deludes himself with the idea
    that his guilt will not be discovered and
    hated.*

---

g Pss 5:9; 51:16; 71:15.—h Prov 5:22; Jer 2:19; Hos 5:5; Rom 3:18.

Ps 36 This psalm combines two contrasting pictures, which were perhaps separated at one time. On the one hand, there is a person destroyed by sin, whose heart holds no sentiment that is not turned to sin (vv. 2-5). On the other, there are creatures dedicated to God, that is, the righteous, who are peaceful and happy (vv. 6ff). These same traditional images of happiness will be found among the Prophets, suggestive of the ideal time for the installment of the future Messiah (Isa 12:2; 25:6; Jer 31:14; Ezek 47).

Christians know better than the psalmist that pride constitutes a maleficent force residing in all humans. In practice, it carries us inevitably along toward evil (see Rom 6:1-11). Through Christ, the Father preserves for us, his faithful, his salvation that shines continually upon us to render us holy and to defend us against outrages on the part of evil and the impious. The New Testament applies images from the second part of this psalm to Christ: light of humankind and inexhaustible wellspring of life (Jn 7:37f; 8:12; Rev 21:6).

36:1 *For the director:* these words are thought to be a musical or liturgical notation.

36:2 *Sin . . . heart:* an alternative translation is: "An oracle is within my heart / concerning the sinfulness of the wicked." *Heart:* see note on Ps 4:8. Paul cites this verse in Rom 3:18.

36:3 *His guilt will . . . be discovered and hated:* because it is an offense against God and hence punished by him.

4 The words his mouth utters are malicious
and deceitful;
he has ceased to be wise and act uprightly.
5 Even when he lies on his bed,*
he is hatching evil plots.
He commits himself to a wicked course
and refuses to reject evil.*i*

6 O Lᴏʀᴅ, your kindness extends to the heavens;
your faithfulness, to the skies.*j*
7 Your righteousness is like the mountains of
God;
your judgments, like the mighty deep;*
you sustain both humans and beasts, O
Lᴏʀᴅ.

8 How precious, O God, is your kindness!*
People seek refuge in the shadow of your
wings.*k*
9 They feast on the abundance of your house,*l*
and you give them to drink from your delightful streams.**m*
10 For with you is the fountain of life,*
and by your light we see light.*n*

---

i Pss 5:10; 144:8, 11; Prov 4:16; Mic 2:1.—j Pss 57:11; 71:19; 89:2.—k
Pss 6:5; 17:8; 57:2.—l Pss 63:6; 65:5; Gen 2:8-10.—m Isa 55:1; Jn 4:14;
Rev 22:1.—n Pss 4:7; 27:1; 80:4, 8, 20; 104:2; Isa 60:1, 19; Jer 2:13.

36:5 *On his bed:* rather than meditating on God's law both day and *night* (Pss
1:2; 119:55), the wicked plots evil even on his bed.
36:6f *Your kindness . . . mighty deep:* God's influence reaches from one end of
the world to the other and into every sphere. *Kindness:* see note on Ps 6:5.
36:8 *Kindness:* see note on Ps 6:5. *Shadow of your wings:* see note on Ps 17:8.
36:9 People rejoice together before the Lord. The image is of the abundance of
meat from the sacrifices. This is already a prefiguration of the Messianic Banquet
of which Jesus will speak, the "Supper of the Lamb" (Rev 19:9). *House:* the earth
that provides food for all living creatures (see Pss 24:2; 104:14). *Streams:* the
means by which God brings forth the rain out of his "storehouses" (Ps 33:7),
which flow into the water sources on earth and give life to creatures.
36:10 *Fountain of life:* an expression to be taken in the widest possible sense as
life implying prosperity, peace, and happiness (see Pss 46:5; 133:3; Isa 12:5; 55:1;
Jer 2:13; 17:13; 31:12). In Proverbs this expression designates wisdom (13:14;
16:22; 18:4) and the fear of the Lord (14:27). The passage is applied to Christ, life
and light of human beings (Jn 4:10, 14). *Light:* through God's loving kindness (see
Pss 4:7; 31:17; 89:16; 97:11; Job 29:3) we enjoy fullness of life and well-being.

11 Continue to bestow your kindness* on those
who know you,
and your saving justice on the upright of
heart.
12 Let not the foot of the arrogant tread upon me,
nor the hand of the wicked drive me out.
13 Behold, the evildoers have fallen;
they are overthrown and unable to rise.

PSALM 37*

Fate of the Wicked and Reward of the Righteous

1 Of David.

Do not fume because of evildoers
or envy those who do wrong.[o]
2 They will wither quickly like the grass
and fade away like the green herb.*[p]

3 Put your trust in the LORD and do good,
that you may dwell in the land* and be secure.[q]

o Prov 3:31; 23:17; 24:1, 19; Mal 2:17; 3:14.—p Pss 90:6; 102:12; 103:15-16; Job 14:2; Jas 1:10.—q Ps 128:2; Deut 30:20; Ezek 34:14; Jn 10:9.

36:11 *Kindness:* see note on Ps 6:5. *Heart:* see note on Ps 4:8.

Ps 37 A peaceful aged psalmist strings together, in alphabetical order (see p. 23), sayings about the opposing lots of the righteous and the wicked. It is a fine lesson in wisdom for those who grow angry at the successes of evildoers: their triumph is ephemeral. Experience and meditation on the word of God have revealed to this sage the happy destiny that the Lord has reserved for his friends; each of the righteous is called to enjoy the promises made to the people of Israel as a reward for their faithfulness: to dwell in the holy land in peace (vv. 3, 11).

The horizon remains limited to this world. Hence, it is a modest happiness if it were not irradiated by the nearness of the Lord and did not contain the still hidden promise of a love that cannot be extinguished, of an eternal joy.

Christ will reveal this infinite perspective: eternal happiness in the Kingdom of God, the true promised land, belongs to the poor, those who forgive and thirst for righteousness and peace (Mt 5).

37:2 See note on Ps 5:11 and introduction to Ps 35 (this also applies to vv. 9f, 15, 20, 35f).

37:3 *The land:* the promised land (Ps 25:13; Deut 16:20), which in the New Testament became a type of heaven (see Mt 5:3-12; Lk 6:20-26; Heb 11:9, 13-16). This word is also used in vv. 9, 11, 22, 27, 29, and 34.

⁴ Take delight in the LORD,
  and he will grant you what your heart*
    desires.ʳ

⁵ Commit your way to the LORD;
  place your trust in him, and he will act.ˢ
⁶ He will make your righteousness shine like
    the dawn,
  and the justice of your cause, like the
    noonday.*ᵗ

⁷ Wait quietly for the LORD
  and be patient until he comes.
  Do not fret over the man who prospers
    because of his evil schemes.

⁸ Refrain from anger and turn away from wrath;
  do not fret—it does nothing but harm.
⁹ For evildoers will be destroyed,
  but those who wait for the LORD will in-
    herit the land.*ᵘ

¹⁰ In a short while, the wicked will be no more;
  no matter how diligently you search, you
    will not be able to find him.
¹¹ But the meek* will possess the land
  and enjoy an abundance of peace.ᵛ

¹² The wicked man plots against the righteous
  and grinds his teeth at the sight of them.

---

r Ps 21:3; Prov 10:24; Mt 6:33.—s Pss 4:6; 51:19; 55:23; Prov 3:5;
16:3.—t Ps 18:25; Wis 5:6; Isa 58:10.—u Pss 25:13; 101:8; 112:3-4; Prov
2:21; Isa 57:13.—v Lev 26:6; Num 14:24; Mt 5:5.

37:4 *Heart:* see note on Ps 4:8.
37:6 *Dawn . . . noonday:* light and brightness symbolize truth, well-being, and
happiness (see Job 22:28; Song 1:7; Wis 5:6).
37:9 Those who hope only in the Lord for their sustenance and their well-being
(i.e., "the poor") will inherit the land, while those who bypass God and by wicked
means try to take hold of it will come to naught (see note on Ps 5:11 and introduction to Ps 35).
37:11 *The meek:* another word for the poor, those who count solely on God and
follow his law (see Mt 5:5). Indeed, the promises of the Lord are only for the meek
who depend solely on him (v. 9) and will enjoy an "abundance of peace." "Peace"
symbolizes the beneficence of the godly (see Ps 72:7) in contrast with the life of
suffering (v. 12; see Ps 119:65f).

¹³ But the L<small>ORD</small> laughs at them,
    knowing that their day* is approaching.ʷ

¹⁴ The wicked draw their swords
    and string their bows
  to bring down the poor* and the needy
    and to slaughter those who are upright.ˣ

¹⁵ Their swords will enter their own hearts,*
    and their bows will be shattered.

¹⁶ Preferable is the little that the righteous possess
    than the great wealth of the wicked.ʸ

¹⁷ For the power of the wicked will be overcome,
    but the L<small>ORD</small> protects the righteous.

¹⁸ The L<small>ORD</small> looks after the lives of the upright,*
    and their heritage will last forever.

¹⁹ They will not be confounded in times of evil,
    and in days of famine they will eat their fill.

²⁰ But the wicked will perish,
    all those who are enemies of the L<small>ORD</small>.
  Like the beauty of the meadows* they will
    wither away;
    like smoke they will disappear.ᶻ

²¹ The wicked man borrows but neglects to repay,
    whereas the righteous man is generous in
    giving.

²² For those blessed by the L<small>ORD</small> will possess
    the land,
    but those who are cursed will perish.

²³ The L<small>ORD</small> makes a man's steps secureᵃ
    when he approves of his conduct.

---

w Pss 2:4; 59:9; Wis 4:18; Ezek 12:23.—x Pss 11:2; 35:10; 57:5; 64:5.—
y Prov 15:16; 16:8.—z Ps 34:22; Wis 5:14.—a Ps 147:11; Prov 20:24.

37:13 *Their day:* the time for their ultimate defeat, their death (see 1 Sam 26:10, where "his day" is translated as "his time").

37:14 *The poor:* see note on Ps 22:27.

37:15 *Hearts:* see note on Ps 4:8.

37:18 *Upright:* those who are God's faithful and obedient servants as was Abraham (see Gen 17:1).

37:20 *Beauty of the meadows:* the beauty of grass and flowers that comes and goes every year (see Pss 90:5f; 102:12; 103:15f; Job 14:2; Isa 40:6-8; Jas 1:10f).

24 Even if he stumbles, he will never fall headlong,
   for the LORD holds him by the hand.*

25 From my youth until my present old age,
      I have never seen the righteous man aban-
         doned
      or his children reduced to begging for
         bread.b
26 He is always compassionate and generous in
      lending,
      and his children will be blessed.*

27 If you shun evil and do good,c
      you will dwell in the land forever.
28 For the LORD loves the just,*
      and he will not forsake his faithful ones.*

   Those who follow evil paths will be destroyed,
      and the children of the wicked will be cut
         off,
29 whereas the righteous will inherit the land
      and dwell in it forever.d

30 The mouth of the righteous man utters wis-
      dom,*
      and his tongue speaks what is right.e
31 The law of his God is in his heart,f
      and his steps do not waver.

---

b Job 4:7; Sir 2:10; Heb 13:5.—c Ps 34:15-16; Am 5:14; 3 Jn 11.—d Ps
25:13; Prov 2:21; Isa 34:17; 57:13.—e Ps 49:4; Prov 10:31.—f Ps 40:9;
Deut 6:6; Isa 51:7; Jer 31:33.

37:24 See Prov 24:16.

37:26 *Blessed:* see note on Ps 1:1.

37:28-29 The righteous will inherit the land and dwell in it forever through
their descendants (see Mt 5:5).

37:28 The psalmist insists that the Lord loves the just (see Prov 2:8) who are
his faithful ones, and he will never forsake them. Hence, Paul could say with
complete confidence: "[Nothing] will be able to separate us from the love of God
in Christ Jesus our Lord" (Rom 8:38f).

37:30-31 The wise man reveres the Lord and desires to do his will. God's law
is written on his heart (see Ps 40:9; Deut 6:6; Isa 51:7; Jer 31:33; Ezek 36:27). He
speaks wisely (see Ps 49:4) and establishes peace (see Ps 36:7). *Heart:* see note
on Ps 4:8. *His steps do not waver:* from the way of the righteous (see Ps 1:6).

³² The wicked man keeps close watch on the
   righteous*
   and seeks an opportunity to kill him.
³³ But the LORD will not abandon the righteous
   to the power of the wicked,
   nor will he allow him to be condemned
   when he is brought to trial.

³⁴ Wait for the LORD
   and follow the path he has laid out;
   then he will exalt you to inherit the land,
      and you will see the destruction of the
      wicked.ᵍ

³⁵ I have seen a wicked man inflicting terror*
   and towering like a verdant tree.ʰ
³⁶ I passed by again, and he was gone;
   I searched for him, but he was not to be
   found.

³⁷ Pay attention to the innocent and behold the
   upright,*
   for the man of peace will have a future.ⁱ
³⁸ But the wicked will be completely destroyed,
   and their children will be cut off.

³⁹ The salvation of the righteous is from the
   LORD;*
   he is their refuge in times of trouble.ʲ
⁴⁰ The LORD will help them and deliver them;
      he will rescue them from the wicked and
      save them
   because they flee to him for refuge.

g Pss 27:14; 31:25.—h Ps 92:8-9; Job 20:6-7; Isa 2:13; Ezek 31:10-11.—i
Pss 11:7; 18:27; Prov 23:18; 24:14.—j Pss 3:9; 9:10; Isa 25:4.

37:32-33 The righteous need not fear the machinations of the wicked, for the
Lord has promised to come to their assistance. He gave Canaan to Israel and the
earth to all who love him (see Isa 65:17-25; 66:22; Rev 21:1).

37:35-36 God confounds the proud (see Job 20:6f; Isa 2:12; 14:13-15; Ezek
31:10f). *Verdant tree: or:* "cedar of Lebanon."

37:37-38 The righteous have a bright future; the wicked have no future at all
(see Prov 23:18; 24:14). *A future:* or "descendants."

37:39-40 The Lord is the protector of all who take refuge in him, all who call
upon him for protection, deliverance, and victory (see Pss 9:10; 12:2; 34:7f).

PSALM 38*

Prayer of a Sinner in Great Peril

¹ A psalm of David. For remembrance.*

² O LORD, do not punish me in your anger
  or chastise me in your wrath.ᵏ

³ For your arrows* have pierced me deeply,
  and your hand has come down upon me.ˡ

⁴ No portion of my body* has been unscathed
  as a result of your anger;
my bones have become weak
  as a result of my sins.ᵐ

⁵ My iniquities tower far above my head;*
  they are a burden too heavy to bear.ⁿ

⁶ My wounds are fetid and fester
  because of my folly.

---

k Pss 6:2; 39:12.—l Pss 31:11; 64:8; Job 6:4; 34:6; Lam 3:12; Ezek 5:16.—m Prov 3:8; Isa 1:5-6; 66:14.—n Pss 40:13; 65:3-4; Gen 4:13; Num 11:14; Ezr 9:6; Lk 11:46.

Ps 38 The psalmist of this third Penitential Psalm (seven in all: Pss 6; 32; 38; 51; 102; 130; 143) is a man prostrated beneath the weight of his sickness and the vilification heaped on him by others, a man marked by the chastisement of God. He utters a suppliant and monotone plaint that seems as interminable as his suffering. Before God, he is pitiable, abandoned, and betrayed. This new Job (Job 6:4; 19:13-21) does not rebel. He thinks of himself as a sinner who deserves his lot and he suffers in silence, leveling neither recriminations nor imprecations against his adversaries. Indeed, hope stirs secretly in him.

The complete abandonment to God that is expressed here is also found in the third Lamentation (Lam 3:26-29) and in the Songs of the Servant of the Lord (see Isa 53:7). The Christian Liturgy sees in this man of sorrows an image of the Christ who was silent during his Passion.

In praying this psalm, we should look to ourselves, scrutinizing our lives and our consciences with a penetrating and impartial honesty, the better to discern the place of sin therein and the better to realize that we are and remain sinners (see Rom 7:14-20; 1 Jn 1:8f). This will in no way prevent us from begging God not to chastise us in his wrath but to save us as soon as possible from our afflictions and our foes.

38:1 *For remembrance:* the meaning is "For the memorial sacrifice" or "portion" (see Lev 2:2, 9, 16; 5:12; Isa 66:3); it occurs elsewhere only in Ps 70; an alternative translation is: *A petition.*

38:3 *Arrows:* i.e., the trials God has sent him (see Deut 32:23; Job 6:4; 34:6; Lam 3:12; Ezek 5:16).

38:4 *Body:* literally, "flesh." *Bones:* see note on Ps 34:20-21.

38:5 *My iniquities tower far above my head:* his guilt has resulted in both physical and psychological suffering.

7 I am bowed down and bent over,
as I spend each day in sorrow.[o]

8 My loins are filled with searing pain;
no part of my body* is unafflicted.
9 I am numb and completely crushed,
and I groan in anguish of heart.*[p]

10 O LORD, all my longing is known to you,
and my sighs are not hidden from you.
11 My heart throbs, and my strength is spent;
even the light has faded from my eyes.[q]

12 My friends and companions stay away from
my affliction,
and my neighbors keep their distance.
13 Those who seek my life set traps;
those who wish me harm threaten violence
and plot treachery all day long.*

14 But I am like a man who cannot hear,*
like one who cannot open his mouth.
15 I am like one who hears nothing
and has no answer to offer.

16 I place my hope in you, O LORD;
you, O LORD, my God, will answer for me.[r]
17 For I prayed, "Never let them gloat over me
or exult should my foot slip."*

18 I am at the point of exhaustion,
and my grief is with me constantly.
19 I acknowledge my iniquity,
and I sincerely grieve for my sin.[s]

---

o Pss 35:14; 57:7.—p Pss 34:19; 102:4-6; Prov 17:22—q Pss 6:8; 31:11; 88:10; Job 37:1.—r Pss 13:4; 27:14.—s Pss 32:5; 51:5; Lev 26:40.

38:8 *Body:* literally, "flesh."

38:9, 11 *Heart:* see note on Ps 4:8.

38:13 This passage recalls the fourth Song of the Servant (Isa 53:4, 7; see also Pss 31:11; 35:20; 37:32; 88:9; Job 12:4f; 19:13f).

38:14-17 Like a man deaf and dumb, the psalmist does not reply to those who slander him; he waits for the Lord to vindicate his cause.

38:17 Passage close to Pss 35:11; 109:3-5. Some Greek manuscripts and many versions add: "They have rejected me, the loved one, like some hideous corpse" (see Isa 14:19 Greek). This allusion to the crucified Christ is made even more explicit in the Coptic version by the words: "They have nailed my flesh."

²⁰ Numerous and strong are my enemies without
　　　cause;
　　　many are those who hate me without good
　　　reason.*
²¹ Those who repay my good deeds with evil
　　　oppose me because I follow a path of righ-
　　　teousness.ᵗ

²² Do not abandon me, O Lᴏʀᴅ;
　　　my God, do not remain far from me.ᵘ
²³ Come quickly to my aid,
　　　O Lᴏʀᴅ, my Savior.ᵛ

PSALM 39*

The Brevity and Vanity of Life

¹ For the director.* For Jeduthun.ʷ A psalm of David.

² I said, "I will be careful of my behavior
　　so as not to sin with my tongue.

---

t Pss 35:12; 109:5.—u Pss 10:1; 22:2, 12, 20; 27:9; 35:22.—v Pss 22:20;
40:14, 18.—w Pss 62:1; 77:1; 1 Chr 16:41; 25:1.

38:20 *Hate me without good reason:* although the psalmist acknowledges that
he sinned against the Lord, he protests his innocence of wrongdoing against his
enemies (see note on Ps 35:19).

Ps 39 The psalmist is not a sage who reflects on existence but a man grap-
pling with God. In the face of the blows that strike him, he realizes the total
frailty of existence and even of life itself. He would like to cast out from his heart
all intentions to rebel, but it is impossible for him to hold back his complaint any
longer. A real faith in the resurrection is still absent and, apart from an intervention of God providing a new breath of life, everything seems a mockery. One
thinks of the lucid reflections of Ecclesiastes (1:2).

This psalm reminds us that while doing our utmost to acquire and develop the
eternal divine life in us, we must regard our bodily life as the highest good, the
most precious natural talent entrusted to us by God for our vigilant concern and
fruitful action. The heavenly Father himself watches over this life, assigning it
food and drink (see Mt 6:25-34) and life itself (see Acts 17:25-28). Jesus himself
watches over material life, looking after the hunger of the crowd (see Mt 15:32),
curing the sick (Mt 4:23), and raising the dead (Mt 9:25). We must thus greatly
value our life and seek to prolong it for the glory of God and our spiritual progress
(see Phil 1:23-26). Christians too have this same feeling in times of great distress: without the Lord what value is there in life?

39:1 *For the director:* these words are thought to be a musical or liturgical
notation. *Jeduthun:* he is believed to be one of the three men appointed choral di-
rectors by David (see 1 Chr 25:1). See note on Ps 89:1.

I will keep a muzzle on my mouth*
    whenever the wicked are in my presence."
³ I kept completely silentˣ
    and refrained from speech,
    but my distress only increased.
⁴ My heart* smoldered within me,
    and, as I pondered, my mind was inflamed,
    and my tongue began to speak:

⁵ "O Lᴏʀᴅ, let me know my end*
    and the number of days left to me;
    show me how fleeting my life is.
⁶ You have allotted me a short span of days;
    my life is as nothing in your sight;
    human existence is a mere breath.ʸ   *Selah*
⁷ Humans are nothing but a passing shadow;
    the riches they amass are a mere breath,
    and they do not know who will enjoy them.*

⁸ "So now, O Lᴏʀᴅ, what do I wait for?
    My hope is in you.
⁹ Deliver me from all my sins;
    do not subject me to the taunts of fools.*

¹⁰ "I was silent and did not open my mouth,
    for it is you who have done it.
¹¹ Remove your scourge from me;
    I am crushed by the blows of your hand.
¹² You rebuke and punish people for their sins;
    like a moth you consume all their desires;
    human existence is a mere puff of wind.
                          Selah

---

x 3-4: Ps 37:1; Jer 20:9.—y Pss 62:10; 89:46; 90:9-10; 144:4; Gen 6:3;
47:9; Job 7:6, 16; 14:1; Prov 10:27; Eccl 6:12; Wis 2:5; Sir 18:8; Isa 65:20.

39:2 *Muzzle on my mouth:* to repress saying anything derogatory in the presence of the wicked.
39:4 *Heart:* see note on Ps 4:8.
39:5-7 The psalmist begs God to help him know and accept the brevity and vanity of life, a brevity and vanity stressed in other psalms (see Pss 62:10; 73:19; 90:10-11) and in Isa 40:17.
39:7 This passage is reminiscent of Ecclesiastes.
39:9 *Fools:* see Ps 14 (introduction and notes on vv. 2 and 3).

¹³ "Hear my prayer, O LORD;*
　　do not be deaf to my cry
　　or ignore my weeping.
　For I am a wayfarer* before you,
　　a nomad like all my ancestors.ᶻ
¹⁴ Turn your eyes away so that I may be glad
　　before I depart and am no more."*

PSALM 40*

Thanksgiving and Prayer for Help

¹ For the director.* A psalm of David.

² I waited patiently for the LORD;*
　　then he stooped down and heard my cry.ᵃ

---

z Ps 119:19; Gen 23:4; Ex 12:48; Lev 25:23; 2 Ki 20:5; Heb 11:13; 1 Pet 2:11.—a Pss 6:10; 31:22; 34:16; 37:7; 116:1; 145:19; Lam 3:25.

39:13-14 The psalmist—a sinner and overcome with adversity—feels like a stranger in God's presence and in his world. Still, he has no doubts about belonging to the Covenant community. So he begs the Lord to remove his judgment from him so that the psalmist may know joy once again.

39:13 *Wayfarer:* that is, one who is only a temporary sojourner on earth (see Lev 25:23: "The land is mine and you are but aliens and my tenants"; see also Ps 119:19; 1 Pet 2:11).

39:14 *Am no more:* in the time of the psalmist there apparently was no idea of any resurrection, even a mitigated one in the netherworld (see note on Ps 6:6).

Ps 40 This psalm, one of the most engaging of the entire Psalter, is divided into two parts. The first (vv. 2-13) is a thanksgiving reminiscent of Jeremiah (7:22; 17:7; 31:33). The second (vv. 14-18) is a lament that appears also as Ps 70.

Every Christian (and the whole Church) can naturally recite this beautiful psalm in his or her own right as one really (though not yet completely) saved.

40:1 *For the director:* these words are thought to be a musical or liturgical notation.

40:2-12 The psalmist expresses a great hope in the Lord. No one knows God's goodness better than one who has experienced abandonment. Purified by trial, the psalmist welcomes God into the depths of his being, his life becomes a kind of inner offering, the only true sacrifice, and he joyfully bears witness to the Lord's righteousness, love, and truth. In reading this psalm, we get the impression of entering into the confidence of Christ himself, of divining his inner attitude toward the course of his action and above all toward his Passion. A few Greek translations have accentuated this resemblance even more; thus, the Letter to the Hebrews cites this psalm to make us understand the profound decision of Christ (Heb 10:5-10).

The best praise of God and the best sacrifice are the gift of one's heart and life. The Prophets often opposed ritual formalism and replaced it with the true religion that is internal (Isa 1:11; Jer 6:20; 31:33; Am 5:22; Hos 6:6). It is this experience to which the Songs of the Suffering Servant bear witness (Isa 50:5; 53:10), which was also the experience of Christ.

3 He raised me up from the desolate pit,
   out of the mire of the swamp;
he set my feet upon a rock,
   giving me a firm footing.*b*
4 He put a new song* in my mouth,
   a hymn of praise to our God.
Many will look on and be awestruck,
   and they will place their trust in the LORD.*c*

5 Blessed* is the man
   who places his trust in the LORD,*d*
who does not follow the arrogant
   or those who go astray after falsehoods.
6 How innumerable, O LORD, my God,
   are the wonders you have worked;
no one can compare with you
   in the plans you have made for us.*e*
I would proclaim them and recount them,
   but there are far too many to enumerate.*f*

7 Sacrifice and offering you did not desire,*
   but you have made my ears receptive.
Burnt offerings and sin offerings
   you did not demand.**g*
8 Then I said, "Behold I come;*
   it is written of me in the scroll of the book.

---

b Pss 18:5; 28:1; 30:4; 69:3, 15-16; 88:5; Prov 1:12; Jer 38:6; Jon 2:6f.—c Ps 33:3; Rev 5:9.—d Pss 1:1; 34:9; Prov 16:20; Jer 17:7.—e Ps 35:10; Deut 4:34.—f Pss 71:15; 75:1; 105:5; 136:4; 139:17-18; Deut 4:34.—g 7-9: Ps 51:18-19; Isa 1:11-15; 50:5; Jer 6:20; Hos 6:6; Am 5:22; Heb 10:5-7.

40:4 *New song:* see note on Ps 33:3. *Many will look on:* see note on Ps 9:2.
40:5 *Blessed:* see note on Ps 1:1.
40:7-9 These verses are applied to Christ by Heb 10:5-10.
40:7 Obedience is better than sacrifice (see Pss 50:7-15; 51:18f; 69:32f; 1 Sam 15:22; Isa 1:10-20; Jer 7:22; Hos 6:6; Am 5:22-25; Mic 6:6-8; Acts 7:42f). *But you have made my ears receptive:* a variant reading from the Greek versions has: "but a body you have prepared for me," which was interpreted in a Messianic sense and applied to Christ (see Heb 10:5ff).
40:8-9 The psalmist presents himself to the Lord, submitting himself to whatever his Master may require (Heb 10:9). He presents himself as an offering to the Lord (see Rom 12:1f). *It is written of me in the scroll:* the scroll is the Torah or the Mosaic Law, transcribed on parchment scrolls. The alternative Greek reading is "with the scroll written for me," which suggests a Messianic sense.

⁹ To do your will, O God, is my delight;
    your law is in my heart."*ʰ

¹⁰ I have proclaimed your righteousness in the
    great assembly;
    I did not seal my lips,
    as you well know, O LORD.ⁱ
¹¹ I have not concealed your righteousness within
    the depths of my heart;
    I have spoken of your faithfulness and sal-
    vation.
I have not concealed your kindness and your
    truth
    in the great assembly.

¹² O LORD, do not withhold your mercy from me;
    may your kindness* and your truth keep
    me safe forever.ʲ
¹³ I am surrounded by evils without number;
    my sins have so engulfed me that I cannot
    see.
They outnumber the hairs on my head,
    and my heart sinks within me.*ᵏ

¹⁴ Be pleased, O LORD, to rescue me.*
    O LORD, come quickly to my aid.ˡ
¹⁵ May all those who seek to take my life*
    endure shame and confusion.
May all those who desire my ruin
    be turned back and humiliated.ᵐ

---

h Ps 37:31; Jn 4:34; 8:29.—i Pss 22:23, 32; 26:12; 35:18; 149:1; Jos
22:22.—j Ps 89:34; Zec 1:12.—k Pss 6:8; 38:4f, 11; 65:4; 69:5; Ezr 9:6.—l
14-18: Pss 70:2-6; 71:12.—m Pss 35:4, 26; 71:13; 1 Sam 20:1; Est 9:2.

40:9, 11, 13 *Heart:* see note on Ps 4:8.
40:12 *Kindness:* see note on Ps 6:5.
40:13 Hyberbolic statements expressing the intense nature of the sinner's sufferings (see Pss 6:8; 38:4f, 11; 69:5), which serve as a transition to the second
part of the psalm.
40:14-18 Distress can remind a person of his attachment to sin. Is there any reason why people should vilify the person who acknowledges his faults? Realizing his
incoercible attraction toward evil, the psalmist cries out to God, and the poor man
rediscovers with astonishment the joyous assurance that God thinks about him.
40:15-16 See note on Ps 5:11 and introduction to Ps 35.

16 May those who cry out to me, "Aha, aha!"*
    be overcome with shame and dismay.[n]

17 But may all who seek you
    rejoice in you and be jubilant.
May those who love your salvation
    cry out forever, "The LORD be magnified."[o]
18 Even though I am poor and needy,*
    the LORD keeps me in his thoughts.
You are my help and my deliverer;
    O my God, do not delay.

PSALM 41*

Trust in God in Sickness and Misfortune

1 For the director.* A psalm of David.

2 Blessed is he who has concern for the weak;*
    in time of trouble the LORD will deliver
    him.[p]

---

n Ps 35:21, 25; Lam 2:16.—o Pss 35:27; 69:7, 33; 104:1; Deut 4:29; 1
Chr 28:9.—p Ps 25:17; Deut 14:29; Job 4:7-11; Prov 14:21.

40:16 *Aha, Aha!:* the mocking words of the psalmist's adversaries.

40:18 *Poor and needy:* see note on Ps 34:7. *My help and my deliverer:* the salvation promised to the faithful (see Isa 25:9), first conceived as natural with reference to the Exodus or the return from the Exile, was later conceived as spiritual without restriction of space or time (see, e.g., Pss 18:1; 19:15).

Ps 41 The psalmist is well aware that mercy is rarely given by human beings. In his illness, he received no mercy from others; instead his enemies gleefully engaged in malicious gossip about him and his coming death and even his friend betrayed him. However, the psalmist does not retaliate in kind; he turns to God for mercy, asking for a rich life with all his powers restored so that he can stand once again in the presence of the Lord.

In praying this psalm, we can recall that the entire psalm is applicable to Christ personally, with the exception of v. 5, which he can assume only in place of and in the role of his sinful members. Since Christ assures us of God's complete solicitude, we can recite this supplication on our account amid our earthly trials.

41:1 *For the director:* these words are thought to be a musical or liturgical notation.

41:2-4 The psalmist voices his confidence that the Lord will restore him to fullness of health and life because of the psalmist's regard for the weak. *Blessed . . . weak:* other psalms use the same designation ("Blessed") for those whom God favors (see Pss 32:1f; 34:9; 40:5; 65:5; see also note on Ps 1:1).

3 The LORD will protect him and keep him alive;
   he will make him happy on earth
      and not abandon him to the will of his ene-
         mies.
4 The LORD will sustain him on his sickbed
   and bring him back to health.

5 Once I prayed, "O LORD, have mercy on me;
   heal me, for I have sinned* against you.
6 In their malice my enemies say of me,
   'When will he die and his name be forgotten?'
7 When someone comes to visit me,
   he utters words without sincerity;
 his heart* harbors slander,
   and on departing he gives voice to it.q

8 "All my enemies whisper against me
   and conjure up the worst in my regard.
9 'He has a fatal disease,' they say;
   'he will never rise up from his sickbed.'

10 "Even my friend whom I trusted,
   the one who dined at my table,
   has risen up against me.*r
11 But you, O LORD, be merciful to me;
   make me well* so that I may pay them back."

12 By this I know that you are pleased with me—
   that my enemy fails to triumph over me.
13 Because of my innocence you uphold me
   and let me stand in your presence forever.

q Pss 12:3; 31:12; 38:12-13; 88:9; 101:7; Job 19:13-19; Jer 20:10; Mt 5:11.—r Ps 55:14-15; Job 19:19; Mt 26:23; Lk 22:21; Jn 13:18.

41:5 *Sinned:* the psalmist acknowledges his sin and asks for forgiveness and healing—in keeping with the idea that sickness was a divine punishment for sin (see Ps 107:17; Job 32:3). In the cure of the man born blind, Jesus was to indicate that such was not the case (see Jn 9:2f).

41:7 *Heart:* see note on Ps 4:8.

41:10 This passage repeats a theme frequently developed (see Pss 31:12; 38:12; 55:15f; 88:9; Job 19:13; Jer 20:10; 38:22). It is cited by Jesus with reference to Judas (Jn 13:18) according to the sense of the Septuagint. *Risen up:* literally, "raised his heel."

41:11 The fact that God heals the psalmist is a judgment in his favor and against his adversaries, but paying them back is not part of God's judgment.

14 Blessed be the LORD, the God of Israel,[s]
   forever and forever.
Amen and Amen.*

BOOK II—PSALMS 42–72*

PSALM 42*

Prayer of Longing for God

1 For the director.* A *maskil* of the sons of Korah.

2 As a deer longs for running streams,
   so my soul longs for you, O God.*[t]

---

s Pss 72:18f; 89:53; 106:48; 150:1-6; Neh 9:5; Dan 2:20.—t 2-3: Pss 36:10; 63:2; 84:3; 143:6; Deut 10:7; Isa 26:9; Joel 1:20; Jn 7:37.

41:14 This doxology is not part of the psalm; it concludes the first of the five books of the Psalter (see Pss 72:18f; 89:53; 106:48; 150). *Blessed:* see note on Ps 18:47.

Pss 42—72 The drama of the righteous confronted with the rise of evil terminated Book I of the Psalter. This conflict remains, but other themes come to the fore with greater insistence. Now the prayer often evinces a desire for God and to be far from human beings, oftentimes with a more mystical note added. At other times, crucial moments of history will appear to provoke alternatively both praise and supplication: the drama of the righteous remains—as that of the people. In short, in the psalms that follow, the collective aspect will be readily underlined.

Ps 42 This psalm, which really forms one with the next psalm, has a fascinating literary beauty but also expresses feeling of a rare kind. It is the lament of the exiled Levite combining nostalgia, distress, and fervent desire. Living in a foreign land, far from the temple of Jerusalem, the sole place where it was believed one would encounter God, the sacred ministers feel the Exile more deeply; the sanctuary is the only place where they find their happiness. They are the first to suffer the mockings of the pagans, who do not recognize the God to whom they have dedicated their lives. Three times the lament is voiced, and three times the chant that gives hope is also uttered, as the psalm vibrantly expresses the fervor for the temple, where the people flocked to celebrate the love and presence of God.

At the heart of this fervor we glimpse the deepest human yearning: the desire for God. It is this that here on earth inspires the candidates who seek to enter the Church, the "house of God," and we also place it on the lips of the dead who are waiting to be admitted into the new Jerusalem, the heavenly city of God. Consecrated men and women also recognize herein the movement of their souls. Is not this the sublime desire at the root of all human restlessness? Down the centuries Augustine has proclaimed: "Our hearts are restless until they rest in you."

42:1 *For the director:* these words are thought to be a musical or liturgical notation. *Maskil:* see note on Ps 32:1a. *Sons of Korah:* Levites (see 1 Chr 26:19). In Book II, seven psalms bear this inscription (Pss 42; 44—49) and four in Book III (Pss 84—85; 87—88).

42:2 *God:* from Ps 42 to Ps 84, the ineffable tetragrammaton ("Yahweh") is generally replaced by "God" ("Elohim"), marking this as the "Elohist Psalter."

³ My soul* thirsts for God, the living God.
    When shall I come to behold the face of
        God?ᵘ

⁴ My tears have become my food
        day and night,ᵛ
    while people taunt me all day long, saying,
        "Where is your God?"ʷ
⁵ As I pour out my soul,ˣ
        I recall those times
    when I journeyed with the multitude
        and led them in procession to the house of
            God,
    amid loud cries of joy and thanksgiving
        on the part of the crowd keeping festival.ʸ

⁶ Why are you so disheartened, O my soul?
        Why do you sigh within me?
    Place your hope in God,
        for I will once again praise him,
        my Savior and my God.*

⁷ My soul is disheartened within me;
        therefore, I remember you
    from the land of Jordan and Hermon,
        from Mount Mizar.*ᶻ

---

u Pss 27:4; 63:2; 143:6; Jos 3:10; Mt 16:16; Rom 9:26.—v Pss 80:6;
102:10; Job 3:24.—w Pss 79:10; 115:2; Joel 2:17; Mic 7:10; Mal 2:17.—x 1
Sam 1:15; Lam 3:20.—y Pss 27:4; 55:15; 122:1, 4; Isa 30:29.—z Pss 43:5;
63:7; 77:12; Deut 3:8.

42:3 *Soul:* see note on Ps 6:4. *Living God:* see Deut 5:26. *Behold the face of God:* here the phrase is taken to mean God's personal presence (see Gen 33:10; Ex 10:28f). In other places the expression "see God" (or "see the face of God") indicates the presence of God in the temple (see Pss 11:7; 17:15; 63:3; Ex 24:10; 33:7-11; Job 33:26).
42:6-7 *Why . . . my God:* this refrain appears three times in this double psalm (42:6, 12; 43:5) and indicates that the two parts were originally one psalm (see note on Ps 42:12).
42:7 *Mount Mizar:* not identified. The translation "from the land . . ." supposes a Levite exiled to the springs of the Jordan, at the foot of Mount Hermon. If we think of him as exiled in Babylon, the translation would be: "I will remember you / more than the land of the Jordan and Hermon, / than the lowly mountain [Zion]."

⁸ The depths of the sea resound
    in the roar of your waterfalls;*
all your waves and your breakers
    sweep over me.ᵃ
⁹ During the day the LORD grants his kindness,
    and at night his praise is with me,
    a prayer to the living God.*

¹⁰ I say to God, my Rock,*
    "Why have you forgotten me?
Why must I go about in mourning
    while my enemy oppresses me?"ᵇ
¹¹ It crushes my bones
    when my foes taunt me,
jeering at me all day long,
    "Where is your God?"*

¹² Why are you so disheartened, O my soul?
    Why do you sigh within me?
Place your hope in God;
    for I will once again praise him,
    my Savior and my God.*

---

a Pss 18:5; 32:6; 69:3; 88:8; 124:4-5; Gen 1:2; 7:11; Jon 2:3.—b Pss 18:3, 33; 31:3-4; 35:14; 106:42; Job 20:19.

42:8 *The depths of the sea resound . . . your waterfalls:* the psalmist alludes to the "waterfalls" that carry God's waters from the "depths" above to the "depths" below (see note on Ps 36:9), bringing God's breakers sweeping over him (see Pss 69:2f; 88:8; Jon 2:3). And God is involved in this danger of water toward the psalmist (see note on Ps 32:6)—he lets it happen.

42:9 Nonetheless, the psalmist is confident of God's kindness, and this sustains him (see note on Ps 6:5). *The living God:* some propose the translation: "the God of my life" and understand it as "the God who gives me life."

42:10 *Rock:* see note on Ps 18:3. *Why. . .? Why. . .?:* see note on Ps 6:4.

42:11 The psalmist has been abandoned by God to his godless enemies, who taunt him with the words "Where is your God?" He resembles a dying man, and his whole being ("bones"; see note on Ps 34:20-21) is distressed by his foes and by God's silence.

42:12 The refrain is voiced for the second time in this double-psalm (see v. 6, above) and will be repeated once more in Ps 43:5. This threefold refrain reflects the attitude of many of God's people during the Exile or any crisis situation. In such loneliness and alienation, faith is tried and leads to salvation. For hope is mindful of the Lord's glorious works of salvation and victory recounted in the Sacred Writings. See Mt 26:38 for the application of these words to Christ's agony in the Garden of Gethsemane.

PSALM 43*

Prayer To Worship God Anew

1 Grant me your justice, O God,
　　and plead my cause against a godless nation;
　　rescue me from those who are deceitful and
　　　　unjust.[c]
2 You, O God, are my refuge;
　　why have you rejected me?
　Why must I go about in mourning,
　　while my enemy oppresses me?

3 Send forth your light and your truth;*
　　they will serve as my guide.[d]
　Let them bring me to your holy mountain,
　　to the place of your dwelling.[e]
4 Then I will go to the altar of God,
　　to the God of my joy and delight,
　and I will praise you* with the harp,
　　O God, my God.

5 Why are you so disheartened, O my soul?
　　Why do you sigh within me?
　Place your hope in God;
　　for I will once again praise him,
　　my Savior and my God.*

---

c Pss 109:2; 119:154.—d Pss 2:6; 18:29; 27:1; 36:10; 57:4; 2 Sam 15:25; Mic 7:8.—e Pss 2:6; 84:2-5; 122:1.

Ps 43 The psalmist asks God for vindication so that he may be able to return to the temple and render him praise once again.

We can pray this psalm to augment our tranquil hope. We place our cause in God, who has sworn that he will obtain redress for us from our enemies (see Rom 12:19; Heb 10:30). He will enable us to journey toward the heavenly Jerusalem in the vast mobile column of his Church, the true liturgical procession and uninterrupted processional march that takes the elect to him (see Heb 10:19-22).

43:3 *Your light and your truth:* the psalmist personifies the divine attributes of light (see note on Ps 27:1) and truth (see Pss 25:5; 26:3; 40:11) and asks that they bring him safely to the temple. *Holy mountain:* see note on Ps 2:6.

43:4 *Altar of God . . . I will praise you:* see notes on Pss 7:18 and 26:6.

43:5 See note on Ps 42:12.

PSALM 44*
Past Glory and Present Need of God's People

¹ For the director.* A *maskil* of the sons of Korah.

² O God, we have heard with our ears,*
    our ancestors have told us,
of the deeds you performed in their days,
    in the days of old.*ᶠ*
³ To establish them in the land,
        you drove out the nations with your own
            hand;
    you crushed the peoples
        so that our ancestors could flourish.*ᵍ*

⁴ It was not their own swords that won them
        the land,
        nor did their own arms make them victori-
            ous;*ʰ*
    rather, it was your right hand and your arm
        and the light of your face,*
        because you loved them.*ⁱ*

⁵ You are my* King and my God,
    who bestowed victories upon Jacob.*ʲ*
⁶ Through you we throw back our enemies;
    through your name* we crush our assailants.

---

f Ps 78:3; 2 Sam 7:22-23; 1 Chr 17:20.—g Pss 78:55; 80:10f; Acts
7:45.—h Deut 8:17f; Jos 24:12.—i Pss 4:7; 31:17; 67:2; 78:54; 80:4; Ex
15:16; Num 6:25; Dan 9:17; Hos 1:7.—j Pss 5:2; 21:6; 145:1.

Ps 44 In the history of Israel, times of joy and defeat alternate with one another. This hymn transmits the strong feeling of the people about the triumphs of
bygone days and the defeat at hand. But they do not believe God can forget forever the people that he loves.

As the true "remnant" and the elite of God's servants, the Church very naturally uses this psalm of the remnant of Israel to beseech the Lord and Master to
take pity on her in the severe trials that assail her. This national lamentation is a
prayer for times when we feel overwhelmed by failure, uncertainty, and confusion.

44:1 *For the director:* these words are thought to be a musical or liturgical
notation. *Maskil:* see note on Ps 32:1a. *Sons of Korah:* see note on Ps 42:1.

44:2-9 The liturgy of the Old Testament transmits with gratitude the memory
of the great hours of the conquest. Isn't God the one who at that time was responsible for this people's victory? A hymn recalls these wondrous deeds.

44:4 *The light of your face:* see notes on Pss 4:7 and 13:2.

44:5 *My:* this psalm is sung in the name of all Israel.

44:6, 9 *Name:* see note on Ps 5:12.

⁷ It is not in my bow that I trust,
  nor can my sword ensure my victory.
⁸ It is you who saved us from our enemies;
  you scattered in confusion those who hate us.
⁹ In God we boast the whole day long,
  and we will praise your name forever.   *Selah*

¹⁰ ᵏ But now you have rejected and humiliated
   us,*ˡ
   and you no longer accompany our armies.*
¹¹ You have forced us to retreat* before the enemy;
   those who hate us plunder us unceasingly.ᵐ
¹² You have handed us over like sheep to be
   slaughtered
   and scattered us among the nations.ⁿ
¹³ You have sold your people for nothing,
   receiving no gain from their sale.ᵒ

¹⁴ You have subjected us to the contempt of our
   neighbors,ᵖ
   to the mockery and scorn of all who are near.
¹⁵ You have made us a byword to the nations;
   the peoples shake their heads* at us.

¹⁶ All day long I am confronted by my disgrace,
   and my face is covered with shame

---

k 10-27: Ps 89:39-52.—l Pss 60:12; 68:8.—m Lev 26:17; Deut 28:25; Jdg 2:14.—n Lev 26:33; Deut 28:64.—o Deut 32:30; Isa 52:3; Jer 15:13.—p 14-17: Pss 79:4; 80:7; 123:3-4; 2 Chr 29:8; Job 12:4; Dan 9:16.

44:10-17 Only a lament can evoke the situation of that moment; we are doubt-less at the time of the Exile, after 587 B.C. This prayer could have been utilized and adapted at other times of national calamity; thus, vv. 18-23 make us think of the Maccabean period when Israel is conscious of being the faithful commu-nity that did not deserve persecution (167-164 B.C.); the people suffer for their faith rather than for punishment of sin. For Paul, this lament (v. 23) reflects the condition of Christians (Rom 8:36).

44:10 *You no longer accompany our armies:* as commander-in-chief (see Pss 60:12; 68:8; Ex 15:3; Jdg 5:4).

44:11 *You have forced us to retreat:* God is responsible for the defeats as well as the victories (v. 5) of Israel.

44:15 Since the People of God have been allowed by God to be conquered, plundered, scattered like sheep, and enslaved by their enemies, their name has been disgraced among the nations (see Deut 28:37; 1 Ki 9:7; Jer 24:10).*Shake their heads:* a gesture of scorn (see Ps 64:9).

¹⁷ as I hear the shouts of taunting and abuse
and see the hateful enemy seeking revenge.

¹⁸ All this has happened to us
even though we have not forgotten you
or been false to your covenant.*
¹⁹ Our hearts* have not turned back,
nor have our feet wandered from your path.
²⁰ Yet you have crushed us,
forced us to live among the jackals,*
and covered us with darkness.^q

²¹ If we had forgotten the name* of our God
or lifted up our hands to a foreign god,
²² would not God have discovered it,
he who knows the secrets of the heart?
²³ For your sake we are put to death all day long;^r
we are treated like sheep destined to be
slaughtered.*

²⁴ Awake, O Lord. Why* do you sleep?
Rise up, and do not abandon us forever.^s
²⁵ Why do you hide your face*
and continue to ignore our misery and our
sufferings?^t

---

q Isa 34:13; Jer 9:10.—r Isa 53:7; Rom 8:36.—s Pss 10:1; 74:1; 77:8; 79:5; 83:2; 89:47.—t Pss 10:11; 13:2; 89:47; Job 13:24.

44:18 Israel's present state is not the result of infidelity to God's Covenant (see Ex 19—24).

44:19 *Hearts:* see note on Ps 4:8. *Your path:* the path or way shown them by the Lord (see Ps 18:31).

44:20 *You have crushed us [and] forced us to live among the jackals:* i.e., relegated Israel to a place unfit for human beings (see Isa 13:22; Jer 9:11; 10:22). Another translation proposed is: "you crushed us as you did the sea monster." *Darkness:* they have been left without "light," which symbolizes the fruits of God's loving kindness (see note on Ps 36:10).

44:21 *Name:* see note on Ps 5:12. *Lifted up our hands:* the usual posture for prayer (see Ex 9:29), with palms turned upward.

44:23 In truth, Israel has suffered the hostility of the peoples because she has been the nation faithful to the Lord. Applying this verse to the Christian community (Rom 8:36), Paul is able to give it a positive slant because of Christ's victory through his Passion and Resurrection (Rom 8:37-39).

44:24 *Why. . .?:* see note on Ps 6:4.

44:25 *Hide your face:* see note on Ps 13:2.

26 We have been brought down to the dust;*u*
  our bodies cling to the ground.*
27 Rise up and come to our aid;
  redeem us for the sake of your kindness.*

PSALM 45*

Nuptial Ode for the Messianic King

1 For the director.* According to "Lilies." A *maskil* of the sons of Korah. A love song.

2 * My heart* is moved by a noble theme
  as I sing my poem to the king;
    my tongue is like the pen of a skillful
      scribe.

---

u Pss 7:6; 12:6; 26:11; 102:14; 119:25; Num 10:35.

44:26 *Our bodies cling to the ground:* posture of those who are defeated, those at prayer, or those in affliction (see Pss 7:6; 119:25; Num 24:4; Deut 9:18).

44:27 *Kindness:* see note on Ps 6:5.

Ps 45 This unique psalm, probably composed for a royal wedding, opens with the dedication to the king, then lets the ceremony unfold before our eyes. First, it celebrates the monarchy, depicting it under the characteristics of a new David, the Anointed One already acclaimed by Isaiah (see Isa 9:5f; 11:3-5). He is a splendid war chief, a lieutenant of God who comes forth with a dazzling cortege; upon him rests the promise made to the House of David (see 2 Sam 7). Next it addresses and celebrates the queen—a foreigner (vv. 11-18)—placed at the right hand of her royal spouse, richly adorned and heaped with gifts. She is ushered into the palace followed by her bridesmaids and offered an array of good wishes.

The psalm also reminds us of a different kind of marriage. The Prophets had spoken of God as espoused to his people (see Isa 62:5; Ezek 16:8f; Hos 2:16), a rich, though bold image. As Jews reread this beautiful lyric text, they had a presentiment of the Covenant that the future Messiah was to establish and extend to include the pagan peoples. The Christian tradition finds in it a prediction of the marriage of Christ and the Church (Mt 9:15; 22:9; Jn 3:29; 2 Cor 11:5; Eph 5:22; Rev 19:9; 21:2), the new and definitive Covenant that is extended to all peoples.

The Liturgy draws upon this psalm in celebrating the most impressive fulfillment of these mystical espousals: the Virgin Mary, Queen and Bride of the King; and those who, following her, have chosen Christ for their Bridegroom.

45:1 *For the director:* these words are thought to be a musical or liturgical notation. *According to "Lilies":* nothing is known about these words. *Maskil:* see note on Ps 32:1a. *Sons of Korah:* see note on Ps 42:1.

45:2-10 The poet addresses the King-Messiah and applies to him attributes of Yahweh (see Ps 145:4-7, 12f, etc.) and of Immanuel (see Isa 9:5f; 11:3-5). He is urged to conduct himself in such a way that his reign will be adorned even more splendidly than the wedding vestments he has on (vv. 4-6). The best way he can do so is to make the glory of his kingdom consist in justice and righteousness (vv. 7-10).

45:2 *Heart:* see note on Ps 4:8.

3 You are the most handsome of men;*
   grace has anointed your lips,
   for God has blessed you forever.[v]
4 Gird your sword upon your thigh, O warrior,
   and advance in splendor and majesty.[w]

5 Ride on triumphantly in truth, humility, and
      justice;
   may your right hand perform wondrous
      deeds.
6 Your arrows are sharp;
   nations will lie beneath your feet;
   the enemies of the king will lose heart.*

7 Your throne, O God,* will last forever and
      ever;[x]
   the scepter of your kingdom will be a
      scepter of justice.
8 You love righteousness and hate wickedness;
   therefore God, your God, has established
      you above your fellow kings
   by anointing you with the oil of gladness.

9 All your robes are fragrant*
   with myrrh and aloes and cassia;
   from palaces of ivory
   stringed instruments bring joy to your heart.

---

v Song 5:10-16; Lk 4:22.—w Pss 21:6; 149:6.—x 7-8: Lam 5:19; Heb 1:8-9.

45:3 *Most handsome of men:* so far above all other men was a king of that era regarded (see 1 Sam 9:2; 16:18) that he is akin to a god (see note on v. 7). Older versions translated this phrase as "fairest among the sons of men." *Grace has anointed your lips:* see Prov 22:11; Eccl 10:12; see also Isa 50:4; Lk 4:22.
45:6 *Heart:* see note on Ps 4:8.
45:7 *O God:* a title of honor applied in the Bible to the Messiah (see Isa 9:6), as well as to the leaders and judges (see Ps 82:6), to Moses (see Ex 4:16; 7:1), to the spirit of Samuel (see 1 Sam 28:13), and to the House of David (see Zec 12:8). The fullest meaning of this description of the Davidic king is attained when it is applied to Christ (see Heb 1:8f).
45:9-10 The psalmist's descriptions and references of the preparations for the wedding ceremony—robes, spices, music, the royal daughters, and the royal bride—all emphasize the rightness of the moment and the anointing of this king, who is a son of David. God's blessing on him ensures the continuity of David's house in accord with God's promise (see 2 Sam 7:16). *Myrrh and aloes and cassia:* Oriental perfumes (see Gen 37:25; Ex 25:6; Song 1:13; 4:14). *From palaces of ivory:* see 1 Ki 22:39; Am 3:15; 6:4. *Heart:* see note on Ps 4:8.

¹⁰ Daughters of kings* are among your women
    in waiting;
    at your right hand is your queen
    adorned in gold of Ophir.

¹¹ My daughter, listen carefully to my words
    and follow them diligently.
    Forget your people and your father's house;*
¹²   then the king will desire your beauty.
    Since he is your lord,
¹³   bow down before him.
    The Daughter of Tyre will bring you gifts,
    people of wealth will seek your favor.*ʸ

¹⁴ Within the palace the king's daughter is
    adornedᶻ
    in robes threaded with gold.
¹⁵ In embroidered garments she is led to the king,
    followed by her virgin companions,
    who are also led to you.*
¹⁶ They are brought in with joy and gladness
    as they enter the palace of the king.

¹⁷ Your* sons will take the place of your ances-
    tors;ᵃ
    you will make them princes in all the earth.

---

y Ps 72:10-11; Jos 19:29; 1 Ki 9:16; Isa 60:5f.—z 14-16: Isa 61:10; Ezek
16:10-13.—a Pss 68:28; 113:8; Gen 17:6; 35:11.

45:10 *Daughters of kings:* in the allegorical sense, these are the pagan nations converted to the true God (see Song 1:3; 6:8; Isa 60:3f; 61:5) and admitted
to his service (v. 16). *Gold of Ophir:* the most prized kind of gold (see 1 Ki 9:28;
10:11; Job 22:24). The location of Ophir is not known; it is sometimes identified
with the southern coast of Arabia or eastern Africa.
45:11 *Forget your people and your father's house:* all her concern should be
with what follows, not with what went before; she is the queen and should be
concerned with her husband the king.
45:13 The reward for joining God's people and for following the new way of life
is exaltation among the nations. The people of Tyre—as well as other wealthy
nations—will bring tribute to Jerusalem. Indeed, during Solomon's rule, precious
gifts were brought to Jerusalem because of his great renown. *Daughter of Tyre:*
the city of Tyre, famous for its wealth, which was the first foreign city to recognize
the Davidic dynasty (see 2 Sam 5:11) and remained close to Solomon (see 1 Ki 5;
9:10-14, 26-28). See also note on Ps 9:15.
45:15 *To you:* i.e., to the king.
45:17 *Your:* i.e., the king's. *Earth:* or "land."

¹⁸ I will extol your name through all generations;
therefore, the nations will praise you for-
ever and ever.*^b

PSALM 46*
God, Refuge of His People

¹ For the director.* A song of the sons of Korah. Accord-
ing to *alamoth*.

² God is our refuge and our strength,*
a well-proved help in times of trouble.*^c
³ Therefore, we will not be afraid, though the
earth be shaken
and the mountains tumble into the depths
of the sea,^d

b Isa 60:15; 61:9; 62:2.—c Pss 9:10; 48:4; Isa 33:2; Jer 16:19; Joel 3:16.—d Pss 3:6; 93:3-4; 97:5; Job 9:5-6; Isa 24:18-20; 54:10.

45:18 The psalmist sees the nations praising the Israelite king, i.e., especially the Messianic King. The Prophets had foretold that in the Restoration the nations would bring him gifts to celebrate the dignity of the People of God among the nations. The Book of Revelation also mentions this aspect of the everlasting state: "The kings of the earth will bring their treasures. . . . The nations will come bringing their treasures and wealth" (Rev 21:24, 26). Filled with blessings (see Gen 17:6; 35:11), the new Zion will be glorious and sovereign (see Isa 60:15, 21; 61:9; 62:2, 7), especially in Messianic times.

Ps 46 This psalm exalts the power of the God of Israel, Master of nature and Ruler of both armies and peace. Upon a horizon of wars and cataclysms rises the city of Zion, peaceful and unshakable. God is in her, a refuge protecting her from all agitations, a river bringing her a richness of life. The psalm lets us relive the explosion of joy prompted by the defeat of the Assyrian armies in 701 B.C. (see 2 Ki 18:13—19:37; 2 Chr 32).

This great moment of the past allows the Prophets to designate in advance the drama at the end of time. Amidst the turmoil of nations, God intervenes to save his people, and the world is turned upside down before obtaining definitive peace. It is an image of the movement of history with its cataclysms and the hope of universal salvation.

In praying this psalm, we should recall that the new and eternal Jerusalem, our mother, is the Church (see Gal 4:26) to whom Christ guaranteed his perpetual protection that renders her indefectible.

46:1 *For the director:* these words are thought to be a musical or liturgical notation. *Sons of Korah:* see note on Ps 42:1. *Alamoth:* probably a musical term.

46:2-4 The divine presence in the temple guarantees the security of the holy city even though creation itself may seem to be falling apart (see Ps 104:6-9; Gen 1:9f).

46:2 *Help in times of trouble:* when people are in trouble they feel the need of God's special protection (see Pss 22:20; 27:9; 40:14; 44:27; 63:8). They experience his presence especially when they go through a time of distress (see Ps 23:4). He is then very close to them (see Deut 4:7).

⁴ though its waters rage and seethe
     and the mountains tremble at the upheaval.*
The LORD of hosts is with us;
     the God of Jacob is our fortress.*   *Selah*

⁵ There is a river* whose streams bring joy to
          the city of God,
     the holy place where the Most High
          dwells.ᵉ
⁶ God is in her midst; she will not be overcome;ᶠ
     God will help her at break of dawn.*

⁷ The nations are in tumult and kingdoms fall;
     when he raises his voice,* the earth melts
          away.ᵍ
⁸ The LORD of hosts* is with us;
     the God of Jacob is our fortress.

                                        Selah

⁹ Come and behold the works of the LORD,
     the astonishing deeds he has wrought on
          the earth.ʰ
¹⁰ He puts an end to wars all over the earth;ⁱ
     he breaks the bow and snaps the spear,
     and he burns the shields with flames.*

---

e Pss 36:9; 48:2-3; 76:2.—f Deut 23:14; 2 Ki 19:35; Isa 17:14.—g Pss
2:1-5; 48:5-8; 76:7-9; Job 12:23; Isa 17:12-14.—h Pss 48:9-10; 66:5.—i Pss
37:15; 76:4; Isa 2:4; 39:9.

46:4 *The Lord of hosts is with us; the God of Jacob is our fortress:* this comfort-
ing refrain occurs three times in the psalm—here and in vv. 8 and 11 (although
the Hebrew lacks it in v. 4). The first part ("The LORD . . . is with us") is similar in
structure and meaning to the name of the royal child in Isaiah: "Immanuel"—
"God is with us" (Isa 7:14; 8:8, 10). *The LORD of hosts:* see note on Ps 24:10.
46:5 *River:* symbol of God's blessings; the symbolic waters (see Ps 36:9) that
spring forth (see Ezek 47:1, 12; Joel 3:18; Zec 14:8) make the holy land fruitful,
purify it (see Zec 13:1), and turn it into a new Eden (see Gen 2:10).
46:6 *At break of dawn:* the most favored time for attacks to be set in motion
against cities but also for God's blessings (see Pss 17:15; 49:15; 101:8; Song
2:17; Isa 17:14). The psalm here most likely alludes to the retreat of Sennacherib's armies in 701 B.C. (see 2 Ki 19:35).
46:7 *His voice:* God's thunder (see Ps 104:7; Jer 25:30; Am 1:2). *The earth
melts away:* under the heat of God's lightnings. But Israel has no need to fear
any of these calamities.
46:10 This verse speaks of universal peace and anticipates the Messianic victory.

11 "Be still and acknowledge that I am God,
    exalted among the nations,*j*
    exalted on the earth."*

12 The LORD of hosts is with us;
    the God of Jacob is our fortress.   *Selah*

PSALM 47*

The Lord, King of All Nations

1 For the director.* A psalm of the sons of Korah.

2 All you peoples, clap your hands,*
    shout to God with cries of gladness.*k*

3 For the LORD, the Most High, is awesome;
    he is the great King over all the earth.*l*

4 He subdued nations under us
    and brought peoples under our feet.*m*

5 He chose our inheritance for us,
    the pride of Jacob,* whom he loved.*n Selah*

6 God has ascended amid shouts of joy;*
    the LORD, amid the sound of trumpets.*o*

---

j Ps 48:11; Deut 32:39; Ezek 12:16.—k Pss 33:3; 89:16; Zep 3:14.—l Ps 95:3; Gen 14:18; Ex 15:18; Isa 24:23; 52:7.—m Pss 2:8; 18:40.—n Ps 16:6; Isa 58:14.—o Pss 24:8, 10; 68:19-20; 98:6; Num 23:21.

46:11 *Exalted . . . on the earth:* because of his wondrous deeds for his people, especially the Life, Passion, and Resurrection of Jesus Christ.

Ps 47 This psalm is concerned with the feast of the New Year. The ark is transported: "God has ascended. . .," and during the procession this chant of the kingdom (see introduction to Ps 93) goes forth. Israel proclaims the kingship of God (see Ex 15:18; Isa 52:7; Zep 3:15) who has handed over to his people the land of Canaan and the city of Jerusalem while also defeating the nearby peoples. The ancient chant remains, but it appears as a prelude to the Lord's reign over the whole universe (see Jer 10:7). The pagans will be converted and join God's people in acclaiming the only true King (see Ezr 6:21; Isa 19:23-25; 25:6; 60:11).

The Roman and Byzantine liturgies see in this text a psalm for the Ascension of Christ: Christ "has ascended amid shouts of joy" and "is seated on his holy throne" as Lord at the right hand of the Father; from there salvation is offered to all peoples (see Acts 2:34; Phil 2:9-11; Rev 5:7-9, 12f).

47:1 *For the director:* these words are thought to be a musical or liturgical notation. *Sons of Korah:* see note on Ps 42:1.

47:2 *Clap your hands:* a gesture used at occasions of great joy, e.g., at enthronements (see Ps 98:8; 2 Ki 11:12; Isa 55:12).

47:5 *Our inheritance . . . the pride of Jacob:* the promised land (see Gen 12:7; 17:8; Ex 3:8; Deut 1:8; Jer 3:18), which God gave Israel by a sovereign act.

47:6-7 God ascends liturgically to the temple in the Ark of the Covenant.

7 Sing praises to God, sing praises;
  sing praises to our King, sing praises.

8 For God is the King of the entire earth;p
  sing hymns of praise to him.

9 God reigns over all the nations;
  God is seated on his holy throne.

10 The princes of the nations assemble
  with the people of the God of Abraham;
 for the rulers of the earth belong to God,q
  and he is exalted on high.*

PSALM 48*

Thanksgiving for the Deliverance of God's People

1 A psalm of the sons of Korah.* A song.

2 Great is the LORD and worthy of high praiser
  in the city of our God.
 His holy mountain,* 3 towering in its beauty,
  is the joy of the entire earth.s

---

p 8-9: Pss 72:11; 93:1; 96:10; 97:1; 99:1; Jer 10:7; Zec 14:9; Col 3:16.—
q Ps 89:19; Ex 3:6; Ezr 6:21; Isa 2:2-4.—r Pss 86:10; 96:4; 135:5; 145:3;
Jer 10:6.—s Ps 50:2; Lam 2:15; Ezek 16:14; Mt 5:35.

47:10 In Messianic times, the reconciled peoples will form only one people with God's chosen ones. The Covenant with Abraham (see Ps 105:6; Ex 3:6; Est C:2-5 [13:9-13]) will be extended to all humankind (see Ps 72:11; Gen 9:9; Isa 2:2; 45:20f; 56:6; Zec 8:20; 14:16). *Princes . . . rulers:* some suggest that these terms refer to the angelic spirits who watch over the nations (see Deut 32:8f; Dan 10:13).

Ps 48 With overflowing joy, this psalm sings of God and the holy city. All the glory of Jerusalem stems from the Lord who dwells, enveloped in mystery, in the temple on the hill in the heart of the city. From there he protects his people; he has even delivered this city from the assaults of the enemy. It is secure from the north (v. 3), east (v. 8), south (v. 11), and west (v. 14). There Israel encounters its God and gives him thanks. And from this dwelling of God, salvation, joy, and praise extend to all peoples and the whole universe. It is a grandiose vision; how can one not love this land of God in the midst of human beings!

To Christians, Zion stands for the Church of Jesus, soul of the world and sign of salvation for humankind, until all are gathered together into the kingdom of God, the heavenly Jerusalem (see Heb 12:22; Rev 14:1; 21:10-26).

48:1 *Sons of Korah:* see note on Ps 42:1.
48:2 *Holy mountain:* see note on Ps 2:6.

Mount Zion, the true heights of the north,*[t]
    is the city of the great King.
4 God is in her citadels
    and has revealed himself as her fortress.*

5 For the kings conspired together*
    and came onward in unison.
6 As soon as they beheld her, they were
    astounded;
    filled with panic, they fled.[u]

7 They were seized with trembling,
    with pains like those of a woman in labor,[v]
8 as though a wind from the east*
    were breaking up the ships of Tarshish.

9 What we had heard,
    we have now beheld for ourselves*
    in the city of the LORD of hosts,
  in the city of our God
    that he established to endure forever.   *Selah*

---

t Isa 14:13.—u Ex 15:16; Jdg 5:19.—v Ex 15:14; Job 4:14; Jer 4:31.

48:3 *The true heights of the north [i.e., Zaphon]:* Mount Zaphon was in the far north, the home of the Canaanite storm-god Baal. The psalmist declares that, although Zion is only a small hill, it is higher than any other mountain because it is the home of the only true God (see Ps 68:16f).

48:4 The psalmist shows that Zion is impregnable not because of her walls but because of the fact that the Lord is present there as the strength of his people (see Pss 18:3; 122:7).

48:5-8 In recalling past defeats of Israel's enemies who attacked Zion, the psalmist may have in mind the victory over the Moab-Ammon coalition at the time of Jehoshaphat (see 2 Chr 20:22-28) or over the Assyrians at the time of Hezekiah (see 2 Ki 19:35f).

48:8 *East:* geographical allusion mentioned in the introduction. *Ships of Tarshish:* i.e., the most powerful ships, built for long voyages—like those that went as far as Tarshish, perhaps Tartessus in southern Spain (see 1 Ki 10:22).

48:9 *Heard . . . beheld for ourselves:* the psalmist may be referring to the glorious things that new pilgrims had heard about the beauty and awesomeness of the holy city and now beheld with their own eyes. He may also be referring to the things the pilgrims had heard from their ancestors about the security of the temple at Jerusalem (see Pss 44:2; 78:3) and now beheld for themselves. They became even more convinced of God's presence in Jerusalem ordering the world's events and working out the redemption of his people. *The LORD of hosts:* see note on Ps 24:10.

¹⁰ O God, as we stand in the midst of your temple,
　　we will meditate on your kindness.*
¹¹ Like your name, O God,
　　your praise extends to the ends of the earth.
　Your right hand* is filled with righteous-
　　　ness; ʷ
¹²　let Mount Zion rejoice.
　Let the towns of Judah exult
　　in your saving judgments.*ˣ

¹³ Walk around Zion; pass throughout her;*
　　count the number of her towers.
¹⁴ Take careful note of her ramparts,
　　walk through her citadels,
　so that you may recount for future genera-
　　　tionsʸ
¹⁵　that such is God;
　our God forever and ever,
　　he will be our guide eternally.*

---

w Ps 113:3; Mal 1:11.—x Pss 97:8; 105:5; Deut 33:21.—y Pss 22:31-32; 71:18; 78:6; 2 Sam 20:15; Isa 26:1; Lam 2:8.

48:10 The godly meditate on God's mighty acts, taking comfort in, rejoicing in, and gratefully making offerings to the revelation of the perfections of the Lord. *Kindness:* see note on Ps 6:5.

48:11 The reaction of praise is a positive response by the godly in contrast to the dread that befell the nations. The godly praise God from one end of the earth to another, declaring his righteousness, i.e., the Lord's victories and glorious work whose benefits his people share. That work is symbolized by his "right hand," which includes power, justice, righteousness, and love. As alluded to in the introduction to this psalm, "right hand" also has a connotation of "south" in Hebrew. *Name:* see note on Ps 5:12.

48:12 *Judgments:* God's actions in human affairs (see Ps 105:7; Isa 26:9), especially his victories over Israel's enemies (see Pss 98:8; 105:5; Deut 33:21).

48:13-14 The psalmist calls upon the people to walk around Jerusalem and see its great defenses (towers, ramparts, citadels). The physical defense system of Jerusalem may have been a symbol of a far greater strength—the protection of the Lord himself. Furthermore, inasmuch as the Lord was present in the temple at Jerusalem, defense of the city was an expression of loyalty to him.

48:15 After seeing the well-nigh impregnable fortifications of Jerusalem, the people will feel more secure and better understand the greatness of the Lord, who protects his city and his people in accord with his promises; they will then recount it to their children and grandchildren. The Lord is their God forever, the great Shepherd-King (see note on Ps 23:1), who will continue to guide them "eternally" (literally, "till death").

PSALM 49*

Deceptive Riches

1 For the director.* A psalm of the sons of Korah.

2 Hear this, all you peoples;*
  listen carefully, all you inhabitants of the
    world,
3 whether lowborn or highborn,
  rich and poor alike.

4 My mouth will speak words of wisdom,z
  and the utterance of my heart will give
    understanding.*
5 I will listen carefully to a proverb,
  and with the harp I will interpret my riddle.*

6 Why should I be afraid in evil times
  when I am beset by the wickedness of my
    foes,
7 those who place their trust in their wealth
  and boast of the abundance of their riches?a

---

z Pss 37:30; 78:2; Mt 13:35.—a Job 31:24; Prov 10:15; Jer 9:23.

Ps 49 The psalmist meditates on the vanity of riches and the problem of retribution (see Pss 37 and 73), after introducing his discourse with a solemnity that is somewhat pretentious. He believes that he has the answer to the problems that torment many (though they are still far from experiencing the crisis of Job). Certainly, fortune is powerless to save the rich from the clutches of death, and no one can buy escape from death; on the contrary, the poor are "filled" because God pays for them when the rich cannot offer despite all their wealth.

The author also seems convinced that death cannot take away from him the divine friendship. The lot of the righteous cannot be the same as that of the wicked, for he suspects (without knowing how to imagine it) that the former will receive some kind of liberation at God's hand (v. 16).

In praying this psalm, we should be mindful that riches cannot assure our physical life and constitute an obstacle to our spiritual life. However, if we remain united with Christ, who has conquered death, we will rise with him (1 Cor 15:45f).

49:1 *For the director:* these words are thought to be a musical or liturgical notation. *Sons of Korah,* see note on Ps 42:1.

49:2-5 Solemn introduction: the first part (vv. 2-3) recalls the Prophets (see 1 Ki 22:28; Isa 34:1; Mic 1:2) and the second (vv. 4-5) recalls Ps 78:2; Job 33:4; 34:19; Prov 8:4f.

49:4 See Mt 12:34. *Heart:* see note on Ps 4:8.

49:5 The psalmist alludes to a kind of inspiration: since all wisdom is from God (see Job 28), he lent his ear to hear it; at the same time, he makes use of the "harp," the instrument that accompanied prophesying (see 1 Sam 10:5f; 2 Ki 3:15).

8 For no one can ever redeem himself[b]
   or pay a ransom to God for his release.*
9 The price to ransom a life would be too costly;
   no one would ever have enough
10 to enable him to live on forever
   and avoid being consigned to the pit.

11 For all can see that the wise die,*
   just as the foolish and the stupid also pass
   away,[c]
   and all leave their wealth to others.*[d]
12 Their graves are their eternal homes,
   their dwelling places for all generations,
   even though they had named lands after
   themselves.
13 Despite his riches,
   a man cannot escape death;[e]
   he is like the beasts that perish.*

14 Such is the destiny of those who trust in
   themselves alone,
   the fate of those who are pleased with their
   lot.*   *Selah*

---

b Job 33:24; Prov 11:4; Ezek 7:19; Mt 16:26.—c Pss 92:7; 94:8; Eccl
2:16—d Ps 39:7; Sir 11:18-19; Lk 12:20.—e Job 14:2; Eccl 3:18-21; 2 Pet
2:12.

49:8-10 Wealth is useless to evade death; only God has the power to bring it
about (see v. 16 and Ps 116:15; Job 33:24-26; Prov 11:4; Ezek 7:19; Mt 16:26;
Rom 3:24). A wealthy person may live lavishly and give the impression that he
will live forever. However, he too must at some point face death—which is a sep-
aration from the land of the living, from all life's comforts, and from social and
economic advantages. *Pit:* a synonym for the netherworld (see Ps 16:10) that signifies death and perhaps retribution for evil done during life (see Ps 94:13).
49:11-12 Those who have amassed wealth for themselves (see Lk 12:20) or
those who have rejected the voice of wisdom (see Prov 1:17f) are "the foolish and
the stupid." These have taken pains to ensure their memory by naming property
after themselves but will be remembered only by the names engraved on their
tombs (v. 12; see Isa 22:16). They will perish, forever bereft of their wealth.
49:11 A passage very close to Eccl 2:16 (see Pss 39:7; 92:7f).
49:13 The psalmist states that death is an inevitable part of earthly existence.
He says nothing about life beyond death or the difference between human and
animal life.
49:14 The psalmist does not condemn riches in themselves but only the attitude of self-sufficiency so often associated with wealth, which then leads to in-
sensitivity, scheming, deception, and arrogance (see Jas 5:1-6) in both the rich
and their followers.

¹⁵ Like sheep* they are destined for the netherworld,
with death as their shepherd.
They descend straight to the grave
where their bodies will waste away;
the netherworld will be their home.
¹⁶ But God will ransom me from the netherworld;
he will take me* to himself.*ᶠ   *Selah*

¹⁷ Do not be afraid when someone becomes rich*
and the splendor of his house increases.
¹⁸ When he dies, he will take nothing with him;ᵍ
his wealth will not accompany him below.*

¹⁹ Although during his lifetime he considered
himself blessed:
"They will praise me because I have done
well,"
²⁰ he will end up joining the company of his
ancestors
who will never again see the light.*ʰ
²¹ Despite his riches,
a man who does not have wisdom
is like the beasts that perish.*

---

f Pss 16:10; 73:24; 86:13; 103:4; 116:8; Gen 5:24.—g Ps 17:14; Eccl
5:15; Sir 11:18-19; 1 Tim 6:7.—h Gen 15:15; Job 10:21-22; 33:30.

49:15 *Like sheep:* death has become their shepherd, leading them to the
grave. *They descend . . . waste away:* an alternative text is: "The upright will rule
over them in the morning, / and their bodies will waste away." *In the morning:*
the customary time for eschatological judgments and the triumph of the righteous (see Pss 17:15; 46:5; 101:8; Song 2:17; Isa 17:14).
49:16 *Take me:* this is the same Hebrew verb that is used for God "taking up" his
favored servants: Enoch (see Gen 5:24), Elijah (see 2 Ki 2:11f), and the righteous
person (see Ps 73:24). The psalmist thus harbors the hope that God will rescue the
righteous from the grave in some way. This hope will become stronger in Israel, as
later Books show (see 2 Mac 7:9f; 12:44f; 14:46; Wis 2:23; 3:9; 6:19; Dan 12:2).
49:17-20 Faith enables the godly to avoid fearing anything that is transitory.
Riches, splendor, and praise (garnered from self or from others) make no difference
in the grave. Although wealth can protect one from the rigors of life, it is powerless
against death, a place of utter darkness without even a ray of hope ("light").
49:18 In contrast, God will glorify the righteous (see Pss 62:8; 73:24; 91:15; 1
Sam 2:30; Wis 3:7; 1 Tim 6:6-8).
49:20 See note on Ps 27:1.
49:21 The psalmist indicates that the godly who are wealthy are different from
the senseless rich. Godly persons have understanding about riches as well as
about their own mortality and about God, and they act accordingly.

PSALM 50*

The Worship Acceptable to God

¹ A psalm of Asaph.*

* The LORD, the God of gods,*
    has spoken and summoned the earth
    from the rising of the sun to its setting.ⁱ
² From Zion, perfect in beauty,
    God shines forth.ʲ

³ Our God is coming, and he will not be silent;
    he is preceded by a devouring fire,ᵏ
    and a raging tempest surrounds him.*
⁴ He summons the heavens above
    and the earth to judge his people:

---

i Ps 113:3; Deut 10:17; Jos 22:22.—j Pss 2:6; 48:3.—k Ps 97:3; Isa 42:14; Dan 7:10.

Ps 50 This psalm takes the form of an indictment against God's people for the formalistic practice of their religion and a request for sacrifices of praise accompanied by obedience. It is divided into three parts: (1) the announcement of the Lord's arrival and the convening of the court (vv. 1-6); (2) the Lord's words of correction (vv. 7-15); (3) his rebuke for the wicked and promise of reward or punishment (vv. 16-23). The psalm itself may have been composed for a temple liturgy for reaffirming commitment to the Covenant.

In praying this psalm, we should recall that Jesus also condemned formalism. Christ does not reproach us for our external worship, our beautiful liturgical celebrations, vows, oblations, or sacrifices. However, all these must truly reflect sentiments of profound religion—"a living sacrifice that is holy and acceptable to God" (Rom 12:1).

50:1a *Asaph:* probably a choral leader in the Jerusalem temple (see introduction to Pss 73—89).

50:1b-6 The author knows how to conjure up the whole apparatus of a divine manifestation. God himself solemnly appears to challenge those who dishonor worship and the Law and to recall for them the great demands of the Covenant. Israel must realize that the God of Zion is the God of Sinai (see Ex 19:16-20). It is a picture of the Last Judgment.

50:1b *The LORD, the God of gods:* in Hebrew, a threefold formula for the divine name that can also be translated as: "The Mighty One, God, the LORD." It is found elsewhere only in Jos 22:22 (but see Deut 10:17). This psalm is notable for the seven names or other titles it uses for God (v. 1: "The God of gods" [or "the Mighty One"], "God," "LORD"; v. 6: "judge"; v. 14: "Most High"; v. 21: "I AM"; v. 22: "God"—alternative word *Eloah*).

50:3 The Lord is the Ruler of the universe and his appearance is attended by phenomena calculated to create awe in his subjects: fire and a tempest. When he comes in judgment, he is like a consuming fire (see Deut 4:24; 9:3; Isa 66:16; Heb 12:29); in his anger, he may also storm like a tempest (see Isa 66:15).

⁵ "Gather before me my faithful servants
    who made a covenant with me by sacri-
    fice."*

⁶ The heavens proclaim his saving justice,
    for God himself is the judge.*ˡ   *Selah*

⁷ "Listen, my people, and I will speak.*
    O Israel, I will testify against you.
    I am God, your God.

⁸ I do not rebuke you for your sacrifices,
    for your burnt offerings are constantly
    before me.

⁹ "I will not accept a young bull from your homes
    or goats from your folds.ᵐ

¹⁰ For all the living creatures of the forest are
    mine,
    animals by the thousands on my hills.

¹¹ I know every bird of the air,
    and whatever moves in the fields belongs
    to me.

¹² "If I were hungry, I would not tell you,
    for the world is mine, and all that it holds.ⁿ

¹³ Do I eat the flesh of bulls
    or drink the blood of goats?

---

l Pss 19:2; 97:6; Gen 16:5; Job 9:15.—m Ps 69:32; Lev 1:5; Num 32:16;
Am 5:21-22.—n Pss 24:1; 89:12; Ex 19:5; Deut 10:14; Jos 3:11; 1 Cor 10:26.

50:5 Those consecrated to the Lord had made a Covenant with him that was
sealed by sacrifices (see Ex 24:4-8).

50:6 *Judge:* a title for God (see Ps 94:2; Gen 18:25; Jdg 11:27).

50:7-15 Pagans might have imagined that they owed food subsidies to their
gods; the Lord has no need of our earthly goods, for everything belongs to him.
This diatribe against purely external worship occurs often in the Bible, notably in
the Prophets (see 1 Sam 15:22; 1 Chr 29:16-19; Isa 1:10-16; 29:13f; 58:1-8; Jer
6:20; 7:21; Hos 6:6; Joel 2:12; Mic 6:5-8; Zec 7:4-6; Mal 1:10) and is also found
elsewhere in the Psalter (see Pss 40:7-9; 51:18f, etc.). The passages do not condemn sacrifices or worship in general, but only the formalism that is satisfied
with performing external rites. We cannot bribe God; we can only acknowledge
him by prayer and thanksgiving: this was the constant attitude of Jesus toward
his Father. Truly religious persons are aware of their limitations; they await everything from God and realize that they owe him everything. The Gospel will lay a
heavy emphasis on this teaching (see Mt 5:23; 12:7; Mk 12:33), and Paul will in
turn repeat it in his instruction on worship in spirit (Rom 12:1; Phil 2:17; 3:3).

14 "Offer to God a sacrifice of thanksgiving
and fulfill your vows to the Most High.[o]
15 Then if you cry out to me in time of trouble,
I will rescue you, and you will honor me."[p]

16 But to the wicked God says:
"How can you recite my statutes*
or profess my covenant on your lips?
17 For you loathe my instruction
and cast my words behind you.

18 "When you meet a thief, you join him;
you revel in the company of adulterers.
19 You employ your mouth for evil,
and your tongue frames deceit.

20 "You willingly speak against your brother
and slander the child of your own mother.
21 When you do such things, can I remain silent?
Do you think that I am* like you?
I will correct you
and set the charge before your face.

22 "Remember this, you who forget God,*
lest I tear you to pieces
and there be no one to rescue you.
23 He who offers a sacrifice of thanksgiving honors me;
to him who follows my way
I will show the salvation of God."[q]

---

o Pss 27:6; 76:12; Hos 14:2; Heb 13:15.—p Pss 3:8; 4:2; 77:3; Isa 58:9.—q Pss 9:15; 91:16; 98:3; Isa 52:10.

50:16-23 Another type of formalism is to have religion or the Law on one's lips more than in one's heart and life. There is no authentic faith unless it includes a moral commitment and notably that of justice and respect toward others: "Not everyone who says to me, 'Lord, Lord,' will enter the kingdom of heaven, but only the one who does the will of my heavenly Father" (Mt 7:21).

50:21 *I AM:* the formula that reveals the name of the Lord in the Old Testament (see Ex 3:14; Isa 41:4, 10, 14; 43:1-3, 10, 13). See notes on Mk 6:50 and 4:26.

50:22 *God:* here the Hebrew is a relatively rare poetic word, *Eloah,* found frequently in Job (see also Pss 18:33; 139:19; Deut 32:15, 17; Hab 3:3).

PSALM 51*

The "Miserere": Repentance for Sin

[1] For the director.* A psalm of David. [2] When Nathan the prophet came to him after he had sinned with Bathsheba.[r]

[3] Have mercy on me, O God,
   in accord with your kindness;*
in your abundant compassion
   wipe away my offenses.
[4] Wash me completely from my guilt,
   and cleanse me from my sin.

---

r 2 Sam 12:1.

Ps 51 This psalm, the "Miserere," the best known of the seven Penitential Psalms (Pss 6; 32; 38; 51; 102; 130; 143), is still the most authentic expression of our prayer as human beings. The kind of sincerity in the confession of sinfulness that it expresses requires a limitless trust in the mercy of God. Whether it voices the repentance of King David after his adultery (see 2 Sam 12:13) or that of the Jewish people after their return from the Exile during which they had become aware of their infidelity, the entreaty shows authentic repentance.

Men and women become conscious of the sin that alienates them from God (see Ezek 2:3; 16:43); evil plunges its roots deep within their being (see Jer 5:23; 7:24; 17:9; Ezek 36:26). A hasty forgiveness, an external purification, is not enough; it is the heart that must be transformed. God alone can effect this new creation and infuse a new Spirit (see Ezek 36:26). He allows sinners to come to their senses and humbly commit themselves to him again. He alone can answer the desire for complete renewal that is inscribed in a true request for forgiveness. Our thoughts turn immediately to Paul who movingly describes the dramatic situation of sinners (Rom 7:14ff) and then contrasts it with the exalted life of Christians who let themselves be led by the Holy Spirit (Rom 8).

Especially striking in this regard is v. 7 of this psalm: the individual—or the people—has been conceived in sin, begotten in guilt. The psalmist is surely not thinking of a sin of the mother that might infect the child, nor does the Old Testament consider the conjugal union to be sinful; by this exceptionally violent image the psalmist intends rather to convey the idea that the human being is born as a prisoner of a sinful environment.

All Christians—whether under the shock of some personal failing or under the at times searing impression of a life of mediocrity and nullity in God's eyes or in union with the entire Church imploring the mercy of the Crucified upon the sinful world—have recited this psalm with its bubbling lyricism to express contrition and distress of soul, and to ask the Savior's mercy and their own inner renewal.

51:1 *For the director:* these words are thought to be a musical or liturgical notation. For the event referred to, see 2 Sam 11:1—12:25.

51:3 *Kindness:* see note on Ps 6:5. *Wipe away:* the psalmist pictures God keeping a record of a person's deeds as earthly kings were wont to do (see Pss 56:9; 87:6; 130:3; 139:16; Ex 32:32f; Neh 13:14; Dan 7:10) on a scroll and then wiping away the evil deeds when forgiveness is given.

5 For I am fully aware of my offense,
　　and my sin is ever before me.[s]
6 Against you, you alone,* have I sinned;
　　I have done what is evil in your sight.

　Therefore, you are right in accusing me
　　and just in passing judgment.[t]
7 Indeed, I was born in iniquity,
　　and in sin did my mother conceive me.*[u]

8 But you desire sincerity of heart;
　　and you endow my innermost being with
　　　wisdom.*
9 Sprinkle me with hyssop* so that I may be
　　cleansed;
　　wash me until I am whiter than snow.[v]

10 Let me experience joy and gladness;
　　let the bones you have crushed exult.
11 Hide your face from my sins,
　　and wipe out all my offenses.

12 Create* in me a clean heart, O God,
　　and renew a resolute spirit within me.[w]

---

s Pss 32:5; 38:19; Isa 59:12; Ezek 6:9.—t 1 Sam 15:24; Lk 15:21; Rom 3:4.—u Lev 5:2; Job 5:7; 14:4.—v Ex 12:22; Job 9:30; Isa 1:18; 44:22; Ezek 36:25; Heb 9:13-14.—w Pss 24:4; 78:37; Ezek 11:19; Eph 4:23-24.

51:6 *Against you, you alone:* the very essence of sin is that it constitutes an offense against God, even though it may also entail an offense against human beings. *Just in passing judgment:* permitted by God, sin calls for the intervention of his judgment (see Rom 3:4).
51:7 All human beings have a congenital inclination toward evil (see Gen 8:21; 1 Ki 8:46; Job 4:17; 14:4; 15:14; 25:4; Prov 20:9). God must take account of this situation, which is a mitigating circumstance, and show mercy. Later, the doctrine of original sin will be made explicit (see Rom 5:12f; Eph 2:3).
51:8 Despite his sins against God's teaching, the psalmist craves that teaching with his whole being; he wants to be among the wise who follow God's law, not the fools who reject it (see Ps 37:30f). *Heart:* see note on Ps 4:8.
51:9 *Hyssop:* a plant with many branchlets that is a convenient sprinkler, prescribed for sprinkling sacrificial blood or water for cleansing (see Ex 12:22; Lev 14:4; Num 19:18). *Whiter than snow:* purity beyond compare (see Isa 1:18; Dan 7:9; Rev 7:14; 19:14).
51:12 *Create:* verb reserved only for God (see Gen 1) and describing the act by which he brings into existence something new and wonderful (see Ex 34:10; Isa 48:7; 65:17; Jer 31:22). The justification of a sinner is the divine work par excellence (see Ezek 36:25f). *Heart:* see note on Ps 4:8.

¹³ Do not cast me out from your presence
    or take away from me your Holy Spirit.*ˣ

¹⁴ Restore to me the joy of being saved,
    and grant me the strength of a generous
        spirit.
¹⁵ I will teach your ways to the wicked,
    and sinners will return to you.

¹⁶ Deliver me from bloodguilt,* O God,
    the God of my salvation,
    and I will proclaim your righteousness.ʸ
¹⁷ O LORD, open my lips,
    and my mouth will proclaim your praise.

¹⁸ For you take no delight in sacrifice;
    if I were to make a burnt offering,
    you would refuse to accept it.*ᶻ
¹⁹ My sacrifice, O God, is a broken spirit;
    a contrite and humble heart, O God,
    you will not spurn.*

²⁰ In your kindness, deal favorably with Zion;*
    build up the walls of Jerusalem.ᵃ

---

x Wis 1:5; 9:17; Isa 57:15; 63:11f; Hag 2:5; Rom 8:9.—y Pss 25:5; 30:10; 35:28; 39:9.—z Pss 40:7; 50:8; 1 Sam 15:22; Isa 1:11-15; Hos 6:6; Am 5:21-22; Heb 10:5-7.—a Ps 147:2; Isa 58:12; Jer 31:4; Ezek 36:33.

51:13 *Holy Spirit:* the full phrase is found in the Old Testament only here and in Isa 63:10f, but the word "Spirit" alone is found throughout. It is by his Spirit that God creates (see Ps 104:30; Gen 1:2; Job 33:4) and redeems (see Isa 32:15; 44:3; 63:11, 14; Hag 2:5), inspires the Prophets (see Num 24:2f; 2 Sam 23:2; Neh 9:30; Isa 59:21; 61:1; Ezek 11:5; Mic 3:8; Zec 7:12) and directs their ministries (see 1 Ki 18:12; 2 Ki 2:16; Isa 48:16; Ezek 2:2; 3:14), prepares his servants for their given work (see Ex 31:3; Num 11:29; Jdg 3:10; 1 Sam 10:6; 16:13; Isa 11:2; 42:1), and bestows on his people a "new heart and . . . a new spirit," enabling them to live in accord with his will (see Ezek 36:26f).

51:16 *Bloodguilt:* the sin that brought about the death of an innocent man (see 2 Sam 12:5, 13) or the judgment passed upon a grave sin requiring the penalty of death (see Ezek 18:13).

51:18 See note on Ps 50:7-15.

51:19 *Broken spirit; a contrite and humble heart:* God is most pleased by a person who trusts in him despite trials of all sorts and who repents of sin and asks forgiveness. *Heart:* see note on Ps 4:8.

51:20-21 Scholars believe that these verses are a postexilic addition, made perhaps before the rebuilding of the walls of Jerusalem in 445 B.C. *Righteous sacrifices:* sacrifices that are not mere empty ritual but filled with praise and thanksgiving to God for his great works.

²¹ Then you will delight in righteous sacrifices,
    in burnt offerings and whole oblations,
    and young bulls will be offered on your altar.

PSALM 52*

Prayer for Help against Calumniators

¹ For the director.* A *maskil* of David. ² When Doeg the
Edomite went and told Saul, "David has gone to the house
of Ahimelech."*b*

³ Why do you boast of your evil deeds,
    you champion of malice? **c*
All day long ⁴ you plot harm;
    your tongue is like a sharpened razor,
    you master of deceit.

⁵ You love evil rather than good,*
    and lies rather than truthful speech.*d*

                                     Selah

⁶ You wallow in destructive talk,
    you tongue of deceit.*e*

b 1 Sam 21:7; 22:6ff.—c Pss 10:3; 12:4; 59:8; 120:2-3; Sir 51:3.—d Ps
58:4; Ex 10:10; 1 Sam 12:25; Jer 4:22; 9:5; Jn 3:19-20.—e Pss 5:10; 10:7;
109:2; 120:2-3; Prov 10:31; Jer 9:4.

Ps 52 The psalmist indicates that a tragic end is reserved for arrogant cynicism
and the perfidious tongue, while the righteous subsist, for they take refuge in God;
they will have the happiness of living in the temple, i.e., in the presence of the Lord.
This psalm constitutes one of the most violent indictments brought against wicked
tongues; it resembles the wisdom psalms (see Pss 57:5; 59:8) and writings (Job 20).
    In praying this psalm, we can dwell on the fact that Jesus teaches us to fear
more than anything else those schemers who seek the death of our souls: the
devil and the corruptive world, the givers of scandal (see 1 Jn 2:16; 1 Pet 5:8).
The workers of evil know how to disguise themselves (see 2 Cor 11:15); by the
power of Satan, they perform even lying works and use all the wicked deceptions
of evil (see 2 Thes 2:9-12).
    52:1-2 *For the director:* these words are thought to be a musical or liturgical
notation. *Maskil:* see note on Ps 32:1a. For the event referred to, see 1 Sam 22:9f.
    52:3 *You champion of malice:* the translation follows the Greek. The Hebrew has:
"the kindness of God lasts all day long." The title is one of scorn; he is a champion
only in his own mind, and God can easily put him in his place (see Isa 22:17).
    52:5-6 The values of the wicked are distorted. He loves to think, speak, and do
evil whenever he can profit from it (see v. 5 and Mic 3:2). His entire being reflects
the evil that is associated with the tongue (see Ps 120:2; Jas 3:1-12).

7 This is the reason why God will crush you*
      and destroy you once and for all.
   He will snatch you from your tent*
      and uproot you from the land of the
      living.*f*   *Selah*

8 The righteous will see and be afraid;
      they will mock him:*g*
9 "This is the man
      who refused to accept God as his refuge.
   Rather, he placed his trust in his abundant
      riches
      and gathered strength by his crimes."*h*

10 * But I am like a green olive tree*
      in the house of God.
   I place my trust forever and ever
      in the kindness of God.*i*

11 I will praise you forever
      for what you have done,*
      and in the presence of the saints
      I will proclaim the goodness of your name.*j*

---

f Pss 27:13; 28:5; 56:14; Deut 28:63; Job 18:14; 28:13; Prov 2:22; Isa
22:19; 38:11; Ezek 17:24.—g Pss 40:4; 44:15; 64:9; Job 22:19.—h Ps 49:7; 2
Sam 22:3; Job 31:24; Prov 11:28; Mk 10:23.—i Pss 1:3; 6:5; 13:6; 92:13-15;
Jer 11:16; 17:8; Rev 11:4.—j Pss 22:23; 25:3; 26:12; 30:13; 35:18; 54:8;
149:1; Deut 7:6.

52:7-9 The wicked will be brought down by God while the righteous will subsist and mock them (see Ps 28:5; Job 18:14; Prov 2:22; Isa 22:17). The end of the
wicked will be that of the foolish rich of Ps 49.
   52:7 *Tent:* the earthly dwelling (see Job 18:14).
   52:10-11 The godly or righteous stands in contrast to the "champion of malice" (v. 3). The latter relies on himself, does evil, and amasses ill-gotten riches
and power; the Lord uproots him like a tree, turns him into a wanderer and de-
stroys him like a building (v. 7). The godly relies on the Lord and is like a tree
flourishing in the Lord's house. The "champion" boasts of his abilities; the godly
praises the Lord for his wondrous works.
   52:10 *Like a green olive tree:* symbol of a long and fruitful life inasmuch as it
lives hundreds of years (see Pss 92:13-15; 128:3). *Kindness:* see note on Ps 6:5.
   52:11 *What you have done:* in punishing the wicked and saving the righteous
(see Pss 13:6; 22:32; 31:23; 57:4). *Saints:* people of God who are and should be
devoted to him (see note on Ps 4:4). *Name:* see note on Ps 5:12.

PSALM 53*

Foolishness of the Wicked

[1] For the director.* According to *Mahalath*. A *maskil* of David.

[2] The fool says in his heart,*
    "There is no God."[k]
Such are depraved and their deeds are vile;
    there is no one who does what is right.[l]

[3] God looks down from heaven
    upon the entire human race,[m]
to see if there are any who act with wisdom,
    if even a single one seeks God.[n]

[4] But they have all turned aside;
    all alike are corrupt.
There is no one who does what is right,
    not even one.[o]

[5] Have all these evildoers no understanding?
    They devour my people as they eat bread,[p]
    and they never call out to God.[q]

---

k 2-6a: Ps 14:2-6a.—l Pss 10:4; 36:2; 74:22; Isa 32:6; Jer 5:12; Mic 7:2; Zep 1:12.—m Pss 11:4; 102:20; Job 41:34.—n 3b-4: Rom 3:11-12.—o Ps 12:2; 1 Sam 8:3.—p Ps 27:2; Isa 9:11.—q Ps 79:6 Isa 65:1; Jer 10:25; Hos 7:7.

Ps 53 The psalmist stresses that when people banish God from their heart, they are led to renounce and exploit their neighbors. A generation turns away from God and erects injustice into a law, but the Lord of the poor and oppressed remains vigilant. The text reproduces Ps 14 with some variants: e.g., "God" is used for "the Lᴏʀᴅ" and v. 5 (which corresponds with vv. 5-6 of Ps 14) is different.

In praying this psalm, we can recall that all the attacks of spiritual or physical tyrants upon us are futile. Christ is with his faithful till the end of time, with the whole Church and with every Christian, to enable them to overcome all external and internal adversities. And without ceasing Christ offers to his Father, out of gratitude for deliverance, a sacrifice of thanksgiving—the Eucharist.

53:1 *For the director:* these words are thought to be a musical or liturgical notation. *Mahalath:* this word may signify a modulation indicating sadness. *Maskil:* see note on Ps 32:1a.

53:2-5 See note on Ps 14:1b-4.

⁶ Later, they will be filled with terror,
    and with good reason,
        although now they do not fear.

For God will scatter the bones
    of those who attack you;
they will be put to shame,
    for God has rejected them.*

⁷ Who will bring about the salvation of Israel
    that is to come out of Zion?*
When God restores the fortunes of his people,
    Jacob will rejoice and Israel will exult.ʳ

PSALM 54*
Prayer in Time of Danger

¹ For the director.* On stringed instruments. A *maskil* of
David. ² When the Ziphites came to Saul and said, "David
is hiding among us."ˢ

³ O God, save me by your name;
    vindicate me by your power.*
⁴ Hear my prayer, O God;
    give ear to the words of my mouth.

---

r Pss 85:2; 126:1.—s 1 Sam 23:19; 26:1.

53:6 This verse corresponds with the theme of Ps 14:6-7 that God crushes
evildoers who attack his people, but the text is quite different. *Scatter the bones:*
bodies left unburied (regarded as a horrible fate) in the wake of a devastating
defeat—an allusion to Israel's divine deliverance from the siege of Sennacherib
in 701 B.C. as a sign of what happens to all who attack God's people (see 2 Ki
19:35f; Isa 37:36f). *Later . . . good reason:* an alternative translation is: "Then
they were overcome with fear, / where there was no reason to fear."
  53:7 *Who will . . . Zion?:* another possible translation: "Oh, if only salvation
for Israel / would come forth from Zion."
  Ps 54 The "name" stands for God himself, the Almighty One. To him the
psalmist directs his supplication, from him help will come, and toward him will
thanksgiving be extended. For Christians, the "name" is that of Jesus Christ, who
saves those who invoke it (see Acts 2:21; Rom 10:9; 1 Cor 1:2). "There is no . . .
other name under heaven given to men by which we can be saved" (Acts 4:12).
The name "Jesus" means "God saves" (see Mt 1:21).
  54:1-2 *For the director:* probably a musical or liturgical notation. *Maskil:* see
note on Ps 32:1a. For the event in David's life, see 1 Sam 23:19.
  54:3 The beleaguered psalmist summons God to give him justice (see Ps 17).
Name: see note on Ps 5:12.

⁵ Strangers* have risen against me;
    those who are ruthless seek my life,
    and they have no thought of God.ᵗ   *Selah*

⁶ Surely God is my helper;
    the LORD is the one who sustains me.ᵘ
⁷ May their own evil recoil on my foes:
    you who are faithful, destroy them.*ᵛ

⁸ I will freely offer sacrifice to you,*
    and I will praise your name, O LORD,
    for it is good.
⁹ For you have rescued me from all my troubles,
    and my eyes have seen the downfall of my
    enemies.ʷ

PSALM 55*

Prayer in Time of Betrayal by a Friend

¹ For the director.* On stringed instruments. A *maskil* of
David.

² Give ear to my prayer, O God,*
    do not ignore my supplication.ˣ

---

t Pss 18:49; 86:14.—u Pss 20:3; 118:7.—v Pss 94:23; 143:12.—w Pss
34:7; 58:10; 59:11; 91:8; 92:12; 112:8; 118:7.—x 2-3: Pss 5:2-3; 27:9;
86:6; 130:1-2; Lam 3:56; Jon 2:3.

54:5 *Strangers:* probably a reference to the people of the desert of Ziph (see 1
Sam 23:19). *They have no thought of God:* the same type of sinners as in Ps 53.
54:7 See note on Ps 5:11 and introduction to Ps 35.
54:8-9 God and his faithful have the same enemies, whose defeat is a subject
for joy and thanksgiving. *Praise your name:* see note on Ps 7:18.
Ps 55 The psalmist, a sensitive and pious Levite, interminably repeats his
lament. Three times he describes his torment as the victim of calumny distressed
to see the holy city corrupted, and abandoned by his best friend. If only he could
escape this misfortune that obsesses him! We are reminded of David in the wake
of Absalom's rebellion against him (see 2 Sam 15—17) as well as of Jeremiah
excoriated by his enemies (Jer 4:19; 5:1; 6:6; 9:1, 3, 7) and of Christ, the man of
sorrows, betrayed by his friend (see Mt 26:21-23, 48-50).
    This psalm is a prayer for days when we feel exhausted by the struggles of life,
by the hostility of people and things, when we would like nothing more than to escape, to flee into some deserted spot and encounter nobody. However, the psalmist
knows that only God's presence can free the heart imprisoned by suffering.
55:1 *For the director:* these words are thought to be a musical or liturgical notation. *Maskil:* see note on Ps 32:1a.
55:2-4 The psalmist begs God to listen to his plight.

³ Listen to my cry and answer me,
  for my troubles afford me no peace.

⁴ I am terrified by the shouts of the enemy
  and the uproar of the wicked.
 For they inflict troubles upon me,
  and in their anger they revile me.

⁵ * My heart* is filled with anguish,
  and I am beset by the terrors of death.
⁶ Fear and trembling overpower me;
  horror overwhelms me.

⁷ I say, "If only I had wings like a dove
  so that I could fly away and be at rest!ʸ
⁸ I would flee away
  and seek shelter in the wilderness.ᶻ   *Selah*
⁹ I would hurry to a place of refuge,
  far from the savage wind and tempest."

¹⁰ * Restrain the wicked, O Lᴏʀᴅ, and confound
  their speech,
  for I see violence and strife in the city.*
¹¹ Day and night they make their rounds on its
  walls,
  and within it are iniquity and malice.
¹² Destruction is also in its midst;
  oppression and treachery pervade its streets.ᵃ

¹³ If it was an enemy who reviled me,*
  I could endure that.
 If a foe had treated me with contempt,
  I could manage to avoid him.

---

y Pss 11:1; 91:4.—z 1 Sam 23:14; Jer 9:1; Rev 12:6.—a Ps 5:10; Jer 5:1; 6:6; Ezek 22:2; Hab 1:3; Zep 3:1.

55:5-9 So great is the physical danger and the mental anguish (see Pss 18:5f; 116:3) that the psalmist wishes he could run away from it all (see Jer 9:1-5).
55:5 *Heart:* see note on Ps 4:8.
55:10-12 The psalmist issues an urgent call for God to come to his assistance.
55:10 See note on Ps 5:11 and introduction to Ps 35. *Restrain . . . confound their speech:* possibly a reference to God's action at Babel (see Gen 11:5-9). Sins of the tongue, calumnies, false witness, and insults are often denounced in psalms of lamentation. *Violence . . . strife:* entities are personified here and in v. 11 *(iniquity . . . malice)*, and vv. 10b-11 recall Jer 5:1; 6:6; 9:6; Ezek 22:2; Zep 3:1.
55:13-15 Doubtless, the betrayer is a Levite; the targum identifies the false friend as Ahithophel (see Ps 44:11; 2 Sam 15:12). See also Mt 26:21-25.

¹⁴ But it was you, one like myself,
      a companion and a dear friend,*b*
¹⁵ with whom I engaged in pleasant conversation
      as we walked with the festive throng
      in the house of God.
¹⁶ Let death strike my enemies by surprise;*c*
      let them descend alive to the netherworld,
   for evil dwells in their homes
      and in the depths of their hearts.*

¹⁷ But I make my appeal to God,
      and the LORD will save me.*
¹⁸ Evening, morning, and noon*
      I will cry out in my distress,
      and he will hear my voice.*d*

¹⁹ He will deliver me in peace and safety*
      from those who are arrayed against me,
      even though there are many of them.
²⁰ God will hear me and humiliate them,
      he who has been enthroned forever.   *Selah*
   For they neither change their ways
      nor have any fear of God.*e*

²¹ My companion treats his friends harshly
      and breaks his covenant.
²² His speech is smoother than butter,
      but war is in his heart.
   His words are more soothing than oil,
      yet in reality they are drawn swords.*f*

---

b Ps 41:10; 2 Sam 15:12; Jer 9:3; Mt 26:21-24 par.—c Pss 49:15; 64:8;
Num 16:33; Prov 1:12; Isa 5:14.—d Ps 141:2; Dan 6:11.—e Pss 29:10; 93:2;
Deut 33:27; Bar 3:3.—f Pss 12:3; 28:3; 57:5; 62:5; 64:4; Prov 12:18; 26:24-
28; Jer 9:7.

55:16 The psalmist calls for the sudden, premature death of his enemies (see
note on v. 10 above), which was the same as the punishment wished on one's
enemies (see Pss 73:19; 102:25; Job 15:32; Prov 1:12; Isa 38:10; Jer 17:11), a
punishment that overtook the rebellious band of Korah (see Num 16:32f). *Hearts
(also v. 22):* see note on Ps 4:8.
   55:17-20 The psalmist believes that God will hear his prayer and come to his aid.
   55:18 *Evening, morning, and noon:* the hours for prayer (see Dan 6:11f). The
legal day begins at the setting of the sun ("evening").
   55:19-24 The psalmist reflects once again on his friend's treachery and then
puts his full trust in the Lord.

23 Entrust your cares to the LORD,
     and he will uphold you;*
     he will never allow the righteous to waver.g
24 But you, O God, will send the wicked
     down to the pith of destruction;*
   those who are bloodthirsty and treacherous
     will not live out half their days.

But as for me,
   I will put my trust in you.i

PSALM 56*

Boundless Trust in God

1 For the director.* According to *Yonath elem rehoqim.* A *miktam* of David. When the Philistines seized him at Gath.j

2 Be merciful to me, O God,
     for people are trampling upon me;
     all day long they keep up their attack.
3 My foes pursue me all day long,
     with their forces too many to number.

---

g Pss 18:37; 37:5; 112:6; Prov 3:5; 16:3; Mt 6:25; 1 Pet 5:7.—h Pss 9:16; 28:1; 30:4; 40:3; 73:18; 88:5; 143:7; Prov 1:12; Ezek 28:8; Jon 2:7.—i Pss 5:7; 25:2; 56:4; 130:5.—j 1 Sam 21:11; 24:3.

55:23 Text cited in 1 Pet 5:7 (see also Ps 121:2; Isa 50:10).
55:24 See note on v. 10 above. *Pit of destruction:* i.e., the grave.
Ps 56 A psalmist subjected to harassment appeals to the Lord to take note of the injustice he is undergoing. He calls for the judgment of God to come upon his persecutors; but, more importantly, a profound religious sense enables him to divine that the prayer and tears of human beings are precious in God's eyes. The spirit of this psalm resides in the refrain: a firm protestation of trust in the word of the Lord (vv. 5, 11-12) despite all the plots of humans. So strong is the psalmist's certitude on this point that it transforms his fervent prayer from a lament into a thanksgiving.
   It is easy to place this psalm on the lips of Christ, for its themes are all found in the Passion: a plea for the Father's mercy, assaults of pagan tyrants, calumnies, plots and snares on the part of enemies, tears, cries of confidence, and a vow of thanksgiving. The psalm also provides Christians with a beautiful prayer of supplication in time of adversity, whether external or internal.
56:1 *For the director:* these words are thought to be a musical or liturgical notation. *According to Yonath elem rehoqim:* nothing is known about this phrase. *Miktam:* see note on Ps 16:1. For the event, see 1 Sam 21:11-16.

4 When I am terrified,
     I place my trust in you.
5 In God, whose word* I praise,
     in God I place my trust and know no fear;[k]
     what can people do to me?[l]

6 All day long they slander me;
     their one thought is to bring evil upon me.
7 In groups they hide in ambush
     and spy on my every step,
     determined to take my life.[m]
8 Shall they escape in their iniquity?
     Strike down the nations, O God, in your
       anger.

9 You have kept count of my wanderings
     and stored my tears in your flask,
     recording all these in your book.*[n]
10 My foes will turn back
     when I call out to you.
Of this I am confident:
     that God is on my side.

11 In God, whose word I praise—
     in the LORD, whose word I praise—
12 in God I place my trust and know no fear;
     what can people do to me?

---

k Pss 27:1; 52:11; 84:13; 130:5.—l Ps 118:6; Mt 10:28; Heb 13:6.—m Pss 59:4; 94:21; 140:5-6; Mk 3:6.—n Ps 10:14; 2 Ki 20:5; Isa 4:3; 25:8; Dan 7:10; Mal 3:16; Rev 7:17.

56:5 *Word:* as in v. 11, God's "word" is the promise by which he committed himself to his faithful; this is a very familiar theme in the Psalter (see Pss 105:8-11; 119:42, 65; 130:5). *People (also in v. 12):* literally, "flesh," representative of human frailty with respect to the divine power. People can indeed inflict pain, suffering, and death upon us, but they cannot rob us of our souls or our eternal future (see Ps 118:6; Heb 13:6). Jesus said: "Have no fear of those who kill the body but cannot kill the soul" (Mt 10:28); thus, we are to fear no one but God alone, who is also our helper.

56:9 God cares for his faithful and keeps a careful record of everything about them (see note on Ps 51:3)—even the tears they shed when they are in trouble. The theme of God's record is frequent (see, e.g., Ps 139:16; Job 19:23; Mal 3:16). Each tear of the righteous will be compensated (see 2 Ki 20:5; Isa 25:8; Rev 7:17). Indeed, Jesus indicated that God has such concern for us that he knows the number of hairs on our head (Mt 10:30).

¹³ I am bound, O God, by vows* to you,
   and I will pay you my debt of gratitude.^o
¹⁴ For you have delivered my life from death
   and my feet from stumbling,
 that I may walk in the presence of God*
   in the light of the living.

PSALM 57*

Trust in God amid Suffering

¹ For the director.* According to "Do not destroy." A
miktam of David. When he fled from Saul into the cave.^p

² Have mercy on me, O God,
   have mercy on me,
   for in you my soul* takes refuge.
 I will seek shelter in the shadow of your
   wings
   until the time of danger has passed.^q

---

o Lev 7:11f; Num 30:3.—p 1 Sam 22:1.—q Pss 2:12; 17:8; 36:8.

56:13 *I am bound . . . by vows:* the psalmist is certain of being delivered and vows to make thanksgiving for it (see note on Ps 7:18).

56:14 *Walk in the presence of God:* an expression that indicates access to the heavenly King, with reference to his presence at the temple (God's royal house on earth). It is legitimate for us to see in this text an allusion to ultimate access to the heavenly temple (see Pss 16:11; 17:15; 23:6; 140:14). *Light of the living:* a happy life on earth (see note on Ps 36:9).

Ps 57 The psalmist pictures evildoers like lions tearing away at him and ravaging his reputation. It is altogether natural for him, then, to call upon God to come in power to chastise the enemy and establish his kingdom on earth. A second tableau ends the psalm: the believer sings of God's deliverance, which comes like a dawn in the midst of the night of danger. Part of this psalm is duplicated in Ps 108 (57:8-12=108:2-6).

This supplication may be justly applied to Christ during his whole Public Life and Passion. Surrounded and attacked by his enemies, he seeks refuge in his Father, who cannot abandon him. It can also fittingly be applied to us who are constantly threatened by our spiritual enemies.

57:1 *For the director:* these words are thought to be a musical or liturgical notation. *According to "Do not destroy":* probably a note by an early scribe intended to prevent his manuscript from being discarded. *Miktam:* see note on Ps 16:1. For the event, see 1 Sam 24:1-3.

57:2 *My soul:* see note on Ps 6:4. *Shadow of your wings:* conventional Hebrew metaphor for protection; it may have been inspired by the wings of the cherubim spread over the Ark in the inner chamber of the temple (see 1 Ki 6:23-28).

³ I call out to God Most High,
   to God who takes care of me.*
⁴ May he send his help from heaven to deliver
      me
      and put to shame those who trample upon
      me;   *Selah*
      may God send his kindness* and his faith-
      fulness.

⁵ I lie prostrate in the midst of lions
   who are hungrily seeking human prey.ʳ
   Their teeth are spears and arrows,
      and their tongues are razor-sharp swords.ˢ
⁶ Be exalted, O God, above the heavens;ᵗ
   let your glory shine over all the earth.*

⁷ They set a trap for my feet,
   and I was overcome with distress.
   They dug a pit in my path,
      but they themselves fell into it.ᵘ

                                             Selah

⁸ My heart is steadfast, O God,*
   my heart is steadfast;*
   I will sing and chant your praise;ᵛ
⁹   awake, my soul!
   Awake, lyre and harp!
   I will awaken the dawn.*ʷ

---

r Pss 17:11-12; 22:22; 35:17; 58:7.—s Pss 11:2; 64:4; Prov 30:14.—t Pss
72:19; 102:16; Num 14:21.—u Pss 7:16; 10:9; 140:5-6.—v Pss 108:2;
112:7.—w Pss 33:2; 39:9; Job 3:9; 38:12.

57:3 *Who takes care of me:* an allusion to God's providence; other translations
given are: "who puts an end to my troubles" and "who perfects his work in me."
   57:4 *Kindness:* see note on Ps 6:5.
   57:6 The psalmist asks that the kingdom of God may be manifested (see Ps
72:19; Num 14:21; 1 Chr 29:11; Isa 6:3; 33:10; Hab 2:14) by the deliverance of
the faithful and the ruin of the wicked (see Pss 79:9; 102:16f; 138:5).
   57:8-12 These verses (with slight variations) are the same as vv. 2-6 of Ps
108.
   57:8 The psalmist is at peace because of his trust in the Lord. *Heart:* see note
on Ps 4:8.
   57:9 *Dawn:* personified as in Ps 139:9; Job 3:9; 38:12. The "night" (v. 5: "lie
prostrate") symbolizes trials; deliverance comes with the "dawn" (see Ps 17:15).

¹⁰ I will give thanks to you among the peoples,
O Lᴏʀᴅ;*
I will sing your praises among the
nations.ˣ
¹¹ For your kindness extends to the heavens;
your faithfulness, to the skies.ʸ

¹² Be exalted, O God, above the heavens;
let your glory radiate over all the earth.

PSALM 58*

The Judge of Unjust Rulers

¹ For the director.* According to "Do not destroy." A *miktam* of David.

² O you rulers,* do you render justice?
Do you judge your people impartially?ᶻ
³ No! You devise wickedness in your hearts,*
and your hands bring about violence on
the earth.

---

x Pss 9:12; 18:50; 30:5; 135:3; 146:2; 2 Sam 22:50; Rom 15:9.—y Pss 36:6; 71:19; 108:5.—z Ps 82:2; Deut 16:19; Prov 31:9.

57:10-11 A vow to offer ritual praise to the Lord for his goodness (see note on Ps 7:18). *Kindness:* see note on Ps 6:5.

Ps 58 This is one of the so-called imprecatory (or cursing) psalms (see introduction to Ps 35) that call upon God to mete out justice to enemies. In their thirst for justice, the authors of these psalms use hyperbole (or overstatement) in order to move others to oppose sin and evil. Such impassioned expressions may seem vengeful to a Western audience not used to the diatribes and curses of Easterners. And the joy exhibited over the justice to be meted out seems ferocious to us. However, we must realize above all that the psalmists were desiring only true justice, a justice that could not be derailed, denied, or mocked—because it was God's justice.

The psalmist and all Israel regard judges as well as rulers to be divine beings (see Pss 45:7; 82:6; Ex 21:6; Deut 19:17), for judging, like ruling, is a power of God. This psalm wars against those who pervert such a divine power.

The early Church applied this psalm to the trial of Jesus before the Sanhedrin (see Mt 26:57-68 par).

58:1 *For the director:* these words are thought to be a musical or liturgical notation. *According to "Do not destroy":* see note on Ps 57:1. *Miktam:* see note on Ps 16:1.

58:2 *Rulers:* literally, "gods": see introduction.

58:3 *Hearts:* see note on Ps 4:8.

⁴ The wicked have gone astray right from the
  womb;
    from birth these liars have taken the
    wrong path.*
⁵ Their venom is like that of a serpent;
    they are as deaf as an asp that stops its ears
⁶ so as not to hear the voice of the charmer*ᵃ*
    no matter how skillful the spells he casts.*

⁷ O God, break the teeth in their mouths;*
    tear out the fangs of these lions, O LORD.*ᵇ*
⁸ Cause them to vanish like water that drains
  off;*ᶜ
    make them wither like grass that is tram-
    pled.*ᵈ

⁹ Let them melt like a snail* that oozes into
  slime
    or like a stillborn child that will never see
    the sun.*ᵉ*
¹⁰ Before they sprout thorns like brambles or
  thistles,*
    may your whirlwind sweep them away.*ᶠ*

---

a Pss 64:4; 140:4; Deut 18:11; 32:33; Eccl 10:11; Isa 3:3; Jer 8:17; Rom 3:13.—b Pss 3:8; 17:12; 22:22; 35:17.—c Job 11:16; Wis 16:29.—d Pss 37:2; 57:4; 90:5-6; 102:12; 103:15-16; Job 14:2; Isa 40:7.—e Num 12:12; Job 3:16; Eccl 6:3.—f Ps 118:12; Job 21:18; Hos 13:13; Nah 1:10.

58:4 The evil ways of the wicked (see Ps 10) are theirs from birth.

58:6 The roles of charmers and enchanters are frequently alluded to in the Old Testament (see Deut 18:11; Eccl 10:11; Isa 3:3; Jer 8:17).

58:7 The psalmist regards teeth as weapons of the mouths by which the wicked harass the righteous (see Ps 57:5); so he begs God to destroy them.

58:8-12 See introduction above and introduction to Ps 35.

58:8b *Make them wither like grass that is trampled:* the meaning of the Hebrew is unclear. Another translation likens the psalmist's foes to archers who shoot blunted arrows. "When they ready the bow, let their arrows be blunted."

58:9 *Snail:* the ancients believed that snails dried up in the sun and evaporated.

58:10 The meaning of the Hebrew for this verse is uncertain. Another translation given is: "Before your pots can feel the heat of the thorns— / whether they be green or dry— / the wicked will be swept away." This accords with the fact that twigs from wild bushes ("thorns") were used to start quick fires for cooking (see Ps 118:12; Eccl 7:6).

¹¹ The righteous will rejoice
   when he sees that justice has been done,
and he will bathe his feet
   in the blood* of the wicked.*g*
¹² Then the people will say,
   "There is truly a reward for the righteous;
   there is a God who dispenses justice on the
      earth."

PSALM 59*

Against Wicked Enemies

¹ For the director.* According to "Do not destroy." A
miktam of David. When Saul sent people to watch David's
house in order to kill him.*h*

² Rescue me, O my God, from my enemies;
   defend me* against those who rise up
      against me.
³ Deliver me from those who do evil;
   save me from the violence of the blood-
      thirsty.

---

g Ps 68:24; Isa 63:1-6; Mal 3:18.—h 1 Sam 19:11.

58:11 *Bathe his feet in the blood:* a vivid expression indicating complete victory over one's foes that was common in the Near East (see Ps 68:24; Isa 63:1-6).

Ps 59 The most realistic situation for this psalm is as follows: a believer, a Jewish group, or the whole people is exposed to persecution; it comes from forces that wish to impose paganism on the exiles or perhaps on Jerusalem itself. Like raging dogs that prowl the night in the cities of the East in search of prey, evil-intentioned persons attack the innocent victim with slander and curses, seeking to destroy his reputation and ultimately his life. The description is ferocious and the imprecation vehement and vengeful; but God will not tolerate lying and perfidy without end; the Almighty One cannot let himself be mocked, for his honor is at stake (v. 14).

We can pray this psalm to God and to Christ in our name in all our temporal struggles, and even more in the bitter spiritual struggles we must constantly wage against our powerful spiritual enemies in the footsteps and image of our Master.

59:1 *For the director:* these words are thought to be a musical or liturgical notation. *According to "Do not destroy":* see note on Ps 57:1. *Miktam,* see note on Ps 16:1. The superscription imagines that the occasion for this psalm was the narrative in 1 Sam 19:11-17. Some believe it might have been when Jerusalem was under siege as at the time of Hezekiah (see 2 Ki 18:19), while others point to the time of Nehemiah (see Neh 4).

59:2 *Defend me:* literally, "lift me to a high, safe place."

⁴ They are lying in wait to take my life;
    the powerful gather together against me.
For no offense or sin of mine, O Lord,
⁵   for no guilt of mine,
    they stand ready to attack me.

Rise up to help me, and look on my plight;
⁶   you, Lord, God of hosts,* are the God of
    Israel.
Rouse yourself and punish all the nations;
    show no mercy to these wicked deceivers.

                                    Selah

⁷ They return each evening,
    snarling like dogs
    as they prowl through the city.*ⁱ*
⁸ See what spews from their mouths—
    they spew out swords from their lips,
    and they assert, "Who is there to hear us?"*
⁹ However, you laugh at them, O Lord;
    you show your disdain for all the nations.*ʲ*

¹⁰ O my strength, I will keep watch for you,*
    for you, O God, are my fortress,
¹¹   O God of mercy.

May God go before me
    and allow me to have my way with my
    enemies.
¹² Do not put them to death,
    lest my people forget.*

---

i Pss 22:17; 55:11.—j Pss 2:4; 37:13; Prov 1:26; Wis 4:18.

59:6 Lord, God of hosts: an expression used first in 1 Sam 1:3 to designate the Lord as the sovereign over all powers in the universe—the God of all armies, both the heavenly army (see Ps 68:17; Deut 33:2; Jos 5:14; Hab 3:8) and the army of Israel (see 1 Sam 17:45). See also note on Ps 24:10. God of Israel . . . punish all the nations: seems to indicate an attack on Israel by the nations.
59:8-9 The wicked curse God as if he cannot see and hear and will not respond. But God laughs at them (see Pss 2:4; 37:13) and listens until the day of reckoning when the curses will fall back in judgment on the wicked themselves.
59:10-14 The psalmist asks God to put his foes to death, so that his people may not be seduced by them and so that the people will remember this particular saving act longer than they have remembered others (see Pss 78:11; 106:13).
59:12ab Another translation possible is: "O God, put them to death / so that they may not seduce my people."

Scatter them in your power
and bring them to their knees,
O LORD, our shield.*

13 For the sins of their mouths
and the words of their lips,
let them be trapped in their pride.
For the curses and lies they speak,*k*
14   put an end to them in your wrath;
put an end to them until they are no more.
Then it will be known to the ends of the earth
that God is the ruler over Jacob.*l*   *Selah*

15 They return each evening,*
snarling like dogs
as they prowl through the city.
16 They roam about searching for food,
and they growl if they do not have their fill.

17 But I will sing of your strength;
when morning dawns, I will proclaim your
kindness.
For you have been my fortress,
my refuge in times of trouble.*
18 O my Strength, I will sing your praises,
for you, O God, are my fortress,
the God who shows me love.*

---

k Ps 10:7; Prov 12:13; 18:7.—l Pss 46:9-11; 83:18-19; Ezek 5:13.

59:12e *O LORD, our shield:* just as the king was regarded as the people's shield in ancient Israel (see Ps 84:10), so the Lord was called the shield of his people (see Pss 7:11; 84:12; 89:19; 91:4; 115:9-11; Deut 33:29; Prov 30:5). Accordingly, the psalmist invokes this attribute of the Lord at this point.

59:14 God's punishment of the nations will show that God, the King of Israel (see Ps 24:1, 6; Isa 41:21ff; 63:19), is also the Master of the universe (see Pss 46:11f; 83:19).

59:15-18 The wicked wreak havoc like a pack of dogs, snarling and howling as they prowl about the city. The godly take courage in hearing of God's laughter (v. 9) and the assurance of his love (vv. 10-11). For the Lord is their Strength and their fortress, who will deliver them from all their enemies and whom they will praise.

59:17 After the night of danger (vv. 7, 15), the psalmist will sing to God on the morning of deliverance (see introduction to Ps 57 and note on Ps 57:9). *Kindness:* see note on Ps 6:5.

59:18 The psalmist vows to offer ritual praise for his deliverance (see note on Ps 7:18).

PSALM 60*
Prayer To End Wars

[1] For the director.* According to "The Lily of . . . ." A *miktam* of David (for teaching). [2] When he fought against Aram-Naharaim and Aram-Zobah; and when Joab, coming back, slew twelve thousand Edomites in the Valley of Salt.[m]

[3] O God, you have turned away from us
   and left us defenseless.
Although your anger was aroused,
   now come to our aid.

[4] You shook the earth* and split it apart;
   repair its cracks, for it continues to shake.[n]
[5] You have inflicted hardships on your people;[o]
   you have given us wine that made us stag-
      ger.*

[6] But for those who fear you,
   you have raised up a banner
   to unfurl against the bow.*   *Selah*

---

m 2 Sam 8:2, 3, 13; 1 Chr 18:2, 3, 12.—n Pss 18:8; 75:4; 2 Chr 7:14; Isa 24:19.—o Pss 71:20; 75:9; Isa 51:17, 21-22; Jer 25:16; Zec 12:2.

Ps 60 God responds to the supplication of the nation of Israel, which is suffering because it has neglected the Covenant. The cry of a holy war sounds forth. God mobilizes Israel from one end to the other (vv. 8-9) to wreak judgment on enemy territory—one feels as if carried back to the time of the Exodus and the Conquest of Canaan. After the Exile, this psalm could have been chanted during a penitential liturgy. Verses 7-14 are also found in Ps 108 as vv. 7-14.

The military casualties and temporal disasters of ancient Israel typify the spiritual disasters that the Church, the new Israel, sometimes suffers. In union with Christ, her risen Head, the Church directs this supplication to the Father in critical moments of her history.

60:1-2 *For the director:* these words are thought to be a musical or liturgical notation. *According to "The Lily of . . . ":* its meaning is unknown. *Miktam:* see note on Ps 16:1. The superscription refers to events that are found in 2 Sam 8:1; 1 Chr 18. However, the accounts make no mention of Edom or of the fact that David's forces met stiff resistance (Ps 60:3-5) and even a temporary defeat (Ps 60:11f). The *Valley of Salt* is unknown (see 2 Sam 8:13).

60:4 *Shook the earth:* the defeat is likened to an earthquake, which is an apocalyptic characteristic (see Isa 24:20).

60:5 *Wine that made us stagger:* God has given them drink from the cup of the divine wrath (see Ps 75:9; Isa 51:17, 22; Jer 25:15) rather than the cup of the divine blessings (see Pss 16:5, including note; 23:5; 116:13).

60:6 *Bow:* symbol of the enemy, which relied on its bows.

7 With your right hand come to our aid and answer us*
so that those you love may be delivered.

8 God has promised from his sanctuary,*
"In triumph I will apportion Shechem
and measure out the Valley of Succoth.
9 Gilead is mine, and Manasseh is mine;
Ephraim is my helmet,*
Judah is my scepter.
10 Moab is my washbasin;*
upon Edom I will plant my sandal;
over Philistia I will shout in triumph."[p]

11 * Who will lead me into the fortified city?*
Who will guide me into Edom?
12 Is it not you, O God, who have rejected us
and no longer go forth with our armies?[q]

13 Grant us your help against our enemies,
for any human assistance is worthless.
14 With God's help we will be victorious,
for he will overwhelm our foes.

---

p Ps 137:7; Deut 2:5; Ru 4:7-8; 2 Sam 8:1-2; Jer 49:7; Lam 4:21-22; Ezek 25:12-14.—q Pss 44:10; 68:8; Jos 7:12; Jdg 5:4-5; Isa 42:13.

60:7-14 These verses occur again as vv. 7-14 of Ps 108.

60:8-10 The Lord gives his people an oracle of hope, reminding them of his promises that the earth is his and no enemy can stand against him. *Shechem* was west of the Jordan, and *Succoth* east of it; therefore, they indicated dominion over all of Palestine. Next are named four Israelite tribes; hence, there are three regions in all that must be reduced to subjection.

60:9 *Helmet:* a symbol of the strength exhibited by the tribe of Ephraim (see Deut 33:17; Jdg 7:24—8:3). *Scepter:* a symbol of the King-Messiah who had been promised from Judah (see Gen 49:10).

60:10 *Moab is my washbasin:* i.e., its people will do menial work for the Israelites (see Gen 18:4). *Plant my sandal:* an Eastern way of signifying possession.

60:11-14 The psalmist asks the Lord to lead him to victory even though the pain of defeat and God's apparent rejection are still with him. For he knows that the Lord remains with his people and will ensure a joyous and victorious outcome (see Pss 44:6; 118:15f).

60:11 *Fortified city:* doubtless Bozrah in Idumea (see Isa 34:6; 63:1; Am 1:12). It was from this inaccessible refuge that the Edomites sent incursions into Judea.

PSALM 61*

Prayer of One in Exile

¹ For the director.* With stringed instruments. Of David.

² O God, hear my cry
    and listen to my prayer.

³ From the ends of the earth* I call to you,
    with a heart that is fainting away;
    set me high upon a rock.
⁴ For you are my refuge,
    a tower of strength against the enemy.ʳ

⁵ I will abide in your tent forever
    and find refuge in the shelter of your
    wings.*ˢ   *Selah*

⁶ For you, O God, have heard my vows
    and granted me the heritage of those who
    fear your name.*

---

r Pss 9:10; 46:2; 59:10; 62:8; Prov 18:10.—s Pss 15:1; 17:8; 36:8; 57:2; Deut 32:11; Mt 23:37.

Ps 61 The psalmist, a Levite deported to Babylon along with the elite of the Jewish people in 598 B.C., voices his ardent desire to return to the holy city and resume his service in the temple. Added to this lament of the exiled Levite is a prayer for the king, probably on behalf of Zedekiah, the last to sit on the throne of David after the first deportation of 598 B.C. This prayer also calls upon the Messiah, who is to come from the royal line (see 2 Sam 7; 1 Chr 17:14), to reign forever, and whose coming Israel awaits.

This prayer beautifully expresses our hope as Christians. Sent by the Father and anointed by the Holy Spirit, Christ has become our Head, our guide and leader to the Father, provided we keep our eyes fixed on him by faith (see Acts 3:15; 5:31; Heb 2:10; 12:2). Long live Christ the King!

61:1 *For the director:* these words are thought to be a musical or liturgical notation.

61:3 *Ends of the earth:* the phrase can also be translated as "from the brink of the netherworld," i.e., the grave. *Heart:* see note on Ps 4:8. *Set me high upon a rock:* a reference to God's sanctuary (see Ps 27:5). Another translation is: "Lead me to the rock that is higher than I": a reference to God, the psalmist's "rock of refuge" (Pss 31:3; 71:3; see also Pss 18:3; 62:3, 7f; 94:22).

61:5 *Shelter of your wings:* see note on Ps 17:8.

61:6 The psalmist is certain of being heard (see Pss 56:14; 66:19) and resuming his functions (see Ps 16:5), for he is among those who fear God (see Mal 3:16; 4:2). *Name:* see note on Ps 5:12.

7 Add length of days to the life of the king;*
   may his years be prolonged for many gen-
      erations.*t*

8 May he be enthroned in God's presence forever,*u*
   and may your kindness and faithfulness
   watch over him.*v*

9 Then I will sing praise to your name forever
   as I fulfill my vows day after day.*

PSALM 62*

Trust in God Alone

1 For the director.* For Jeduthun. A psalm of David.

2 In God alone is my soul* at rest;
   it is from him that my salvation comes.*w*

---

t Ps 21:5; 1 Ki 3:14.—u Pss 72:5; 89:5.—v Pss 40:12; 85:11; 89:15, 25;
Prov 20:28.—w 2-3, 6-7: Pss 18:3; 31:3-4; 42:10; 118:8; 146:3; Mic 7:7.

61:7-8 As in Pss 85:11f and 89:15, 25, these personified divine attributes were
thought to accompany the Messiah just as they protect the king (see Prov 20:28) or
the simple Levite (see Ps 40:12). They were then applied to Christ, "Son of David,"
by the Fathers of the Church. The insistence on an eternal reign recalls the prophecy
of Nathan (see 2 Sam 7:16; 1 Chr 17:14), which is frequently alluded to in the
Psalter (see Pss 18:51; 45:18; 72:5, 17; 89:5; 132:12). *Kindness:* see note on Ps 6:5.

61:9 See note on Ps 7:18. To fulfill one's vows meant to make an offering or
sacrifice promised to God, normally in a single ceremony. To do so *day after day*
shows a commitment to a debt that could never be paid off or an awareness that
God's blessings are new every morning. *Name:* see note on Ps 5:12.

Ps 62 This psalm recalls the malice of human beings (see Ps 4:3), the nothingness of creatures (see Ps 39:6f; Isa 40:15), the vanity of riches (see Ps 49:13;
Prov 11:28; 27:24), and the impartiality of the heavenly Judge (see Pss 9:8f, 17;
11:7; 33:5; 140:13). It provides an unsurpassable lesson of wisdom and simple
trust in God to those who are deeply hurt and deceived (see Ps 31). Human
beings seek success in wickedness, falsehood, and violence. The believer knows
the futility of this manner of acting; it is of no avail in the sight of God's judgment. Entirely different is the strength of the faithful: the Lord, who renders to
each what they merit (Job 34:11; Prov 24:12; Sir 16:14; Ezek 18), will never fail
them—and he is the only one who will never do so.

At the invitation of Christ and in union with him, we must learn to abandon
ourselves to the heavenly Father in all the trials and difficulties of life and seek
in him our rest and inner peace. We could thus recite this entire psalm to celebrate the wonderful fruits of this filial confidence and to exhort our life companions to practice similar abandonment.

62:1 *For the director:* these words are thought to be a musical or liturgical notation. *Jeduthun:* see note on Ps 39:1.

62:2 *Soul:* see note on Ps 6:4.

³ He alone is my rock and my salvation,
    my fortress, so that I stand ever unshaken.
⁴ How long will you assault someone,
    and all of you beat him down,
as if he were a leaning wall
or a tottering fence?*
⁵ They devise plots to dislodge me
    from my place on high*
    and delight in spreading lies about me.
They bless with their lips,
    but they curse in their hearts.ˣ   *Selah*

⁶ In God alone be at rest,* O my soul;
    it is from him that my hope comes.
⁷ He alone is my rock and my salvation,
    my fortress, so that I stand unshaken.

⁸ My deliverance and my glory depend on God;
    he is my mighty rock and my refuge.ʸ
⁹ Trust in him at all times, my people,
    and pour out your heart before him,*
    for God is our refuge.   *Selah*

¹⁰ Ordinary people are no more than a breath,
    and the great are no more than a delusion.
When they are placed on scales all together,
    they are lighter than air.*ᶻ
¹¹ Do not place your trust in extortion,
    and set no vain hopes in stolen goods;*

---

x Pss 12:3; 28:3; 55:22; Prov 26:24-25.—y Ps 3:4; Isa 26:4; 60:19; Jer 3:23.—z Pss 39:6-7; 144:4; Job 7:16; Wis 2:15; Isa 40:15.

62:4 *Leaning wall . . . tottering fence:* metaphor for the psalmist's state of weakness—real (in God's eyes) or imagined (by his enemies).

62:5 *Place on high:* either a throne in the case of David or a place of safety such as a fortress on a cliff in the case of another psalmist. *Hearts:* see note on Ps 4:8.

62:6 *Be at rest:* see Pss 27:13f; 42:6, 12; 43:5.

62:9 *Pour out your heart before him:* a call for true prayer and meditation with God (see Lam 2:19). *Heart:* see note on Ps 4:8.

62:10 A reference to the manner of weighing precious objects; the lighter one would rise. On God's scale, the wicked are a puff of air. The image of the scale recurs in Job 31:6; Prov 16:2; 21:2; 24:12; Isa 40:15.

62:11 The Prophets inveighed against social crimes (see Isa 30:12; Ezek 22:29). The consequence was the recommendation to be detached from riches (see Job 27:12ff; 31:25; Eccl 5:8ff; Jer 17:11; Mt 6:19f, 24). *Heart:* see note on Ps 4:8.

no matter how greatly your wealth increases,
do not set your heart* on it.*a*

¹² One thing God has revealed;
two things have I heard:
that power belongs to you, O God,*b*
¹³ and so does kindness, O LORD.
You reward each person*c*
in accordance with his deeds.*

PSALM 63*

Thirst for God

¹ A psalm of David. When he was in the wilderness of
Judah.**d*

² O God, you are my God,
for whom I have been searching earnestly.*
My soul yearns for you
and my body thirsts for you,

---

a Job 31:25; Eccl 5:9; Jer 17:11; Ezek 22:29; Mt 6:19-21, 24.—b Job
40:5; Rev 19:1.—c Pss 28:4; 31:24; 86:5; 2 Sam 3:39; Job 34:11; Jer 17:10;
Mt 16:27; Rom 2:6; 2 Tim 4:14; Rev 22:12.—d 1 Sam 24; 2 Sam 15:23-28.

62:13 The doctrine of personal retribution, taught by the Prophets, above all
Ezekiel (see Ezek 18), is taken up by the sages and the psalmists (see Pss 28:4;
31:24; Job 34:11; Prov 24:12; Sir 16:13) and passes into the New Testament (see
Mt 16:27; Rom 2:6; 2 Tim 4:14; Rev 2:23)—but only good deeds have eternal
value. *Kindness:* see note on Ps 6:5.

Ps 63 A deported Levite thinks back to the time when he lived in the temple,
close to God; in the silence of the night he meditates on those happy hours, the
remembrance of which comforts him. And the desire rises in him and becomes
more and more intense; already it is as if he is once again in the sanctuary with
no other occupation than to offer unceasing praise to the One whose love surpasses every other good. In that time of deliverance the king will be filled with
blessings by God while the oppressors will receive the severest of chastisements.

By its movement and style, this engaging prayer finds a place among the most
beautiful psalms of longing (see Pss 42; 61; 73; 84). It enables us to rediscover—amid the difficulties of daily life and all that distracts us from the spiritual life—the longing for God, whose love is the only thing that makes life worth
living. It can also serve as the song of the prodigal son (see Lk 15), enabling us
to put into words the distress, hope, and penitence of the repentant sinner.

63:1 This superscription ascribes the psalm to a time when David was in the
wilderness (see 1 Sam 24; 2 Sam 15:23-28; 16:2, 14; 17:16, 29).

63:2 *Earnestly:* literally, "in the morning" (see introduction to Ps 57 and note
on Ps 57:9). *My soul . . . my body:* i.e., my whole being.

like the earth when it is parched,
    arid and without water.*e*

3 I have gazed upon you in the sanctuary
    so that I may behold your power and your
       glory.
4 Your kindness* is a greater joy than life itself;
    thus my lips will speak your praise.

5 I will bless you all my life;
    with uplifted hands* I will call on your name.
6 My soul* will be satisfied as at a banquet
    and with rejoicing lips my mouth will
      praise you.

7 I think of you while I lie upon my bed,*
    and I meditate on you during the watches
      of the night.
8 For you are my help,
    and in the shadow of your wings I rejoice.**f*
9 My soul clings tightly to you;
    your right hand holds me fast.

10 * Those who seek my life will incur ruin;*
    they will sink down into the depths of the
      earth.

---

e Pss 36:8-10; 42:3; 84:3; 143:6; Isa 26:9.—f Pss 17:8; 27:9; 36:8;
118:7; Ru 2:12.

63:4 *Kindness:* see note on Ps 6:5. For the Old Testament, the greatest good
was earthly life; but God's kindness is better even than life.

63:5 *Uplifted hands:* a gesture of prayerful praise. *Name:* see note on Ps 5:12.

63:6 *Soul:* see note on Ps 6:4. *As at a banquet:* literally, "marrow and fat," the
preferred meats of the Palestinian Arabs and a symbol of the best of foods (see
Ps 36:9).

63:7 *Upon my bed:* during the night of darkness, the psalmist anxiously looks
for the morning of God's deliverance (see introduction to Ps 57 and note on Ps
57:9). *Watches of the night:* the night was divided into three watches, and if
someone were aware of all three of them he was passing a sleepless night—in
this case at prayer (see Ps 119:148; Lam 2:19).

63:8 See note on Ps 17:8.

63:10-12 See note on Ps 5:11 and introduction to Ps 35.

63:10-11 The psalmist's enemies will lose their lives for having sought to kill
him, and they will become *food for jackals,* i.e., they will remain unburied, a
cause for shame (see note on Ps 53:6).

11 They will be slain by the sword
and their flesh will become food for jackals.
12 But the king will rejoice in God;
all who swear by him* will exult,
for the mouths of liars will be silenced.g

PSALM 64*

Thanksgiving for Recovery from Illness

1 For the director.* A psalm of David.

2 Listen, O God, to my cry of lament;
from the dreaded enemy preserve my life.
3 Protect me from the council of the wicked,
from the band of those who do evil.

4 They sharpen their tongues* like swords,
and they shoot forth their venomous words
like arrows,h
5 while they attack the innocent from ambush,
shooting suddenly and without fear.

---

g Pss 21:2; 107:42; Deut 6:13; Isa 45:23; 48:1; Jer 12:16; Dan 13:43, 61;
Zep 1:5.—h Pss 7:13; 11:2; 37:14; 55:22; 57:5; 58:7; Isa 49:2; Jer 9:2.

63:12 *All who swear by him:* to swear by the Lord signified devoted adherence
to him (see Isa 45:23; 48:1; Zep 1:5). God will acquit his followers (see Deut 6:13;
Jer 12:16; Dan 13:42, 60) but will chastise the wicked (see Ps 52:3-7).

Ps 64 The psalmist shows that the righteous are often defenseless before the
cynicism of the machinations and calumnies to which they are prey. Those who
weave their intrigues act in shadows and believe they are hidden from view. However, God sees everything, even secret human actions and designs. His judgment
overtakes those who evade justice. Basing himself on the law of talion ("an eye
for an eye"), the author imagines that, even here below, God will turn their evil
against the wicked while publicly acquitting the righteous. Each life will be
brought before the judgment of God; the righteous will find their joy in the Lord.
Such is the lesson of the psalm, even though the ways of God follow a more mysterious course than its author yet suspected.

This psalm was applied to the Passion of Jesus by St. Augustine. It also finds
a ready place in the prayer of the Church and the faithful who experience the
physical and spiritual attacks of the world, the flesh, and the devil as we await
the coming of Christ to dispense true justice (see Rev 19:1f).

64:1 *For the director:* these words are thought to be a musical or liturgical notation.

64:4 *Tongues:* see note on Ps 5:10.

⁶ They agree on their evil plan,*
    and they resolve to lay snares,
    saying, "Who will see us?"
⁷ They plot evil schemes
    and devise shrewd plots;
    the thoughts of their hearts* are hidden.*ⁱ*

⁸ * However, God will shoot his arrows at
        them,*
    and they will suddenly be struck down.*ʲ*
⁹ Their own tongues will bring them down,
    and all who see them will wag their
        heads.**k*

¹⁰ Then everyone will be in awe,*
    as they proclaim God's mighty deeds
    and contemplate what he has done.*
¹¹ The righteous will rejoice in the LORD
    and take refuge in him;
    all the upright in heart will praise him.*l*

---

i Ps 140:3; Prov 6:14; Jer 11:20f.—j Pss 7:13-14; 38:3; Deut 32:42; Job 6:4; 34:6; Lam 6:12; Ezek 5:16.—k Pss 5:10-11; 44:15; 52:6; 59:13.—l Pss 5:12; 36:8; 57:2.

64:6-7 These verses enlarge the portrait of the wicked set forth in vv. 3-5; there the wicked are shown opposing the innocent, while here their common plotting is shown. The wicked lay snares to trap their victims (see Pss 35:7; 119:110; 140:6; 142:4; Deut 7:16; Prov 22:24f; Jer 7:9f).
64:7 *Hearts:* see note on Ps 4:8. *Hidden:* literally, "deep" (see Prov 18:4; 20:5).
64:8-10 See note on Ps 5:11 and introduction to Ps 35.
64:8-9 God will turn on the wicked the harm they wanted to do to the psalmist, as demanded by the law of talion (see Pss 7:13f; 9:16f; 35:7f; 37:15; 59:13f; 140:10). He will shoot his arrows at them (see Ps 38:3; Deut 32:42). The shame they had intended to bring upon the godly will fall back upon themselves (see Pss 22:8; 52:7-9; 59:11; Jer 48:26).
64:9 *Wag their heads:* a common gesture of ridicule (see Pss 22:8; 44:15; 109:25; Jer 48:27).
64:10-11 The psalmist encourages all to proclaim and ponder the acts of God (see Ps 2:10; Isa 41:20) and to turn to him in adversity. He will vindicate his servants who are righteous (see Pss 7:11; 11:2-7), and they will be in a position to give him praise (see Ps 7:18).
64:10 The wicked asked derisively, "Who will see us?" (v. 6) and were unafraid of the consequences of their actions. But when all humanity sees the power of God, fear will come upon everyone.

PSALM 65*

Thanksgiving for Divine Blessings

1 For the director.* A psalm of David. A song.

2 It is fitting* to offer praise to you,
   O God, in Zion.
 To you our vows must be fulfilled,*
3   for you answer our prayers.
 To you all flesh* must come,*m*
4   burdened by its sinful deeds.*n*
 Too heavy for us are our sins,
   and only you can blot them out.*

5 Blessed* is the one whom you choose
   and invite to dwell in your courts.

---

m Pss 22:28; 66:4; 86:9; Isa 66:23; Zec 14:16; Rev 15:4.—n Pss 32:1-2; 40:13; 78:38; 79:9; Isa 1:18; Heb 9:14.

Ps 65 In Israel, the harvest feast (see Lev 23:29) directly follows the Day of Atonement (to which reference is made in v. 4; see Lev 16). At this time the people celebrate a season of abundance. Joy and gratitude pervade this poem. At the beginning, there is a first acclamation to the Lord who dwells in Zion; in this privileged place God receives worship and dispenses pardon while the Levites are overwhelmed with joy and filled with grace. Then the horizon is expanded to include the very ends of the earth: the people praise the Master of the world whose exploits are proclaimed by all creation and history. Lastly, gratitude is offered for the huge harvest: the poet evokes the miracle that comes in the form of rain (for these regions ever threatened by drought); the springtime of Judea shines forth, and the country experiences a sumptuous rebirth.

The modern—scientific—way in which we look at the succession of the seasons and harvests need not deprive us of the wisdom of the ancients, which saw God at work and extolled his splendor and goodness. It is God who acts through the regular course of nature (see Mt 6:26, 30).

This psalm reminds us to offer God unceasing praise and thanksgiving (see Col 3:16f; Eph 5:19f).

65:1 *For the director:* these words are thought to be a musical or liturgical notation.

65:2 *It is fitting . . . praise to you:* another translation is: "Praise awaits you." The debt of giving praise to God is fulfilled when people carry out the vows they made in time of need (see note on Ps 7:18).

65:3 *To you all flesh must come:* i.e., all humankind will come to God. It recalls the universalism of the psalmists (see Pss 64:10; 66:1, 4, 8; 67:4-6) and of Isaiah (see Isa 17:12; 26:15; 66:19, 23).

65:4 *Blot them out:* or "make atonement for them." God forgives sins when his people repent and observe his rules for pardon (as he did for the Israelites who observed the Day of Atonement—see Lev 16:20-30).

65:5 *Blessed:* see note on Ps 1:1.

We will be filled with the good things of your
    house,*
  of your holy temple.

6 Through your awesome deeds* of righteous-
    ness,
    you respond to us, O God, our Savior;
  you are the hope of all the ends of the earth
    and of the far-off islands.o

7 Clothed in your great power,
    you hold the mountains in place.
8 You quiet the roaring of the seas,
    the turbulence of their waves,p
    and the turmoil of the nations.*q
9 Those who dwell at the ends of the earth
    are awestruck by your wonders.*
  You call forth songs of joy
    from sunrise to sunset.

10 You care for the earth and water it,
    making it most fertile.
  The streams of God* are filled with water
    to provide grain for its people.r
  Thus, you prepare the earth for growth:
11   you water its furrows
    and level its ridges;
  you soften it with showers
    and bless its yield.

---

o Ps 18:47; Isa 66:19.—p Pss 89:10; 93:3-4; 107:29; Job 26:12; 38:11;
Mt 8:26.—q Isa 17:12.—r Ps 68:11; Lev 26:4; Isa 30:23, 25; Joel 2:22-23.

65:5 *Good things of your house:* see note on Ps 36:9.
65:6 *Awesome deeds:* God's creative acts as reflected in the beauty and
bounty of Nature and his saving acts as seen in the deliverance of Israel from
Egypt and its establishment in the promised land (see Pss 106:22; 145:6; Deut
10:21; 2 Sam 7:23; Isa 64:3).
65:8 Just as God tamed the turbulence of the primeval waters of chaos (see
notes on Pss 32:6 and 33:7), so he brings to an end the *turmoil of the nations*
(see Isa 2:4f; 11:6-9; Mic 4:3f).
65:9 *Wonders:* the great saving acts of God indicated in note to v. 6.
65:10 *Streams of God:* the poet evokes the means by which God brings forth the
rain out of his "storehouses" (Ps 33:7), which flow into the water sources on earth
and give life to creatures (see Ps 46:5; Isa 33:21).

¹² You crown the year with your bounty,*
　　and your tracks dispense fertility.
¹³ The pastures of the wilderness overflow,
　　and the hills are covered with rejoicing.
¹⁴ The meadows are clothed with flocks,
　　　and the valleys are decked out with grain;
　　in their joy they shout and sing together.*s

PSALM 66*

Thanksgiving for God's Deliverance

¹ For the director.* A song. A psalm.

Shout joyfully to God, all the earth;*
²　　sing to the glory of his name;*
　　offer to him glorious praise.t

---

s Pss 72:16; 98:8; 144:13; Isa 44:23.—t Pss 65:14; 79:9; Isa 44:23.

65:12 *Bounty:* literally, "goodness"; the reference is to both material and spiritual gifts, God's Covenant promises. *Tracks:* God's royal chariot tours the heavens dispensing fertility throughout the earth (see Pss 18:11; 68:5; Deut 33:26; Isa 66:15; Am 9:13).

65:14 *In their joy they shout and sing together:* all creation joins in the praise of God for his goodness (see Pss 89:13; 96:11-13; 98:8f; 103:22; 145:10; 148:3f, 7-10; Job 38:7; Isa 44:23; 49:13; 55:12).

Ps 66 This psalm is made up of two wholly autonomous parts: in the first, Israel praises God for his saving acts on its behalf, and in the second, an individual fulfills his vow to God for some favor. In its liturgy, Israel always contemplates anew the great days of the past: the Exodus from Egypt and the passage of the Jordan (v. 5). This does not constitute nostalgia for a past favor; yesterday's event is the sign of God's presence today. God always manifests himself as the savior of his people: now he delivers them from the distress of an invasion or possibly from the great trial of the Exile (vv. 8-11). A spirit of universalism pervades the first part of this poem: the whole earth is invited to proclaim the deliverances of God.

In the individual's prayer of thanksgiving, a man saved from a great trial comes to give praise by his offerings and his proclamation amidst his friends. The person who announces a deliverance at God's hands makes himself the spokesman of the community of believers.

This psalm is an apt reminder to offer God a fitting sacrifice of thanksgiving in the Eucharist. Such is the living sacrifice we offer God, placing ourselves in it as other living victims (see Rom 12:1) in order to thank him for the wonders accomplished in our souls, especially for our spiritual resurrection achieved in union with Christ's Resurrection (see Rom 6:5-8).

66:1a *For the director:* these words are thought to be a musical or liturgical notation.

66:1b *All the earth:* see note on Ps 65:3.

66:2 *Name:* see note on Ps 5:12.

3 Say to God: "How awesome are your deeds!
    Because of your great power,
    your enemies grovel before you.ᵘ
4 The whole earth bows down in worship be-
    fore you,
    singing praises to you,
    singing praises to your name."   *Selah*

5 Come and behold* the works of God,
    the awesome deeds he has done for people.
6 He changed the sea into dry land;
    they crossed the river* on foot.
  There we rejoiced in him,ᵛ
7   for he rules forever by his power.
  His eyes keep watch over the nations
    so that the rebellious not exalt themselves.
                           Selah

8 Bless our God, all you peoples;*
    let the sound of his praise be heard.
9 For he has preserved our lives*
    and has kept our feet from stumbling.ʷ

10 For you, O God, have put us to the test;
    you have purified us as silver is refined.ˣ
11 You allowed us to be snared in the net*
    and placed heavy burdens on our backs.

---

u 3-4: Pss 18:45; 81:16; Mic 7:17.—v Pss 74:15; 114:3; Gen 8:1; Ex
14:21f; Lev 23:40; Jos 3:14ff; Isa 44:27; 1 Cor 10:1.—w Pss 30:4; 91:12;
121:3; Deut 32:35; 1 Sam 2:9; Job 12:5; Prov 3:23.—x Ps 12:7; Ex 15:25;
Isa 48:10; Dan 11:35; 12:10.

66:5 *Come and behold:* in the eyes of the psalmist, God's saving acts are
present and can be seen in the liturgical celebration in the temple.
66:6 *Sea . . . river:* the passages through the Red Sea (see Ex 14:1—15:21)
and through the Jordan (see Jos 3:11—4:24) became typical of God's power and
wondrous deeds in the history of Israel (see Ps 114:3; Isa 44:27; 50:2).
66:8-12 Praise for a new deliverance that God has worked on his people's behalf.
66:9 *Preserved our lives:* sometimes translated as "brought us to life," which
accounts for the name "Resurrection Psalm" given this psalm in Greek and Latin
manuscripts and its use in the Easter Liturgy.
66:11-12 The Israelites experienced imprisonment, slavery, and total defeat before being delivered by God and brought into a place of abundance (see Pss 18:20;
23:4-6; 119:45). The Lord does not permit his people to succumb to their trials (see
Ps 37:24; 1 Cor 10:13) and rewards a persevering faith (see 1 Pet 1:7).

12 You let our captors ride over our heads,*
        and we went through fire and water,
        but now you have afforded us relief.*y*

13 I will enter your house with burnt offerings*
        and carry out my vows to you,
14 the vows that my lips pronounced
        and my mouth promised when I was in dis-
        tress.
15 I will offer burnt offerings of fat animals
        with the smoke of burning rams;
        I will sacrifice to you bulls and goats. *Selah*

16 Come and listen, all you who fear God,
        while I relate what he has done for me.
17 * I lifted up my voice in prayer to him;
        his praise* was on my tongue.

18 If I had harbored evil in my heart,*
        the LORD would not have listened.
19 But God truly did listen,
        and he was attentive to the words of my
        prayer.

20 Blessed* be God,
        because he did not reject my prayer
        or withhold his kindness from me.

---

y Pss 32:6; 81:18; Isa 43:2; 51:22f.

66:12 *You let our captors ride over our heads:* literally, "you let men mount our head," which suggests the ancient practice of victors in war placing their feet on the necks of their enemies as a sign of total subjugation (see Isa 51:23). *Fire and water:* conventional metaphors for the gravest of trials (see Pss 32:6; 81:8; Isa 43:2; 51:22f).

66:13-20 An individual fulfills the vows he promised to God when he was in trouble (see note on Ps 7:18; see also Pss 50:14; 116:17-19).

66:17-20 The psalmist's celebration of his deliverance includes a lament ("I lifted up my voice," v. 17), a profession of commitment ("his praise was on my tongue," v. 17), a protestation of innocence ("if I had harbored evil in my heart," v. 18; see Pss 17:1f; 18:21f; 59:4f; Jn 9:31), and praise ("God truly did listen," v. 19; see Pss 28:6; 31:22; 68:20, 36).

66:17 *I lifted up my voice . . . his praise:* prayer always entails praise in both the Old Testament and the New (see Phil 4:6; 1 Tim 2:1). Even while the psalmist was praying for help, he was also praising God for his goodness and mercy.

66:18-19 Because the psalmist acknowledged his sin, he was forgiven by God, and his prayer was heard. *Heart:* see note on Ps 4:8.

66:20 *Blessed:* see note on Ps 22:27. *Kindness:* see note on Ps 6:5.

PSALM 67*
Prayer That All May Worship God

1 For the director.* With stringed instruments. A psalm. A song.

2 O God, be gracious to us and bless us
   and let your face shine upon us.*z   *Selah*
3 Then your ways will be known on earth*
   and your salvation among all nations.*a*
4 Let the peoples praise you, O God;
   let all the peoples praise you.

5 Let the nations rejoice and exult,*
   for you judge the peoples fairly
   and guide the nations upon the earth.*b* *Selah*
6 Let the peoples praise you, O God;
   let all the peoples praise you.

7 The earth has yielded its harvest;
   God, our God, has blessed us.*c*

---

z Pss 4:7; 31:17; 44:4; 80:4; Num 6:24-26; Dan 9:17.—a Ps 98:2; Isa 40:5; 52:10; Jer 33:9.—b Pss 82:8; 98:9; 100:2-3.—c Ps 85:13; Gen 12:2; Lev 26:4; Isa 55:10; Ezek 34:27; Hos 2:23-24; Zec 8:12.

Ps 67 This psalm recounts the assembly of the people for the feast of the harvest (see Ex 23:16; Lev 26:4) and their prayers of praise to God. They recall first all that he has done in Israel; the abundance of the fruits of the earth is like a new sign of his power and goodness. And more and more, they want the whole world to take part in this thanksgiving to God. The Lord is no longer merely the God of Israel; he is the Master and Judge of the whole world and all its peoples.
   This psalm enables us to thank God for his material blessings on us. However, it also reminds us to ask God to continue to shower upon us his spiritual blessings so as to elicit admiration, envy, and divine praises even from nonbelievers.
   67:1 *For the director:* these words are thought to be a musical or liturgical notation.
   67:2 This verse was inspired by the priestly blessing (see Ps 31:17; Num 6:24-26). *Face shine upon us:* a radiant face is the sign of a joyous and benevolent heart (see Pss 4:7; 31:17; 44:4; 80:4; 119:135; see also note on Ps 13:2).
   67:3-4 The history of the chosen people is a lesson that God gives to the pagan nations, enabling them to discover his power and goodness. They too are called to serve the one God and must join their praises to those of God's people. The refrain of the psalm (vv. 4, 6) insists on the universalism that the Prophets (see Jer 33:9), especially Second Isaiah, have impressed on the religious conscience of Israel. Many psalms bear witness to this spirit.
   67:5 The psalmist prays that the nations may see the goodness of God's rule and respond with joy and praise (see Pss 98:4-6; 100:1).

⁸ May God continue to bless us
    and be revered to the ends of the earth.

PSALM 68*

Song of Victory

¹ For the director.* A psalm of David. A song.

² May God rise up, and his enemies be scat-
      tered;*
    may his foes flee before him.ᵈ
³ As smoke is blown away in the wind,
    so will they be blown away.

---

d Pss 12:6; 18:15; 89:11; 92:10; 132:8; 144:6; Num 10:35; Isa 17:13; 21:15; 33:3.

Ps 68 This psalm may have been used in a processional liturgy celebrating the triumphal march of Israel's God to his sanctuary, possibly as part of the Feast of Booths or Tabernacles that included a procession of the tribes (vv. 25-28). With the words "May God rise up . . .," the poet sets in motion the procession with the ark, as at the time when it went before the marches of the people (v. 2; see Num 10:35). And he lets the whole history of Israel unfold before our eyes like a grand march of God, like his procession into the heart of Jerusalem. God rises, and the darkness dissipates; he takes the head of his people, and the adversaries are thrown into disorder. This epic poem assembles a series of allusive images, many of which remain obscure for us.

In this coming of God, however, we will recognize stirring moments in the destiny of Israel: the Exodus from Egypt and the divine manifestation at Sinai (vv. 8-9; see Ex 19:16), the wonders of the Exodus (vv. 10-11), the exploits of the Judges (vv. 12-15; see Book of Judges), the Conquest of Jerusalem (vv. 15-19), the sad fate of the criminal Ahab (v. 24; see 1 Ki 21:19), and the solemn Passover of Hezekiah who had reunited all the tribes of Israel (vv. 25-38; see 2 Chr 30), which foreshadowed the gathering in the holy city of the pagans who had finally come to render homage to the Lord of all nations.

The important thing in this psalm is not so much to grasp all the allusions as it is to let ourselves be carried along by the rhythm of the chant; we should listen to it as to an heroic march, as the glorious epic that draws Israel out of the dreary atmosphere of everyday life. It is the ideal psalm for processions to the temple.

In the ascent of God, who rises to take possession of the sacred hill of Jerusalem, the apostle Paul sees the Ascension of Christ, who draws after him the redeemed people, the Church that is filled with the gifts of the Holy Spirit (v. 19; see Eph 4:8-11). When Christians sing this hymn, they recall the presence of God in the working out of the world's destiny and the march of humanity, which is continually called by God until it is made one again in glory.

68:1 *For the director:* these words are thought to be a musical or liturgical notation.

68:2-4 This first of nine parts prays that God will come at the head of his people to defeat their enemies and enter his sanctuary in triumph.

As wax melts away before a flame,
   so will the wicked perish before God.*e*
4 But those who are righteous will rejoice;
   they will exult before God,
   crying out with great delight.

5 * Sing to God, sing praise to his name;*
   exalt him who rides upon the clouds.
Rejoice in the presence of this God
   whose name is the LORD.*f*

6 The Father of orphans and the defender of
   widows:*g*
   such is God in his holy dwelling place.
7 He gives a home to those who are forsaken
   and leads out prisoners amid chants of exultation,
   while rebels are forced to live in an arid
   land.

8 O God, when you set out at the head of your
   people,*
   when you went marching through the
   wilderness,*h*   *Selah*
9 the earth quaked,*
   and rain poured down from the heavens,

---

e Pss 9:4; 37:20; 97:5; Jud 16:15; Wis 5:14; Mic 1:4.—f Pss 7:18; 18:10;
104:3; Deut 33:26; Isa 19:1.—g 6-7: Pss 10:14; 25:16; 103:6; 146:7, 9; Ex
22:21; Bar 6:37.—h 8-9: Pss 44:10; 114:4, 7; Ex 13:21; Deut 33:2; Jdg 5:4-
5; Heb 12:26.

68:5-7 This second part calls for God to be praised as savior.
68:5 *Name:* see note on Pss 5:12 and 8:1. *Who rides upon the clouds:* the
psalmist applies to Yahweh the image of the Canaanite storm-god Baal riding to
battle on storm clouds; he thus stresses that Yahweh rather than Baal is the exalted God who makes the storm clouds his chariot (see v. 34; Pss 18:10f; 104:3;
Deut 33:26; Isa 19:1; Hab 3:8; Mt 26:64).
68:8-11 This third part recalls God's march at the head of his people from
Egypt, through the desert of Sinai, and into the promised land (see Ps 60:14; Ex
13:21; 19:16; Num 14:14; Deut 33:2; Hab 3:3).
68:9 *Earth quaked:* a reference to the "trembling" of Mount Sinai (see Ex
19:18). *Rain poured down from the heavens:* although there is no record of rain in
the Sinai story, there is mention of "thunder and lightning, with a thick cloud"
(see Ex 19:16), which would usually indicate rain. In addition, rain is connected
with the shaking of the earth (see Jdg 5:4).

at the presence of God, the One of Sinai,
　　at the presence of God, the God of Israel.

¹⁰ You poured down rain in abundance, O God,*
　　and revived your exhausted inheritance.
¹¹ It was there that your people settled;
　　and in your great goodness, O God,
　　you provided for those who were needy.

¹² * The Lord issues the word,*
　　and a vast army proclaims good tidings:
¹³ "Kings and their armies are beating a hasty
　　　　retreat;
　　even those who remained in camp are di-
　　　　viding up the spoils.ⁱ

¹⁴ "While you linger by the sheepfolds,
　　the wings of the dove are covered* with
　　　　silver,
　　its feathers brilliant with shining gold."ʲ
¹⁵ When the Almighty* routed the kings there,
　　it was like snow fallen upon Zalmon.

¹⁶ The mountains of Bashan are God's moun-
　　　　tains;*
　　the mountains of Bashan are mighty peaks.

---

i Jos 10:16; Jdg 5:19, 30.—j Gen 49:14; Jdg 5:16.

68:10-11 These two verses evoke the miracles of the Exodus: the cloud (see Ex 13:21; Num 14:14), the manna and quail (see Ps 78:24f; Ex 16:4f), and the entrance into the promised land (v. 11: "it was there").
68:12-15 This fourth part recalls the defeat of the Canaanite kings by God.
68:12 *Issues the word:* God foretells his victory over the Canaanites (see Ex 23:22f, 27f, 31; Deut 7:10-24; 11:23-25; Jos 1:2-6).
68:14 *Wings of the dove are covered:* even while in camp, before the battle, Israel (God's "dove": see Ps 74:19; Hos 7:11) is already assured of enjoying the booty ("silver" and "gold") of the Canaanite kings, for God had guaranteed it (see Jos 2:8-11; 5:1; 6:16).
68:15 *Almighty:* the Hebrew is *Shaddai,* "the Mountain One." The name by which God revealed himself to the patriarchs was *El-Shaddai:* "God Almighty" (see Gen 17:1), which stressed God's power or his home in the mountains (see Ps 121:1). *Zalmon:* a mountain near Shechem (see Jdg 9:46-48) or a dark volcanic mountain in Bashan or Hauran east of the Sea of Galilee. It was known as the "dark one" in opposition to the "white one," Lebanon.
68:16-19 This fifth part celebrates the taking of Jerusalem to which God ascends and from which he will rule the world.

17 Why, O rugged mountains, do you gaze enviously
   at the mountain* that God has chosen as his abode,
   where the LORD himself will dwell forever?[k]

18 The chariots of God* are myriad,
   thousands upon thousands;
   the LORD has come down from Sinai
   and entered into the holy place.

19 You ascended on high,
   leading captives in your train;
   you accepted slaves as tribute,
   so that even rebels might dwell with the LORD God.*[l]

20 Blessed be the LORD, day after day,*
   the God of our salvation, who carries our burden.[m]   *Selah*

21 Our God is a God who saves;
   the LORD God delivers from death.*

22 God himself will smite the heads of his enemies,
   the hairy crowns of those who persist in their sins.[n]

23 The LORD has said:
   "I will bring them back even from Bashan,

---

k Ps 132:13-14; Deut 12:5; Ezek 43:7.—l Pss 7:7; 47:6; Eph 4:8-10.—m Pss 34:2; 145:2; Deut 32:11; Isa 46:3-4; 63:8.—n Ps 74:14; Deut 32:42.

68:17 *The mountain:* Mount Zion, a little mount, which God has made the highest mountain because he has placed his temple there and dwells in it.

68:18 *Chariots of God:* the heavenly hosts (see Hab 3:8, 15), later termed "legions" by Jesus (see Mt 26:53). It may also refer to the heavenly chariots seen by Elisha (see 2 Ki 6:17) rather than the chariots of Solomon (see 1 Ki 10:26).

68:19 When God went up to his place of enthronement on Mount Zion (see Ps 47:6f), he had captives in his train and received gifts like a victor in battle. The apostle Paul applies this verse in its Greek translation to the ministry of the ascended Christ (Eph 4:8: "When he ascended to the heights, / he took prisoners into captivity / and gave gifts to men"). It assures all who believe in Christ that by trusting him they can overcome evil.

68:20-24 This sixth part offers joyous praise and the fervent hope that God's victories will continue.

68:21 *Delivers from death:* see notes on Pss 6:6; 11:7; 16:9-11.

I will bring them back even from the depths of the sea,*
24 so that you may bathe your feet in the blood of your foes
and the tongues of your dogs may have their share."*[o]

25 Your procession, O God, comes into view,*
the procession of my God and King into the sanctuary.
26 The singers enter first,
with musicians trailing behind them,
while in their midst are the maidens playing tambourines.*[p]

27 Bless God in the assembly;
the LORD, the source of Israel.
28 In the lead is Benjamin, the smallest in number,
with the princes of Judah in a council,
as well as the princes of Zebulun and Naphtali.[q]

29 Marshal your power once again, O God,*
the power of God that you have often wielded for us.

---

o Ps 58:11; 1 Ki 21:19; 22:38; 2 Ki 9:36; Isa 63:1-6.—p Pss 81:3-4; 87:7; 149:3; 150:3-5; 2 Sam 6:5; Rev 18:22.—q Jdg 5:18; 1 Sam 9:21; Isa 9:1.

68:23 *From Bashan . . . from the depths of the sea:* i.e., the heights and the depths, the farthest places to which enemies might flee.

68:24 A vivid expression indicating complete victory over one's foes that was common in the Near East (see Ps 58:11). It alludes to the predictions of Elijah (1 Ki 21:19f) about the death of Ahab (1 Ki 22:38), his son Joram, wounded at Ramoth Gilead and brought back to Jezreel (2 Ki 8:29; 9:15), and Jezebel (2 Ki 9:36).

68:25-28 This seventh part describes the procession as it approaches the temple and renews God's taking up residence there (see Pss 24; 47) in the presence of all Israel, both north and south. It also alludes to the Passover of Hezekiah in which all the tribes participated (see Ps 80:2f; 2 Chr 30:1ff; Isa 9:1).

68:26 *Tambourines:* instruments played especially after a victory in battle (see Ex 15:20; 1 Sam 10:5; 18:6; 2 Sam 6:5; Jer 31:4).

68:29-32 This eighth part gives the prayer that God may continue to rule over the enemies of his people and exact tribute from them.

30 For to your temple in Jerusalem
    kings will come to you bearing gifts.*

31 Rebuke those wild beasts of the reeds,
    the herd of mighty bulls, the calves of
    nations,
who bring bars of silver and prostrate them-
    selves;
    rout the nations that delight in war.*

32 Envoys will come from Egypt;*r*
    Cush will stretch out its hands to God.**s*

33 Sing to God, all you kingdoms of the earth;*
    sing the praises of the LORD,*t*   *Selah*

34 who rides the ancient heavens above
    and speaks with his voice of thunder.*

35 Acknowledge the power of God,
    whose majesty is over Israel
    and whose power is in the skies.

36 Awesome is God in his sanctuary,
    the God of Israel, who gives power and
    strength to his people.**u*

    Blessed be God!

---

r Ezek 17:15; 29:2ff.—s Isa 18:7; 43:3; 45:14; Zep 3:10.—t Pss 7:18; 67:5; 138:4.—u Pss 18:2; 28:8; 29:11; Deut 7:21.

68:30 The defeated nations, led by their kings, will bring tribute to the Lord who has established his majesty in his temple at Jerusalem (see Ps 76:12; Isa 18:7; 60:3-7; 66:20; Hag 2:7; Zec 2:11-13; 6:15; 8:21f; Rev 21:24).

68:31 The prayer contains a petition to strike the nations that will not submit to the Lord. *Wild beasts of the reeds:* the reference is to the crocodile, a symbol for Egypt (see Ezek 29:3), which in turn stands for all the hostile nations. *Herd of mighty bulls:* the "lords of nations" who oppress and seduce their peoples. *Bars of silver:* tribute from the foreign nations brought to Zion.

68:32 Egypt will submit, as will Cush (i.e., the upper Nile region), which usually formed an alliance with Egypt (see Isa 18:1—19:15; 20:1-6).

68:33-36 This ninth part calls upon all nations to praise the God of Israel who dwells in the temple and acclaim him as the God of all nations (see Ps 47).

68:34 The words "who rides the ancient heavens above" indicate the Lord's majesty, for he rules the highest heavens (see Deut 10:14; 1 Ki 8:27). The thunder symbolizes the power and majesty of his rule (see Pss 18:14; 29:3) on behalf of his people (see Deut 33:26).

68:36 Although the Lord is awesome in his deeds (see Pss 47:3; 65:6; Ex 15:11; Deut 10:17; Rev 15:3f), he condescends to be present to his people in the sanctuary in order to aid them.

PSALM 69*

Cry of Anguish in Distress

¹ For the director.* According to "Lilies." Of David.

² Save me, my God,
   for the waters have risen to my neck.ᵛ
³ I am sinking in muddy depths*
   and can find no foothold.
 I have fallen into deep waters,
   and the floods* overwhelm me.ʷ

⁴ I am exhausted from crying out;
   my throat is parched.
 My eyes have been worn out
   searching for my God.ˣ

⁵ More numerous than the hairs of my head
   are those who hate me for no reason.*
 Many are those who seek to destroy me,
   and they are treacherous.
 How can I restore
   what I have not stolen?ʸ

---

v Pss 18:5; 32:6; 93:3-4; Job 22:11; Jon 2:5.—w Pss 40:3; 42:8; 124:4-5;
Job 30:19.—x Pss 6:7; 25:15; 27:8; 119:82; 123:2; 141:8; Isa 38:14.—y Pss
35:19; 38:20; 40:13; Lam 3:52; Jn 15:25.

Ps 69 This Messianic psalm encompasses the laments of two different people
in distress; the first may have been accused of thievery (v. 5), and the second
may have been tormented because of his piety and derided for his faith. The
swamp in which they are sinking and the waters by which they are engulfed are
the images of the despair that afflicts a person facing death. The tragic state of
the suppliants resembles that of the righteous person whom we have encountered in Ps 22 and who makes us think of the prophet Jeremiah (see Jer 15:15)
and the Suffering Servant (see Isa 53:10). Their prayer, which appeals to God's
justice as well as his compassion, concludes with a vast thanksgiving; the salvation that they await must be extended to all the lowly who rely only on God.

In their sufferings, Jesus sees his own suffering (Jn 15:25), and the evangelists have applied themselves to underscore this likeness (see Mt 27:46; Jn 2:17;
19:28; etc.). No psalm except Ps 22 is cited more often in the New Testament, a
fact that led the Fathers of the Church to classify this psalm as Messianic.

69:1 *For the director:* these words are thought to be a musical or liturgical notation. *According to "Lilies":* nothing is known about this phrase.

69:2-3 *Waters . . . muddy depths . . . deep waters . . . floods:* a common means
of indicating extreme distress (see note on Ps 30:2).

69:5 *Hate me for no reason:* see note on Ps 35:19. These words were completely fulfilled in the hatred his enemies had for Jesus (see Jn 15:25).

⁶ O God, you know how foolish I am;
      my guilty deeds are not hidden from you.*
⁷ Do not allow those who hope in you
      to be put to shame because of me,
      O Lᴏʀᴅ of hosts.
   Do not let those who seek you
      suffer disgrace because of me,
      O God of Israel.ᶻ

⁸ It is for your sake that I endure reproach
      and that shame covers my face.ᵃ
⁹ I have become alienated from my brothers,*
      a stranger to my mother's sons.ᵇ
¹⁰ Zeal for your house* consumes me,
      and the insults directed at you fall on me.ᶜ

¹¹ When I mortified myself with fasting,ᵈ
      I exposed myself to scorn.
¹² When I clothed myself in sackcloth,
      I became a laughingstock.
¹³ Those who sit at the gate taunt me,
      and drunkards make me the target of their
         ditties.

¹⁴ But I lift up my prayer to you, O Lᴏʀᴅ,
      in the time of your favor.*
   In your great kindness, O God,
      respond to me with your certain help.ᵉ
¹⁵ Draw me out of the mire,ᶠ
      and do not let me plunge any deeper.

---

z Pss 25:3; 40:17.—a Ps 44:16; Jer 15:15.—b Pss 31:12; 38:12; Job 19:13-15; 53:3; Jn 7:5.—c Pss 89:51-52; 119:139; Jn 2:17; Rom 15:3.—d 11-13: Pss 35:13; 109:24-25; Job 30:9; Lam 3:14.—e Pss 32:6; 102:14; Isa 49:8; 2 Cor 6:2.—f 15-16: Pss 28:1; 30:4; 32:6; 40:3; 88:5; 144:7; Num 16:33; Prov 1:12.

69:6 The psalmist admits his guilt, but he is innocent of the great crimes attributed to him by his enemies. This verse can be applied to Jesus only as an indication of the sins of the world that he took upon himself.

69:9 *I have become alienated from my brothers:* i.e., he is mocked by them; this text lies behind Jn 7:5, where Jesus' relatives ("brothers") do not believe in him.

69:10 *Zeal for your house:* cited in Jn 2:17 with reference to Jesus. *Insults directed at you:* cited in Rom 15:3 as an example of Jesus' selflessness.

69:14 *Time of your favor:* i.e., the special time when God is very near (see Ps 32:6; Isa 49:8; 61:2; 2 Cor 6:2). *Kindness:* see note on Ps 6:5.

Deliver me from my enemies
and from the deep waters.
16 Do not let the floodwaters sweep over me,
or the depths swallow me up,
or the pit close its jaws around me.

17 Answer me, O LORD, for your kindness* is
wonderful;
in your great compassion turn toward me.
18 Do not hide your face* from your servant;
answer me quickly, for I am in distress.*g*
19 Draw near to me and redeem me;
deliver me from my enemies.

20 You know my reproach, my shame, and my
dishonor;
all my oppressors are in your sight.
21 Insults have so broken my heart
that I am near the end of my strength.
I looked for compassion, but in vain,
for some consolers, but I found none.*h*
22 They put gall in my food,
and in my thirst they gave me vinegar* to
drink.*i*

23 Let their table become a trap for them;*
let their well-being become a snare.*j*
24 Let their eyes dim so that they cannot see,
and let their limbs tremble constantly.

---

g Pss 22:25; 50:15; 102:3; 143:7.—h Ps 142:5; Job 6:14ff; Isa 63:5; Lam 1:2.—i Lam 3:15; Mt 27:34, 48; Mk 15:23; Lk 23:36; Jn 19:28-30.—j Job 18:10; Rom 11:9-10.

69:17 *Kindness:* see note on Ps 6:5.
69:18 *Hide your face:* see note on Ps 13:2.
69:21 *I looked for . . . consolers, but I found none:* see Job 6:14ff; 16:2; Lam 1:2; and in reference to Jesus, see Mt 26:40; Jn 16:32.
69:22 *Gall . . . vinegar:* the evangelists suggest that the sufferings of the psalmist as described in this verse foreshadowed the sufferings of Jesus on the cross (see Mt 27:34, 48; Mk 15:23; Lk 23:36; Jn 19:29).
69:23-29 Prayer for divine justice to prevail (see note on Ps 5:11 and introduction to Ps 35).
69:23-24 These two verses are applied by Paul to the divine hardening of sinners' hearts that God allows (see Rom 11:9f). *Table:* a single tablecloth spread on the ground; hence the possibility of tripping over it.

²⁵ Vent your wrath on them,
　　and let your burning anger take hold of
　　　them.

²⁶ Let their camp be left desolate;^k
　　let there be no one to dwell in their tents.*

²⁷ For they pursue the one you struck down
　　and tell of the pain of the one you hurt.

²⁸ Charge them with crime after crime;
　　let them not share in your salvation.

²⁹ Blot them out from the book of the living;*
　　do not number them among the upright.^l

³⁰ But I am filled with pain and suffering;
　　may your saving power, O God, raise me up.

³¹ I will praise the name of God with a song*
　　and glorify him with a hymn of thanksgiving.

³² This will gratify the LORD more than an ox
　　or a young bull with horns and hoofs:*^m

³³ "Let the poor* see this and rejoice;
　　let those who seek God take heart.ⁿ

³⁴ For the LORD hears the needy
　　and does not turn his back on captives.

³⁵ Let the heavens and the earth offer praise,
　　the seas and everything that moves therein."

³⁶ For God will deliver Zion
　　and rebuild the cities of Judah.^o

---

k Acts 1:20; Mt 23:38.—l Ps 139:16; Ex 32:32; Isa 4:3; Ezek 13:9; Dan 12:1; Mal 3:16; Rev 3:5; 20:12.—m Pss 40:7; 50:8-9, 14; 51:18; Isa 1:11-15; Hos 6:6; Am 5:21-22; Heb 10:5-8.—n Pss 22:27; 35:27; 70:5; 119:144.—o Ps 102:21-22; Isa 44:26; Ezek 36:10.

69:26 Peter applies this verse to the replacement of Judas (see Acts 1:20).

69:29 *Book of the living:* a figurative expression denoting God's record of the righteous (see note on Ps 51:3). From the human point of view, individuals may be blotted out of that book, but from the divine point of view it contains only the names of the elect who will not be blotted out (see Phil 4:3; Rev 3:5; 13:8; 17:8; 20:15).

69:31-34 A vow to praise God for hearing his prayer (see note on Ps 7:18). *Name:* see note on Ps 5:12.

69:32 Prayer is worth more than the sacrifice of animals (see Pss 40:7; 50:13f; 51:18f), even the most perfect ones (see Lev 11:3; 1 Sam 1:24). See notes on Pss 40:7 and 50:7-15.

69:33 *Poor:* see note on Ps 22:27. *Heart:* see note on Ps 4:8.

His people will live there and possess it;
37 his servants' children will inherit it,
     and those who love his name will dwell
     there.*p*

PSALM 70*

Insistent Prayer for Divine Assistance

1 For the director.* Of David. For remembrance.

2 Make haste, O God, to rescue me;**q*
   O LORD, come quickly to my aid.*r*
3 May all those who seek to take my life*
   endure shame and confusion.

May all those who desire my ruin
   be turned back and humiliated.*s*
4 May those who cry out to me, "Aha! Aha!"*
   be forced to retreat in shame.*t*

5 But may all who seek you
   rejoice in you and be jubilant.
May those who love your salvation
     cry out forever, "May God be magni-
     fied."**u*

---

p Pss 25:13; 102:29; Isa 65:9.—q 2-6: Ps 40:14-18.—r Pss 22:20;
71:12.—s Pss 6:11; 35:4, 26; 71:13; 1 Sam 20:1; Est 9:2.—t Ps 35:21, 25;
Lam 2:16.—u Pss 35:27; 69:7, 33; 104:1; Deut 4:29; 1 Chr 28:9.

Ps 70 The psalmist's cry is that of all who cannot endure suffering any longer
and have no hope except in God. He calls upon God to come to his aid quickly. It
is a slightly revised duplicate of Ps 40:14-18.

Every Christian (and the whole Church) can naturally recite this psalm in his
or her own right as one really (though not yet completely) saved.

70:1 *For the director:* these words are thought to be a musical or liturgical notation. *For remembrance:* see note on Ps 38:1.

70:2-6 Distress can remind us of our attachment to sin. Is there any reason why
people should vilify the person who acknowledges faults? Realizing his strong attraction toward evil, the psalmist cries out to God, and the poor man rediscovers
with astonishment the joyous assurance that God thinks about him.

70:3-4 The psalmist prays for the downfall of his enemies, somewhat as
Christians pray for the kingdom of God to come, which includes the petition that
the Lord will come to vindicate his own and avenge the wrongs done by his enemies (see 2 Thes 1:5-10; see also note on Ps 5:11 and introduction to Ps 35).

70:4 *Aha! Aha!:* the mocking words of the psalmist's adversaries.

70:5 When the Lord works his deliverance, his people will rejoice in his salvation (see Ps 35:27) and give him praise.

6 As for me, I am poor and needy;*
    hasten to my aid, O God.
You are my help and my deliverer;
    O LORD, do not delay.

PSALM 71*

Prayer of the Righteous in Old Age

1 In you, O LORD, I have taken refuge;ᵛ
    let me never be put to shame.ʷ
2 In your righteousness rescue me and deliver
        me;
    hear my plea and save me.

3 Be to me a rock of refuge
    to which I can always go;
  proclaim the order to save me,
      for you are my rock and my fortress.ˣ

4 O my God, rescue me from the hands of the
        impious,
    from the grasp of cruel and ruthless foes.ʸ
5 You, O LORD, are my hope,
    my confidence, O GOD, from my youth.

v 1-3: Ps 31:2-4.—w Pss 22:6; 25:2; Deut 23:15; Ru 2:12.—x Pss 18:3;
28:8; 31:2-4.—y Ps 140:2; 2 Ki 19:19.

70:6 *Poor and needy:* see note on Ps 34:7. *My help and my deliverer:* the salvation promised the faithful (see Isa 25:9), first conceived as natural with reference
to the Exodus or the return from the Exile, was later conceived as spiritual without restriction of space or time (see, e.g., Ps 18:3; 19:15).

Ps 71 Accustomed to being exposed to malevolence, an aged person, probably
a cantor in the service of the temple, casts a look backward. From his childhood,
every day of his long life he has endeavored to remain faithful to the Lord and to
live in union with him; he has made praise of God his life companion. Profoundly
confident, he begs God to come to his aid, resolute in his will to praise him with
all his might. This lament resembles the "confessions" of the prophet Jeremiah
(Jer 17:14-18) and could have been later applied to Israel itself. We could regard
it as primarily a prayer of fidelity in difficult moments of old age; it is a fine
prayer for the evening of life.

   This supplication is appropriate for Christians in their temporal and spiritual
trials, and even more on the lips of the Church who is looked upon by her enemies
as old, failing, and vulnerable to receive the finishing blow.

⁶ I have relied upon you since birth,
　　and you have been my strength from my
　　　　mother's womb;
　　my praise rises unceasingly to you.*ᶻ

⁷ I have become a portent to many,*
　　but you are my sure refuge.
⁸ My mouth is filled with your praises
　　as I relate your glory all day long.

⁹ Do not cast me off in my old age;
　　do not forsake me when my strength is
　　　　completely spent.
¹⁰ For my enemies speak against me,
　　and those who seek my life plot together.ᵃ
¹¹ They say: "God has abandoned him;
　　go after him and seize him,
　　for no one will come to his rescue."

¹² O God, do not remain aloof from me;
　　come quickly to help me, O my God.ᵇ
¹³ Let those who accuse me
　　be put to shame and perish;
　　let those who are determined to harm me
　　incur contempt and disgrace.*ᶜ

¹⁴ But I will hope in you continually
　　and will render even more praise to you.
¹⁵ My lips will proclaim your righteous deeds*
　　and your salvation all day long,ᵈ
　　though I do not know their extent.*

---

z Ps 22:11; Jer 17:14.—a Pss 3:2; 10:8; 22:8.—b Pss 22:20; 38:23.—c
Pss 25:3; 35:4; 40:15; 70:3.—d Pss 35:28; 109:30.

71:6 *My praise . . . to you:* an alternative translation is: "my hope has always
been in you."
71:7 *I have become a portent to many:* more by his trials (see Ps 31:12; Deut
28:46; Isa 52:14) than by the benefits received from God, for people are surprised
to see a righteous person suffering.
71:13 A prayer for the divine justice to be done (see note on Ps 5:11 and introduction to Ps 35).
71:15-18 A vow to offer praise to God for his help (see note on Ps 7:18).
71:15 The psalmist does not know the full extent of God's goodness toward
him. For God's acts of "salvation," consisting of his "mighty deeds" (v. 16) and
"marvelous works" (v. 17), are too numerous to count (see Pss 40:6; 139:17f).

¹⁶ I will speak of your mighty deeds, O Lord
GOD,
and declare your righteousness, yours alone.

¹⁷ O God, you have taught me from my youth,
and to this day I proclaim your marvelous
works.*
¹⁸ Now that I am old and my hair is gray,*
do not abandon me, O God,*e*
until I have extolled your might
to all the generations yet to come,*f*
your strength ¹⁹ and your righteousness, O God,
to the highest heavens.

You have done great things;*g*
O God, who is there who is like you?*h*
²⁰ You have shown me many afflictions and
hardships,
but you will once again revive me.
From the depths of the earth*
you will once again raise me up.
²¹ You will restore my honor
and console me once again.

²² Then I will also praise* you with the harp
for your faithfulness, O my God.
I will sing praises to you with the lyre,
O Holy One of Israel.

---

e 1 Sam 12:2; Isa 46:4.—f Pss 22:31-32; 48:14-15; 145:4; Ex 9:16; Job
8:8.—g Pss 36:5; 72:18; Lk 1:49.—h Pss 35:10; 86:8.

71:16-17 *Mighty deeds . . . righteousness . . . marvelous works:* God's "mighty
deeds" on behalf of his people flow from his "righteousness"—and show forth
that righteousness (see also v. 24). See also note on Ps 9:2.

71:17-18 *Youth . . . old and gray:* this passage can be applied without difficulty to Israel to whom the Prophets apply images of youth (see Jer 2:2; Hos 2:15)
and old age (see Isa 46:4; Hos 7:9); see also Ps 129:1f. *Might:* literally, "arm," a
prophetic image (see Isa 51:9; 53:1), used often with respect to the miracles of
the Exodus. This passage (see Pss 22:31f; 78:5f; 102:19) shows how conscious
the psalmists were of being bearers of tradition.

71:20 *From the depths of the earth:* the realm of the dead, which is entered by
the grave (see note on Ps 30:2).

71:22 *I will praise:* a vow to praise God for his help (see note on Ps 7:18). *Holy
One of Israel:* a frequent expression of the Book of Isaiah but used infrequently in
the Psalter (see Pss 78:41; 89:19).

²³ When I sing to you, my lips will rejoice,
       and so will my soul, which you have re-
       deemed.
²⁴ All day long my tongue
       will relate your righteousness.
   For those who intended to do me harm
       will suffer shame and disgrace.

PSALM 72*

The Kingdom of the Messiah

¹ Of Solomon.

O God, endow the king with your judgment,
    the son of kings with your righteousness.*ⁱ*
² He will govern your people fairly*
    and deal justly with your poor ones.*ʲ*

³ The mountains will yield peace for the people,
    and the hills, righteousness.*ᵏ*
⁴ He will defend the afflicted among the people,
    save the children of the poor,
    and overwhelm the oppressor.

---

i Pss 9:9; 99:4; Jer 23:5.—j Prov 31:8-9; Isa 9:6.—k Isa 45:8; 52:7; 55:12.

Ps 72 Only the expected Savior will fulfill all the hopes placed on the ideal leader described in this psalm, of whom the Prophets also speak (see Isa 9:7; 11:1-9; Jer 23:5f; 33:15f; Zec 9:9-17). The portrait bears more than one facet of King Solomon the Sage, but it is Messianic, i.e., it sketches a mysterious King who is to come. Promised a reign without end (v. 5), he will rescue the needy and poor from oppression and uphold their rights (vv. 12-14). He will establish definitive peace (v. 7), and the pagan nations that he subdues—even the most distant—will come to do homage to him (vv. 10-11). Finally, he will rule over the idealized promised land (v. 8) and transform it into a new heavenly paradise (vv. 6, 16).

Since Israel has never yielded to the temptation to make gods out of its kings, this king, too, is not divinized; the psalmist prays for him. This psalm is like a chart or mirror for a true reign in the name of God. It will be marked by the work of justice and peace, the effort for the deliverance of the poor and needy.

In proclaiming the beatitudes, Jesus was to provide the authentic content of this perfect happiness that is promised for the reign of the Messiah. In the adoration of the Magi, Matthew (2:11) sees a visit from pagan kings who prostrate themselves at the feet of the promised Savior (vv. 10-11); hence, this psalm is read in the Liturgy during the Epiphany time.

72:2-3 Righteousness will rain down God's blessings on the people (see Pss 5:13; 65:10-14; 133:3; Lev 25:19; Deut 28:8).

5 He will reign as long as the sun,
      as long as the moon, through all genera-
         tions.[l]
6 He will descend like rain on the meadow,
      like showers that water the earth.[m]
7 Justice will reign in his days,
      and peace will abound
      until the moon is no more.

8 His rule will extend from sea to sea,*
      and from the River to the ends of the earth.[n]
9 His foes will bow down before him,
      and his enemies will lick the dust.*[o]

10 The kings of Tarshish and the Islands
      will offer him tribute;
    the kings of Sheba and Seba
      will present him with gifts.*[p]
11 All kings will pay him homage,
      and all nations will serve him.[q]

12 For he will save the poor who cry out
      and the needy who have no one to help them.
13 He will have pity on the lowly and the poor;
      the lives of the needy he will save.[r]
14 He will free them from oppression and vio-
         lence,
      for their blood is precious in his sight.

15 Long may he live!*
      May the gold of Sheba be given to him.

---

l Pss 61:8; 89:37-38; Jer 31:35.—m Deut 32:2; Isa 45:8; Hos 6:3.—n Ex
23:31; Deut 11:24; Zec 9:10.—o Isa 49:23; Mic 7:17.—p Ps 68:30; 1 Ki
10:1ff; Est 10:1; Isa 60:5-6.—q Ps 47:8; Ezr 1:2.—r Prov 31:9; Lk 10:33.

72:8 *From sea to sea:* the Red Sea and the Mediterranean. The *River* is the Euphrates. Both details indicate the universality of the Messianic reign. *Ends of the
earth:* an alternative translation is: "end of the land."
    72:9 *His foes:* literally, "the Beast," a word referring to the tribes of the Ara-
bian Desert, east of the promised land. *Lick the dust:* a sign of abject fear and
defeat (see Mic 7:17).
    72:10 All kings, whether near or far, will acknowledge the Messiah's rule.
Tarshish: a seaport located in southern Spain, hence to the far west; *Sheba:* a
city of southwest Arabia, hence to the far south; *Seba:* probably a region in modern Sudan, south of Egypt (see Gen 10:7; Isa 43:3). This verse is applied by Matthew to the visit of the Magi at Christ's birth (see Mt 2:11).

May people pray for him unceasingly
and invoke blessings* on him all day long.

16 May grain abound throughout the land,
even growing abundantly on the mountain-
tops.
May its crops be as plenteous as those of
Lebanon,ˢ
and may its people flourish like the grass
of the field.*

17 May his name* be blessed forever;
may it endure as long as the sun.ᵗ
May all peoples be blessed in him;
may all the nations proclaim his greatness.ᵘ

18 Blessed be the LORD, the God of Israel,*
who alone can perform such wondrous
deeds.ᵛ
19 May his glorious name be blessed forever,
and may the whole world be filled with his
glory.
Amen. Amen.ʷ

20 The end of the psalms of David, son of Jesse.*

---

s Ps 4:8; Isa 27:6; Hos 14:6-8; Am 9:13.—t Ps 89:37.—u Gen 12:3; Zec
8:13.—v Pss 41:14; 89:53; 106:48; 150.—w Ps 57:6; Num 14:21; Hab 3:3.

72:15-17 The psalmist prays that the Messiah-King may enjoy a long and prosperous reign acknowledged by the whole world and a blessing for all the nations.
72:15 *May people pray . . . and invoke blessings:* an obscure passage. As it is
translated, it means: may the people pray for the Messiah that he will benefit the
poor with the treasures he has received, and may they bless and thank him. But Israel could also pray to ask God for a perfect Messiah and so offer vows for the extension of the Messianic kingdom (see Ps 61:8f). Hence, one could also translate:
"He [the Messiah] will pray [intercede] for him [the poor] / and bless him" (see 1 Ki
8:14, 28).
72:16 Fertility of the land was one of the blessings of the Messianic age (see
Hos 14:6f; Am 9:13). *May its crops . . . Lebanon:* may its crops possess the same
vital power that the majestic cedars of Lebanon display.
72:17 *Name:* see note on Ps 5:12. *All peoples:* an echo of the promise to the
patriarchs (see Gen 12:3; 18:18; 22:18; 26:4; 28:14).
72:18-19 This doxology is not part of the psalm; it concludes the second of the
five books of the Psalter (see Pss 41:14; 89:53; 106:48; 150). Praise of the Lord is
the most profound religious attitude and ends every authentic prayer.
72:20 Colophon added by a redactor.

BOOK III—PSALMS 73–89*

PSALM 73*

False Happiness of the Wicked

¹ A psalm of Asaph.

God is truly good to the upright,*
    to those who are pure in heart.

² * But as for me, I nearly lost my balance;*
    I was almost at the point of stumbling.
³ For I was filled with envy of the arrogant
    when I perceived how the wicked prosper.ˣ

---

x Ps 37:1; Job 9:24; 21:13; Prov 3:31; Jer 12:1; Mal 3:15.

Pss 73—89 This third book of the Psalter combines the collections of psalms of Asaph (probably a choral leader in the Jerusalem temple; see 1 Chr 25:2-6; 2 Chr 29:30) with the end of the Psalter of the Sons of Korah, which began in the second book (Pss 42—49). The prayers are varied in accord with the experience of believers; we pass from the lament of the innocent to the exultation after victory. We read, by turns, canticles of Zion, chants of joy and hope, and historical retrospectives that often take the tone of great national lamentations. Each prayer expresses in a new way the longing for God and his salvation.

Ps 73 The psalmist is taken back by the prosperity of the wicked and the sufferings of the righteous (see Job; Eccl 7:15; Jer 12:1; Mal 3:15). Those who make sport of God seem to succeed in life much more then believers, and their example becomes a scandal for the righteous and the wise: what is the good of remaining faithful? Still he knows that no one should deny God. Tempted by doubt, the faithful psalmist reflects and seeks light in God's presence; in such a meditation, his faith deepens and a conviction imposes itself on him with new force: human glory has no tomorrow, but the friendship of God remains forever precious; it cannot end or deceive. The psalmist-sage who expresses himself here begins to suspect that the joy of being with the Lord could become eternal happiness (v. 24).

In times of trouble, at moments when people grow weary of being faithful, this psalm brings the grace of refreshment to the interior life.

73:1a *Asaph:* see introduction to Pss 73—89.

73:1b *The upright:* literally, *"Israel,"* i.e., the group of the "poor" (see v. 15; Pss 72:2ff; 149:4; 1 Mac 1:53; Isa 49:3, 13). *Pure in heart:* see note on Ps 24:4. *Heart:* see note on Ps 4:8.

73:2-3 Like many of the godly, the psalmist envied the prosperity of the wicked and their arrogance. Everything seemed to go well for them. They experienced "prosperity," i.e., well-being, full family life, and success in business. Hence, the psalmist was miserable, filled with self-pity and discontent with God's justice. But, although he almost lost his foothold on the "way" of the Lord, he righted himself with the help of the Lord, who sustains his saints (see Ps 37:23ff).

73:2 *I nearly lost my balance:* see note on Ps 37:30-31.

⁴ They endure no painful suffering;*
  their bodies are healthy and well fed.
⁵ They are not plagued with burdens common
    to all;
  the troubles of life do not afflict them.

⁶ So they wear arrogance like a necklace
  and don violence like a robe.
⁷ Their callous hearts overflow with malice,
  and their minds are completely taken up
    with evil plans.ʸ

⁸ They mock and pour forth their malevolence;
  in their haughtiness they threaten oppres-
    sion.ᶻ
⁹ Their mouths rage against the heavens
  while their tongues are never stilled on the
    earth.

¹⁰ So the people blindly follow them*
  and find nothing offensive in their words.*
¹¹ They say: "How does God know?
  Does the Most High notice anything?"ᵃ
¹² Such are the wicked,
  as they pile up wealth, without any concerns.

¹³ Is it in vain that I have kept my heart clean*
  and washed my hands in innocence?ᵇ

---

y Ps 17:10; Job 15:27.—z Pss 17:10; 41:6; Ezek 25:15; Col 3:8.—a Pss 10:11; 64:6; Job 22:13.—b Ps 26:6; Job 9:29-31; 21:14f; Mal 3:14.

73:4-12 The psalmist describes the reasons that led the godly to envy the wicked. Evildoers seem to be carefree and unconcerned for the future. They have wealth and power and enjoy freedom of movement and speech. They appear untouched by life's frustrations: frailty, adversities, diseases, and hard labor. They disregard God and his laws with apparent impunity. They decree what can be done on earth and even what God can do in heaven. In short, it seems that God lets the wicked get away with their wickedness. *Hearts:* see note on Ps 4:8.
73:10-12 From the mistaken viewpoint of an afflicted person, the wicked enjoy power, glory, and prosperity without end.
73:10 The meaning of the Hebrew for this verse is unclear. Another translation is: "So the people turn to them / and find no fault in them."
73:13-14 The psalmist begins to have doubts about his effort to keep himself holy (see Pss 24:4; 119:9). He questions himself about the troubles and sufferings that he experiences while the wicked seem to have no such problems.

14 For I am stricken day after day
    and punished every morning.

15 If I had decided, "I will speak like them,"
    I would not have been true to your chil-
        dren.*
16 When I tried to understand all this,*
    I found it too difficult for me,
17 until I entered the sanctuary of God*
    and realized what their final end would be.

18 Indeed, you set them on a slippery slope*
    and cast them headlong into utter ruin.
19 How suddenly they are destroyed,c
    completely wiped out by terrors!
20 When you arise, O LORD,
    you will dismiss them
    as one discards a dream on awakening.

21 When my heart was embittered*
    and my soul was deeply tormented,
22 I was stupid and unable to comprehend—
    like a brute beast in your presence.

---

c 19-20: Pss 49:14; 78:65; Job 20:8; Isa 29:8; 47:11.

73:15 If he had expressed in public what he had been thinking, the psalmist would have denied the ancestral traditions and beliefs (see note on Ps 139:19-24) and betrayed the "poor." For the Lord is a father to Israel (Ex 4:22; Isa 63:16; Hos 11:1).

73:16-17 Understanding did not come to the psalmist until he entered into the "sanctuary of God." There he regained his perspective in the light of God's greatness, glory, and majesty. He realized once again that the Lord is just and will judge the wicked in accord with their evil deeds.

73:17 *Sanctuary of God:* literally, "the divine sanctuaries." Rather than the temple (see Jer 51:51) where he would have been enlightened by God, or the divine mysteries (see Wis 2:22) in which he would have received revelation, this expression indicates the teaching contained in the Scriptures, the abode of wisdom (see Ps 119:130; Prov 9:1ff; Sir 39:1).

73:18-20 In reality, God makes the state of the wicked so precarious that they will not be stable but will vanish like the figures of a dream. The assurance of Scripture is that the wicked will incur sudden and complete judgment. They will be assailed by all kinds of terrors and death itself.

73:21-22 The psalmist stresses his former embittered state once again. In his grief he was irrational (see Ps 94:8) and not ruled by wisdom; he was like the fools who are compared to brute beasts (see Ps 49:13, 21; Isa 1:2f). He was assailed by doubt and mired in self-pity—but God used this experience to make him a better person and bring him closer to himself. *Heart:* see note on Ps 4:8.

²³ Yet I am always with you;*
    you grasp me by the right hand.*d*
²⁴ You guide me with your counsel,
    and afterward you will receive me into
    glory.*

²⁵ Whom do I have in heaven except you?
    And besides you there is nothing else I de-
    sire on earth.
²⁶ Even should my heart and my flesh* fail,
    God is the rock of my heart
    and my portion forever.

²⁷ But all those who are far from you will perish;*
    you destroy those who are unfaithful to you.
²⁸ As for me, my happiness is to be near God,
    and I have made the Lord GOD my refuge;
    I will proclaim all your works*
    at the gates of the Daughter of Zion.

---

d Pss 63:8; 121:5; Gen 48:13.

73:23-26 The psalmist's experience of anguish is transformed into the joy of God's presence and his greatness. God protects him by holding his "right hand" (v. 23; see Ps 63:8; Isa 41:10, 13; 42:6; Jer 31:32), by strengthening his resolve ("rock," v. 26; see Ps 18:3), and by taking care of all his needs ("portion," v. 26; see Ps 16:5). God gives his servant wisdom and insight ("counsel") as he journeys toward everlasting glory (v. 24; see Ps 32:8).

73:24 *Receive me into glory:* is it a question here of heavenly glory? The text does not make clear. It states that God will preserve the righteous from a brutal and premature death and rehabilitate them (see Job 19:9; 29:18; 42:7), while he despises the wicked who will suddenly disappear (vv. 18f). Nothing obliges us to give the verb "receive" a stronger meaning than in Pss 18:17 ("snatched me up") and 49:17 ("take"—see also note there) based on the assumption into heaven of Enoch (Gen 5:24; Sir 44:16) and Elijah (2 Ki 2:3; Sir 48:9). However, as in Ps 16:9f, the psalmist's fervor and the demands of his love for God lead him to long never to be separated from him; it constitutes a stage in the explicit belief in the resurrection, attested in Dan 12:2.

73:26 *My heart and my flesh:* the whole being (see Ps 84:3). *Heart:* see note on Ps 4:8. *Portion:* as a Levite, the psalmist has the Lord for his portion (or inheritance) of the promised land, i.e., he lives off the tithes that the people present to the Lord (see Num 18:21-24; Deut 10:9; 18:1-8).

73:27-28 The psalmist now understands that all who are unfaithful to God must perish. Their judgment is a consequence not only of their failure to profess faith in God but also of their immoral and unjust practices.

73:28 *I will proclaim all your works:* the psalmist expresses the vow to praise the Lord's mercies (see note on Ps 7:18). *At the gates of the Daughter of Zion:* this phrase is added to the final line of the Septuagint. It is taken from Ps 9:15, which may be a liturgical adaptation.

PSALM 74*

Prayer in Time of Calamity

1 A *maskil** of Asaph.

Why, O God, have you cast us off forever?*e*
    Why* does your anger blaze forth
    against the sheep of your pasture?*f*
2 Remember the people that you purchased
        long ago,
        the tribe that you redeemed as your own
            possession,
        and Mount Zion that you chose as your
            dwelling.**g*

3 Direct now your steps to the endless ruins,
        toward the sanctuary destroyed by the
            enemy.*

---

e Pss 10:1; 43:2; 44:27; 77:8.—f Pss 79:13; 80:5; 95:7.—g Pss 68:17;
132:13; Ex 15:16; Deut 7:6; Isa 63:17; Jer 10:16; 51:19.

Ps 74 This lamentation expresses the soul of a stricken people who feel abandoned even by God. The deportees who have returned from the Exile (538-529
B.C.) or else the Jews persecuted by Antiochus IV Epiphanes (167-164 B.C.)
mourn over their sanctuary, which the pagans have profaned (see 2 Ki 25:9-12;
Isa 64:10 for the former and 1 Mac 4:38; 2 Mac 1:8 for the latter). Has the Lord
forgotten the Covenant and the wonders he once accomplished to free his people
(vv. 13-14), to sustain them in the journey through the wilderness, and to open
the promised land for them (v. 15)?

Rightly, the past prevents the psalmist from despairing and enables him to
believe in a better future. Israel has now lost all pretense of power; it is the community of the poor (vv. 19-21), conscious of its weakness; it is like the timid dove
that God cannot abandon to the ferocity of the beasts (v. 19).

Prolonging Christ's presence and even identifying mysteriously with him, the
Church is now God's people on earth (see 1 Pet 2:9f). She is also the earthly visible temple of God, his city and the spiritual capital of the world (see 1 Cor 3:16; 1
Pet 2:4-6). Hence, her members can pray this psalm in trials when Christ seems
to have delivered them over to persecution without end.

74:1a *Maskil:* see note on Ps 32:1a. *Asaph:* see introduction to Pss 73—89.

74:1b *Why . . .? Why . . .?:* see note on Ps 6:4. *Forever:* figuratively speaking; it
seemed like forever. *Flock of your pasture:* see introduction to Ps 23.

74:2 In this time of great calamity, the psalmist begs God to recall his exploits
at the Exodus, the Conquest, and the establishment of the temple. *You redeemed
as your own possession:* see Deut 9:29.

74:3 The psalmist begs the Lord to hasten ("direct . . . steps") to restore the
sanctuary that the pagans have destroyed.

⁴ Your foes exulted triumphantly in the place
    of your assembly
    and set up their memorial emblems.

⁵ They set upon it with their axes
    as if it were a thicket of trees.
⁶ And then, with hatchets and hammers,
    they bludgeoned all the carved work.

⁷ They set your sanctuary ablaze;
    they razed and defiled the dwelling place
    of your name.*ʰ
⁸ They said to themselves, "We will utterly
    crush them,"
    and they burned every shrine of God* in
    the land.

⁹ Now we see no signs,
    there are no longer any prophets,
    and none of us knows how long this will last.*ⁱ

¹⁰ How long, O God, will the foe mock you?
    Will the enemy blaspheme your name for-
    ever?*ʲ
¹¹ Why do you hold back your right hand?
    Take it out from your robe and destroy
    them.*

¹² Yet you, O God, are my King from of old,
    working deeds of salvation throughout the
    earth.

---

h Ps 79:1; Lev 20:3; Isa 64:10; Acts 21:28.—i Ps 77:9; Ex 4:17; Lam 2:9;
Ezek 7:26.—j Pss 6:4; 80:4; 89:47.

74:7, 10 *Name:* see note on Ps 5:12.
    74:8 *Every sacred shrine of God in the land:* i.e., shrines, whether legitimate or
not (see 1 Ki 3:2; 2 Ki 18:4).
    74:9 The people were used to asking the Prophets how long a divine punish-
ment would last (see 2 Sam 24:13). In this case, they have had no miraculous
signs of any kind, and the voice of the Prophets is absent as it has been for some
time (see Ps 77:9; 1 Mac 4:46; 9:27; 14:41; Lam 2:9; Ezek 7:26).
    74:10 Jeremiah had announced that there would be 70 years of exile (see Jer
25:11; 29:10), a round figure symbolizing a very long time (see Pss 6:4; 89:47).
    74:11 To do battle, the warrior bared his arm from his garment (see Isa
52:10).

13 By your power you split the sea in two*[k]
      and shattered the heads of the dragons in
         the waters.[l]

14 You crushed the heads of Leviathan[m]
      and gave him as food for the wild beasts.
15 You opened up springs and torrents
      and turned flowing rivers into dry land.*

16 Yours is the day, and yours also is the night,[n]
      for you set in place both sun and moon.
17 You fixed all the boundaries of the earth
      and created both summer and winter.

18 Remember, O LORD, how the enemy has
         mocked you,*
      how a foolish people has blasphemed your
         name.
19 Do not surrender the soul of your dove* to
         wild beasts;
      do not forget forever the life of your poor.

20 Have regard for your covenant!
      For the land is filled with darkness,
      and the pastures are haunts of violence.
21 Do not let the oppressed turn back in shame;
      let the poor and needy* bless your name.

---

k Ps 89:10; Ex 14:21.—l Isa 27:1; 51:9-10; Ezek 29:3.—m Job 3:8; 41:1;
Isa 27:1; Jer 50:39.—n 16-17: Ps 136:7-9; Gen 1:16.

74:13-14 Allusion to the crossing of the Red Sea (see Ex 14:30) and the defeat
of the Egyptians (see Isa 27:1; Ezek 29:3; 32:4). *Leviathan:* a mythological multi-
headed monster of chaos; here it seems to stand especially for Egypt (for Egypt's
crocodiles, see Job 40:25f).

74:15 Allusion to the miracles of the Exodus (see Ex 17:6; Num 20:11) and the
crossing of the Jordan (see Jos 3:15f) where God's creative power is exercised
(see Ps 89:11).

74:18-21 The godly beg God to "remember" (see v. 2) the evil conduct of their
oppressors (v. 19) who blaspheme his name and afflict his people. The Lord's name
is sacred to them for it ensures that he will fulfill his Covenant promises (see Ex 6:6-
8). They ask him to come to their aid so that they will have reason to bless his name.

74:19 *Your dove:* a term of endearment for "Israel" (see Ps 68:14; Song 2:14;
5:2; 6:9; Hos 7:11; 11:11).

74:21 *Poor and needy:* see note on Ps 34:7. *Name:* see note on Ps 5:21.

²² Rise up, O God, and defend your cause;
  remember how fools mock you all day long.
²³ Do not ignore the outbursts of your enemies,
  the unceasing tumult of your foes.

PSALM 75*

God Is Judge of the World

¹ For the director.* According to "Do not destroy!" A
psalm of Asaph. A song.

² We give thanks* to you, O God,
  we give thanks to you.
 For your wondrous deeds
  declare that your name is near.

³ You say, "When I receive the assembly;*
  I will judge with equity.
⁴ When the earth quakes, with all its inhabitants,ᵒ
  it is I who will hold its pillars firm.*   *Selah*

---

o Pss 46:3f; 60:4; 93:1; 96:10; 104:5; 1 Sam 2:8; 2 Sam 22:8; Isa 24:19.

Ps 75 This psalm has parallels to the Song of Hannah (see 1 Sam 2:1-10).
Freed from the Exile but always dependent on and pestered by those who had
taken their place in the land, the People of God give thanks to the Lord. They
know that in the end God will make right triumph on earth; the righteous will obtain glory and the wicked will receive the chastisement they deserve. These oracles proclaim once again the reversal worked by true justice: the proud will be
abased, and the humble will be lifted up.
  We can pray this psalm with the same sentiments of the psalmist and apply
the role of Judge to the risen Christ, to whom the Father has given it. We can proclaim the wondrous deeds of our Savior, who will come to save the righteous and
punish the wicked on the last day.
  75:1 *For the director:* thought to be a musical or liturgical notation. *According
to "Do not destroy":* see note on Ps 57:1. *Asaph:* see introduction to Pss 73—89.
  75:2 *Give thanks:* this is given in the form of praise (see Pss 7:18; 28:7; 30:13;
35:18). *Wondrous deeds:* see note on Ps 9:2. *Name:* see note on Ps 5:12.
  75:3-6 This is a reassuring word from God, possibly through prophetic words
already uttered by the Prophets (e.g., Isaiah in 2 Ki 19:21-34). *When I receive the
assembly:* another possible translation is: "I choose the appointed time."
  75:4 God is the Master of the moral order as well as the physical universe, and
he keeps them stable (see Pss 93:1f; 96:10; 1 Sam 2:8) or makes them quake
(see Ps 18:8; Job 26:11); no cataclysm escapes his will (see Pss 46:3f; 60:4), and
he alone establishes the hour of the judgment (see Hab 2:3).

⁵ "I say to the arrogant, 'Do not boast,'*
   and to the wicked, 'Do not lift up your
      horns.'*ᵖ
⁶ Do not rebel against heaven
   or speak with arrogance against the Rock.' "*q

⁷ For judgment does not come from east or west,*
   nor from the wilderness or the mountains.*ʳ
⁸ Rather, it is God who judges rightly,ˢ
   humbling one and exalting another.*

⁹ The LORD holds in his hand a cup
   filled with foaming wine and richly spiced.
   When he pours it out,
      all the wicked of the earth must drink;ᵗ
      they will drain it down to the dregs.*

---

p Ps 5:6; 1 Sam 2:3; Zec 1:21.—q Ps 94:4; Job 15:25.—r Mt 24:23-27.—s
Job 5:11; 1 Sam 2:7; Dan 2:21.—t Ps 60:5; Job 21:20; Prov 23:30; Isa
51:17, 21-22; Jer 25:15ff; Hab 2:16.

75:5-6 This passage recalls Ps 94:4; 1 Sam 2:3; Job 15:25f. The wicked are
fools (see Pss 14:1; 94:7). The horn is the symbol of arrogant and aggressive
force (see Pss 89:18; 92:11; Deut 33:17; 1 Ki 22:11); it will be broken (see Jer
48:25; Zec 1:19).
75:5 The Lord speaks to those who incite chaos and immorality: "the arrogant"
and "the wicked" who live without God and his laws (see Pss 52:3; 73:3ff).
75:6 The wicked even dare to place themselves in direct opposition to God by
"rebelling," i.e., raising their horns "against heaven" and speaking "with arrogance," i.e., with outstretched neck—a common gesture of opposition.
75:7-8 Concerning these first two verses of the response from earth (vv. 7-8),
possibly by a Levite, see 1 Sam 2:7; Dan 2:21. The oracles against the nations en-
visaged such a power, in the north (see Zep 2:13), in the south (see Isa
30:6), or in the wilderness (Isa 21:1); other oracles were directed against the
mountains of Israel (see Ezek 6:2; 36:1), or the forests of the south (see Ezek 21:2f).
Here the wilderness represents the south, and the mountains (Lebanon) stand for
the north (see note on v. 7, below). As in Zec 1:16, the accent is placed on the universality of the divine judgment (see v. 9) on the Day of the Lord (see Mt 24:23ff).
75:7 *For judgment does not come . . . the mountains:* another possible translation is: "No one from the east or the west / or from the wilderness can exalt a man."
In other words, search where we may, there is no other arbiter but God; therefore,
no earthly honor is anything but provisional. Furthermore, no one can escape God's
judgment (see Ps 139); God will bring down anyone who exalts himself.
75:8 Indeed, judgment belongs to God alone, for he is sovereign in judgment
and in redemption.
75:9 All the wicked will be vanquished by God. The image of the cup full of
foaming and dizzying wine is taken from the Prophets (see Isa 51:17; Jer 25:15;
49:12; Lam 4:21; Ezek 23:31; Hab 2:15); it has already appeared in Ps 60:5 (see
Job 21:20) and will reappear in Rev 14:10. See also note on Ps 16:5.

¹⁰ As for me, I will proclaim this forever;
>   I will sing praises to the God of Jacob.*
¹¹ "I will cut off all the horns of the wicked,
>   but the horns of the righteous will be exalted."*^u

PSALM 76*

God, Defender of Zion

¹ For the director.* With stringed instruments. A psalm of Asaph. A song.

² God is renowned in Judah;*
>   his name is great in Israel.^v
³ His tent has been established in Salem,
>   his dwelling place in Zion.

---

u Pss 89:18; 92:11; 112:9; 148:14.—v Ps 99:3; Hab 3:2.

75:10 It is unclear who is speaking in this verse. It may be the Levite in his own name or as a representative of his people. *Sing praises:* see note on Ps 7:18. *Jacob:* i.e., Israel (see Gen 32:28).

75:11 This verse appears to be another word from the Lord to go with vv. 2-5, above. He indicates that even if godlessness now triumphs and justice is subverted, at the end of time the Messiah will come to judge the nations in fulfillment of the promise about the victory of the righteous.

Ps 76 In 701 B.C., the mighty army of Sennacherib had camped beneath the walls of Jerusalem. One night the attacker suddenly lifted the siege. What mysterious terror did the Lord employ to put to rout the forces of that haughty ruler? It is the victory of God at Jerusalem; and in the holy city, God reveals himself through his triumphs (see 2 Ki 19:35). The memory of this event remained engraved in the minds of the people (see 2 Mac 8:19; Sir 48:21) and became the symbol for the salvation awaited by the poor, the remnant of God.

Like Ps 46, this hymn to the glory of Zion is doubtless inspired by that event; it restores the courage and hope of the exiles returning from Babylon after 538 B.C. The fearsome God prostrates the powerful of the world and saves the lowly. This confidence of the poor will continuously rise from the heart of humankind in protest against haughty dominators as an announcement of the judgment of God.

It is by the glorious Christ that God the Father dwells in and protects his new People, the Church. With this psalm, we can rightly celebrate our Savior, who is terrible for his enemies: the devil, sin, and death.

76:1 *For the director:* these words are thought to be a musical or liturgical notation. *Asaph:* see introduction to Pss 73—89.

76:2-3 The Lord has chosen "Salem" (ancient name for Jerusalem; see Gen 14:18; Heb 7:1-3) as his royal city so that both the southern kingdom ("Judah") and the northern kingdom ("Israel") may gain reassurance that God is in their midst (see Ps 46).

4 There he shattered the flashing arrows,
    shields and swords and weapons of war.ʷ
                        Selah

5 You are awesome and resplendent,*
    more majestic than the everlasting moun-
    tains.
6 The bold warriors lie plundered
    and sleeping their last sleep.*
And not one of the men of war
    can lift up his hands.ˣ
7 At your rebuke, O God of Jacob,
    both chariots and horses lie prostrate.

8 You indeed are awesome;
    who can stand in your presence when your
    anger is aroused?ʸ
9 You thundered your verdicts from the heav-
    ens;
    the earth in its terror was silent
10 when you arose, O God, to judge,
    to rescue all the afflicted of the land.*
                        Selah
11 Human wrath only serves to praise you;*
    those who survive your anger will cling to
    you.

---

w Pss 46:10; 48:4-8; 122:6-9; Ezek 39:9.—x Ps 13:4; Jdg 20:44; 2 Ki 19:35; Jer 51:39; Nah 3:18; Mt 9:24.—y Deut 7:21; 1 Sam 6:20; 1 Chr 16:25; Nah 1:6; Mal 3:2; Rev 6:17.

76:5-11 Praise of God's mighty deed against the Assyrians and his judgment of evildoers.

76:6 *Last sleep:* allusion to the night of which 2 Ki 19:35 speaks (see Ps 13:5; Jer 51:39, 57; Nah 3:18).

76:10 *Rescue all the afflicted of the land:* the psalmist widens his perspectives to include not only the inhabitants of Zion but also all the lowly who will be saved by God's defeat of the rulers and war leaders.

76:11 Everyone must give honor to the Most High—even those who rebel against the Lord and his kingdom must proclaim his honor and glory. When wrath leads men to do evil, it also leads to God's praise when he defeats them. The same theme is found in an alternative translation: "your wrath against men brings you praise"; in his wrath he brings down the wicked and obtains praise from those he has thus rescued. Furthermore, God's wrath against evil is never exhausted. This should gain him the praise and fear of all peoples.

¹² Make vows to the LORD, your God, and keep
    them;*
    let all the lands nearby
    bring gifts to the Awesome One,ᶻ
¹³ who breaks the spirit of rulers
    and inspires fear in the kings of the earth.

PSALM 77*

Lament and Consolation in Distress

¹ For the director.* For Jeduthun. A psalm of Asaph.

² I cry aloud to God,*
    for when I cry out to God, he hears me.*
³ In the time of my distress I seek the LORD;
    at night I stretch out my hands unceasingly,
    and my soul refuses to be consoled.ᵃ

---

z Ps 50:14; Num 30:3; Eccl 5:4-5.—a Pss 50:15; 88:2; Isa 26:16; Mt 2:18.

76:12-13 All people must respond wisely to the Lord. His Covenant people must keep their vows to him. The Gentiles must offer homage to this "Awesome One" who rules over everyone including kings.

Ps 77 During a difficult period that the people of Israel are experiencing after the return from exile, more than one fervent Israelite can think that God has abandoned his own. But the Lord does not act after the fashion of human beings: has he not from Egypt to Canaan by means of the wonders of the Exodus (vv. 14-20) transformed a motley group of slaves into a people of his own?

The striking evocation of the passage through the Red Sea and the coming of God at Sinai enables the psalmist to rediscover the great certitude that God still guides his people. Such a certitude is present even when one must realize that God's ways are mysterious. Hope is reborn, purified by adversity and more unshakable than ever.

This psalm is a reminder of the Father's faithfulness toward Christ and calls us to remain faithful in times of distress and spiritual dryness. "Let us remain firm in the confession of our hope without wavering, for the one who made the promise is trustworthy" (Heb 10:23). We must imitate the ancients and, even more, Christ by remaining faithful even in the darkest of times, for "we are not among those who draw back and are lost. Rather, we are among those who have faith and are saved" (Heb 10:39).

77:1 *For the director:* these words are thought to be a musical or liturgical notation. *Jeduthun:* see note on Ps 39:1. *Asaph:* see introduction to Pss 73—89.

77:2-10 To the psalmist, God seems to have deserted his people; he no longer responds to appeals for help in time of distress and intense prayer.

77:2-3 The psalmist looked to God as the the sole comforter of his distressed soul (see Gen 37:35; Jer 31:15). He cried out ceaselessly in prayer with hands outstretched—but remained uncomforted. *Soul:* see note on Ps 6:4.

⁴ I groan as I think of God;*
    my spirit grows faint as I meditate on
      him.ᵇ   *Selah*

⁵ You keep my eyes from closing in sleep;
    I am much too distraught to speak.

⁶ I reflect on the days of old
    and recall the years long past.
⁷ At night I meditate in my heart,*
    and as I reflect, my spirit questions:ᶜ

⁸ "Will the LORD cast us off forever*
    and never again show us his favor?ᵈ
⁹ Has his kindness* vanished forever?
    Has his promise ceased for all time?
¹⁰ Has God forgotten how to be merciful?
    Has he shut up his compassion in anger?"
                          Selah

¹¹ And I say: "This is my grief—*
    that the right hand of the Most High has
      changed."*ᵉ
¹² I will remember the works of the LORD;
    I will call to mind your wonders in the past.ᶠ

---

b Ps 6:3, 7; Jon 2:8.—c Ps 143:5; Deut 32:7.—d 8-10: Pss 13:2; 44:24;
74:1; 80:5; 89:47; 102:14; Lam 3:31.—e Pss 17:7; 18:36; Ex 15:6, 12.—f
Ps 143:5; Num 14:1-4; Neh 9:17.

77:4-7 Sleeplessness and dryness in prayer lead the psalmist's faith to be shaken, but he puts his mind on the origins of his people as God's people and attempts to rediscover hope (see Ps 119:52; Deut 32:7ff).
77:7 *Heart:* see note on Ps 4:8.
77:8-10 These verses follow the style of laments (see Pss 74:1; 89:47ff; Isa 63:15; Lam 3:21-24, 31ff). The prophetic word had ceased (see Ps 74:9); still God remained faithful to his promises, inscribed in the ancient writings on which the psalmist meditated endlessly (see Pss 1:2; 105:3ff) to convince himself that God had not changed in his love for his people (see Isa 49:14ff; Mal 3:6).
77:9 *Kindness:* see note on Ps 6:5.
77:11-21 The psalmist takes up the Book of History, so to speak, and meditates upon the great deeds of the Lord, the miracles he wrought in the past. He is so captivated by the reading that in meditating on the glorious deeds that the Lord did for Israel in former times he obtains peace of mind and forgets his present distress.
77:11 The psalmist remembers the years when God—by means of his right hand—provided strong guidance and protection for his people (see Pss 17:7; 18:35; Isa 41:10). And he laments the loss of this protection once accorded them by their God.

¹³ I will reflect on all your deeds
and ponder your wondrous works.*

¹⁴ O God, your way is holy.*
What god is as great as our God?*g*

¹⁵ You are the God who works wonders;
you have displayed your might to the
nations.*h*

¹⁶ With your strong arm you redeemed your
people,
the descendants of Jacob and Joseph.*i* *Selah*

¹⁷ When the waters beheld you, O God,*
when the waters beheld you, they writhed;*
the very depths trembled.*j*

¹⁸ The clouds poured forth their water,
the skies thundered,*k*
your arrows flashed back and forth.*

¹⁹ The crash of your thunder resounded in the
heavens;
your flashes of lightning lit up the world;
the earth trembled and shook.**l*

---

g Ps 18:31; Ex 15:11.—h Pss 86:10; 89:7; Ex 3:20.—i Gen 46:26-27; Ex
6:6; Neh 1:10.—j Pss 18:16; 114:3; Nah 1:4; Hab 3:10.—k Pss 18:14-15;
29:3; 144:6; Deut 32:23; Job 37:3-4; Wis 5:21; Hab 3:11; Zec 9:14.—l Pss
18:8; 97:4; 99:1; Ex 19:16; Jdg 5:4-5; 2 Sam 22:13.

77:13 The psalmist reflects on the Lord's works in their great variety—in creation, redemption, judgment, and salvation. See also note on Ps 9:2.

77:14 *Your way is holy:* see Ps 18:31; Deut 32:4. Another translation is: "your ways are seen in the sanctuary" (see Ps 63:3).

77:16 *Descendants of Jacob and Joseph:* those who emigrated to Egypt ("Jacob") and those who were born there ("Joseph") (see Ps 81:5ff; Gen 46:26f; 48:5).

77:17-20 The miracle of the crossing of the Red Sea is presented in a cosmic perspective, possibly to heighten the description of God's majesty in bringing his people from slavery to freedom, which led to the Passover. For Christians, the culminating miracle was God's deed in bringing Jesus from death to life after the crucifixion (see Mt 28:2; Eph 1:18-22), which led to the Christian Passover, Easter.

77:17 The waters are at the mercy of the Creator (see Pss 89:10; 93:3f; 104:7; 106:9; 114:3; Job 7:12; 38:10; Nah 1:4; Hab 3:10).

77:18 This verse is inspired by Hab 3:11. See also Pss 18:16; 68:9; 144:6. *Arrows:* i.e., lightning bolts.

77:19 This verse evokes the theophany at Sinai (see Ps 97:4; Ex 19:18).

²⁰ Your path led through the sea,
    your way, through the mighty waters,
        though none could trace your footsteps.*ᵐ
²¹ You led your people like a flock
    by the hand of Moses and Aaron.*ⁿ

PSALM 78*

God's Goodness in the Face of Ingratitude

¹ A *maskil* of Asaph.*

Give ear, my people, to my teaching;*
    pay attention to the words of my mouth.

---

m Ex 14:22; Neh 9:11; Job 9:8; Wis 14:3; Isa 43:16; 51:10; Hab 3:15.—n
Ps 78:52; Ex 4:16; 13:21; 15:20-21; Num 33:1; Isa 63:11-14; Hos 12:14;
Mic 6:4.

77:20 See Neh 9:11; Wis 14:3; Isa 43:16; 51:10. God's action reveals his invisible presence as Shepherd and Savior (see Ps 78:52; Isa 63:11ff; Mic 6:4).

77:21 The conclusion to the thought expressed in v. 16: God led his people through the wilderness under the care of Moses and Aaron.

Ps 78 This lengthy sermon is given us as a lesson in wisdom: if the People of God wish to understand their destiny, they must reflect on their origins and meditate on the Exodus, which is a history of divine grace and human infidelity. In effect, their ancestors never responded with anything but ingratitude to the miracles that God multiplied for them. He rolls back the sea and brings water from a rock; the people already clamor for another prodigy (vv. 12-20). Filled with the manna and the quail, the people still murmur (vv. 23-30)! Then the Lord becomes angry and metes out punishment, but he soon grants pardon to them out of pity for their human weakness (vv. 31-39). On their behalf, he had also brought about the plagues (vv. 43-51), and guided them through the wilderness and into the promised land (vv. 52-56). Still, offenses multiplied; so he also resorted anew to chastisement. But ultimately he reserved for his people the privileged holy place, Zion, and the shepherd after his own heart, David (vv. 59-72).

Thus, the psalm emphasizes the infidelity of Ephraim (the ancestor of the Samaritans), the choice of Judah, and the call of David. Its lesson is that in spite of the successive about-faces of the people, God accomplished his design.

Is this not also our history? To acknowledge God's love does not keep us from infidelities; at such times, the word of God challenges us but also brings pardon, and the Eucharist is given to sustain our steps. In Jesus, the new David and Good Shepherd, the People of God find a model and perfect guide to the new promised land, the heavenly Jerusalem, where the Father waits.

78:1a *Maskil:* see note on Ps 32:1a. *Asaph:* see introduction to Pss 73—89.

78:1b-8 Remembrance of the great deeds of the Lord should serve to strengthen the people's faith in his power and fidelity. Thus, they will not forget what the Lord has done for their ancestors, which was a blessing for their descendants, and what God has demanded from his Covenant people.

² I will open my mouth in parables⁰
   and expound the mysteries of the past.*

³ These things we have heard and know,*
   for our ancestors have related them to us.ᵖ
⁴ We will not conceal them from our children;
   we will relate them to the next generation,
   the glorious and powerful deeds of the Lᴏʀᴅ
   and the wonders he has performed. q

⁵ He instituted a decree in Jacob
   and established a law in Israel,
   which he commanded our ancestors
   to make known to their descendants,ʳ
⁶ so that they would be known to future gener-
       ations,
   to children yet to be born.

   In turn they were to tell their children,ˢ
⁷   so that they would place their trust in God,
   and never forget his works
   but keep his commandments.
⁸ Nor were they to imitate their ancestors,
   a stubborn and rebellious generation,ᵗ
   a generation whose heart* was not steadfast
   and whose spirit was unfaithful to God.ᵘ

⁹ The Ephraimites, who were skilled archers,*
   fled in terror on the day of battle.*

---

o Ps 49:5; Mt 13:35; Lk 8:10.—p Pss 44:2; 145:4.—q Ex 10:2; Deut 4:9;
Job 8:8; 15:18.—r Pss 19:8; 147:19; Deut 33:4.—s Pss 22:31-32; 48:14-15;
Deut 4:9; 6:7.—t Deut 31:27; 32:5; Isa 30:9.—u Ps 95:10; Num 14:34.

78:2 *Parable* in Hebrew means a comparison, or any saying with a deeper
meaning, which is to be understood via the hidden comparison; in this case, the
parable is the whole psalm. This passage is used by Mt 13:35 as a foreshadowing of Christ's teaching in parables (see also Ps 49:5; Ezek 17:2; 24:3).
78:3-5 Israel is the people of tradition (see Deut 4:9; 32:7; Job 8:8; 15:18; Isa
38:19; Joel 1:3); what its people hand down is above all the remembrance of the
Exodus (see Ex 10:2; 13:14) and the Covenant statutes (Deut 4:9-14; 6:20-25).
78:8 *Heart:* see note on Ps 4:8.
78:9-16 The psalmist stresses that the northern kingdom, in which Ephraim
had the lead, has been unfaithful to the Covenant (a theme of the prophets Amos
and Hosea). It constitutes the last in a series of infidelities committed by Israel.
78:9 There is no record of flight from battle on the part of Ephraimites; it may
be a metaphor for Ephraim's failure to keep the Covenant.

¹⁰ They failed to keep God's covenant
    and refused to live in accord with his law.

¹¹ They forgot the works he had done,
    the wonders he had performed for them.

¹² He worked marvels in the sight of their ances-
      tors
    in the land of Egypt, in the Plain of Zoan.*ᵛ

¹³ He divided the sea so that they could pass,ʷ
    heaping up the waters as in a mound.ˣ

¹⁴ He led them with a cloud by day,
    and with the light of a fire by night.ʸ

¹⁵ He split open rocks in the wilderness
    and gave them water to drink from limit-
      less depths.ᶻ

¹⁶ He brought forth streams from a rocky crag
    and caused water to flow down in torrents.

¹⁷ * But they still sinned* against him,
    rebelling against the Most High in the
      wilderness.ᵃ

¹⁸ They tested God's patience ᵇ
    by demanding the food they craved.*

¹⁹ They railed against God, saying:
    "Can God provide a banquet in the wilder-
      ness?ᶜ

²⁰ Certainly when he struck the rock,
    water gushed forth and the streams over-
      flowed.

---

v Ps 106:7; Neh 9:17.—w 13-14: Pss 74:15; 136:13; Ex 14—15.—x Pss 66:6; 114:3; Ex 14:21-22; 15:8.—y Pss 99:7; 105:39; Ex 13:21; Wis 18:3.— z Pss 105:41; 114:8; Ex 17:1-7; Num 20:2-13; Deut 8:15; Wis 11:4; Isa 48:21; 1 Cor 10:4.—a Deut 9:7, 22; Ezek 20:13; Heb 3:16.—b Ps 106:14; Ex 16:2-36; 1 Cor 10:9.—c Ps 23:5; Num 21:5.

78:12 *Zoan:* a city in the Nile delta, capital of Egypt at the time of the Exodus.

78:17-31 The psalmist indicates that the Israelites rebelled against the Lord in the wilderness despite all kinds of marvels that he worked on their behalf. This led to the Lord's anger against them.

78:17 *Still sinned:* the psalmist has mentioned no sin, but because of the theme of water in v. 16 he is reminded of the people's murmuring over the lack of water at Marah (see Ex 15:24).

78:18 See Ex 16:2f.

But can he also give us bread
or provide meat for his people?"*

21 When the LORD heard this, he was filled with
anger;[d]
his fire blazed forth against Jacob,
and his wrath mounted against Israel,
22 because they had no faith in God
and put no trust in his saving might.

23 Yet he issued a command to the skies above
and opened the doors of the heavens.
24 He rained down manna for them to eat,
giving them the grain of heaven.[e]
25 Mere mortals ate the bread of angels;*
he sent them an abundance of provisions.

26 He made the east wind blow in the heavens
and brought forth the south wind in force.
27 He rained down meat upon them like dust,
winged birds like the sands on the seashore.
28 He let them fall within the camp,
all around their tents.

29 They ate and were completely satisfied,
for he had given them what they desired.
30 But when they did not curb their cravings,
even while the food was in their mouths,
31 the anger of God blazed up against them;
he slew their strongest warriors
and laid low the chosen of Israel.[f]

32 Despite this, they continued to sin;*
they put no faith in his wonders.

---

d 21f: Num 11; Deut 32:22; Heb 3:19.—e Ps 105:40; Ex 16:4, 13-15; Num 11:31ff; Deut 8:3; Wis 16:20; Jn 6:31.—f Num 14:29; Isa 10:16.

78:20 See Ex 16:2f and Num 11:4.
78:25 *Bread of angels:* literally, "bread of mighty ones," which clearly refers to angels (see Ps 103:20; Wis 16:20; see also Jn 6:32, 50; 1 Cor 10:3). Ps 105:40 speaks of "the bread of heaven" (see Deut 8:3).
78:32-39 The people's infidelity to the Lord continued unabated throughout the entire sojourn in the wilderness (see Isa 26:16; 29:13; Hos 5:15; 8:1). However, the Lord tempered his punishment, for he knew they shared the inherent weakness of human beings (see Pss 65:4; 85:4; 103:13f; Ex 32:14; Num 14:20; 21:7ff; Isa 48:9; Ezek 20:22).

33 So he brought their days to an abrupt end
and cut off their years with sudden terror.*

34 When death afflicted them,
they sought him;
they searched eagerly for God.[g]
35 They remembered that God was their Rock,*
that God Most High was their Redeemer.

36 However, while they flattered him with their mouths
and lied to him with their tongues,
37 their hearts* were not right with him,
nor were they faithful to his covenant.[h]

38 Even so, he was compassionate toward them;
he forgave their guilt
and did not destroy them.
Time after time he held back his anger,
unwilling to stir up his rage.[i]
39 For he remembered that they were flesh,
like a breath of wind that does not return.

40 How often they rebelled against him in the wilderness*
and pained him in the wasteland.
41 Again and again they tested God's patience,
provoking the Holy One of Israel.*

42 They did not keep in mind his power
or the day when he delivered them from their oppressor,[j]

---

g Num 21:7; Deut 32:15, 18; Isa 26:16.—h Ps 95:10; Isa 29:13; Hos 8:1.—i Ps 85:4; Ex 32:14; Num 14:20; Isa 48:9; Ezek 20:22; Hos 11:8-9.—j Ps 106:21; Jdg 3:7.

78:33 Nonetheless, the Lord decreed that the faithless generation of the Exodus would never set foot on the promised land (see Num 14:22f, 28-35).

78:35 *Rock:* see note on Ps 18:3.

78:37 *Hearts:* see note on Ps 4:8.

78:40-55 The Israelites continued to rebel against God in the wilderness. They failed to recall how he had delivered them from Egypt by such wonders as the plagues and the passage through the Red Sea. Nonetheless, the Lord went on to lead them to the conquest and settlement of the promised land.

78:41 *Holy One of Israel:* see note on Ps 71:22.

43 when he manifested his wonders in Egypt[k]
   and his portents in the plain of Zoan.

44 He turned their rivers into blood;*
   they could not drink from their streams.
45 He sent swarms of flies that devoured them
   and frogs that devastated them.[l]

46 He assigned their harvest to the caterpillars
   and their produce to the locusts.
47 He destroyed their vines with hail
   and their sycamore trees with frost.[m]

48 He exposed their cattle to hailstones
   and their flocks to bolts of lightning.[n]
49 He sent upon them his blazing anger,
   wrath, fury, and hostility,
   a band of destroying angels.*

50 He gave his anger free rein;
   he did not spare them from death
   but delivered their lives to the plague.
51 He struck down all the firstborn in Egypt,[o]
   the firstfruits of their manhood in the tents
   of Ham.*

52 Then he led forth his people like sheep
   and guided them through the wilderness
   like a flock.[p]
53 He led them in safety, and they were not afraid,
   while the sea engulfed their enemies.[q]

---

k 43f: Pss 105:27-36; 135:9; Ex 7:14—11:10; 12:29-36; Wis 16—18.—l
Ps 105:31; Ex 8:2, 6f, 17, 24.—m 46-47: Pss 105:32-35; 147:17; Ex 9:23;
Wis 16:16.—n Ex 9:3, 25.—o Pss 105:36; 135:8; 136:10; Ex 12:29.—p Pss
28:9; 77:21; Isa 66:11-14; Hos 12:14; Mic 6:4.—q Ps 106:10-11; Ex 14:26-
28.

78:44-51 The psalmist is not concerned about a complete, chronological, and
exact narrative of the plagues. He gives them in a different order and enumeration, while also omitting the third, fifth, sixth, and ninth (see Ex 7—12).
78:49 *Destroying angels:* the psalmist here generalizes the theme of the "destroyer" of the firstborn (see Ex 12:23), personifying the Lord's wrath, fury, and
hostility as agents of his anger (see Ex 9:14; Deut 32:24; Job 20:23).
78:51 *Tents of Ham:* usually linked with Egypt (see Pss 105:23, 27; 106:21f;
Gen 10:6).

⁵⁴ He brought them to his holy land,
    to the mountain his right hand had pur-
        chased.ʳ
⁵⁵ He drove out the nations before them,
    apportioning a heritage for each of them
    and settling the tribes of Israel in their tents.*

⁵⁶ Even so, they put God to the test*
    and rebelled against the Most High,
    refusing to observe his decrees.
⁵⁷ They turned away and were disloyal like
        their ancestors;
    they were as unreliable as a faulty bow.
⁵⁸ They angered him with their high places*
    and made him jealous with their idols.ˢ

⁵⁹ When God saw this, he became enraged
    and rejected Israel totally.*
⁶⁰ He forsook his dwelling in Shiloh,*
    the tent where he dwelt among mortals.ᵗ

⁶¹ He surrendered his might into captivity
    and his glory* into the hands of the enemy.ᵘ
⁶² He abandoned his people to the sword
    and vented his wrath on his own heritage.

---

r Ps 44:4; Ex 15:17.—s Ex 20:4; Deut 32:16, 21; Jdg 2:12.—t Jos 18:1, 8; 21:1f; Jdg 18:31; 1 Sam 1:3; Jer 7:12; 26:6; Ezek 8:6.—u Ps 132:8, 17; 1 Sam 4:11, 22; 2 Chr 6:41.

78:55 The psalmist here summarizes the story of the Conquest told in Joshua.

78:56-64 This part, like its predecessors, begins with the remembrance of Israel's sins and evokes the time of Samuel and Saul in the Book of Judges. Because of the people's infidelity, God rejected Israel (see Jer 7:12ff).

78:58 *High places:* the Canaanites were accustomed to build altars to their gods on hills ("high places"), a custom followed by the Israelites who built altars to Yahweh on hills. However, this led to the adoption of pagan practices and idols by God's people. *Jealous:* see Ex 20:5 ("I . . . am a jealous God").

78:59 The psalmist is here not speaking of a permanent abandonment of Israel by God.

78:60 *Shiloh:* a shrine located in Ephraim (see Jdg 21:19) that was the center of Israelite worship from the time of Joshua (see Jos 18:1, 8; 21:1f; Jdg 18:31; 1 Sam 1:3; Jer 7:12; 26:6). It was destroyed by the Philistines when the Ark of the Covenant was captured (see 1 Sam 4:1-11).

78:61 *His might . . . his glory:* the divine attributes of which the Ark of the Covenant was the symbol (see Ps 132:17; 1 Sam 4:19ff; 2 Chr 6:41).

⁶³ Fire devoured their young men,
    and their maidens had no wedding song.ᵛ
⁶⁴ Their priests fell by the sword,
    and their widows sang no lamentation.

⁶⁵ Then the LORD awakened as from sleep,*
    like a warrior flushed from the effects of
        wine.
⁶⁶ He struck his enemies and routed them,
    inflicting perpetual shame on them.

⁶⁷ He rejected the tent of Joseph
    and did not choose the tribe of Ephraim.
⁶⁸ Rather, he chose the tribe of Judah,
    Mount Zion,* which he loved.ʷ
⁶⁹ He built his sanctuary like the high heavens,
    and like the earth* that he founded forever.

⁷⁰ He chose David* to be his servant
    and took him from the sheepfolds.ˣ
⁷¹ From tending sheep he brought him
    to be the shepherd of his people Jacob,
    of Israel, his heritage.ʸ
⁷² He shepherded them with an unblemished
        heart
    and guided them with a knowing hand.*

---

v Num 11:1; Deut 32:25; Jer 7:34.—w Pss 48:2; 50:2; 87:2; 108:9; Lam 2:15.—x Ps 89:21; 1 Sam 13:14; 2 Chr 6:6; Ezek 34:23; 37:24.—y Gen 37:2; 1 Sam 16:11-13; 2 Sam 7:8.

78:65-72 After the Israelites had been cleansed by the divine chastisement, the Lord had mercy on them and fought by their side once more in vanquishing their enemies. But afterward God chose Judah instead of Ephraim as the leading tribe, Mount Zion instead of Shiloh as the royal seat (the place of his sanctuary), and David instead of Saul as his king and regent. David is the ideal shepherd (see Ezek 34:23; 37:24), the Lord's anointed (see Ps 89:21), and the type of the Messiah to come (see Ps 110). What the Lord did for the people in the wilderness, David did in his name for the people of Judah.

78:68 *He chose . . . Mount Zion:* see Ps 132:11, 17.

78:69 *High heavens . . . earth:* the Lord built his sanctuary to last like the heavens and the earth (see note on Ps 24:2) and to reflect his glory as they do (see Pss 19:2; 29:9; 97:6).

78:70 *He chose David:* see Ps 132.

78:72 The Prophets regarded Israel led by David as the hope of God's people (see Ezek 34:23; 37:24; Mic 5:2—fulfilled in Jesus: see Mt 2:6; Jn 10:11; Rev 7:17).

PSALM 79*

Prayer for Restoration

¹ A psalm of Asaph.*

O God, the nations have invaded your heritage;*
  they have profaned your holy temple
  and turned Jerusalem into a heap of ruins.ᶻ
² They have given the corpses of your servants
  as food to the birds of the air,
the flesh of your saints
  to the beasts of the earth.ᵃ

³ They have poured out their blood like water
  all around Jerusalem,
  and no one is left to bury them.*ᵇ
⁴ We have become the scorn of our neighbors,ᶜ
  mocked and derided by those around us.*

---

z 2 Ki 25:9-10; Neh 4:2; Jer 26:18; Lam 1:10.—a Ps 80:13-14; Deut 28:26; Jer 7:33.—b 1 Mac 7:17; Jer 14:16; 16:4; Zep 1:17.—c Pss 39:9; 44:14; 80:7; 123:3-4; Job 12:4; Ezek 6:14; Dan 9:16; Zep 2:8.

Ps 79 In this poem the psalmist is speaking of the darkest days of Israel's history: in 587 B.C. the Chaldeans captured and sacked Jerusalem; the neighboring Moabites and Edomites then attacked them as they were in their death-throes. Israel is aware now that it deserved to be punished for its infidelities, and it appeals to God's mercy. In this lamentation, the distress of the oppressed calls upon the Lord for redress. The pagans dishonor the divine name; this is tantamount to a defeat for the Lord. In avenging his own, God must first save his honor in the eyes of the world, and his people will be grateful to him. Such is the theme of this national lamentation.
  Must vengeance be paid back seven times (i.e., in full measure) upon one's neighbors? Christ has told us to pardon seventy times seven (Mt 18:22)—so that we cannot take this psalm literally. Still it remains a poignant appeal to God's mercy, an act of faith in the Lord when everything seems to be collapsing around us. We do not demand the total destruction of our enemies but a salutary punishment, in keeping with the divine justice, which brings evildoers low in order to pardon and save them.
  79:1a *Asaph:* see introduction to Pss 73—89.
  79:1b-4 God's city and temple have been desecrated and so have his worshipers, whose dead bodies have been left unburied. *Saints:* see note on Ps 16:3.
  79:2-3 *They have given . . . the flesh . . . to bury them:* these verses are cited freely in 1 Mac 7:17 in application to the massacre of sixty pious Jews in Jerusalem during the Maccabean wars.
  79:4 A secular hostility opposed Israel to its neighbors, as is shown by the oracles of the Prophets against the nations (see Lam 3:45; Zep 2:8).

5 * How long, O LORD?* Will you be angry forever?
  How long will your rage continue to blaze
  like a fire?*d*
6 Pour out your wrath on the nations*
  that refuse to acknowledge you,
on the kingdoms
  that fail to call on your name.**e*
7 For they have devoured Jacob
  and ravaged his homeland.

8 Do not hold against us the sins of our ancestors;
  let your mercy come quickly to meet us,
  for we are in desperate straits.**f*
9 Help us, O God, our Savior,*
  for the glory of your name;
deliver us and wipe away our sins
  for your name's sake.**g*

10 Why should the nations ask,
  "Where is their God?"*h*
Before our eyes make it clearly known among
  those nations
  that you avenge* the blood of your servants.*i*

---

d Pss 13:2; 44:24; 74:1; 89:47; Deut 4:24.—e Ps 14:4; Sir 36:1-5; Jer
10:25.—f Pss 116:6; 142:7.—g Ps 25:11; 31:4; Ezek 20:44; 36:22.—h Pss
42:4; 115:2; Joel 2:17; Mal 2:17.—i Deut 32:43; Joel 3:2; Rev 6:10.

79:5-8 The divine justice cannot remain inactive in the case of such wickedness, which calls out for retribution.
79:5 *How long . . . ?:* see note on Ps 6:4. *Rage:* i.e., a jealous rage (see Ps
119:139; Nah 1:2). *Blaze like a fire:* see Deut 4:24; 6:15; Zep 1:18; 3:8.
79:6-7 Cited in Jer 10:25. Concerning the call for redress, see note on Ps 5:11.
79:6, 12 See note on Ps 5:11 and introduction to Ps 35.
79:8 The exiles beg God to show mercy on them and not hold the sins of their
ancestors against them (see 2 Ki 17:7-23; 23:26f; 24:3f; Dan 9:4-14).
79:9-13 The psalmist beseeches God to pardon Israel for his name's sake so
that the Most High may no longer be dishonored and blasphemed by the nations.
Then the People of God will praise him from generation to generation.
79:9 The divine pardon is always gratuitous; it is the effect of his mercy and
love (see Ps 78:38; Ezek 20:44; 36:22; see also note on Ps 65:4).
79:10 *You avenge:* God is the avenger of blood in Israel (see Pss 18:48; 19:15;
58:11f; 94:1; 149:7; Deut 32:43).

¹¹ Let the groans of the captives come before you;
　　through your great power
　　　save those who have been sentenced to
　　　death.*ʲ

¹² Repay our neighbors sevenfold in their breasts,
　　O LORD,*
　　　for the insults with which they taunted you.ᵏ
¹³ Then we, your people, the sheep of your pasture,
　　will offer thanks to you* forever;
　from generation to generation
　　we will proclaim your praise.

PSALM 80*

Prayer for the Persecuted People

¹ For the director.* According to "Lilies." *Eduth.* A psalm
of Asaph.

² * Listen to us, O shepherd of Israel,*
　　you who lead Joseph like a flock.

---

j Pss 79:11; 102:21; 126:1; Lk 4:18.—k Pss 12:7; 89:51-52; Gen 4:24; Isa 65:6-7; Jer 32:18.

79:11 *Captives . . . those who have been sentenced to death:* literally, "the sons of death," i.e., the exiles in Babylonia (see Ps 102:21) who are under threat of death if they seek to escape.

79:12 *Sevenfold:* a symbolic phrase meaning fullness or superabundance (see Ps 12:7; Gen 4:24; Lev 26:21).

79:13 *Offer thanks to you:* see note on Ps 7:18.

Ps 80 At the time of this psalmist, the northern kingdom of Israel and the southern kingdom of Judah have disappeared in turn (721 and 587 B.C.). For the time being, Israel will be nothing but a scattered flock, a ruined vineyard. Whence can restoration come if not from God? This psalm is well adapted to our prayer during Advent: so deep is our wretchedness that we await the coming of God; he alone can turn us to himself by his presence and lead us to conversion.

80:1 *For the director:* these words are thought to be a musical or liturgical notation. *According to "Lilies." Eduth:* nothing is known about this phrase. *Asaph:* see introduction to Pss 73—89.

80:2-8 God is the Shepherd of Israel (see Isa 40:11; Jer 31:10; Ezek 34:31), and Jesus will call himself the Good Shepherd (see Jn 10). This image evokes profound links between Israel and God—affectionate solicitude on one side and confident belonging on the other. Hence, those who are in distress do not address an unknown and distant God.

80:2 *Shepherd of Israel:* see Pss 74:1; 77:21; 78:52, 71f; 79:13. *Joseph:* see note on Ps 77:16. *Cherubim:* see note on Ps 18:11.

As you sit enthroned upon the cherubim,
  shine forth[l]
3 over Ephraim, Benjamin, and Manasseh.*
Stir up your power
  and come to save us.

4 Restore us, O LORD of hosts;
  let your face shine* upon us,
  and we will be saved.[m]

5 O LORD of hosts,*
  how long will you be angry
  at your people's prayers?[n]

6 You have fed them with the bread of tears
  and made them drink tears beyond measure.[o]

7 You have made us an object of contention to
  our neighbors,
  a source of mockery to our enemies.[p]

8 Restore us, O LORD of hosts;
  let your face shine upon us,
  and we will be saved.

9 * You brought a vine* out of Egypt;
  you dispersed the nations and planted it.

---

l Pss 23:1-3; 77:21; 95:7; 100:3; Gen 48:15; Ex 25:22; 1 Sam 4:4; 2 Sam 6:2; Ezek 34:2; Mic 7:14.—m 4, 8, 20: Pss 4:7; 31:17; 67:2; 85:5; Num 6:25; Jer 31:18.—n Pss 13:2; 44:24; 74:1; 79:5; 89:47; Deut 4:24; 29:20.—o Pss 42:4; 102:10.—p Pss 44:14; 79:4; 123:3-4; Job 12:4; Dan 9:16.

80:3 *Over Ephraim, Benjamin, and Manasseh:* Ephraim and Manasseh were the two principal tribes of the northern kingdom, with which Benjamin was at times associated (see Num 2:18f). It was also in front of these three tribes that the Ark of the Covenant advanced during the sojourn from Sinai to the promised land (see Num 10:21-24).

80:4 *Let your face shine:* see notes on Pss 4:7 and 13:2.

80:5 *LORD of hosts:* see note on Ps 59:6. *How long. . . ?:* see note on Ps 6:4.

80:9-17 Israel is God's magnificent garden whose ideal limits extend as far as the Euphrates ("River" of v. 12). God is like the vinedresser who cherishes his vine-vineyard and takes pleasure in it. How could he not be saddened to see it devastated (see Isa 5:1-7; 27:2-5; Jer 2:21; 12:10)? This image will pass into the New Testament (see Mt 20:1; 21:33-41; Jn 15:1-5).

80:9 *Vine:* a familiar allegory in the Prophets (see Isa 5:1; 27:2; Jer 2:21; 12:10; Ezek 17:6-8; 19:10-14; Hos 10:1; 14:7; Mic 7:1), as is that of the shepherd (see Ps 23:1; Gen 48:15; Ezek 34:11). See also Mt 20:1; Jn 15:1.

¹⁰ You prepared the ground for it;
  then it took root and filled the land.

¹¹ The mountains were covered with its shade
  and the cedars of God* with its branches.
¹² It sent out its boughs as far as the Sea,
  its branches as far as the River.*

¹³ * Why * have you broken down its walls
  so that all who pass by pluck its grapes?q
¹⁴ The boars from the forest ravage it,
  and wild beasts of the field feed on it.r

¹⁵ Turn once again to us, O LORD of hosts;*
  look down from heaven and see;
 take care of this vine,
¹⁶   this shoot* that your right hand has planted,
  the son that you yourself made strong.

¹⁷ Let those who would burn it or cut it down
  perish when confronted by your rebuke.
¹⁸ Let your hand rest upon the man at your right,*
  the son of man that you yourself made
  strong.

¹⁹ Then we will never again turn away from you;
  give us life and we will call upon your name.*

²⁰ Restore us, O LORD of hosts;
  let your face shine upon us,
  and we will be saved.

---

q Ps 89:41; Jer 12:7-13; 39:8.—r Jer 5:6; Hos 2:12.

80:11 *Cedars of God:* cedars that were so huge that they were regarded as being planted by God.
80:12 *Sea:* i.e., Mediterranean. *River:* i.e., Euphrates River.
80:13-20 The psalmist begs God to attend once again to his wasted vine. Then the people will once again praise their savior.
80:13 *Why. . . ?:* see note on Ps 6:4.
80:15 *Lord of hosts:* see note on Ps 59:6.
80:16 *Shoot:* i.e., Israel. *Son:* i.e., Israel. The word may also be translated as "branch." Some versions omit v. 16b.
80:18 *Man at your right:* probably a reference to Israel, beloved son of the Lord (see Ex 4:22) or to the Davidic king who will lead the army in battle. Other suggestions put forth by scholars are Zerubbabel and Ezra who presided over the restoration. *Son of man:* another word for "man" in the first half of this verse.
80:19 A vow to offer praise to God (see note on Ps 7:18).

PSALM 81*

Exhortation To Worship Worthily

1 For the director.* "Upon the *gittith*." Of Asaph.

2 Sing out your joy to God our strength;
   shout aloud to the God of Jacob.*s
3 Raise the chant and sound the tambourine;
   play the pleasant harp and the lyre.

4 Sound the trumpet at the New Moon,
   and also at the full moon on the day of our
   Feast.*t

---

s Pss 43:4; 66:1; 68:27; 81:2-3; 87:7; 149:3; 150:3-4; 2 Sam 6:14; Jud 16:1; Jer 31:4.—t Pss 81:4; 98:6; Ex 19:13; Lev 23:24; Num 10:9-10; 29:1; 31:6; Jos 6:4; 2 Ki 11:14; 1 Chr 15:28.

Ps 81 The blasts of the trumpet call Israel to an assembly. The time is the full moon of September, the feast of Booths or Tabernacles (see Num 10:10; Lev 23:34, 39-43). The Covenant is renewed. At such a time, it is also important to rediscover the demands of fidelity. The psalmist, who is completely pervaded by the spirit of Deuteronomy, makes everyone aware of them. Let the people be on guard not to close their hearts to God. Today (v. 14) as yesterday (vv. 8, 12-13) the fidelity of God is checkmated by the infidelity of human beings.

In the last verse (v. 17) of this psalm, Christians cannot fail to be reminded of the blessings of the Eucharist in which we are filled with the "finest of wheat" (words found in the Mass texts of the Holy Thursday Evening Mass and the Easter Season), with bread that has become the Body and Blood, Soul, and Divinity of our Lord Jesus Christ. Each Eucharist is a renewal of the New Covenant, enabling us to relive the saving events of Christ's Passion and Resurrection. And in each Eucharist we pledge ourselves to Christ by hearing and keeping his word proclaimed and by receiving his Body and Blood.

81:1 *For the director:* these words are thought to be a musical or liturgical notation. *Upon the gittith:* see note on Ps 8:1. *Asaph:* see introduction to Pss 73—89.

81:2 *Jacob:* i.e., Israel (see Gen 32:28-29). Concerning the ritual "shout," see Ps 33:3.

81:4 The first day of the lunar month (New Moon) was for a long time celebrated as a feast (see 2 Ki 4:23; Isa 1:13; Hos 2:11; Am 8:5). Here it is a question of the beginning of the seventh month, long considered as the New Year (see Lev 23:24; Num 29:1); on the following full moon (on the fifteenth of the month) the Feast of Tabernacles was celebrated (see Lev 23:34; Num 29:12), five days after the Day of Atonement (see Lev 16:29). It concluded the cycle of feasts that began with the Passover and Unleavened Bread six months before (see Ex 23:14-17; Lev 23; Deut 16:13-15). Every seventh year the Covenant law was to be read to all the people (see Deut 31:9-13; Neh 8:2-15).

The purpose of the Feast of Tabernacles was to proclaim aloud the mighty deeds of the Lord in the History of Salvation. During the Feast, the assembly recalled God's wondrous works in Egypt.

5 For this is a law in Israel,
    a decree of the God of Jacob.*u*
6 He imposed this testimony on Joseph*
    when he departed from the land of Egypt.

I now hear an unfamiliar voice:
7   "I lifted the burden from their shoulders;*v*
    their hands put aside the laborer's basket.*
8 When you cried out to me in distress, I res-
        cued you;*
    from the thunderclouds I answered you;
    I tested you at the waters of Meribah:*w*

                                        Selah

9 " 'Listen to me, O my people, while I warn
        you.
    O Israel, if only you would listen to me!*x*
10 You must not accept a foreign god in your
        presence;*y*
    you must not bow down to an alien deity.
11 I am the Lord, your God,
    who brought you up from the land of
        Egypt;
    open your mouth wide so that I may fill
        it.'*

---

u Ex 23:14ff.—v Ex 1:14; 6:6; Isa 9:4.—w Ps 95:8; Ex 2:23ff; 17:7;
19:16; Num 20:13; 27:14; Deut 33:8.—x Ps 50:7; Ex 15:26; Isa 55:2-3.—y
10-11: Ex 20:2-6; Deut 5:6-10; Ezek 2:8.

81:6 *Joseph:* see note on Ps 77:16. *I now hear an unfamiliar voice:* the "voice"
is the "thunder" of God's judgment against Egypt (v. 8). Some translate: "We
heard a language we did not understand," and regard it as referring to the fact
that the people were aliens in a foreign land (see Ps114:1; Deut 28:49; 33:19).
Some also regard this as a reference to inspiration.
81:7 *Burden . . . basket:* allusion to the forced labor that the Israelites had to
endure in Egypt (see Ex 1:11-14).
81:8 *When you cried out . . . I rescued you:* see Ex 3:7-10; see also Ps 106:9; Ex
14:21, 24; 15:8, 10). *From the thunderclouds:* allusion to the theophany at Sinai
(see Ex 19:16ff). *I tested you . . . Meribah:* see Ps 95:8; Ex 17:1-7.
81:11 The Lord challenges Israel to obey the first commandment of fidelity
to God after the proclamation of the Exodus (see Ps 78:23-29; Deut 11:13-15;
28:1-4). *Open your mouth wide:* i.e., trust in the Lord alone for every need. *So that
I may fill it:* as he did in the wilderness (see v. 17 and Ps 78:23-29; see also Ps
37:3-4; Deut 11:13-15; 28:1-4).

¹² "But my people did not listen to my voice;
  Israel refused to obey me.*
¹³ So I abandoned them to their stubborn
   hearts*z*
  and let them follow their own devices.*

¹⁴ "If only my people would listen to me,*
  if only Israel would walk in my ways,*ᵃ
¹⁵ I would quickly subdue their enemies*
  and raise my hand against their foes.ᵇ

¹⁶ "Then those who hate the LORD would tremble before him,
  for their doom would last forever.*
¹⁷ But Israel he would feed with the finest of
   wheat*
  and fill them with honey from the rock."ᶜ

---

z Jer 3:17; 7:24; Acts 7:42.—a Deut 5:29; Isa 48:18.—b Lev 26:7-8; Am 1:8.—c Ps 147:14; Ex 29:2; Deut 32:13-14; Ezek 16:19.

81:12 Instead of remaining loyal to the Lord out of gratitude for their redemption and his promise of the future, the people continued to rebel against him—a characteristic typical of their history beginning with the generation in the wilderness (see Pss 78; 95; 106).

81:13 God gives the people over to their sins (see Ps 78:29; Isa 6:9f; 29:10; 63:17; see also Rom 1:24, 26, 28) because of their "stubborn hearts"; but he always reserves the right to "circumcise" their hearts and bring them back to him (see Deut 30:6; 1 Ki 8:58; Jer 31:33; Ezek 11:19; 36:26). *Hearts:* see note on Ps 4:8.

81:14-17 An allusion to the Covenant blessings; the era of wars and persecutions will cease (see Lk 21:24), their enemies will be vanquished, and the people will enjoy the best of everything.

81:14 The Lord cannot abandon his people completely. He calls them to return to him and follow his "ways," i.e., his commandments (see Pss 27:11; 86:11; 128:1; 143:8). For if they listen to God's word, they will respond by faith and repentance, and carry out his will rather than their own.

81:15 If his people return to him, the Lord will quickly come to their aid with his "hand" pressing hard against their enemies.

81:16 If his people return to him, the Lord will mete out to their enemies— "those who hate the LORD"—their just deserts, inflicting on them an everlasting punishment.

81:17 *Finest of wheat:* a staple of life. For Christians, of course, wheat is associated with the Eucharist, and this phrase has given rise to one of the finest modern Eucharistic hymns: *Gift of Finest Wheat,* composed for the 1976 Eucharistic Congress that took place in the United States. *Honey from the rock:* the purest of honey, since it came from places usually not attainable (from a cleft of rock in which bees in Canaan sometimes built their hives). The phrase is reminiscent of God's promise to Moses of a "land flowing with milk and honey" (Ex 3:8).

PSALM 82*

Judgment on Abuse of Authority

¹ A psalm of Asaph.*

God takes his place in the divine council;*
    in the midst of the gods he pronounces
    judgment:*^d
² "How long will you issue unfair judgments
    and rule in favor of those who are
    wicked?*^e   *Selah*

³ "Grant justice to the weak and the orphan;*
    defend the rights of the lowly and the poor.

---

d Pss 7:9; 58:11; Job 21:22; Isa 3:13-14; 66:16; Joel 4:2.—e Ps 58:3; Deut 1:17; Prov 18:5.

Ps 82 The psalmist sets forth a word about just and unjust judges (somewhat similar to Ps 58). He reminds rulers and magistrates that they are earthly members of God's tribunal, associated in the government of the world, and in this respect "gods" (v. 6). Why then does the cause of the poor find such little regard among them! By establishing injustice rather than justice, these powerful people disturb the very order of the world (v. 5). They themselves will therefore be judged by the great King (see Ps 47) and Judge of all the earth (see Ps 94:2; Gen 18:25; 1 Sam 2:10) who "loves justice" (Ps 99:4) and judges the nations in righteousness (see Pss 9:9; 96:13; 98:9). Furthermore, God's justice turns human judgments topsy-turvy; the kingdom of God and his justice will overcome the evildoers and the powers of oppression (see Isa 24:21f).

Even in nations that are not concerned with God or openly deny him, rulers and judges receive their powers from God and are bound to exercise them for justice in accord with his will: "[Civil authorities] are . . . God's representatives for your welfare . . . [and] God's servants to mete out punishment to wrongdoers" (Rom 13:4). This same truth is proclaimed by 1 Pet 2:13f. See also Ps 2:6-11; Isa 44:28; Jer 27:6; Dan 2:21; 4:14, 28f; 5:18; Jn 19:11; Rom 13:1.

82:1a *Asaph:* see introduction to Pss 73—89.

82:1b *Divine council:* the psalmist pictures a kind of heavenly assembly (see Ps 89:6; 1 Ki 22:19; Job 1:6; 2:1; Isa 6:1-4) in the Hall of Justice, patterned after the Solomonic one (see 1 Ki 7:7), in which God is dispensing justice. *Gods:* a word applied to rulers and judges who are "godlike" in their function of establishing justice on the earth (see note on Ps 45:7).

82:2 Like other authors of the Old Testament, the psalmist reproaches those in power with the sin of administering justice inequitably and showing partiality toward the wicked (see Ex 23:6; Lev 19:15; Deut 1:17; 2 Chr 19:7; Prov 18:5; Mic 3:1-12).

82:3-4 Rulers and judges are exhorted to protect the powerless against exploiters and oppressors (see Ps 72:2, 4, 12-14; Job 29:11f; Prov 31:8f; Isa 11:4; Jer 22:3, 16; Ezek 22:27, 29; Zec 7:9f). Indeed, to see to it that the weak do not fall into the hands of unscrupulous exploiters is one of the most important functions of government. *Poor:* see note on Ps 34:7.

⁴ Rescue the wretched and the needy;
    free them from the hand of the wicked.*f

⁵ "They neither know nor understand;
    they wander around in darkness
        while all the foundations of the earth are
            crumbling.*
⁶ I declare, 'Although you are gods,*
    all of you sons of the Most High,*
⁷ you will die as all men do;
    like any ruler you will fall.' "*

⁸ Rise up, O God, and judge the earth,
    for all the nations belong to you.*

---

f Pss 35:10; 72:4; 140:13; Deut 1:17; Isa 1:16f; 10:1-3; Zec 7:7-10; Jas 1:27; 2:1.

82:4 This verse can also be looked upon as the end of a two-verse didactic poem, in which the Lord reminds his people of his expectations for them under the Covenant (see Isa 1:16f; Zec 7:7-10; Mal 3:9; Jas 1:27). Failure to live up to those expectations on their part leads to condemnation (see Isa 10:1-3).

82:5 When those in authority, instead of sharing in God's wisdom (see 1 Ki 3:9; Prov 8:14-16; Isa 11:2), have no understanding of their most important duty or of the divine norm and standard and do not walk in the light of the revealed will of the eternal Judge (see Job 21:22), then all the supports upon which a well-ordered State rests will crumble (see Pss 11:3; 75:4). *Foundations of the earth:* a metaphor for God's rule on earth (see Pss 11:3; 75:4; 96:10). The Lord has established some order even in pagan nations, and he condemns the ungodly for undermining that order for their own ends.

82:6-7 These verses can be interpreted to apply to judges or rulers but also to pagan gods. The Lord pronounces sentence and dethrones such gods. Indeed, his judgment is pronounced upon all manifestations of evil both in the human world and in the angelic world (see Mt 25:41; Rev 20:10, 14f; 21:8).

82:6 Rulers and judges are representatives of God, appointed by him (see Ps 2:7; Isa 44:28; Jer 27:6; Dan 2:21; 4:14, 28f; 5:18; Jn 19:11; Rom 13:1). *Gods:* see note on v. 1b. This passage is applied by Christ, in an entirely different context, to Jews instructed by the word of God (see Jn 10:34; see also Acts 17:28; 2 Cor 6:18).

82:7 These corrupt rulers will see death like all other human beings and be judged in the same way. *Like any ruler you will fall:* another possible translation is: "as one man, rulers, you will fall." God will humble the great of the world as he annihilated the false gods likened to personages of the ancient mythology (see Isa 14:12; Ezek 28:11ff).

82:8 The psalmist prays that God's just judgment (see Pss 9:21; 10:12-15; 76:10) will come soon. Whenever we encounter injustice, we can fittingly say our Lord's prayer: "Your kingdom come" (Mt 6:10). This verse can be fittingly applied to Christ, to whom all judgment has been entrusted by the Father (see Jn 5:22).

PSALM 83*

Against a Hostile Alliance

¹ A song. A psalm of Asaph.*

² O God, do not remain silent;*
    do not be quiet and inactive, O God.ᵍ
³ Note how your enemies rage about,*
    how your foes increase in arrogance.*

⁴ They formulate shrewd plans against your
    people,
    conspiring against those you love.ʰ
⁵ They say, "Come, let us wipe them out as a
    nation;
    let the name of Israel be totally forgotten."

---

g Pss 10:1; 44:24; 50:3; 109:1.—h Ps 31:14; Jer 11:9.

Ps 83 After the deportation in 587 B.C., Israel ceased to exist as a political entity. The community that has been reestablished in Jerusalem after the return is subjected to the tutelage of great powers and the vexation of their neighbors. The communities that had been scattered among foreign peoples have already experienced more than one persecution. In their struggles with pagan religions and cultures, believers feel threatened in their faith. It seems that all forces have formed a coalition to destroy Israel because it wishes to remain faithful to its vocation as the People of God. As a result the psalmist directs the following challenge to the Lord: May he let himself be known by crushing the pride of the nations; indeed, may the latter meet the cruel fate of the petty kings who wanted to destroy Israel at the time of the Judges (see note on Ps 5:11 and introduction to Ps 35).

Obviously, this is a prayer of vengeance, but even more of salvation. It wishes to provoke Heaven: how could a polytheistic and idolatrous world come to worship the one and all-powerful God if he abandons his people? The chosen people could never resign themselves to such a collapse; that would be tantamount to the defeat of the Lord himself.

Although as Christians we are constantly under threat from the godless, we can ceaselessly implore God the Father (by this psalm) to grant his new People a complete victory over our enemies. We do not desire the eternal death of our foes but ask that God will bring them low and lead them to himself as God and Father.

83:1 *Asaph:* see introduction to Pss 73—89.

83:2 *Do not remain silent:* i.e., spring into action (see Pss 35:22; 109:1).

83:3-5 The words "Come, let us" are the very ones used by the leaders of the rebels at the tower of Babel when humanity attempted to usurp the power of the Lord (see Gen 11:3f). They obviously identify the enemies of God and of his people who cunningly plot to show their independence from the Lord and to exterminate Israel as a nation. *Name:* see note on Ps 5:12.

83:3 *Increase in arrogance:* literally, "rear their heads."

⁶ They conspire with a single mind,ⁱ
　forming an alliance* against you:
⁷ the tents of Edom and the Ishmaelites,*
　Moab and the Hagrites,ʲ
⁸ Gebal, Ammon and Amalek,ᵏ
　Philistia, and the inhabitants of Tyre;ˡ
⁹ Assyria has also joined them as an ally,
　offering aid to the descendants of Lot.

Selah

¹⁰ * Deal with them as you did with Midian,*
　and with Sisera and Jabin at the brook of
　Kishon,*ᵐ
¹¹ who were destroyed at Endor
　and became manure for the ground.ⁿ

---

i Pss 2:2.; 14:4—j Ps 137:7; Num 20:23; Deut 2:5; 1 Chr 5:10, 19; Am 1:11.—k Gen 19:38; Ex 17:8; Jos 13:5.—l Jos 13:2; Isa 23:3.—m Ex 2:15; Jdg 4:2; Isa 9:3; 10:26.—n 1 Sam 28:7; Jer 8:2.

83:6 *Alliance:* there is no record of such a vast alliance of nations ever arrayed against Israel at one time. It may be that only some of them were attacking at the moment while passively being supported by the others. Some point to the time when Moab, Ammon, and Edom were invading Judah during the reign of King Jehoshaphat (see 2 Chr 20). *Against you:* the invaders acknowledge openly that the war is intended not only against the people but also against their God.

83:7-9 The members of the hostile alliance are all well-known foes of Israel. The psalmist alludes to the *Edomites*, descendants of Esau, the son of the patriarch Isaac (see Gen 36), and the *Ishmaelites* who descended from Ishmael, the son of Abraham and Hagar (see Gen 16:15f); he also mentions the *Moabites* (see 2 Chr 20:1) and *Ammonites*, descendants of Lot, the nephew of Abraham (see Gen 19:38); next he includes the *Hagrites*, an Arabian bedouin tribe that was encamped on the border of the Syro-Arabian desert (see 1 Chr 5:10, 19f). Other members were the inhabitants of *Gebal*, in the territory of the Edomites south of the Dead Sea (see Jos 13:5), and the *Amalekites* (see Gen 14:7). The *Philistines,* Israel's foes along the Mediterranean coast of Palestine (see Ex 15:14), were also part of the alliance as were the inhabitants of *Tyre* (see Isa 23:3). *Assyria* (see Gen 10:11) is mentioned as rendering assistance to the alliance.

83:10-19 See note on Ps 5:11 and introduction to Ps 35.

83:10-13 The psalmist takes heart by recalling two great victories won with God's help against superior forces during the time of the Judges: the victory of Gideon over the Midianites (see Jdg 7) and the defeat of King Jabin (see Jdg 4). He knows that in order for God's kingdom of righteousness and peace to come his foes must be defeated (see note on Ps 5:11).

83:10 *Midian:* it was at Midian (see Ex 2:15) that Gideon defeated the Midianites and slew the leaders named in v. 12 (see Jdg 7:24-25; 8:5). *Sisera and Jabin:* commander and king, respectively, of the army defeated by Deborah and Barak in the plain of Esdraelon near Endor at the foot of Mount Tabor (see Jdg 4—5).

12 Make their chieftains like Oreb and Zeeb,*
     and all their princes like Zebah and Zal-
          munna,
13 who boasted, "Let us seize for ourselves
     the pastures of God."

14 O my God, treat them like tumbleweed,*
     like chaff blown before the wind.o
15 As a fire rages through a forest,
     as a flame sets mountains ablaze,p
16 so hound them with your tempestsq
     and terrify them with your stormwinds.*

17 Fill their faces with shame
     so that they will seek your name,* O LORD.
18 Let them be humiliated and terrified forever;*
     let them be disgraced and perish.
19 Let them know that you alone,
     whose name is the LORD,
     are the Most High over all the earth.r

---

o Pss 1:4; 35:5; 58:10; Job 27:21; Isa 5:24; 10:17; 17:13; 29:5; Jer 13:24; Ezek 21:3.—p Ps 50:3; Deut 32:22.—q Job 9:17; 27:20; Jer 25:32.— r Pss 46:11; 97:9; Deut 4:39; Dan 3:45.

83:12-13 The Midianites had despoiled the croplands (v. 13: "Let us seize for ourselves the pastures of God") and driven fear into the hearts of the Israelites. In their defeat at the hands of the Lord through Gideon, their leaders Oreb, Zeeb, Zebah, and Zalmunna were captured and put to death (see Jdg 7:25; 8:21).

83:14-15 The psalmist likens the fate of the enemies to that of "tumbleweed" and "chaff" carried away by the wind and a "forest" or "mountains" destroyed by fire (common figures of destruction at the hand of the Lord: see Pss 1:4; 35:5; Isa 5:24; 10:17; 17:13; 29:5; Jer 13:24).

83:16 *Tempests . . . stormwinds:* for God in the thunderstorm, see Pss 18:8-16; 68:34; 77:18f; Ex 15:7-10; Jos 10:11; Jdg 5:4, 20f; 1 Sam 2:10; 7:10; Isa 29:5f; 33:3. See also note on Ps 68:5.

83:17 *They will seek your name:* the psalmist prays that God will humiliate the enemies and lead men to seek his name, i.e., realize and accept that the Lord alone is God (see v. 19).

83:18-19 The Chronicler (2 Chr 20:22-29) records the defeat of the alliance and mentions that all the nations were terrified when they learned that the Lord fought on the side of the Israelites. This is precisely what the psalmist asks so that his people will be saved and the Lord will be praised by the whole world.

PSALM 84*

Longing for God's Dwelling

¹ For the director.* "Upon the *gittith*." A psalm of the sons of Korah.

² How lovely is your dwelling place,
    O LORD of hosts.**ˢ*
³ My soul* yearns and is filled with longing
    for the courts of the LORD.
My heart and my flesh cry out
    for the living God.*ᵗ*

⁴ Just as the sparrow searches for a home
    and the swallow builds a nest for herself
    where she may place her young,
so do I seek your altars,*
    O LORD of hosts, my King and my God.*ᵘ*

⁵ Blessed* are those who dwell in your house;
    they offer continuous praise to you.   *Selah*

---

s Pss 27:4; 43:3; 122:1; 132:5.—t Pss 42:2-3; 63:2-3; 143:6; Jos 3:10; Job 19:27; Isa 26:9.—u Pss 2:6; 5:3; 43:4; 44:5; 68:25; Jer 44:11.

Ps 84 During one of the pilgrimages prescribed by the Mosaic Law (see Ex 23:17; 1 Sam 1:3; Lk 2:42), perhaps the one for the harvest, a pilgrim expresses his joy at finding himself near God in the temple. At the last stage, the Lord has already manifested his favor to the pilgrims (vv. 6-7). He reserves even more happiness for those who follow his Law. Another opinion holds that this psalm recalls Ps 42 and reflects its circumstances. The psalmist is a Levite who has no access to God's house, possibly at the time when Sennacherib was overrunning Judah (see 2 Ki 18:13-16), and expresses his longing for the closeness in the temple that he experienced in the past.

This pilgrim song, overflowing with the desire for and joy of God, becomes the song of hope and confidence for all Christians en route to the house of the Father where they will sing an Alleluia (or Hallelujah) without end. It also translates the sentiments of all who love Christ's Eucharistic Presence in the tabernacle. Those who in one way or another have consecrated their life to the Lord will find herein words to express their deepest aspirations.

84:1 *For the director:* these words are thought to be a musical or liturgical notation. "*Upon the gittith*": see note on Ps 8:1. *Sons of Korah,* see note on Ps 42:1.

84:2 *LORD of hosts:* see note on Ps 24:10.

84:3 *Soul:* see note on Ps 6:4. *Heart . . . flesh:* i.e., entire being (see Ps 73:26).

84:4 God sees to it that even the "birds of the air have nests" (Mt 8:20); hence, he will welcome his faithful to the shelter of his altars.

84:5, 6, 13 *Blessed:* see note on Ps 1:1.

⁶ Blessed are those who find strength in you,
      who set their hearts upon your ways.*

⁷ As they pass through the valley of Baca,
      they turn it into a region of springs,
      and the early rain covers it with pools.*

⁸ They move forward with increasing strength
      as they behold the God of gods in Zion.*

⁹ O LORD of hosts,* hear my prayer;
      listen to my pleas, O God of Jacob.   *Selah*

¹⁰ O God, look upon our shield;*
      behold the face of your anointed one.ᵛ

¹¹ It is better to spend one day in your courts
      than a thousand elsewhere.
   I would rather be a doorkeeper* in God's house
      than dwell inside the tents of the wicked.

¹² The LORD God serves as our sun and our shield;
      the LORD showers us with grace and glory.
   He does not withhold any good thing
      from those who walk in integrity.*

¹³ O LORD of hosts,
      blessed is the man who puts his trust in you.

---

v Pss 2:2; 18:51; 59:12; 89:19; 132:17.

84:6 *Who set their hearts upon your ways:* literally, "in whose hearts are the open roads."

84:7 Through God's care, even the most fearsome path becomes a path of blessings and praise (see 2 Chr 20:26). *Valley of Baca:* valley of "weeping" or "balsam trees"; in the Vulgate, it is called "the Valley of Tears," which gave rise, in the ascetical and preaching tradition, to the familiar expression, "vale of tears," for our earthly pilgrimage (see the popular Marian prayer "Hail, Holy Queen"). *Pools:* or "blessings."

84:8 *Zion:* see note on Ps 9:12.

84:9 *LORD of hosts:* see note on Ps 24:10. *Jacob:* i.e., Israel (see Gen 32:28-29).

84:10 *Our shield:* the king (see Ps 89:19). *Anointed one:* either the king (who was God's earthly regent over his people) or the high priest (who led the community of Israel after the disappearance of the royalty).

84:11 *Doorkeeper:* some of the sons of Korah (see v. 1) were doorkeepers or gatekeepers in the temple (see 1 Chr 26:1).

84:12 There is no joy in the world that can outweigh and replace supernatural joys that have their source in God alone. For he denies no grace to his faithful ones. *Sun:* see note on Ps 27:1 on God as "light."

PSALM 85*

Prayer for the People's Salvation

¹ For the director.* A psalm of the sons of Korah.

² O Lᴏʀᴅ, you showed favor to your land;
  you restored the good fortune of Jacob.*ʷ
³ You forgave the iniquity of your people;
  you canceled all their sins.   *Selah*
⁴ You cast aside all your wrath;
  you put an end to your great anger.ˣ

⁵ Restore us once again, O God, our Savior,*
  and cease your displeasure toward us.ʸ
⁶ Will you remain angry with us forever?
  Will you hold onto your wrath for all gen-
    erations?ᶻ

⁷ Will you not once again give us life
  so that your people may exult in you?
⁸ Show us, O Lᴏʀᴅ, your kindness*
  and grant us your salvation.

---

w Pss 14:7; 126:4; Deut 30:3.—x Pss 78:38; 106:23; Ex 32:14; Num 14:20; Isa 48:9; Ezek 20:22; Hos 11:8-9.—y Pss 71:20; 80:4.—z Pss 50:21; 79:5; 89:47.

Ps 85 This psalm is a national lament recalling God's goodwill in bringing his people back from exile to their homeland (538 B.C.) but also indicating that the repatriates are having difficulty in reestablishing themselves in Judea. The psalmist as much as says: "You have enabled us to come back to our land; now let us come back to our lives." The lament becomes a prayer of hope, for the Prophets had announced a better future (see Isa 58:8; Zec 8:12). The temple of Jerusalem is being rebuilt (520-515 B.C.) and will be a visible sign of the presence of God, of his "glory" (v. 10; see Ezek 43:2). Happiness is promised to those who remain faithful. All these thoughts are similar to those expressed by the postexilic Prophets (see Hag 1:5-11; 2:6-9; Mal 3:13-21).

In praying this psalm, we can keep in mind that in Jesus, the Son of God, the promise becomes reality (see Jn 14:27; Col 1:20). When love and truth, justice and peace dwell on the earth, a new world is being born and God is there.

85:1 *For the director:* these words are thought to be a musical or liturgical notation. *Sons of Korah:* see note on Ps 42:1.

85:2 *Restored the good fortune of Jacob:* another translation possible is: "brought Jacob back from exile." *Jacob:* i.e., Israel (see Gen 32:28-29).

85:5-8 The psalmist begs God to favor his penitent people with pardon and peace.

85:8 *Kindness:* see note on Ps 6:5.

⁹ I will listen for God's response;*
     surely the LORD will proclaim peace to his
       people, his saints,*
     to those who turn to him with their whole
       heart.
¹⁰ His salvation is indeed near for those who
       fear him;
     his glory will dwell in our land.*

¹¹ * Kindness and faithfulness* will meet;
     righteousness and peace will embrace.ᵃ
¹² Faithfulness will spring forth from the earth,
     and righteousness* will look down from
       heaven.ᵇ

¹³ The LORD will grant us prosperity,*
     and our land will yield its harvest.ᶜ
¹⁴ Righteousness will go forth in front of him,
     and he will set us on the way he treads.

---

a Pss 61:8; 89:15; 97:2.—b Ps 72:6; Isa 45:8.—c Pss 67:7; 84:11; Lev 26:4; Ezek 34:27; Hos 2:22-23; Zec 8:12; Jas 1:17.

85:9-14 God answers the prayer through a reassuring word of a priest or Levite.

85:9 *Saints:* see notes on Pss 4:4; 16:3; and 34:10. *To those . . . heart:* other translations possible are: "and to those who turn from folly" and "but let them not return to folly" (the Hebrew word for "folly" includes the connotation of moral deficiency).

85:10 Only those who fear God in the spirit of wisdom (in contrast to the spirit of folly, v. 9) will inherit his benefits, which will be their glory. They will experience a renewed spirit since they are the heirs of the new age of restoration, which is described by various terms: salvation and glory (v. 10), kindness, faithfulness, righteousness, and peace (vv. 11-12), good and harvest (v. 13). *Glory:* the Lord's glory—a visible manifestation of his power and divinity—had left the temple and the holy city (see Ezek 11:23); it would return there once the temple was restored (see Ezek 43:2; Hag 2:9). See also Jn 1:14.

85:11-12 People will regulate their lives by the divine norms. The divine attributes as well as the moral virtues that correspond to them are here personified (see Pss 89:15; 97:2) as courtiers of the returning king.

85:11 *Kindness and faithfulness:* often found together to express God's loyalty (see Pss 25:10; 40:12f; 57:11; 61:8; Ex 34:6).

85:12 *Righteousness:* personification of God's attribute, which expresses his kingship in and over his people (see Pss 4:2; 22:31, alternative translation).

85:13-14 The goodness and blessings that the psalmist sees in a vision of the future are, for Christians, fulfilled in Christ. Yet the completion of salvation is also for Christians an object of promise and of longing expectation.

85:13 *Prosperity:* the benefits of God's kingdom enjoyed by those who fear him: forgiveness (v. 3), reconciliation, renewal of Covenant status (vv. 9-10), and fullness of restoration (vv. 10-14). Thus, faith in God leads to hope in a new age of righteousness (see Gal 5:5; 2 Pet 3:13).

PSALM 86*
Prayer in Suffering and Distress

[1] A prayer of David.

Incline your ear, O LORD, and answer me,
    for I am poor and needy.*
[2] Preserve my life, for I am faithful to you;
    save your servant who puts his trust in you.

[3] You are my God;* have pity on me, O Lord,
    for to you I cry out all day long.
[4] Give joy to the soul of your servant,
    for to you, O Lord,
    I lift up my soul.*d

[5] O Lord, you are kind and forgiving,
    filled with kindness* for all who cry to you.e
[6] Hear my prayer, O LORD,
    and listen to my voice in supplication.f
[7] In the time of trouble I call to you,
    for you will answer me.

[8] There is no one among the gods like you, O
    Lord,g
    nor can any deeds compare with yours.

---

d Pss 25:1; 143:8.—e Ex 34:6; Joel 2:13.—f Pss 5:3; 17:1; 130:1-2.—g Pss 35:10; 89:9; Ex 15:11; Deut 3:24; Job 21:22; Jer 10:6.

Ps 86 The psalmist passes in turn from supplication to an act of trust and gratitude toward God. This poem, composed most likely after the Exile, is the prayer of devout Israelites who believe in the Lord's goodness as a result of their own experience. After all, he brought Israel back to life in the most somber moment of her history! The Lord seemed so close to them that he could listen, pardon, and save; the psalmist contemplates the mystical experience of Moses encountering God (see Ex 34:6). The conviction of God's goodness overwhelms us by its evidence and its simplicity of expression. It already paves the way for a "missionary" sensitivity. The imprecations against the pagans lose their vehemence and one foresees the day when, touched by the Lord, they will render glory to the only God.

By means of this psalm, Christians can pray for their well-being in this world and beyond. Prolonging Christ's Passion, the Church and Christians experience the same anguish he did and seek to take refuge in the same heavenly Father.

86:1 *Poor and needy:* see note on Ps 34:7.

86:3 *You are my God:* indeed, God himself has chosen David to be his servant (see 1 Sam 13:14; 15:28; 16:12; 2 Sam 7:8).

86:4 *My soul:* see note on Ps 6:4.

86:5 *Kindness:* see note on Ps 6:5.

9 All the nations* you have made
    will come and bow down before you, O
      Lord,
    and glorify your name.*h*

10 For you are great and you do marvelous deeds;*
    you alone are God.

11 Teach me your ways, O LORD,
    so that I may walk in your truth;*i*
  let me worship your name
    with an undivided heart.*

12 I will praise you with all my heart,
    O Lord, my God,
    and I will glorify your name forever.*

13 Your kindness toward me is great;*
    you have rescued me from the depths of
      the netherworld.*j*

14 Arrogant men are rising up against me, O God;
    a violent mob seeks my life;
    they do not keep you before their eyes.*

15 But you, O Lord, are a merciful and compas-
      sionate God,
    slow to anger and abounding in kindness
    and faithfulness.*k*

16 Turn to me and grant me your gracious favor;
    endow your servant with strength
    and rescue the child of your handmaid.*l*

h Pss 22:28; 66:4; Zec 14:16; Rev 15:4.—i Pss 25:4; 26:3; 27:11; 119:12, 35; 143:8, 10; Jer 24:7; 32:39.—j Pss 30:3; 40:2; 88:6; Jon 2:7.—k Pss 103:8; 111:4; 130:7; 145:8; Ex 34:6.—l Pss 18:3; 25:16; 116:16; Wis 9:5.

86:9 *All the nations:* see note on Ps 46:11. *Your name:* see note on Ps 5:2.
86:10 *Marvelous deeds:* see note on Ps 9:2.
86:11 The psalmist asks God to save him from his enemies and also from himself (see Pss 25:5; 51:9, 12). *Undivided heart:* see Ezek 11:19 as well as 1 Chr 12:33; 1 Cor 7:35.
86:12 The psalmist vows to praise the Lord for his help (see note on Ps 7:18). *Heart:* see note on Ps 4:8.
86:13 The psalmist anticipates being heard. *Kindness:* see note on Ps 6:5. *Depths:* see note on Ps 30:2.
86:14 These haughty foes disregard God—to their ruin (see Ps 54:5; Jer 20:11).
86:15 This verse recalls Ex 34:6.
85:16 *Child of your handmaid:* another translation is: "faithful child." See also Ps 116:16.

¹⁷ Grant me a sign of your favor,*
    so that those who hate me
    may see it and be put to shame,
because you, O LORD,
    have helped and comforted me.

PSALM 87*

Zion, Home of All Nations

¹ A psalm of the sons of Korah.* A song.

The LORD has founded a city*
    on the holy mountains.ᵐ
² He loves the gates of Zion
    more than* any dwelling in Jacob.

---

m 1-2: Pss 2:6; 48:2; 76:2-3; 78:68-69; Zec 2:16.

86:17 *Favor:* the good things promised in the Covenant (see notes on Pss 27:13 and 31:20). *Those who hate me . . . put to shame:* the imprecations against enemies that conclude a good number of the psalms are here kept to a minimum.

Ps 87 The psalmist here paints a picture of Jerusalem as the spiritual mother of all peoples and thus prefigures the Church of Christ (see Acts 2:5ff; Gal 4:26). No other canticle has given greater exaltation to the holy city, Zion, the chosen city of God. Not only is she at the heart of Israel, but in her God lays the basis for the spiritual rebirth of all peoples, even the sworn enemies of Israel such as Egypt and Chaldea, through their worship of the true God (see Ps 45:15f; Zec 2:15; 8:23). All will be admitted into her bosom, and God will declare her mother of all peoples.

After having encountered the conflicts of peoples and the persecution of Israel in so many psalms, here is a symphony with unforgettable melodies. We are enchanted by this universalist aspect and the perspective of a humanity reunited by God in his presence, in accord with the vision of the Prophets (see Isa 2:2-4; 19:19-25; 25:6; 45:14, 22-24; 56:6-8; 60:3; 66:23; Dan 7:14; Mic 4:1-3; Zec 8:23; 14:16). Such is also the vocation of the Church, the new Jerusalem, to be a leaven for the ingathering of all peoples.

Thus, in praying this psalm, Christians keep in mind not only the earthly Zion with its fulfillment, the Church, but also the heavenly Jerusalem, the heavenly Church, which is our true and definitive home, the source of eternal life and perfect blessedness. At the end of time, this new Jerusalem will come down out of heaven from God, prepared as a bride for her husband (see Rev 21:2, 24).

87:1a *Sons of Korah:* see note on Ps 42:1.

87:1b *LORD has founded a city:* it is the Lord himself who has made Zion his city (see Isa 14:32) and the temple his dwelling. *Mountains:* see note on Ps 2:6.

87:2 *Loves . . . more than:* Zion is more cherished by the Lord than any other Israelite city or town (see Pss 9:12; 78:68; 132:12-14). *The gates of Zion:* a common Hebrew idiom for the city. *Jacob:* i.e., Israel (see Gen 32:28-29).

3 Glorious things are said of you,
    O city of God.   *Selah*

4 "I number Rahab and Babylon*
    among those who acknowledge the L ORD,
  as well as Philistia, Tyre, and Cush;
    concerning them it can be said,
    'This one was born there.' "*   *Selah*

5 However, of Zion it will be said,
    "They were all born there,^n
    for the Most High himself establishes
    her."*o

6 The L ORD records in the register of the
    peoples,^p
    "This one was born there."*   *Selah*

7 And as they play, they all sing,*q
    "In you are all my fountains."

---

n Gal 4:26.—o Ps 48:9; Isa 62:4-5.—p Ps 69:29; Ex 32:32; Isa 4:3; Ezek 13:9; Mal 3:16.—q Pss 36:10; 68:25; 149:3.

87:4-5 These verses foresee a wholesale conversion to the Lord on the part of peoples who were longtime enemies of God and his kingdom (see Isa 19:21).

87:4 The Gentiles will be incorporated into the People of God and adopted by Zion, their religious homeland. As the representatives of all the Gentile nations, the psalmist mentions the arrogant Egypt ("Rahab"—the name of an ocean monster used poetically for Egypt) and Babylon, the two world kingdoms on the Nile and Euphrates, both of which had fought for centuries for the possession of Palestine. We also hear of the Philistines, archenemy of Israel, wealthy Tyre proud of its independence, and the ambitious Ethiopians ("Cush").

87:5 The privileges of the holy city and her spiritual motherhood are divine in origin and hence indefectible. The eschatological community of the faithful is established by the Lord (see Ps 48:9; Isa 14:32; 28:16; 54:11f).

87:6 Here it is a case simply of a list ("register") of the citizens of Zion (see Isa 4:3; Ezek 13:9) rather than the apocalyptic book of destinies (see Ps 69:28). Each people will thus have two homelands—one material and one spiritual. The basis for the people's security and inclusion in Zion lies in the promise of the Lord and the fact that he is its builder (see Heb 11:10, 16).

87:7 Zion is associated with "the fountain of life" (Jer 2:13), of "salvation" (Isa 12:3), "a river whose streams bring joy to the city of God" (Ps 46:5; see Ezek 47; Rev 22:1-5). *As they dance, they all sing:* an alternative translation is: "As they make music, they will sing." Hence, the peoples will be admitted to the official liturgical worship (see Isa 66:21) and will at least be able to participate in the ritual dances (see Pss 149:3; 150:4; 2 Sam 6:5).

PSALM 88*

Prayer in Affliction

1 A song. A psalm of the sons of Korah.* For the director. According to *Mahalath.* For singing. A *maskil* of Heman the Ezrahite.

2 O LORD, the God of my salvation,*
   day and night I cry out to you.*r*
3 Let my prayer come before you;
   give ear to my cry for help.*s*

4 * For my soul* is filled with misery,*t*
   and my life draws near to the netherworld.

---

r Pss 3:5; 77:3.—s Ps 119:170.—t 4-7: Pss 6:3; 25:17; 28:1; 30:4; 40:3; 86:13; 143:7; Num 16:33; Job 17:1; Lam 3:55; Jon 2:6-7.

Ps 88 The anguish of death has rarely found expression in such touching images as those of the present psalm: prison, shipwreck, solitude, and darkness. The suppliant has experienced the depths of misfortune. Has God abandoned him? Despite the depths of his distress, the believer refuses to admit such a thing; he puts down all thought of rebellion within himself. For although no expressions of hopeful expectation (as in most psalms) are present and the last word speaks of darkness as "my closest friend," the psalmist firmly believes that the Lord is "the God of [his] salvation."

This psalm illustrates the hazy ideas that the ancients harbored about life after death before they arrived at faith in the resurrection: in the netherworld ("Sheol"), in the subterranean pit, the dead have no more communication with God; they are no more than dull shadows of themselves in the land of no recall. It is a prayer of a man who experiences the depths of human misery, a prayer of Israel at the edge of collapse, but also a prayer of everyone on the brink of hopelessness.

This psalm furnishes Christians with a prayer during times of spiritual dryness as well as human calamities of all kinds. We can then express to the heavenly Father our sufferings and distresses in the face of hostility, the weight of our spiritual and human solitude, and our fear in the light of his persistent silence. It will enable us to accept our cup without recrimination and to renew our trust in our God.

88:1 *Sons of Korah:* see note on Ps 42:1. *For the director:* these words are thought to be a musical or liturgical notation. *According to Mahalath:* possibly a tune. *Maskil:* see note on Ps 32:1a. *Heman the Ezrahite:* he is thought to be the son of Zerah (hence, Ezrahite) and member of the tribe of Judah (see 1 Chr 2:6) as well as leader of the Korahite guild (see 1 Chr 6:33, 37).

88:2-3 The psalmist, despite his wretched state, has not lost hope; he believes that the Lord is the God who saves and so he cries out to him for help.

88:4-6 His soul is full of troubles; indeed, he is accounted as one already in the grave and cut off from God (see Ps 143:7; Job 10:15; 17:1).

88:4 *Soul:* see note on Ps 6:4. *Netherworld:* see note on Ps 6:6.

5 I am numbered among those who go down to
     the pit;*
  all strength has failed me.

6 I have been abandoned among the dead,
     like the slain who lie in the grave,
  like those whom you remember no longer
     and whom your hand has abandoned.*

7 You have lowered me into the depths of the
     pit,*
  into the darkest regions of the abyss.

8 Your wrath lies heavy upon me;
     all your waves engulf me.ᵘ   *Selah*

9 You have caused my closest friends to shun
     me
  and made me hateful in their sight.*
  I am shut in with no means of escape,ᵛ
10   and my eyes grow dim* with my suffering.

  Every day I call out to you, O LORD,*
     and spread out my hands to you.
11 Do you perform wonders* for the dead?
  Do the shades rise up and give you
     praise?ʷ   *Selah*

---

u Pss 7:12; 18:5; 32:6; 42:8; 69:2; Jon 2:3.—v Pss 31:12; 38:12; 79:4;
80:7; 123:3-4; 142:8; Job 12:4; 19:13; Lam 3:7; Dan 9:16.—w Pss 6:6; 9:2;
30:10; 115:17; Isa 38:18.

88:5 The psalmist is alive but dead (see Pss 6:6; 107:18) as to his contempo-
raries (see Pss 22:30; 28:1; 143:7; Prov 1:12). He is like a shade, "a man without
strength" (see Isa 14:19f). *Pit:* see note on Ps 30:2.
   88:6 As far as the psalmist is concerned, he is already in the pit (see note on
Ps 6:6), where he cannot call upon God to remember him and come to his aid
(see Pss 25:7; 74:2; 106:4).
   88:7-10a For some reason God has let a flood of troubles overwhelm the suppliant so that he remains deprived of all human consolation (see Ps 142:7; Lam 3:7).
   88:9 Friends interpret the suffering of the suppliant as a punishment from
God and remain aloof from him lest they also be struck with it.
   88:10a *Eyes grow dim:* see note on Ps 6:8.
   88:10b-13 The psalmist prays to be saved in order to continue to praise the
Lord for his wondrous deeds, for those in the grave can no longer do so (see notes
on Pss 6:6 and 9:2).
   88:11 *Wonders:* see note on Ps 9:2. *Rise up:* i.e., a simple act of rising to give
praise in the kingdom of the dead (see Isa 14:9)—not a bona fide resurrection
from the dead.

¹² Is your kindness celebrated in the grave,
     or your faithfulness in the tomb?*
¹³ Are your wonders known in the region of
     darkness,
     or your righteous deeds in the land of obliv-
        ion?*

¹⁴ But for my part, I cry out to you, O LORD;*
     in the morning my prayer rises before you.
¹⁵ Why do you cast me away, O LORD?
     Why do you hide your face from me?*

¹⁶ Since infancy I have been wretched and close
        to death;
     I have borne your terrors
     and have now reached the point of exhaus-
        tion.
¹⁷ Your wrath has weighed down upon me;
     your terrors have destroyed me.ˣ

¹⁸ All day long they surround me like a flood;
     they encircle me completely.
¹⁹ You have caused my friends and neighbors to
        shun me;ʸ
     my sole companion now is darkness.*

---

x Ps 7:12; Job 6:4; 20:25.—y Ps 38:12; Job 17:13-17; 19:13.

88:12 The psalmist would be unable to render praise to God if he were to go to
the "grave," also known as the "pit." *Kindness . . . faithfulness:* see notes on Pss
6:5 and 36:6f. *The tomb:* literally, "Destruction," another name for the grave or
the pit; in Hebrew it is *Abaddon* (see Job 26:6; 28:22; Prov 15:11; Rev 9:11).
88:13 The psalmist speaks of death as a place of total darkness, also known
as the "land of oblivion" in contrast with the "land of the living" (Pss 27:13;
52:7; 116:9; 142:6), because those who die are quickly forgotten by the living
(see Pss 6:6; 31:13; Eccl 9:5).
88:14-19 Even when human consolation is lacking, suffering can still be bear-
able if God gives his perceptible consolation; however, the psalmist also feels
himself abandoned by God.
88:15 *Why . . . ?:* see note on Ps 6:4. *Hide your face:* see note on Ps 13:2.
88:19 The lamentation ends on a cry of sadness, like Ps 39. However, it is not
a cry of despair, for God cannot remain deaf to the prayers of his faithful ones
(see Ps 79:9-11; Job 16:18-20).

PSALM 89*

Prayer for the Fulfillment of God's Promise

1 A *maskil** of Ethan the Ezrahite.

2 * I will sing forever of the LORD's kindness;
    with my lips I will proclaim your faithful-
      ness*
    throughout the generations.z

3 You said, "My kindness lasts forever;
    my faithfulness is as firmly established as
      the heavens.

4 "I have made a covenant with my chosen
    one;
    I have sworn to my servant David:

---

z Pss 30:10; 36:6; 40:11; 57:11; 59:17; 71:19; 100:5; 108:5; 117:2; Isa 63:7.

Ps 89 This psalm constitutes a beautiful hymn to God the Creator and a grand acclamation to the Lord who has given his word and his promise to Israel. And although the facts in Israel's history seem to give the lie to such splendid visions, the believer refuses to rely on appearances. God's word and his promise are solid in spite of a temporary present roadblock, as a long history bears witness. The temporary roadblock may have been the attack on Jerusalem by Nebuchadnezzar and the exile of King Jehoiachin in 597 B.C. (see 2 Ki 24:8-17) or the disappearance of the Davidic dynasty after the Exile (from the sixth century on).

The psalmist sketches a wonderful catalog of God's work: the origins of the world and the election of David; the order of the cosmos and the stability of the royal throne; heaven and earth and the present, past, and future. In time of incertitude, one must make use of this sublime contemplation and continue to believe in the faithfulness of God. Then the Messianic Hope will be renewed; it is the expectation of the coming of the Lord by his "anointed," the Messiah.

Through David, it is principally to his Son Jesus Christ that God the Father promised love and faithfulness, prosperity and perpetual royal stability upon the new Israel, the Church. Even though catastrophes of all kind seem to belie God's loving faithfulness, we can pray this psalm with complete confidence.

89:1 *Maskil:* see note on Ps 32:1a. *Ethan the Ezrahite:* he is thought to be the son of Zerah (hence, Ezrahite) and member of the tribe of Judah (see 1 Chr 2:6) as well as founder of one of the three choirs (see 1 Chr 15:19) and identical with the *Jeduthun* of Ps 39 (see 2 Chr 5:12).

89:2-5 God is true. If anything is certain, it is his kindness and faithfulness. They endure without fail in creation and they endure in the Covenant with David (see 2 Sam 7:8-16; 1 Chr 17:10-15), on which Israel's Messianic Hope is based.

89:2 *Kindness . . . faithfulness:* see notes on Pss 6:5 and 36:6f. These words are each repeated eight times in the psalm: *kindness* (vv. 2, 3, 15, 18, 25, 29, 34, 50) and *faithfulness* (vv. 2, 3, 6, 9, 15, 25, 34, 50).

⁵ 'I will establish your descendants forever
　　and allow your throne to endure for all
　　generations.' "*a   *Selah*

⁶ * Let the heavens* praise your wonders, O
　　LORD,
　　your faithfulness in the assembly of your
　　holy ones.ᵇ

⁷ For who in the skies can be compared to the
　　LORD?ᶜ
　　Is there any heavenly being who is like the
　　LORD,*

⁸ a God who is feared in the council of the holy
　　ones,
　　greater and more awesome than any who
　　stand in his presence?

⁹ O LORD, God of hosts,* who is like you?
　　Almighty LORD, your faithfulness is never
　　absent.

¹⁰ You control the raging sea,
　　calming its surging waves.ᵈ

¹¹ You crushed Rahab* with a deadly blow;
　　you scattered your foes with your mighty arm.

---

a Pss 61:7-8; 132:11-12; 2 Sam 7:8-16; 1 Ki 8:16.—b Pss 19:2; 29:1;
82:1; Job 1:6; 5:1.—c 7-9: Pss 35:10; 86:8; 111:1; 113:5; Ex 15:11; Isa 6:3;
Jer 10:6.—d 10-11: Pss 65:8; 68:2; 74:13-15; 107:29; Job 7:12; Isa 51:9-10.

89:5 Despite the fall of the Davidic monarchy, God remains faithful to his
Covenant, which is an eternal Covenant (see 2 Sam 7:16; Isa 54:10; 55:3; 61:8;
Jer 31:31-34; Ezek 16:60; 37:26) and the foundation of the Messianic Hope.
89:6-19 The psalmist sings of God's greatness in the secret of heaven where
he is surrounded by angels (the "holy ones" and "any heavenly being," vv. 6-7).
He declares the power of the One who created the earth and rules the primitive
chaos, symbolized by the mythological monster Rahab. The more deeply the believer divines the mystery of God, the more overwhelmed he becomes with joy.
89:6 *The heavens:* i.e., all beings who are part of God's heavenly kingdom.
Wonders: see note on Ps 9:2. *Assembly of your holy ones:* the great council in
heaven (see Ps 82:1).
89:7 *Heavenly being:* literally, "son of God" (see note on Ps 29:1).
89:9-10 *LORD, God of hosts:* see note on Ps 59:6. *Sea:* see note on Ps 65:8.
89:11 *Rahab:* a mythical sea monster that may be another name for Leviathan
(see Pss 74:14; 104:26) and is used in the Old Testament primarily as a personification of the primeval chaos. Here it is a symbol of God's dominance of the sea
and all rebellious creatures. *You scattered . . . arm:* cited in Lk 1:51.

12 Yours are the heavens and yours is the earth;
   you founded the world* and all that is in it.*e*

13 You created the north and the south;*
   Tabor and Hermon joyously praise your
      name.

14 Mighty is your arm and strong is your hand;
   your right hand is forever raised high.

15 Righteousness and justice are the foundation
      of your throne;
   kindness and faithfulness go before your
      face.**f*

16 Blessed* are the people who know how to ac-
      claim you, O LORD,
   who walk in the light of your countenance.

17 In your name they rejoice all day long,
   and they exult in your righteousness.*g*

18 You are the strength in which they glory,*
   and by your kindness our horn* is exalted.*h*

19 For the LORD is our shield,
   the Holy One of Israel, our King.*i*

---

e Pss 24:1-2; 50:12; Deut 10:14; 1 Chr 29:11; 1 Cor 10:26.—f Pss 85:11-
12; 97:2; Ex 34:6-7.—g Pss 30:5; 47:2; 105:3; Zep 3:14.—h Pss 18:2;
75:11; 92:11; 112:9; 148:14.—i Pss 18:3; 47:9; 96:10; 97:1; 99:1; Isa 6:3;
16:5; 33:17, 22.

89:12 *Heavens . . . earth . . . world:* the Lord is the almighty Creator of the heavens and the earth as well as everything in them. He is the benign Ruler of these
same areas with a love that extends through them to the Messianic kingdom, symbolized by David (vv. 4, 21). Thus, he not only created but also redeemed them.

89:13 *The north and the south:* some believe that the Hebrew words for these
two geographical poles (*saphon* and *yamin*) are the names of two sacred mountains in northern Syria: Mount Zaphon (see Ps 48:3 and note; Jos 13:27; Jdg 12:1;
Isa 14:13) and Mount Amana (see Song 4:8), paralleling the mountains Tabor
and Hermon (which also stand for east and west). *Tabor:* a low mountain in the
Valley of Jezreel in northern Israel. *Hermon:* a tall mountain in Lebanon that
marks the southern limit of the Anti-Lebanon range. *Joyously praise:* see note on
Ps 65:14.

89:15 The divine attributes are personified (see Pss 85:11-12; 97:2).

89:16 *Blessed:* see note on Ps 1:1. *How to acclaim you:* literally, "the joyful
shout."

89:18-19 These verses serve as a transition to the great oracle that follows.
The lot of the Davidic dynasty and the coming of the Messiah-King depend completely on the Lord.

89:18 *Horn:* symbolizes strong one (see also Ps 18:3, with note, and Ps 75:11).

20 * On one occasion you spoke in a vision*
    and said to your faithful servants:[j]
    "I have appointed as leader one who is mighty;
    I have exalted one chosen from the people.
21 I have found David, my servant,
    and with my holy oil I have anointed him.

22 "My hand will sustain him;[k]
    my arm will make him strong.
23 No enemy will overcome him;
    no one who is wicked will oppress him.

24 "I will crush his foes before him
    and strike down those who hate him.
25 My faithfulness and my kindness will be with
    him;
    through my name his horn will be exalted.

26 "I will stretch his hand as far as the Sea
    and his right hand as far as the rivers.*
27 He will cry to me, 'You are my Father,[l]
    my God, the Rock of my salvation.'

28 "I will designate him as my firstborn,*
    the highest of all earthly kings.
29 Forever I will maintain my kindness for him,[m]
    and my covenant with him will never end.
30 I will establish his dynasty forever
    and his throne as long as the heavens.

---

j 20-21: Pss 78:70; 132:11-12; Ex 29:7; 2 Sam 7:4, 8:16; 1 Ki 1:39; 1 Chr 17:3, 7-14; Isa 42:1; Acts 13:22.—k 22-25: Ps 18:36; 1 Sam 2:9-10.—l 27-28: Pss 2:6; 110:2-3; 2 Sam 7:9, 14; Jer 3:19; Col 1:15; Jn 20:17; Rev 1:15.—m 29-30: Pss 18:51; 61:8; 144:10; 2 Sam 7:11; Isa 55:3.

89:20-38 This powerful and faithful God has revealed to his "faithful people" (the prophets Samuel and Nathan) his plan for David and his posterity. It is a promise that cannot be effaced, a Covenant that will never be revoked. It is guaranteed by God's kindness and faithfulness.

89:20 *Vision:* the revelation made to Samuel (see 1 Sam 16:12) or to Nathan (see 2 Sam 7:4-16). *Faithful servants:* those faithful to his Covenant.

89:26 *Sea . . . rivers:* David's dominion would extend from the Mediterranean Sea (west) to the Tigris and Euphrates rivers (east) (see Pss 72:8; 80:12).

89:28-30 The only one in whom these promises are fulfilled is Jesus Christ. This is hinted at by the use of *firstborn* and *highest,* which in Hebrew is *elyon,* a divine name (see Ps 83:19), applied to the Messiah, the Son of God (see 2 Sam 7:14; Jn 20:17) and supreme king (see Col 1:18; Rev 1:5).

31 "If his descendants forsake my law*
 and refuse to conform to my decrees,[n]
32 if they break my statutes
 and do not keep my precepts,
33 I will punish their disobedience with the rod
 and their iniquity with scourges.

34 "But I will not deprive him of my kindness
 or fail to observe my faithfulness.*[o]
35 I will not violate my covenant*
 or alter the promise I have spoken.[p]

36 "By my holiness I have sworn once and for all:
 never will I break faith with David.[q]
37 His dynasty will last forever,[r]
 and his throne will endure before me like
 the sun.
38 It will endure forever like the moon,
 a faithful witness in the sky."   *Selah*

39 But now you have spurned and rejected him,*
 you have become filled with wrath against
 your anointed one.[s]
40 You have repudiated your covenant with your
 servant
 and dishonored his crown in the dust.
41 You have breached all his walls[t]
 and turned his strongholds into ruins.
42 Every passer-by has despoiled him;
 he has become a laughingstock to his
 neighbors.

---

n 31-33: Lev 26:14-33; 2 Sam 7:14.—o Ps 40:12; 2 Sam 7:15; Sir 47:22.—
p Num 23:19; Jer 33:20-21.—q Ps 110:4; Am 4:2.—r 37-38: Pss 61:8; 72:5;
Sir 43:6.—s 39-47: Ps 44:10-25.—t 41-42: Ps 80:13-14; Isa 22:5.

89:31-38 God's promises can be said to be partly provisional and partly absolute. As provisional promises, they were not fulfilled in David's descendants who
did not carry out the conditions of the Covenant (vv. 31-33). As absolute promises
they were fulfilled in the Son of God who is also the Son of David (vv. 34-38).

89:34 *Fail to observe my faithfulness:* see 2 Sam 7:15.

89:35-36 See Ps 110:4; Isa 31:2; 55:3; Jer 33:20ff; Am 4:2.

89:39-46 Seemingly, God has renounced his Covenant. The temple is sacked,
the village ruined, the kingship laid open to scorn contrary to the word given to
David. It is of little import as to why such an evil has occurred; the important
thing is that God seems inconsistent.

⁴³ You have exalted the right hand of his foes
   and caused all his enemies to rejoice.ᵘ
⁴⁴ You have driven back his drawn sword
   and left him to fight without your support.

⁴⁵ You have put an end to his glory
   and toppled his throne to the ground.
⁴⁶ You have curtailed the time of his youth*
   and enveloped him in shame.   *Selah*

⁴⁷ How long, O LORD? Will you remain hidden
   forever?*
   How long will your wrath blaze like a fire?ᵛ
⁴⁸ Remember how brief is my span of life
   and how weak you have made all mortals.ʷ

⁴⁹ Who can live and never experience death?
   Who can save himself from the power of
   the netherworld?ˣ   *Selah*
⁵⁰ Where is your kindness of old, O LORD,*
   which you swore to David in your faithfulness?

⁵¹ Remember, O LORD, the insults hurled at
   your servant;
   recall how I have borne in my heart the
   slanders of all the peoples.ʸ
⁵² Your enemies have leveled insults at us, O
   LORD;
   they have taunted the footsteps of your
   anointed one.

---

u Pss 13:3; 44:14; 79:4; 123:3-4; Job 12:4; Lam 1:15; Dan 9:16; Zep 2:8.—v Pss 13:2; 44:25; 74:10; 79:5; Deut 4:24.—w Pss 39:5-6; 62:10; 90:9-10; 144:4; Gen 47:9; Job 7:6, 16; 14:1, 5; Wis 2:5; Eccl 6:12; 1 Pet 1:24.—x Pss 22:30; 90:3; Gen 5:24.—y Pss 69:20; 79:12.

89:46 *Curtailed the time of his youth:* the Israelite royalty enjoyed only four and a half centuries of independence: this was the time of its youth (see Ps 129:1) after its birth in the wilderness (see Isa 46:3; Jer 2:2; Hos 11:1).

89:47-49 To give himself hope, the psalmist begs God not to let him die without having assisted at the renewal of the Covenant. *How long . . . ?:* see note on Ps 6:4.

89:50-52 May the God who made the promise to David not prove insensitive to the king removed from his throne and the people exiled from their kingdom and forced to experience the taunts of the Gentiles. The believer awaits a new discovery of God, as happened in days gone by at the beginnings of love.

53 Blessed be the LORD forever.
    Amen! Amen!*z

BOOK IV—PSALMS 90–106*

PSALM 90*

Prayer To Use Time Wisely

1 A prayer of Moses the man of God.*

LORD, you have been our refuge
    from generation to generation.
2 Before the mountains were brought forth
    or the earth and the world came into exis-
      tence,
    from everlasting to everlasting you are
      God.a

---

z Pss 41:14; 72:18f; 106:48; 150.—a Pss 48:14f; 55:20; 93:2; 102:13; 135:13; 145:13; Gen 1:1; Ex 15:18; 2 Sam 7:16; Prov 8:25; Isa 55:13; Lam 5:19; Hab 1:12.

89:53 This doxology is not a part of the psalm but a conclusion to Book III of the Psalter added by a redactor (see note on Ps 41:14).

Pss 90—106 Joined to a series of very diverse psalms, many of which lack superscription or indication of origin, is a well-defined group: the psalms of the kingdom of God (Pss 93; 96-99). In this part of the Psalter, praise comes to the fore. The psalmists acclaim the Creator who brought the world into being as well as the Lord who intervenes in history. They await the God who comes to make all things new.

Ps 90 The psalmist (who is well versed in the Scriptures) herein depicts the dismal human condition as contrasted with the majesty and eternity of God. The Lord alone remains. Man passes away, a derisory creature undermined by sin; even if his life is lengthy, it remains precarious. The ancient account of the fall and the malediction of Adam (see Gen 3:19) illustrates the origin of our human condition: the ancients accept it with some distress and resignation (see the Book of Ecclesiastes). Man's days are numbered, and it is wisdom to reflect on this fact.

However, such lucidity does not exclude the joy that comes when God's presence illumines the days that he accords to each one and the times that he prepares for his people. This meditation of wisdom becomes a prayer of conversion.

Praying with the expressive formulas of the psalmist will teach us to contemplate the eternity of God and aid us to be detached from the present life, sin, and death, which can prevent us from entering into eternal life.

90:1 *Man of God:* a phrase usually applied to prophets (see 1 Sam 2:27), including Moses (see Deut 33:1; Jos 14:6).

3 You turn men back to dust,
   saying, "Return,* you children of men."[b]
4 For to you a thousand years
   are like a yesterday that has passed[c]
   or one of the watches of the night.*

5 You snatch them away like a dream;[d]
   they are like the grass of the field,*
6 which at dawn flourishes and is green
   but by nightfall is withered and dry.[e]

7 We have been brought low by your anger*
   and overwhelmed with terror by your
   wrath.
8 You have not forgotten our iniquities;
   our secret sins are clearly visible in your
   sight.[f]

9 All our days pass away under your wrath;[g]
   our years are consumed like a sigh.
10 The span of our life numbers seventy years,
   or perhaps eighty, if we have enough
   strength.
   Most of them are marked by toil and emptiness;
   they pass swiftly, and then we fly away.

---

b Pss 103:14; 104:29; 146:4; Gen 3:19; 1 Mac 2:63; Job 34:14-15; Eccl 3:20; 12:7; Sir 40:11; 1 Cor 15:47.—c Job 10:5; 2 Pet 3:8.—d Ps 89:48; Gen 19:15.—e Pss 37:2; 102:12; 103:15-16; Job 14:1-2; Isa 40:6-8; Mt 6:30; Jas 1:10.—f Ps 109:14-15; Hos 7:2; Eph 5:12.—g 9-10: Pss 39:5-7; 62:10; 78:33; 102:24-25; 144:4; Gen 6:3; 2 Sam 19:35; Job 7:6, 16; 14:5; Prov 10:27; Wis 2:5; Eccl 6:12; Sir 18:8; Isa 65:20.

90:3 *Return:* by a word of the Lord, human beings return to the dust from which they were made (see Gen 2:7; 3:19).

90:4 A thousand years are for God like one day or, even less, like a fraction of one night—like one of the three watches into which the night was divided (see Jdg 7:19). This verse is cited by 2 Pet 3:8.

90:5 The life of people is like that of the new grass that appears at dawn and disappears by nightfall under the burning rays of the sun (see Pss 103:16f; 129:6; Job 14:1f; Isa 40:6f). They have no longevity.

90:7-10 Short though it is, human life is filled with trouble because of sin and God's righteous wrath.

90:10 *Most of them are marked by toil and trouble:* an alternative translation is: "Yet their span is but trouble and sorrow" (see Gen 6:3; Job 20:8; Prov 10:27; Eccl 12:1ff; Sir 18:8f).

11 Who understands the might of your anger*
    and rightly fears the power of your wrath?
12 Teach us to comprehend how few our days
    are
    so that our hearts may be filled with wisdom.

13 Return, O Lord. How long must we wait?
    Show compassion to your servants.*
14 Fill us with your kindness in the morning[h]
    so that we may exult and be glad all our
    days.*

15 Grant us joy for as many days as you have
    afflicted us
    and for as many years as we have known
    misfortune.[i]
16 Manifest your works to your servants
    and your glory to their children.

17 May the favor* of the Lord, our God, rest
    upon us.
    And may the work of our hands prosper—
    indeed, may the work of our hands pros-
    per.[j]

---

h Pss 5:12; 17:15; 31:8; 65:5; 85:7; 103:5.—i Num 14:34; Jer 31:13.—j Ps 33:22; Isa 26:12; Hab 3:2.

90:11-12 The psalmist prays that God may teach his people to appreciate the number of years given them and to use them in doing God's will. He asks that they may acquire a correct view of life so as not to challenge God's wrath but rather work out their salvation throughout their life. All this is given us in wisdom, which discerns the true values and gives the righteous a realistic attitude in accord with the divine will and adapted to circumstances (see Deut 4:6; 32:29). *Hearts:* see note on Ps 4:8.

90:13 The psalmist now extends to Israel the meditation and prayer that concerned all humanity. *Return:* i.e., "relent." *How long . . .?:* see note on Ps 6:4.

90:14 The psalmist prays that *in the morning* (the typical time for deliverance and salvation: see note on Ps 49:15) God's love will put an end to the long night of their trial. The fulfillment of this prayer is found in the resurrection (see Rom 5:2-5; 8:18; 2 Cor 4:16-18). *Kindness:* see note on Ps 6:5.

90:17 *Favor:* another translation is "beauty," which constitutes the Lord's "goodness" (see Ps 27:4 and note). Thus, the psalmist asks for God's loving help to his people, so that their work may be effective and enduring, even though the workers are apt to disappear quickly. *Indeed, may the work of our hands prosper:* this second occurrence of these words may be an accidental repetition.

PSALM 91*

Security under God's Protection

¹ You who abide in the shelter of the Most
High,*
who rest in the shadow of the Almighty,
² say to the LORD, "You are my refuge and my
fortress,
my God in whom I place my trust."ᵏ

³ He will rescue you from the snare of the
fowler*
and from virulent pestilence.
⁴ With his feathers he will shelter you,*
and you will take refuge under his wings;
his faithfulness serves as a protective
shield.ˡ

---

k Pss 9:10; 18:3; 31:3-4; 42:10; 142:6; 2 Sam 22:2.—l Pss 17:8; 35:2; 36:8; 57:2; 63:8; Deut 32:10; Ru 2:12; Isa 31:5; Mt 23:37.

Ps 91 This pilgrimage psalm is a glowing testimony to the security that God bestows on those who come to the temple to place themselves under his protection. They will be strengthened by God and his angels all along the path of life in which perils and snares proliferate on every side: the terror by night, the arrow by day, the fowler's snare, pestilence, and plague as well as the asp and viper, lion and dragon—in a word, every possible threat. Death itself seems to retreat, and one gets a glimpse of the peace and joy of the Messianic Age.

En route toward Jerusalem, or toward God, every believer is a pilgrim. The itinerary is not an idyllic dream; rather, amidst risks and dangers, the Lord delivers us from fear and leads us to salvation, to life in his presence. This peaceful psalm is especially suited to be an evening prayer.

We can regard this psalm as an exhortation of Christ developing the invitation that he addressed to his disciples after the Last Supper: "Do not let your hearts be troubled. You place your trust in God [the Father]. Trust also in me" (Jn 14:1). We are to journey along the path of life with the constant certitude that the divine Persons surround us with a never-ending solicitude.

91:1 *The shelter of the Most High:* a designation in the psalms for the temple (see Pss 27:5; 31:21; 61:5). *The shadow of the Almighty:* literally, "the shadow of the wings of the Almighty" (see Pss 17:8; 36:8; 57:2; 63:8). As indicated by v. 4, the shadow is an image of the safety to be found under the outstretched wings of the cherubim in the holy of holies. *Almighty:* literally, "Shaddai," an ancient name for God (see note on Ps 68:15).

91:3 *Snare of the fowler:* a proverbial phrase for danger (see Ps 124:7; Prov 6:5; Hos 9:8).

91:4 *With his feathers he will shelter you:* traditional Biblical image (see note on Ps 17:8).

5 You will not fear the terror by night*
    nor the arrow that flies by day,*m*
6 nor the pestilence that stalks in darkness,
    nor the plague* that lays waste at midday.*n*

7 Even though a thousand may fall at your side,
    ten thousand at your right hand,
    such evils will not afflict you.
8 Rather, your own eyes will behold*
    the punishment inflicted on the wicked.*o*

9 You have made the LORD your refuge
    and chosen the Most High to be your dwell-
        ing.
10 Therefore, no evil will threaten you,
    no calamity will come near your dwelling.*p*

11 * For he will command his angels* about you—*q*
    to guard you wherever you go.*r*
12 They will lift you up with their hands,*s*
    lest you dash your foot against a stone.*
13 You will tread upon the asp and the viper;*t*
    you will trample the lion and the dragon.*

---

m Job 5:21; Prov 3:25; Song 3:8.—n Deut 32:24; Jer 15:8.—o Pss 37:34;
92:12.—p Deut 7:15; Prov 12:21.—q 11-12: Mt 4:6; Lk 4:10f.—r Ps 34:7;
Heb 1:14.—s Ps 121:3; Prov 3:23.—t Job 5:22; Isa 11:8; Dan 6:22; Lk
10:19.

91:5 *Terror by night:* resulting from true or false alerts of enemy attacks; attacks by day were announced by flying *arrows.*

91:6 *Pestilence . . . plague:* dreaded mortal diseases that frequently grew into
epidemics (see Deut 32:24; Hos 13:14; Hab 3:5). In place of the "plague that lays
waste at midday" the versions have: "devil at noon" or the "noonday devil" (apparently a mythological expression for a contagious disease presumed to be
caused by the noonday sun).

91:8 *Your own eyes will behold:* the righteous will be merely a spectator to the
threats mentioned and not be harmed by them.

91:11-12 These words were cited by Satan when tempting Christ to presump-
tion against divine providence (Mt 4:6; Lk 4:10f).

91:11 *His angels:* the teaching on guardian angels is common in the Old Testament (see Ps 34:7; Gen 24:7; Ex 23:20).

91:12 *Against a stone:* along the stony paths of Canaan (see Ps 23:3).

91:13 *Asp . . . viper . . . lion . . . dragon:* these terms correspond to the references found in vv. 5-6 and complete the list of deadly threats against God's servants (see Am 5:19)

[14] "Because he loves me, I will deliver him,*
  I will raise high* the one who acknowledges my name.[u]
[15] When he calls to me, I will answer,
  and I will be with him in time of distress;
  I will rescue him and cause him to be honored.[v]
[16] I will reward him with a long life
  and show him my salvation."*[w]

PSALM 92*

Praise of God's Just Rule

[1] A psalm. A song. For the Sabbath.*

[2] It is good to give thanks to the LORD,[x]
  to sing praise to your name, O Most High,*

---

u Pss 9:11; 119:132.—v Isa 43:2; Jer 33:3; Zec 13:9; Jn 12:26.—w Pss 21:5; 50:23; Deut 6:2; Prov 3:2.—x Pss 9:3; 27:6; 33:1; 135:3; 147:1.

91:14-16 The psalmist reinforces his message by utilizing the form of a prophetic oracle in which God promises Messianic blessings to all who put their trust in him (see Ps 50:15, 23; Rom 8:30).

91:14 *Raise high:* i.e., "raise him to a high, safe place." *My name:* see note on Ps 5:12.

91:16 *With a long life . . . my salvation:* for the Sages of Israel, a long life is the reward of the righteous (see Ex 23:26; Deut 4:40; 1 Sam 2:30; Job 5:26; Prov 3:2, 16; 10:27).

Ps 92 This is a didactic psalm, that is, both a praise of the Lord and an instruction for the faithful. The psalmist meditates on God's way of acting. His love and faithfulness are reflected in everything he does, but they must be comprehended. Ultimately the happiness of the wicked will fade like seasonal grass, whereas the lot of the righteous will be like the great trees whose roots are planted in solid ground. For the latter, new seasons are promised in the courts of God. God's joy is like a new spring in the life of believers.

We can make use of this psalm in following Christ's lead to praise the triune God, to sing of the wondrous divine work that delivers us from our spiritual enemies and mysteriously introduces us into eternal life.

92:1 *For the Sabbath:* these words indicate that in the postexilic temple liturgy this psalm was sung at the time of the morning sacrifice on the Sabbath or seventh day. Psalms sung on the other days were: Ps 24: first day; Ps 48: second day; Ps 82: third day; Ps 94: fourth day; Ps 81: fifth day; and Ps 93: sixth day.

92:2 Human beings have the duty to praise the Lord Most High (see note on Ps 7:18). *Name:* see note on Ps 5:12.

3 to proclaim your kindness* in the morning
    and your faithfulness during the night,
4 with the ten-stringed harp,
    to the melody of the lyre.*y*

5 Your deeds, O LORD, have caused me to exult;*
    at the works of your hands I shout for joy:
6 How great are your deeds, O LORD!*z*
    How profound are your thoughts!
7 * A senseless person cannot grasp this;
    a fool* is unable to comprehend it.

8 Even though the wicked may sprout like grass
    and all evildoers may prosper,*a*
they are doomed to eternal destruction,
9   whereas you, O LORD, are exalted forever.*
10 Surely your enemies, O LORD,
    surely your enemies will perish,
    and all evildoers will be scattered.*b*

11 You have given me the strength of a wild bull*c
    and anointed me with fresh oil.*d*
12 My eyes have witnessed the downfall of my
    enemies;
    my ears have heard the rout of my wicked
    foes.*e*

---

y Pss 33:2; 71:22; 144:9.—z 6-7: Pss 111:2; 131:1; 139:6, 17; Wis 13:1;
17:1; Rev 15:3.—a Ps 37:2, 35.—b Pss 45:5; 68:2-3; 125:5.—c Pss 75:11;
89:18; Deut 33:17.—d Ps 23:5.—e Pss 54:9; 91:8.

92:3 *Kindness:* see note on Ps 6:5.
92:5-6 God's great deeds (of creating, redeeming, and ruling human beings)
bring joy to the psalmist and all who have understanding through his grace.
92:7-10 Evildoers have no knowledge of the Lord's deeds or his dispensing of
justice; they are seemingly happy and prosperous now, but they will soon perish
under the just judgment of the Lord.
92:7 *Senseless person . . . fool:* enemies of God and his faithful (see notes on
Pss 14:1 and 14:2; see also Pss 37:33ff; 68:3; 83:4; 94:8-11).
92:9 *Exalted forever:* since God reigns forever, there is no hope of escape for
the senseless.
92:11-12 The psalmist has experienced victory over his enemies thanks to the
Lord's doing. He is overjoyed with God's favors (see vv. 5-6). The Lord has enabled him to gain the victory (see Ps 89:23-26) and anointed him with *fresh oil*,
i.e., "the oil of gladness" (Ps 45:8; see also Ps 23:5). *Strength:* literally, "horn"
(see Ps 75:11; Deut 33:17; Lk 1:69).

¹³ The righteous will flourish like the palm tree;*
      they will grow like a cedar of Lebanon. *f*
¹⁴ They are planted in the house of the LORD*
      and will flourish in the courts of our God.

¹⁵ They still will bear fruit, in their old age,
      and they will remain fresh and green,
¹⁶ proclaiming, "The LORD is upright;
      he is my Rock, in whom no injustice can be
      found."*g*

PSALM 93*

Glory of the Lord's Kingdom

¹ The LORD is King,* adorned in splendor;
      the LORD has clothed and girded himself
      with strength.

---

f Pss 1:3; 52:10; Jer 17:8; Hos 14:6.—g Deut 32:4; Job 34:10.

92:13-16 In contrast to the lot of the wicked, the righteous are exalted and re-newed in their strength and happiness.

92:14 *Planted in the house of the LORD:* the righteous are likened to trees growing in the temple itself, which is a source of life and fertility because of the divine presence (see Ps 36:8-10; Ezek 47:1-12).

Ps 93 This is one of the nine psalms of the kingdom (Pss 47; 93-100), most of which feature the liturgical acclamation "The LORD is King," in which is centered the whole faith of Israel. All these hymns exalt the kingdom of God that extends over the entire universe and dominates the course of time. God reveals his king-ship when he brings forth the world; he does so even more when he chooses Is-rael. Nonetheless, creation and history are still only the beginning and promise; the kingdom of God will be manifested in all its glory at the end of time (see Rev 4:11; 11:15-17): a new heaven, a new earth, and a new Jerusalem—such are the images that allow us to glimpse the joy of a new humanity gathered together in the glory of God (see Rev 21:1—22:5). The acclamation of the psalms of the kingdom already vibrates with this ineffable hope.

Psalm 93 exalts the Lord who reigns, robed in majesty. He affirms his great-ness by the forces of creation that he rules, by the Law—or "decrees"—that he gives to his people, and by the temple of Jerusalem that he consecrates to his mysterious presence. From his earthly experience, the believer acclaims the splendor of a kingdom that can have no end.

In all truth, we can regard this psalm as applicable to Christ's kingship and sing: "Christ is King." For he vanquishes in himself and in his followers all hostile powers (Satan, death, and sin), delivering believers from the reign of death and transferring them into his kingdom (see Eph 1:2). This is the extraordinary wonder that he continues across the centuries until the full deliverance of his Church and the definitive destruction of his enemies will occur (see Rev 20—22).

93:1a-b *The LORD is King:* a liturgical acclamation that sums up the entire faith of Israel (see Pss 96:10; 97:1; 99:1; see also Zec 14:9).

He has made the world firm,*
  never to be moved.[h]
2 Your throne has stood firm from the begin-
    ning;
  you have existed throughout eternity, O
    LORD.[i]

3 The waters* have lifted up, O LORD;
  the waters have lifted up their voice;
  the waters have lifted up their roar.
4 More powerful than the roar of mighty wa-
    ters,
  more powerful than the crashing waves of
    the sea,[j]
  mighty on high is the LORD.*

5 Your decrees* are firmly established;
  holiness adorns your house,
  O LORD, throughout the ages.

---

h Pss 47:8; 75:4; 96:10; 97:1; 99:1; 104:5; Isa 52:7.—i Pss 55:20; 90:2;
102:13; 2 Sam 7:16; Hab 1:12.—j Pss 18:5; 65:8; Jer 6:23; Mk 8:39.

93:1c-2 The Lord established his kingdom on earth when he created the world
and everything in it (see Ps 24:1). Hence, the world will not be moved no matter
what pressure is brought to bear on it by hostile forces (see Pss 10:6; 104:5), because the Lord has established his rule over it. Indeed, the Lord is eternal (see Ps
90:2), but his rule was established when his throne was set up at the beginning
of history with the creation ("from the beginning"; see Isa 44:8; 45:21; 48:3-8).

93:3 *Waters:* the waters of the primeval chaos that the Lord mastered through
his creative word (see Pss 33:7; 104:7-9; Gen 1:6-10; Job 38:8-11; see also note
on Ps 65:8). They can also stand for the enemies of God and his people (see Job
7:12; Isa 8:7; 17:12; Jer 46:8; Dan 7:2; Rev 17:15) as well as the ocean currents,
whose powers were feared by the pagan nations as indicated in the mythical account of Baal's victory over the sea god Yamm.

93:4 The Lord is the Master of the thundering storms and surging waves by his
simple word (see Christ's calming of the storm by a single word in Mk 4:39).

93:5 *Decrees:* these divine judgments constitute revelation in the wide sense
insofar as they are the norm of human life (see Ps 119). As stable (see Ps 19:8)
as the physical universe and as inviolable (see Ps 95:8-11) as the sanctuary of
Jerusalem, this revelation will be the foundation of the Lord's definitive kingdom,
inaugurated from the creation and already effective in Israel (see Isa 51:9f, 13;
52:7). *Holiness adorns your house . . . throughout the ages:* the temple, home of
the King of Israel, is consecrated forever (1 Ki 8:13; 9:3; Jud 9:18; Ezek 42:13f;
Rev 21:27). Those who approach the most holy God (see Ps 99) are also consecrated (see Ex 19:6; Lev 10:3; 19:2).

PSALM 94*

God, Judge and Avenger

¹ O LORD, you are an avenging God;*
　　shine forth, O God of vengeance.ᵏ

² Rise up, O judge of the earth;
　　repay* the arrogant as they deserve.ˡ

³ O LORD, how long will the wicked,
　　how long will the wicked be triumphant?*ᵐ

⁴ Their mouths pour forth their arrogant words*
　　as these evildoers never cease to boast.ⁿ

⁵ They crush your people, O LORD,
　　and they oppress your heritage.

⁶ They slay the widow and the foreigner
　　and put the orphan to death.ᵒ

---

k Deut 32:35, 41; Nah 1:2.—l Num 10:35; Jer 51:56; Lam 3:64.—m Pss 13:3; 75:5; Jer 12:1—n Ps 73:7-12; Jer 43:2; Mal 2:17; 3:14.—o Ex 22:21-22; Deut 24:17-22; Isa 1:17.

Ps 94 Distressed at God's delays in dispensing justice, the psalmist utters this cry of impatience. Why does God not intervene immediately against the wickedness that crushes the lowly? The reflection of this sage tells him that despite appearances the lot of the righteous is in the final analysis the only one that matters. Certainly God's hour will come when the Lord will avenge his "heritage," the true Israel, that is, the poor. He cannot remain indifferent to wrongs and evils that the innocent endure nor suffer the scorn of haughty spirits and wicked hearts. As "an avenging God," he authorizes no one to launch individual reprisals; it is he himself who reestablishes a justice that is troubled by the arrogance of men to the plight of the poor. These comparative tableaus of the arrogant and the innocent have the astonishing power to challenge us: is our life marked by this sense of justice?

Placed in a condition similar to that of the psalmist, we can pray this psalm to implore the divine intervention against those who exploit our brothers and sisters. At the same time, we can use it to proclaim that trials, far from crushing us, instruct us and enable us to discover true joy and happiness in the love of God (see Jn 15:9-11).

94:1 *An avenging God:* i.e., one who redresses wrongs (see Deut 32:35, 41). It is God's prerogative to avenge as Paul declares in Rom 12:19.

94:2 *Repay:* the central theme of the psalm: God is righteous and repays both the good and the bad as they deserve (see Pss 7:7; 28:4; 62:13; Lam 3:64; Joel 3:4).

94:3 *How long . . . ?:* see note on Ps 6:4.

94:4-7 Not only do the wicked hurl arrogant words, but they also attack God's people, especially those to whom the Lord has promised his protection: the widows, orphans, and aliens (see Ex 22:21; Deut 24:17; Isa 1:17; 10:2; Ezek 22:7). They no longer believe that God is concerned with their activities or demands an accounting from them (see Ps 10:2-11).

7 They say, "The LORD does not see;
  the God of Jacob* pays no attention."p

8 Try to comprehend, you senseless people.*
  You fools, when will you gain some wisdom?q

9 Does the one who made the ear not hear?
  Does the one who fashioned the eye not
  see?r

10 Does the one who guides the nations* not
   punish?
   Does the one who instructs people lack
   knowledge?

11 The LORD is well aware of our thoughts*
   and how foolish they are.s

12 * Blessed* is the man you admonish, O LORD,
   the man you teach by means of your law,t

13 giving him respite in times of misfortune
   until a pit is dug for the wicked.

14 For the LORD will not abandon his peopleu
   or forsake his heritage.*

---

p Pss 10:11; 64:6; 73:11; Job 22:13-14; Ezek 9:9.—q Deut 32:6; Prov
1:22; 8:5.—r Ex 4:11; Prov 20:12.—s Ps 33:15; Eccl 1:2; 1 Cor 3:20.—t Ps
119:71; Job 5:17; Heb 12:5.—u 1 Sam 12:22; Sir 47:22; Rom 11:1-2.

94:7 *Jacob:* i.e., Israel (see Gen 32:29).
94:8-11 The wicked are "senseless" like animals (see Ps 92:7), "fools" (see Ps
49:11) without understanding. The Lord not only hears and sees and knows everything that takes place on earth but also metes out punishment for all wicked
deeds.
94:10 *Guides the nations:* through chastisement (see Lev 26:18; Jer 31:18). *Instructs people:* about the natural and the supernatural order (see Deut 20:1-17;
Isa 28:26).
94:11 *The LORD is well aware of our thoughts:* contrary to what the proud profess to believe. This verse is cited by Paul in 1 Cor 3:20.
94:12-15 Blessed are those who are instructed by God, for they know that God
sees all and rewards and punishes in his own good time.
94:12 *Blessed:* see note on Ps 1:1. *Law:* in the wide sense, revelation and
moral doctrine, as often used in the wisdom writings. This verse recalls Ps
119:71 and Job 5:17.
94:14 God guides his people, especially the powerless, through difficult times
because they are his possession, and he never rescinds his promises. On the Day
of the Lord, divine retribution will be meted out and justice will triumph. This
verse is cited by Paul in Rom 11:1f.

¹⁵ Judgment will again be based on righteousness,
    and all the upright in heart will uphold it.

¹⁶ Who will stand up for me against the wicked?*
    Who will defend me against evildoers?

¹⁷ If the LORD had not come to my aid,
    I would long ago have been consigned to
    the kingdom of silence.*ᵛ

¹⁸ When I realized that my foot was slipping,
    your kindness,* O LORD, raised me up.ʷ

¹⁹ When my anxious thoughts multiplied,
    your comfort filled my soul with joy.*

²⁰ Can evil rulers have you as an ally,*
    those who make use of the law to oppress
    the helpless?*

²¹ They conspire against the righteous*
    and condemn the innocent to death.

²² But the LORD has been my stronghold,*
    my God, the rock in whom I find refuge.

²³ He will repay the wicked for their iniquity
    and destroy them for their evil deeds;ˣ
    the LORD, our God, will destroy them.ʸ

---

v Pss 115:17; 124:2.—w Ps 145:14; Deut 32:35f.—x Pss 7:17; 9:17; 35:8; 57:7; Prov 5:22; 26:27; Eccl 10:8; Sir 27:26.—y Pss 107:42; 145:20.

94:16-19 The faithful psalmist puts his trust in God alone. When he was burdened with cares, temptations, difficulties, and trials, God was always there to help, console, and encourage him and bring joy to his soul.

94:17 *Kingdom of silence:* i.e., the silence of the netherworld (see Pss 88:4-6; 115:17).

94:18 The psalmist experienced the Lord's presence (see Ps 24:1) through the support of God's loving "kindness" (see note on Ps 6:5).

94:19 The psalmist was overcome with anxiety and close to despair because of his situation, but the Lord came to his aid and infused him with consolation and joy (see 2 Cor 1:5). *Soul:* see note on Ps 6:4.

94:20-23 The psalmist is confident that the Lord will save his people and call the wicked to account.

94:20 The Lord will never allow evil to be victorious over himself and his faithful ones for long.

94:21 *Righteous:* see note on Ps 1:5.

94:22-23 The Lord is the "fortress" and "rock" of those who take refuge in him (see Pss 18:2f; 31:3) and the judge and chastiser of those who do evil (see Ps 7:12-17).

PSALM 95*

A Call To Praise and Obey God

¹ Come, let us sing with jubilation to the LORD;*
    let us cry out to the Rock of our salvation.ᶻ
² Let us come before him with thanksgiving
    and extol him with our songs.

³ For the LORD is the great God,
    the King who surpasses all other gods.*ᵃ
⁴ In his hands are the depths of the earth,
    and the peaks of the mountains are his.
⁵ To him belongs the sea, for he created it,ᵇ
    and also the dry land* that his hands have
    molded.

⁶ Come forth! Let us bow down to worship him;
    let us kneel before the LORD, our Maker.*

---

z Ps 5:12; Deut 32:15.—a Pss 47:3; 96:4; 135:5.—b Pss 24:1-2; 146:6.

Ps 95 This psalm calls upon the Israelites assembled in the temple to worship the Lord: "Come, let us sing with jubilation to the LORD." All are invited to give praise, and all acclaim the God of the Covenant. He is the Creator and sovereign Ruler of the world; he is the Shepherd who loves and saves Israel, his flock (see Ezek 34:11, 31; Jn 10).

The Prophets address their oracle to the crowd: "If only you would listen to his voice today. . . ." It is an exhortation to faithfulness, placing them on guard against the sins of yesteryear. The spirit of rebellion has no place in God's land (see Ex 17:1-7; Num 20:13; Deut 6:16; 33:8).

The Letter to the Hebrews gives a long commentary on this exhortation (3:7—4:11), and this invitation to praise God opens the Church's official prayer, the Liturgy of the Hours. Like Israel in the wilderness, the Church journeys on earth. Christians know God's promises but they are equally familiar with temptation. If we wish to enter into the new promised land, that is, share God's life, we must persevere in the struggle for fidelity. Each day is the "today" in which we must heed the voice of God.

95:1-2 The first duty of his faithful toward God is one of praise and adoration (see Isa 66:18-23; Zec 14:16-21). *Rock:* see note on Ps 18:3.

95:3 As the pagans had different gods for different peoples, regions of the earth and sky, and spheres of life (war, fertility), so, the psalmist indicates, do the Israelites. However, in their case, it is only the Lord who is God of every one of these spheres ("who surpasses all other gods") (see Pss 47:3; 96:4; Job 36:22; Dan 2:47).

95:4-5 *Depths . . . peaks of the mountains . . . sea . . . dry land:* depths, heights, waters, and dry land—all are God's as well as everything in them.

95:6 Worship is a concrete expression of the people's devotion to their God. The reason for it is made clear by its placement between the Lord's universal kingship (vv. 3-5) and his Covenant love for his people (v. 7).

7 For he is our God,
  and we are the people he shepherds,*
  the flock he protects.*c*

If only you would listen to his voice today:*d*
8   "Harden not your hearts as you did at
    Meribah,*
  as on the day of Massah in the wilderness.
9 It was there that your ancestors sought to
    tempt me;*e*
  they put me to the test
  even though they had witnessed my works.*

10 "For forty years* I loathed that generation;
  I said, 'They are a people whose hearts go
    astray,
  and they do not know my ways.'*f*
11 Therefore, in my anger I swore,
  'They will never enter my rest.' "*

---

c Pss 23:1-3; 80:2; 100:3; Ezek 34:11; Mic 7:14.—d 7d-11: Pss 81:8;
106:32; Ex 19:5; Deut 12:9; Heb 3:7-11, 15; 4:3, 5, 7.—e Ex 17:1-7; Num
14:22; 20:2-13; Deut 6:16; 33:8; 1 Cor 10:9.—f Ps 78:8; Ex 16:35; Num
14:34; Deut 32:5f; Job 21:14; Prov 12:26; Isa 53:6.

95:7 As the "Maker" of his people (v. 6) because he has brought them into
being as his Covenant people (see Deut 32:6, 15, 18; Isa 44:2; 54:5), the Lord is
also their shepherd, and they are "the people he shepherds" (see Pss 23:1;
79:13; 100:3; Jer 23:1; 25:36; Ezek 34:21; Jn 10:11-14). *If only you would listen to
his voice today:* see Ps 81:8, 13; Ex 19:5; beginning with these words, vv. 7-11
are cited in Heb 3:7-11.

95:8 *Meribah:* this word means "quarreling" and is the name of the place during the journey in the wilderness where the Israelites *sought to tempt* the Lord;
Massah: this word means "testing" and is the name of the place where they
tested the Lord (see Ex 17:7; Num 20:13). Scholars assign the first episode to a
place near and to the southwest of Sinai and the second to a place near Kadesh
Barnea in southern Palestine.

95:9 *Had witnessed my works:* God's wonders in Egypt, at the Red Sea, and in
the wilderness (see Ex 16; Num 14:11, 22).

95:10 *Forty years:* Israel was condemned to wander forty years in the wilderness when the people refused to advance into Canaan and opted to return to
Egypt instead (see Num 14:1-4, 34). *That generation:* the adults who were freed
from Egypt and made a Covenant with the Lord at Sinai (see Num 32:13). *Hearts:*
see note on Ps 4:8. *My ways:* see note on Ps 25:4-7.

95:11 *My rest:* where the Lord has his dwelling (see Ps 132:7, 14) in the land
of Canaan (see Deut 12:9; Ezek 20:15). In Heb 3:7ff, this rest is interpreted in the
spiritual sense of heavenly beatitude.

PSALM 96*

God, Sovereign and Judge of the Universe

¹ Sing to the LORD a new song;*
   sing to the LORD, all the earth.^{g}
² Sing to the LORD and bless his name;
   proclaim his salvation* day after day.

³ Declare his glory* among the nations,
   his wondrous deeds to every people.^{h}
⁴ For great is the LORD and worthy of all praise;
   he is more to be feared than all other gods.^{i}

---

g Pss 30:4; 33:3; 98:1; Isa 42:10.—h Pss 98:4; 105:1; Rev 15:3.—i Pss 48:2; 89:8; 95:3; 145:3.

Ps 96 Partially cited in 1 Chr 16:23-33, this hymn is comprised of Old Testament reminiscences, especially from the Psalter and Isaiah (e.g., 42:10; 55:12). The peoples and nations of which it speaks were originally the neighbors who attempted to prevent Israel from becoming established in Canaan; later, they were all the peoples of the world who failed to recognize the one true God. Israel, which had been saved at the time of the Judges and brought back from an exile through which she had suffered a kind of annihilation, had experienced the Lord's deliverance more than once. She could well bear witness before the whole world of the power and superiority of the one sole God: the Lord had created the world and had given his people new life.

All peoples are invited to acknowledge him as the sovereign Master; all are summoned to the liturgy, to adoration. Deep emotion will grip the entire universe when God comes as Judge; he who has brought into being an unshakable world will establish all human beings in justice and righteousness.

This song of universal joy is always new with the newness of God himself; the New Testament (see Acts 17:31; Rev 19:11) refers to v. 13 in announcing the final coming of Christ on the day of judgment, when he will make all things new. Thus, by means of it Christians call upon the whole universe to praise God the Father as well as the risen Jesus, whom the Father has made "Lord and Messiah" (Acts 2:36), "Leader and Savior" (Acts 5:31), and "ruler of the kings of the earth" (Rev 1:5).

According to the superscription in the Septuagint and Vulgate, this psalm was sung at the dedication of the postexilic temple. Its Messianic content made it suitable for that occasion.

96:1 *New song:* see note on Ps 33:3. *All the earth:* see note on Ps 9:2; see also Pss 97:1; 100:1.

96:2 *Salvation:* the psalmist does not specify the precise nature of the "salvation" he mentions (see note on Ps 67:3-4). Most likely, it included all God's acts in redemptive history: Creation and Redemption (vv. 2, 11-12; see Ps 136:4-25). The People of God must assume the lead by praising the Lord ("bless his name"—see note on Ps 5:12) every day.

96:3 *Glory:* see note on Ps 85:10. *Wondrous deeds:* see note on Ps 9:2.

5 The gods of the nations are merely idols,*j*
    but it was the LORD who made the heavens.*
6 Majesty and splendor surround him;
    power and beauty are in his sanctuary.*

7 Render to the LORD, you families of nations,
    render to the Lord glory and power.**k*
8 Render to the LORD the glory due to his
    name;
    bring an offering and enter his courts.*

9 Worship the LORD in the splendor of his holi-
    ness;
    tremble before him, all the earth.
10 Say among the nations, "The LORD is King.*
    The world is firmly established, never to be
    moved.
    He will judge the peoples fairly."*l*

11 Let the heavens exult and the earth be glad;
    let the sea resound and all that fills it.*m*
12 Let the fields rejoice and all that is in them;
    let all the trees* of the forest shout for joy

---

j Ps 97:7; Lev 19:4; Isa 40:17; 1 Cor 8:4.—k Pss 22:28; 29:2.—l Pss 67:5; 75:4; 93:1; 97:1.—m Pss 97:1; 98:7; Isa 49:13; Rev 12:12.

96:5 *Made the heavens:* since the Lord made the heavens, which were suppos-edly the home of the gods, it follows that he is far greater than all the gods; but he is also greater because they are nothing more than idols.

96:6 The Lord is surrounded by personifications of divine attributes ("majesty and splendor . . . power and beauty") that extol his universal kingship.

96:7 The psalmist makes use of Ps 29:1f, eliminating any allusion to the theme of "heavenly beings" (i.e., "sons of God") and accentuating the universal-ist tone (see Ps 47:10; Zec 14:17). All peoples are specifically summoned to pledge their obedience to the Lord.

96:8 *Courts:* i.e., of the temple where the Lord dwells (see Ps 84:3, 11; 2 Ki 21:5; 23:11f). The psalmist may have been thinking of the outermost court of the temple, which was the court of the Gentiles.

96:10 *The LORD is King:* see note on Ps 93:1a-b. The Lord is not only the Cre-ator of all (as well as the Redeemer of all) but also the Judge of all. Greek and Latin mss have a Christian addition: "from the wood" [of the cross]—a splendid expression of the theology of the cross found in the Gospel of John.

96:11-12 *Heavens . . . sea . . . fields . . . trees:* i.e., the whole world. By being what it is, God's creation gives him glory. However, it will rejoice even more when the fullness of redemption is attained, which it is presently awaiting together with all humanity (see Rom 8:21f).

[13] before the LORD, for he is coming,
   coming to judge the earth.
He will judge the world with justice
   and the nations with equity.*[n]

PSALM 97*

Divine King and Universal Judge

[1] The LORD is King;* let the earth exult;
   let the distant isles rejoice.[o]
[2] * Clouds and darkness* surround him;
   righteousness and justice are the foundation of his throne.[p]

---

n Pss 7:12; 86:11; 98:9; Acts 17:31; Rev 19:11.—o Pss 75:3; 93:1; 96:11;
99:1; Ex 15:18; Isa 52:7.—p Pss 85:11; 89:15; Ex 19:16; Deut 4:11; 5:22; 1
Ki 8:12; Job 22:14.

96:13 The psalmist may have been thinking of the Lord's coming as the one in
which he led the exiles back to Jerusalem. But the Lord comes in many ways. In
Christ, the Lord came to fulfill the words of this psalm, bringing all peoples back
to God, and he will come again at the end of time to judge the living and the
dead (Acts 10:42; 17:31). His judgment is righteousness and truth.

Ps 97 Here is another hymn to King Yahweh, the only Lord and Savior. His
coming is described with the grandiose and traditional images of divine manifestations (see Ex 19:16-20). These produce terror among idolaters and joy in Israel. By the time this song was written, all fear of foreign deities had disappeared among the Israelites; the gods themselves, or at least their worshipers,
are invited to come and prostrate themselves before the only God. The people's
faith in the only Lord is henceforth unshakable.

This majestic Lord is also the God who comes, the one who loves every righteous heart. Furthermore, this God of the universe who is praised is the very same
God who is close to us along the paths of life.

The theme of the kingdom of God was dominant in the teaching of Jesus. According to John's Gospel, Jesus was enthroned on the cross and in his Resurrec-
tion-Ascension. Hence, as Christians pray this psalm, we can rejoice in Christ's
rule.

According to the superscription in the Septuagint and Vulgate, this psalm was
sung when David's land was established, hence after the return from the Exile.

97:1 *The LORD is King:* see note on Ps 93:1a-b. *The distant isles:* distant coun-
tries accessible only by sea (see 1 Ki 9:26-28; 10:22; Isa 60:9; Jon 1:3).

97:2-6 The psalmist portrays the Lord's appearance by traditional signs of his
manifestation at Sinai. These went on to become the signs used to describe the
future Day of the Lord, when he would come in glory to establish true justice on
the earth (see notes on Pss 18:7 and 18:8-16).

97:2 *Clouds and darkness:* these served to veil God's ineffable glory from
human eyes (see Ex 19:9; 1 Ki 8:12). *Righteousness and justice:* divine attributes
personified (see Pss 61:8; 85:12; Prov 16:12; 25:5).

3 Fire* precedes him,
   consuming his enemies on every side.
4 His flashes of lightning illumine the world;
   the earth sees this and trembles.q

5 The mountains melt like wax before the LORD,
   before the LORD of all the earth.r
6 The heavens proclaim his righteousness,*
   and all the nations behold his glory.s

7 All who worship images are put to shame,
   those who boast of their worthless idols;
   bow down before him, all you gods.*t

8 Zion hears and rejoices,
   and the cities* of Judah exult
   because of your judgments, O LORD.u
9 For you, O LORD, are the Most High over all
   the earth;
   you are exalted far above all gods.v

10 Let those who love the LORD hate evil,*
    for he protects the souls of his faithful ones
    and rescues them from the hand of the
       wicked.w
11 Light* dawns for the righteous,
    and joy for the upright in heart.x

12 Rejoice in the LORD, you who are righteous,
    and give thanks to his holy name.*y

---

q Pss 18:8; 50:3; 77:19; 99:1; 104:32; Jdg 5:4-5.—r Ps 68:3; Jud 16:15;
Mic 1:4.—s Pss 50:6; 98:6.—t Ps 96:5; Jer 10:14.—u Pss 9:3; 48:12.—v Pss
7:8; 83:19.—w Ps 121:7; Prov 8:13.—x Ps 4:7f; 112:4.—y Pss 30:5; 104:34.

97:3 *Fire:* symbol of God's wrath (see Pss 21:10; 50:3; 83:15; Deut 4:24; 1 Ki
19:12; Isa 10:17).
97:6 *The heavens proclaim his righteousness:* the heavens show forth the
glory of their Creator to all peoples (see Ps 19:2-5a).
97:7 Those who trust in false gods are put to shame. For "our God is in
heaven; he does whatever he pleases. Their idols are merely silver and gold, the
work of human hands" (Ps 115:3f).
97:8 *Cities:* literally, "Daughters." *Judgments:* see note on Ps 48:12.
97:10-12 Those who are loyal to the Covenant (the righteous) live in the light
of God's presence, where there is fullness of joy. They glorify his holy name, that
is, they honor him by their lives.
97:11-12 *Light:* see notes on Pss 27:1 and 36:10. *Name:* see note on Ps 5:12.

PSALM 98*

Praise of the Lord, King and Judge

[1] A psalm.

Sing to the LORD a new song,[z]
    for he has accomplished marvelous deeds.
His right hand and his holy arm [a]
    have made him victorious.*

[2] The LORD has made known his salvation;
    he has manifested his righteousness for all
       the nations to see.*

[3] He has remembered his kindness and his fidelity
    to the house of Israel.
The farthest ends of the earth have witnessed
    the salvation of our God.*

[4] Sing joyfully to the LORD, all the earth;
    raise your voices in songs of praise.

[5] Sing praise to the LORD with the harp,
    with the harp and melodious singing.

---

z Pss 30:4; 96:1; Isa 42:10.—a Ps 44:3; Jos 24:4; Isa 59:16; 63:5; Lk 1:51.

Ps 98 Israel has returned from the Exile; God has saved her, and the whole world is a witness of it. Hence, the Lord is pursuing his project of salvation. Let all peoples acclaim him as their sovereign and let joy burst out over the whole face of the earth, for God comes to inaugurate a kingdom of peace and justice for all humanity. The same worldwide perspective is glimpsed in the second part of the Book of Isaiah (Isa 40—55) with which the psalms of the kingdom have much in common.

The previous psalm brought to mind the second coming of Christ. This psalm recalls the first coming of the Lord and the faith of all peoples. Hence, the Christian Liturgy uses it during the Christmas season, since the latter is so filled with joy at the coming of the Lord, the Savior of all human beings.

98:1 God's deliverance of Israel from exile, a type of the Messianic redemption, is such a wondrous deed that it deserves to be praised in song. *New song:* see note on Ps 33:3. *Marvelous deeds:* see note on Ps 9:2. *His right hand and his holy arm:* God is portrayed as a champion warrior.

98:2 Reminiscent of his wonders during the Exodus, God has once again revealed his infinite power and greatness (see note on Ps 46:11; see also Isa 52:10).

98:3 God has kept the promise he made to the house of Israel, and it is fully visible to all nations. The complete fulfillment of this promise was what God performed in the redemption worked by his Son Jesus Christ—which also was seen by all nations. *Kindness:* see note on Ps 6:5.

⁶ With trumpets and the sound of the horn
   sing joyfully to the King, the LORD.*b

⁷ Let the sea resound and everything in it,*
   the world* and all its inhabitants.c
⁸ Let the rivers clap their hands
   and the mountains shout for joy.d

⁹ Let them sing before the LORD, who is coming,
   coming to judge the earth.e
He will judge the world with justice
   and the nations with fairness.*f

PSALM 99*

God, King of Justice and Holiness

¹ The Lord is King;*
   let the nations tremble.
He sits enthroned on the cherubim;
   let the earth quake.g

---

b Ps 47:6-7; Ex 19:16.—c Pss 93:3; 96:11.—d Ps 148:9; Isa 44:23; 55:12.—e Pss 75:3; 96:13.—f Pss 7:12; 9:9; 67:5; 96:10.—g Pss 18:8-11; 48:2; 80:2; 93:1; 97:1; Ex 15:18; 25:20, 22; 1 Sam 4:4; 2 Sam 6:2; 1 Chr 16:30f; Isa 52:7.

98:6 The whole of creation is summoned to acclaim the Lord as King, as Israel acclaimed her kings at their coronation, with trumpets and horns (see 1 Ki 1:34).
98:7-9 All creation is exhorted to honor its King (see note on Ps 96:11-12).
98:7 *Sea . . . world:* the two major areas that contain living things.
98:9 The Lord will come to rule everyone impartially. Jesus announced that the long-awaited coming of the Lord to rule the earth had begun in his ministry (see Mk 1:15: "The kingdom of God is close at hand"). See also note on Ps 96:13.
Ps 99 Each of the two parts of this eschatological hymn is followed by a refrain (vv. 5, 9) that stresses the holiness of the King of Israel (see Isa 6:3-5). In the temple at Jerusalem, the Ark of the Covenant had two winged creatures, the cherubim, which were considered to be the throne of God. It is a weak image of the greatness of the Almighty, for whom Mount Zion is a "footstool." God is so holy that he infinitely transcends all the realities of the universe. However, his holiness is not a far-off greatness, indifferent to human life. In adoring him we are brought face to face with the demands of justice, right, and faith. The holiness of a God is truly astounding. In the final analysis, it constitutes God's intimate presence in our lives.
We can pray this psalm in honor of Christ the King who is all-holy and always obedient to the will of his Father (see Jn 4:34; 14:31). His whole life Jesus carried out what the Father had given him to accomplish, one lengthy self-sacrifice for the salvation of the world (Heb 7:27; 9:28).
99:1 *The LORD is King:* see note on Ps 93:1a-b. *Cherubim:* see note on Ps 18:11.

2 The LORD is great in Zion;
  he is exalted above all the peoples.
3 Let them praise your great and awesome
    name:*
  holy is he!*h*

4 Mighty King, you love justice,
    and you have established fairness;
  in Jacob you have brought about
    what is just and right.**i*
5 Exalt the LORD, our God,
    and worship at his footstool;*j*
  holy is he!*

6 Moses and Aaron were among his priests,
    and Samuel was among those who invoked
      his name;*k*
  they cried out to the LORD,
    and he answered them.*
7 He spoke to them from the pillar of cloud;*
    they obeyed his decrees and the law he
      gave them.*l*

---

h Ps 33:21; Isa 6:3.—i Pss 2:6; 72:1; Jer 23:5.—j Ps 132:7; Ex 15:2.—k
Ex 28:1; 1 Sam 7:5; Jer 15:1.—l Ps 19:10; Ex 19:18-19; 33:9; Num 12:5.

99:3 *Name:* see note on Ps 5:12. *Holy is he:* God is so holy that he infinitely transcends all the realities of our universe; furthermore, because he is holy himself, God calls upon his people to be holy too (see Lev 11:44). They must consecrate themselves wholly to him (see also Mt 5:48; Rom 12:1).

99:4 God is completely just by nature. He gave the Law to his people so that they could live in his ways. Paul characterizes the Gospel as the revelation of the justice ("righteousness") of God (see Rom 1:17). *Jacob:* i.e., Israel (see Gen 32:29).

99:5 God is portrayed seated in heaven with his feet resting on the earth as on a footstool (see Isa 66:1), and more specifically on Mount Zion (see Ps 132:7; 1 Chr 28:2; Lam 2:1). The people are to praise and worship the Lord at his footstool.

99:6 The psalmist wishes to show that the Lord is a gracious King who hears the prayers of all who come to him with the right disposition. To do so, he mentions three great figures who at various stages interceded with the Lord for the nation (see Ex 32:30; Num 17:12f; 1 Sam 7:2-11).

99:7 *Spoke to them from the pillar of cloud:* the pillar of cloud was the symbol of God's presence with his people during the Exodus (see Ex 13:21f), and God spoke to Moses (see Ex 33:9) and to Aaron (see Num 12:5) in the pillar of cloud. But though he spoke to Samuel, we have no record of it being in the pillar of cloud. Hence, the psalmist may here be alluding to the communication itself rather than how God communicated.

8 O LORD, our God,
   you answered them;
 you were a forgiving God to them,
   but you punished their wrongdoings.*m
9 Exalt the LORD, our God,
   and worship at his holy mountain,
   for the LORD, our God, is holy.*

PSALM 100*

Processional Entrance Hymn

1 A psalm of thanksgiving.*

Acclaim the LORD* with joy, all the earth;
2   serve the LORD* with gladness;
   enter his presence with songs of joy.

---

m Ex 22:26; 32:11; Lev 26:18; Num 14:20; 20:12.

99:8 *Punished their wrongdoings:* among those punished for wrongdoings were Moses and Aaron, neither of whom was allowed to enter the promised land (see Ps 106:22f; Num 27:14; Deut 3:26).

99:9 Refrain similar to that in v. 5.

Ps 100 Although it does not explicitly mention the theme of the Lord as King, this psalm is linked with the group of psalms of the kingdom by its style and ideas and serves as a kind of general conclusion for them. The Lord is King of the world and especially of Israel his flock. This is the Good News that calls for praise and joy.

The psalmist intimates that in a few brief moments, the sacrifice will be offered by which the people enter into communion with God (see Lev 7:11-15). He invites the throng to celebrate the one God and his providence for the people he has created and chosen for himself. Although this hymn is short, it must have filled the hearts of believers with great wonder since they knew themselves to be in the hand of God. The entire universe is invited to share this endless joy of Israel.

By this hymn, the Church calls Christians to sing to the Lord Jesus with a similar enthusiastic joy, for he too is our Lord and God (see Jn 20:28). In cooperation with his Father he has created and then re-created us (see Jn 1:1-3, 12). Because of this, we belong entirely to him (see 1 Cor 3:22f).

100:1a *Thanksgiving:* this word may indicate that the psalm was to be used in conjunction with a "thank offering" (see Lev 7:12).

100:1b *Acclaim the LORD:* a similar opening phrase occurs in Pss 66; 81; and 95. *All the earth:* the entire world is to worship God for all that he is and all that he has done for his people (see Pss 47:2f; 66:1, 4; 97:1; 117:1 for this theme of universalism).

100:2 *Serve the LORD:* the psalmist reminds the people that their first duty is to worship the Lord with mind, heart, and voice in complete gladness.

³ Proclaim that the LORD is God.*
   He made us and we are his possession;
   we are his people, the flock he shepherds.ⁿ

⁴ Offer thanksgiving as you enter his gates,*
   sing hymns of praise as you approach his
      courts;
give thanks to him and bless his name,ᵒ
⁵ for the LORD is good.
His kindness endures forever,
   and his faithfulness is constant to all gen-
      erations.*

PSALM 101*

Norm of Life for a Good Ruler

¹ A psalm of David.

I will sing of kindness and justice;
   to you, O LORD, I will offer praise in song.ᵖ

---

n Pss 23:1; 95:7; Deut 32:39; Isa 40:10, 13; 64:8; Mic 7:14.—o 4-5: Pss 42:4; 106:1; 107:1; 118:1; 136:1; 138:8; Ezr 3:11; Jer 33:11.—p Pss 33:1; 51:17; 89:2; 145:7.

100:3 *Proclaim . . . God:* acknowledge that the Lord is God and be faithful to him; it is a statement of monotheism (see Deut 4:39; 32:39; Isa 43:10, 13). *Made us . . . his people:* through his choice and the wonders he did for them (see Ps 95:6). *Flock he shepherds:* see note on Ps 95:7. Christians know that God made us his people through Jesus, the Good Shepherd, who gave his life for his sheep (see Jn 10:11).

100:4 *His gates:* of the temple (see note on Ps 24:7, 9). *Courts:* of the temple (see Pss 84:3, 11; 2 Ki 21:5; 23:11f).

100:5 The psalm concludes with the reasons why the Lord is to be praised: he is good (i.e., generous), kind (i.e., merciful), and faithful to his promises from generation to generation (see Pss 106:1; 107:1; 118:1; 136:1; 138:8; 2 Chr 5:13; Ezr 3:11; 1 Mac 4:24; Jer 33:11; Mic 7:18-20; Mt 19:17; 1 Jn 4:7ff).

Ps 101 The Lord's Covenant comprises a rule of life for every Israelite, including the king. This psalm constitutes the mirror of the ruler in whom it inculcates essential resolutions: personal integrity, choice of loyal counselors, ferreting out the arrogant, the deceitful, and the slanderous from the royal court, and the battle against injustice. The teaching is classic in the Bible, but its application is rarely carried out. Nonetheless, its main ideas continue to be vitally relevant.

We can pray this psalm in honor of Christ the King, constituted by the Father as supreme Head of the Church and of the world (Eph 1:20-23), who alone has perfectly fulfilled the commitments mentioned herein. He is thus the invisible Suzerain from whom all visible leaders (both spiritual and temporal) derive their authority (see Jn 21:15-17; Rev 1:5). Since Christ makes them his representatives, all these leaders must be loving and faithful images before their subjects.

2 I will walk in the path of blamelessness;
     when will you come to me?*

Within my house* I will act
     with integrity of heart.*q*
3 I will not allow any shameful act
     to be done before my eyes.

I will refuse to associate*
     with people who do evil.*r*
4 Let the perverse of heart remain far from me;
     I will not tolerate the wicked.

5 Anyone who secretly slanders a neighbor*s*
     I will reduce to silence.
Anyone with haughty glances and an arro-
          gant heart
     I cannot endure.*t*
6 The faithful in the land are the ones
     whom I will choose to be my companions.
Only the one who follows the path of integrity
     will be allowed to be my servant.*u*

7 No one who practices deceit
     will be permitted to remain in my house.
No one who utters lies
     will be numbered among my companions.*v*

q Ps 26:11; 1 Ki 3:14; Isa 33:15.—r Prov 11:20; Jer 16:18.—s Ex 20:16;
Prov 17:20.—t Prov 21:4.—u Pss 26:11; 119:1; Prov 20:7.—v Ps 5:5; Prov 25:5.

101:2ab In imitation of the heavenly King, the psalmist himself will lead a
blameless life. But to do so he will need God's help, which he prays will be forth-
coming (see 1 Ki 3:7-9; see also Ps 72). *When will you come to me?:* some see in
these words an allusion to the awaited coming of the Messiah, who was at times
called "He who comes" (see Mt 11:3; Jn 4:25). Others offer an alternative translation: "I will attend to the wholehearted man / whenever he comes to me."
     101:2c-3b *House:* the king promises to make his household free of those who
abuse power. *Heart . . . eyes:* in the Old Testament, people were thought to act
after inner ("heart") and/or external ("eye") influence (see note on Ps 4:7; see
also Ps 119:36f; Num 15:39; Job 31:7; Prov 21:4; Eccl 2:10; Jer 22:17).
     101:3c-4 The psalmist will not desire or do evil himself nor condone it in
others and will avoid all evildoers.
     101:5-6 The norms of the king's private life are also the fundamental principles
of his governing. He will bring into his service only the "faithful" and those who follow "the path of integrity." *Reduce to silence:* i.e., destroy (see Pss 54:7; 94:23).
Proud: i.e., the haughty; see note on Ps 31:23.
     101:7 *Will . . . companions:* another translation is: "will stand in my presence."

⁸ Morning after morning I will banish
   all the wicked from the land,
      removing all evildoers from the city of the
      LORD.*

PSALM 102*

Prayer of an Exile

¹ The prayer of one afflicted. When he is wasting away
and pours out his anguish before the LORD.*

² O LORD, give heed to my prayer;*
   let my plea for help reach you.
³ Do not conceal your face* from my sight
   in the time of my distress.
Incline your ear to me;
      on the day when I call out to you answer
      me speedily.ʷ

⁴ For my days are fading away like smoke,ˣ
   and my bones are burning like live coals.

---

w Pss 22:25; 31:3; 37:2; 69:18; 143:8.—x 4-6: Ps 38:4-9; Lam 1:13.

101:8 Evildoers will be eradicated from the kingdom. *Morning after morning:* the customary time for administering justice (see 2 Sam 15:2; Jer 21:12) and for receiving God's help (see Pss 59:17; 143:8; Isa 33:2). *City of the LORD:* see Pss 46:5f; 48:2f, 9; 87:3).

Ps 102 Known as the fifth of the seven Penitential Psalms (Pss 6; 32; 38; 51; 102; 130; 143), this psalm combines the lament of an afflicted person overwhelmed with pain and the prayer of the community of poor returned exiles waiting to be able to rebuild the walls of Jerusalem, their holy city. It shows that humanity and the universe pass away, while God remains (vv. 12, 13, 26, 28). This is the proof of the Lord's power and the reason for their hopes.

It is also the reason for the hopes of Christians, since we know that in Jesus and in his Church God has built an imperishable dwelling place for his people, a point emphasized by the Letter to the Hebrews (1:10-12) when it comments on vv. 26-28 of this psalm.

102:1 This superscription is unique, giving neither author nor liturgical or historical note; instead it assigns the prayer to a life situation—when one afflicted is close to giving up, i.e., *wasting away* (see Pss 61:3; 77:4; 142:4; 143:4).

102:2-12 One day, possibly during a grave sickness, the psalmist reaches the bitter conclusion of the inconsistency of human life. And the supreme outrage is that all who see him attribute his sad state to punishment sent by God, for his prayer and repentance receive no answer. The poor man experiences the depths of anguish where everything is falling apart; he can do nothing except cry out to God.

102:3 *Conceal your face:* see note on Ps 13:2.

⁵ My heart* is stricken, withered like grass;
    I am too exhausted to eat my bread.

⁶ As a result of my incessant groaning,
    I am now nothing more than skin and bones.

⁷ I am like a pelican* of the wilderness,
    like an owl among the ruins.

⁸ I am sleepless* and I moan
    like a lone sparrow on a rooftop.

⁹ All day long my enemies revile me;*
    those who rage against me use my name as
        a curse.

¹⁰ I eat ashes as though they were bread,*
    and I mingle tears with my drink.ʸ

¹¹ Because of your indignation and wrath,
    you have raised me up only to cast me down.

¹² My days are like a lengthening shadow,ᶻ
    and I am withering away like grass.ᵃ

¹³ But, you, O LORD, are enthroned forever,*
    and your renown will endure for all gener-
        ations.ᵇ

y Pss 42:4; 80:6; Isa 44:20.—z Pss 109:23; 144:4; 1 Chr 29:15; Job 8:9;
14:2; Eccl 6:12; Wis 2:5.—a Ps 90:5-6; Job 8:12; Jas 1:10.—b Pss 55:20;
90:2; 93:2; 135:13; 145:13; Ex 15:18; Isa 55:13; Lam 5:19; Hab 1:12.

102:5 *Heart:* see note on Ps 4:8. *Withered like grass:* see note on Ps 90:5.

102:7 *Pelican:* a bird that in Christian times became a symbol of Christ all alone in Gethsemane and of the Eucharist. The word is also translated as "owl." *Owl:* a symbol of desolateness and destruction (see Isa 34:11, 15; Jer 50:39; Zep 2:14).

102:8 *I am sleepless:* some translations omit the words: "and I moan."

102:9 *Enemies revile me:* see note on Ps 5:10; see also Ps 109:25. *Use my name as a curse:* his enemies point him out as an example of divine malediction, saying: "May you become as wretched as so-and-so."

102:10-12 The Israelites indicated their penance externally by covering their heads with ashes and uttering lamentation accompanied by copious tears. To obtain God's pity, the sick psalmist does not hold back. He covers himself with such an abundance of ashes that they are interspersed with his food, and he gives way to so many tears that they mingle with his drink. All the same, he is inexorably on his way toward death.

102:13-23 The people thus experience a time of scorn. Uprooted from their temple and their land, they are too overwhelmed by the loss of what they most cherish for them to think of revenge. They have recourse to God's tender mercies. In their misfortune, they fall back on a single certitude—the goodness of the Lord. At once, hope of restoration begins shining forth, for "the appointed time has come" (v. 14)—so much so that they do not stop at imagining the sole reestablishment of Israel, but their perspective of renewed happiness embraces all humanity.

14 You will arise and show mercy to Zion,
    for it is time for you to have pity on her;
    the appointed time* has come.
15 For her stones are precious to your servants,
    and her dust causes them to weep.*

16 The nations will revere your name, O LORD,
    and all the kings of the earth will sing of
      your glory.*c
17 For the LORD will rebuild Zion
    and reveal himself in all his glory.*
18 He will answer the prayer of the destitute,
    and he will not ignore their petition.

19 Let this be written* for future generations
    so that a people yet unborn may praise the
      LORD:d
20 "The LORD looked down from his sanctuary
    on high
    and gazed on the earth from heaven,e
21 to hear the sighs of the prisoners
    and to set free those under sentence of
    death."*f

22 Then the name of the LORD will be proclaimed
    in Zion,
    and his praise* in Jerusalem

---

c Pss 77:8; 119:126; Deut 32:36; 1 Ki 8:43; Isa 59:19; 66:18.—d Ps 22:31-32; Rom 4:24.—e Pss 11:4; 14:2; 53:2.—f Ps 79:11; Lk 4:18.

102:14 *Appointed time:* the time established by God for judgment and salvation (see Ps 75:3; Ex 9:5; 2 Sam 24:15; Dan 11:27, 35).
102:15 The psalmist intimates that Zion must be highly cherished by the Lord for she is so dear to his servants.
102:16 See note on Ps 46:11. *Name:* see note on Ps 5:12.
102:17 *And reveal himself in all his glory:* may also be translated as: "and thus appear in his glory" (see v. 16 and note on Ps 46:11; see also Isa 40:1-5). The ultimate fulfillment of this hope will occur in the "new Jerusalem" (see Rev 21).
102:19 *Written:* this is the only place in the Psalter that calls for a written record of God's saving deed. The usual reference is to an oral record (see Pss 22:32; 44:2; 78:1-4).
102:21 *Prisoners . . . those under sentence of death:* see note on Ps 79:11.
102:22 *Name . . . praise:* see notes on Pss 5:12 and 9:2.

²³ when all peoples and kingdoms come together
to worship the LORD.*ᵍ

²⁴ He has taken away my strength on my life's
journey;*
he has cut short my days.
²⁵ So I said: "Do not carry me off, O my God,
before half my days are done,*
for your years endure from age to age.ʰ

²⁶ "Long ago you laid the foundations of the
earth,*
and the heavens are the work of your hands.ⁱ
²⁷ They will pass away but you endure;
they will all wear out like a garment.
You will change them like clothing,
and they will perish.*

²⁸ "However, you remain always the same,
and your years will have no end.*
²⁹ The children of your servants will be secure,
and their descendants will dwell in your
presence."*ʲ

---

g Ps 22:28; Isa 60:3-4; Zec 2:11; 8:22.—h Pss 39:5; 90:10; Job 14:5;
36:26.—i 26-28: Isa 51:6; Heb 1:10-12.—j Pss 25:13; 69:37.

102:23 See notes on Pss 46:11 and 47:10; see also Pss 96; 98; 100; Isa 2:2-4;
Mic 4:1-3. *Name:* see note on Ps 5:12.
102:24-29 Here the individual lament and the national supplication are combined. Upon meditating on the precariousness of existence before the God who
endures forever, a hope arises, the hope of not being abandoned. The Letter to
the Hebrews (13:8) will proclaim: "Jesus Christ is the same yesterday, today, and
forever."
102:25 *Before half my days are done:* when the normal life span is only half-
completed (see Isa 38:10; Jer 17:11).
102:26-28 This passage is inspired by Isa 51:6-8 and applied to the Messiah
(Heb 1:10-12). The restoration of Israel and the coming of the Messiah will be the
preface to the eschatological renewal or regeneration that will accompany the
end of time (see Isa 65:17; 66:22; Rev 20:11; 21:1).
102:27 Both the "foundations of the earth" and the "heavens" (which the
ever-living God has made) will perish (see Pss 1:6; 90:4; 2 Pet 3:8ff) and be of no
use, like discarded clothing (see Isa 51:6).
102:28 By contrast, the Lord remains forever the same (see Heb 13:8); he is
the "first and the last" (see Deut 32:39; Isa 41:4; 46:4; 48:12).
102:29 Because God does not change, the children of his people will be secure
in the Lord (see Mal 3:6). *Dwell in your presence:* another translation is: "dwell in
the [promised] land" (see Pss 25:13; 69:37; see also Ps 37:3, 29; Isa 65:9).

PSALM 103*
Praise of God's Providence

¹ Of David.

Bless the LORD, O my soul;*
　　my entire being, bless his holy name.
² Bless the LORD, O my soul,
　　and do not forget all his benefits.

³ He forgives all your sins
　　and heals all your diseases.*
⁴ He redeems* your life from the pit
　　and crowns you with kindness and mercy.ᵏ
⁵ He satisfies your years with good things
　　and renews your youth like an eagle's.*

---

k Pss 28:1; 30:4; 34:23; 40:3; 69:16; 88:5; 143:7; Prov 1:12; Jon 2:6.

Ps 103 In its literary construction and sublime concepts, this psalm is one of the most pure and joyous of the Psalter. Healed of a grave sickness that he considers to have been caused by sin, the psalmist regards this cure doubled by God's pardon as a privileged experience of the love of the Lord. By this favor, God has shown his love for the psalmist in concrete fashion, thus powerfully confirming for him the revelation he made of this love to Israel through the Exodus and to Moses in the meeting on Sinai.

God's love is boundless for the righteous and magnanimous for sinners, disconcerting for the ephemeral creatures that we are and long-suffering to the point of extending to the far-off descendants of his faithful ones. Such is the love of the infinite God whose name is holy, whose throne is in heaven, and whose reign is eternal. He is the Father who will reveal Jesus and whose ineffable goodness Paul will proclaim (see 1 Cor 2:9). We can thus understand how right the psalmist is in calling upon heaven itself to celebrate such a God.

The signal corporal and spiritual cure obtained by the psalmist constitutes only a pale figure of the Resurrection that definitively snatches Jesus from corporal death and the sinful world and shows him his Father's love with incomparable force. By sharing in the Resurrection of Christ through the sacraments, Christians discover that "God is love" in an experience derived from that of Christ and far superior to that of the psalmist. In all truth, every Christian can recite this psalm to praise the God who is love.

103:1 *Soul:* see note on Ps 6:4. *Name:* see note on Ps 5:12.

103:3 Following the Old Testament understanding, the psalmist considers sufferings as the punishment for sin (see Ps 41:5; Ex 15:26).

103:4 *Redeems:* i.e., "delivers." *Pit:* i.e., the grave (see note on Ps 30:2).

103:5 *Like an eagle's:* because of its acknowledged long span of life, which at times reaches one hundred years, the eagle was regarded as a symbol of perennial youth and vigor (see Isa 40:31). It was thought that when an eagle became old and its eyes grew dim, it flew toward the sun, so that the film was burned away from its eyes and its plumage was renewed by the sun's scorching rays.

⁶ The LORD performs acts of righteousness
    and administers justice for all who are op-
    pressed.*l*
⁷ * He made known his ways* to Moses,
    his wondrous deeds to the people of Israel.

⁸ The LORD is merciful and gracious,*
    slow to anger and abounding in kindness.*m*
⁹ He will not always rebuke,
    nor will he remain angry forever.
¹⁰ He does not treat us as our sins deserve
    or repay us according to our offenses.

¹¹ As high as the heavens are above the earth,
    so great is his kindness toward those who
    fear him.*n
¹² As far as the east is from the west,
    so far has he removed our transgressions
    from us.*

¹³ As a father has compassion for his children,*
    so the LORD has compassion for those who
    fear him.

---

l Pss 9:9; 146:6-7.—m Pss 86:15; 145:8; Ex 34:6-7; Num 14:18; Jer 3:12; Joel 2:13; Jon 4:2; Mic 7:18-19; Jas 5:11.—n Pss 13:6; 57:11; Isa 55:9; Eph 3:18.

103:7-12 God made known his ways to Moses on Mount Sinai, telling him that his attitude toward human beings and his great works find their inspiration in his loving kindness. Passing mysteriously before Moses, God cried out: "The LORD, the LORD, the compassionate and gracious God, slow to anger, abounding in love and faithfulness, maintaining love to thousands, and forgiving wickedness, rebellion, and sin. Yet he does not leave the guilty unpunished" (Ex 34:6f).

103:7 *His ways:* see note on Ps 25:10.

103:8-10 God pardons sinners who repent, a truth often affirmed (see Pss 86:15; 145:8; Ex 34:6; Neh 9:17; Isa 57:16; Jer 3:12; Joel 2:13; Jon 4:2). *Kindness:* see note on Ps 6:5.

103:11 *Those who fear him:* see note on Ps 15:2-5. *Kindness:* see note on Ps 6:5.

103:12 God places a huge gulf between his faithful and their sins, extending, as it were, from one end of the earth to the other (see Isa 1:18; 43:25; Jer 31:34; 50:20; Mic 7:18f).

103:13-17 What an amazing condescension on the part of God's love. Although he is well aware that we are fragile and ephemeral creatures who, like grass or flowers, are carried off by the slightest breeze, God keeps in his love the whole lives of his servants. He presents a just account of their merits and blesses their descendants who are faithful to his Covenant.

14 For he knows how we were formed;
he remembers that we are only dust.*[o]

15 The days of mortal man are like grass;
he flourishes like a flower of the field.[p]
16 The wind sweeps over him, and he is gone,
and his place never sees him again.

17 But from everlasting to everlasting
the kindness* of the LORD is with those who fear him,
and his righteousness with their children's children,
18 with those who keep his covenant
and diligently observe his commandments.*

19 The LORD has established his throne in heaven,
and his kingdom rules over all.*
20 * Bless the LORD, O you his angels,*
you mighty in strength who do his bidding,[q]
who obey his spoken word.

21 Bless the LORD, O you his hosts,
his ministers who do his will.
22 Bless the LORD, all his works,
everywhere in his domain.

Bless the LORD, O my soul.*

o Pss 90:3; 119:73; 139:13-15; Gen 2:7.—p Pss 37:2; 90:5-6; 102:12; Job 14:2; Isa 40:6.—q Pss 91:11; 148:2; Dan 3:58.

103:14 The Lord has compassion on those "who fear him" (v. 13) because he knows their frailty, that they are but "dust" (see Gen 2:7; 3:19; Job 4:19; Eccl 3:20; 12:7).

103:17 *Kindness:* see note on Ps 6:5.

103:18 Keeping the Covenant entails obeying the Lord's commandments (see Ex 20:6; Deut 7:9), i.e., doing the will of God (see Mt 6:9-15).

103:19 *His kingdom rules over all:* see Pss 22:29; 145:11-13. The Book of Obadiah concludes with this cry of triumphant eschatology (v. 21: "And dominion will belong to the LORD").

103:20-22 The psalmist calls upon all creatures to join him in praising the heavenly King who rules all things with love (see note on Ps 9:2).

103:20 The angels are God's messengers (see Ps 91:11).

103:22 *Bless the LORD, O my soul:* this last line was probably added by the redactors of the Psalter to show that God's word is efficacious by itself and needs no intermediary.

PSALM 104*

Praise of God the Creator

¹ Bless the LORD, O my soul.
   O LORD, my God, you are indeed very great.
   You are clothed in majesty and splendor,
²   wrapped in light* as in a robe.

   You have stretched out the heavens like a tent;ʳ
³   you have established your palace upon the
         waters.
   You make the clouds serve as your chariot;
      you ride forth on the wings of the wind.*

r Ps 19:2; Gen 1:6-7; Job 9:8; Prov 8:27-28; Isa 40:12; Jer 51:15; Am 9:6.

Ps 104 This hymn calls to mind the majestic poem that opens the Book of Genesis (see Gen 1); perhaps it is even older. The text seems to have undergone the influence of an Egyptian hymn to the sun. It is a rarity at this period for the author to look at the world with the curious eyes of a scientist who is seeking the cause of things and the laws that govern them. The author nevertheless conceives of the universe primarily as a song to God who gives it life. While Ps 103 celebrates the Lord insofar as he shows himself animated by a powerful love in the moral and spiritual order, this psalm—possibly composed by the same poet—invites us to praise him insofar as he reveals himself as a prodigious artist in the initial creation and a benevolent organizer in the governance of the universe.

The power of the creative act brings worlds forth: perfectly mastered, nature and creatures come alive. Divine providence has foreseen everything and organized it all: the seasons, the rhythm of existence, nourishment, and the home of animals and humans. Animated by the Spirit, that is, the divine Breath, creatures sing of the glory of their Creator. The only shadow in this tableau is sin, which risks destroying the beautiful harmony; hence, the author prays that it be eliminated. In the creative Breath (v. 30), the Church sees the Spirit of Pentecost who renews the broken harmony and gives rise to the "new creation" the new human being who is reborn in Christ (see 2 Cor 5:17).

Enlightened by science concerning the unsuspected and amazing wonders of the material universe, all Christians sing to their heavenly Father this psalm of enthusiastic praise. They will also sing it to Christ, intimately associated with the Father both in the creation of these wonders and in their continuance in being (see Col 1:16f). We will praise above all the eminent greatness and power of Father and Son in sending their Spirit to re-create sinful human beings and to renew the spiritual cosmos, the Church (v. 30).

104:2 *Light:* created on the first day (see Gen 1:3-5). In general, the psalmist follows the order of creation found in Gen 1. *Heavens:* created on the second day (see Gen 1:6-8).

104:3 As the ancients represented the world, the rains were stored in reservoirs in the vault of the heavens, which they thought were solid. *Your palace:* God's heavenly dwelling above the upper waters of the sky (see notes on Pss 29:10 and 36:9; see also Gen 1:6f). *Clouds . . . your chariot:* see note on Ps 68:5.

⁴ You have appointed the winds as your messengers
    and flames of fire as your ministers.*ˢ

⁵ You established the earth on its foundations
    so that it will remain unshaken forever.*
⁶ You covered it with the deep like a cloak;
    the waters rose above the mountains.

⁷ At your rebuke* the waters took to flight;
    at the sound of your thunder they fled in
      terror.ᵗ
⁸ They rose up to the mountains
    and flowed down to the valleys,*
      to the place that you had designated for
        them.
⁹ You established a boundary that they were
    not to cross
      so that they would never again cover the
        earth.ᵘ

¹⁰ You made springs gush forth in the valleys*
    and flow between the mountains.
¹¹ They supply water to every beast of the field,ᵛ
    and from them the wild asses quench their
      thirst.

---

s Ps 148:8; Gen 3:24; 2 Ki 2:11; Heb 1:7.—t Pss 18:16; 29:3; Ex 9:23;
Job 7:12.—u Gen 9:11-15; Job 38:8-11; Jer 5:22.—v 11-14: Pss 135:7;
147:8-9; Gen 1:11-12; Jer 10:13; 51:16.

104:4 The Letter to the Hebrews cites this verse to show that Christ is superior
to the angels. Since God makes use of mere wind and lightning ("flames of fire")
as his messengers and servants, the ministering spirits in heaven that he also
uses as his messengers must be infinitely inferior to the eternal Son of God. The
cogency of the argument is much greater in Greek (in which the Letter was written) because the word *pneuma* means both "wind" and "spirit" while the word
angelos means both "messenger" and "angel."
104:5 The ancients regarded the earth as resting upon firm foundations (see
note on Ps 24:2).
104:7 *Rebuke:* see Ps 76:7. *Waters took flight:* poetic description of what took
place on the third day of creation (see Gen 1:9f).
104:8 *They rose up to the mountains and flowed down to the valleys:* the
sources of the Jordan and the other great rivers of the Near East are in the mountains. Another translation offered is: "The mountains rose high and the valleys
went down."
104:10-12 God refreshes the ravines by means of the lower waters.

¹² On the banks the birds of the air build nests
    and sing among the branches.
¹³ From your dwelling you water the mountains,*
    enriching the earth with the fruit of your
    labor.

¹⁴ You provide grass for the cattle,
    and the plants for man to cultivate.
  You bring forth food from the earth
¹⁵   and wine to gladden the heart* of man,
  oil to make his face shine
    and bread to strengthen his body.

¹⁶ The trees of the LORD have fruit in abundance,
    the cedars of Lebanon* that he planted.
¹⁷ In them the birds build their nests;
    in the fir trees the stork makes its home.ʷ
¹⁸ The high mountains are inhabited by the wild
      goats;
    in the rocky crags the badgers* find refuge.

¹⁹ You created the moon that marks the seasonsˣ
    and the sun that knows its time for setting.*
²⁰ You bring on darkness, and it is night,
    when all the beasts of the forests go on the
      prowl.
²¹ The young lions* roar for their prey,
    seeking their food from God.ʸ

---

w Ezek 31:6, 13.—x Ps 19:6; Sir 43:6.—y Job 38:39; Am 3:4.

104:13-15 God refreshes his creatures by means of the reservoir of upper waters (see v. 3 above and Gen 7:11; Job 38:22; Sir 43:14).
104:15 *Heart:* see note on Ps 4:8.
104:16 *Cedars of Lebanon:* see note on Ps 80:11.
104:18 *Badgers:* the hyrax or rock badger, a small, harelike, ungulate mammal (see Lev 11:5; Deut 14:7; Prov 30:26).
104:19 The ancients governed their lives by the cycles of the sun and moon, which God created on the fourth day for that purpose (see Gen 1:14-19).
104:21-23 The "young lions" and "man" represent the animal and the human kingdom. The psalmist, in accord with the beliefs of his day, postulates that animals come out at night to search for their food and humans do their working and eating by day. See Jn 9:4, where Jesus uses the inability of humans to work at night (because of the circumstances of his time—absence of light at night) to impart a greater spiritual truth.

22 When the sun rises, they steal away
     and return to their lairs to rest.
23 People go forth to their work
     and to their labor until darkness descends.

24 How countless are your works, O LORD;*
     by your wisdom you have made them all;
     the earth abounds with your creatures.ᶻ
25 There is the sea, vast and broad,
     filled with numberless species,
     living creatures both great and small.ᵃ
26 There the ships sail forth,
     and the Leviathan that you formed to play
        therein.*ᵇ

27 All of them look to you*
     to give them their food at the appropriate
        time.*ᶜ
28 When you provide it for them,*
     they gather it up;
  when you open your hand,
     they are filled with good things.

---

z Pss 8:2; 92:6; Sir 39:16.—a Ps 69:35; Sir 43:26.—b Job 3:8; 40:20;
Ezek 27:9.—c Pss 136:25; 145:15-16; Job 36:31.

104:24-26 The psalmist now takes up God's creation of the sea and everything in it on the fifth day (see Gen 1:20-23). He calls upon the people to worship the Lord's wisdom and creative diversity. Here he emphasizes sea creatures to complement the wild and domesticated animals and humans mentioned
in vv. 10-18.

104:26 See note on Ps 74:13-14. Here "Leviathan" is a whale or large
cetacean. The name is that of a fabled dragon and is already found in Ugaritic
poems of the fifteenth century B.C.

104:27-30 On the sixth day, God enabled everything he had made to fructify
(see Gen 1:24-31). All living things on earth and in the sea, whether wild or domesticated, birds, sea creatures, and human beings have some idea of the living
Presence by whom they exist (see Pss 145:15f; 147:9). They have their being in
God (see Acts 17:24f), and the Lord gives and sustains life by his Spirit. Indeed,
God has supreme power over the universe, creating, preserving, and governing
all. The lives of all creatures are in his hands.

104:27 All nature depends on its Creator for provisions, and he has arranged
for everyone to have enough food.

104:28-29 Creatures are governed by the Lord; they are gladdened by his provisions, terrified by his absence, and encounter death by the withdrawal of his
breath.

²⁹ When you turn away your face,*
    they are dismayed;
  when you take away their breath,
    they die and return to the dust.ᵈ
³⁰ When you send forth your Spirit,*
    they are created,
    and you renew the face of the earth.

³¹ * May the glory of the Lᴏʀᴅ abide forever,
    and may the Lᴏʀᴅ rejoice in his works.*
³² When he looks at the earth, it quakes;
    when he touches the mountains, they
       smoke.*ᵉ

³³ I will sing to the Lᴏʀᴅ as long as I live;*
    I will sing praise to my God while I have life.ᶠ
³⁴ May my meditation be pleasing to him,
    for I find my joy in the Lᴏʀᴅ.
³⁵ May sinners be banished from the earth,*
    and may the wicked no longer exist.

  Bless the Lᴏʀᴅ, O my soul.

  Alleluia.

---

d Ps 90:3; Gen 3:19; Deut 31:17; Job 34:14-15; Eccl 3:20.—e Ps 97:4; 144:5; Ex 19:18.—f Pss 7:17; 108:2; 146:2; Ex 15:1.

104:29 *Turn . . . face:* see note on Ps 13:2. *Return to dust:* see note on Ps 90:3.
    104:30 *Your Spirit:* the Spirit or "Breath" of God is the divine creative power, source of all natural life (see Gen 1:2; 2:7). So also the Holy Spirit is the source of all supernatural life (see Jn 3:5f). Hence, this verse is applied by the Church to the third Person of the Blessed Trinity.
    104:31-34 The psalmist concludes the psalm the way it began—with praise (vv. 1-4). The Lord, who reveals himself in creation in all his splendor (vv. 1-4), has bestowed his glory on it (see Ps 19:2; Isa 6:3), and his handiwork will endure as long as he undergirds it. Hence, his faithful should respond with praise, devotion, and an intention to please the Lord (see Ps 19:15).
    104:31 *Rejoice in his works:* as he did at the end of creation (see Gen 1:31).
    104:32 The Lord is so much greater than his creation that even a mere look or touch on his part is enough to wreak havoc in it.
    104:33 *I will . . . I live:* a perpetual vow to praise the Lord (see note on Ps 7:18).
    104:35 Before concluding, the psalmist prays that sin may disappear from creation. However, because the hymn cannot end with a malediction (see Ps 139:19), he repeats the words of v. 1 as a refrain: "Bless the Lᴏʀᴅ, O my soul." *Alleluia:* i.e., "Hallelujah" or "Bless [or praise] the Lᴏʀᴅ," which most likely belongs to the beginning of Ps 105 (see Ps 105:45; 106:1, 48).

PSALM 105*

God's Faithfulness to the Covenant

1 * Give thanks to the LORD, invoke his name;*g
　　proclaim his deeds among the peoples.h
2 Offer him honor with songs of praise;
　　recount all his marvelous deeds.
3 Glory in his holy name;
　　let the hearts* of those who seek the LORD
　　　exult.

4 Reflect on the LORD and his strength;
　　seek his face continually.i
5 Remember the marvels he has wrought,
　　his portents, and the judgments* he has set
　　　forth.

---

g 1-15: 1 Chr 16:8-22.—h Pss 18:50; 96:3; 145:5; Isa 12:4-5; Joel 3:5; Acts 2:21.—i Pss 24:6; 27:8; Deut 4:29.

Ps 105 The magnificent hymn in praise of God for creation (see Ps 104) does not suffice for believers. God is he who comes among human beings; hence, they proclaim God's greatness in history by delivering the human race from slavery and leading it to salvation. In order to voice its joy and thanks, Israel loves to recall the events that marked the beginnings of its adventure: the promise made to Abraham and renewed to the patriarchs (vv. 8-15), the adventure of Joseph (vv. 16-23; see Gen 37—50), Moses and the plagues in Egypt (vv. 24-36; see Ex 1—13), the Exodus and the miracles in the wilderness (vv. 37-43; see Ex 14—15), and lastly the entrance into Canaan, the land promised as an inheritance (v. 44).

Contrary to the following psalm (Ps 106), the author is silent about Israel's sins; he wishes to sing of nothing but the action of God. The Lord has always kept his word; he has multiplied wonders for his people, and his providence has guided their steps. Now he has a right to expect them to be faithful to him (v. 45).

This psalm becomes the song of the Church, a people chosen by God in Christ and saved by his Passover (see Eph 1). Since our God is the God of Abraham, Isaac, and Jacob (see Mk 12:26), unchanged and also faithful, we can legitimately base our confidence in him on the promises and proofs he gave to our distant spiritual ancestors. Let us not forget, however, that these promises have received eminent confirmation in the life of Christ, whom God has led—through the dreadful detour of death—from this exile to the true promised land. This last proof constitutes the primary foundation of our enthusiasm and confidence.

The first fifteen verses of this psalm are found again in 1 Chr 16:8-22.

105:1-3 These three verses can be regarded as a prelude, and they are counterbalanced by the conclusion comprising verses 44-45.

105:1 *Name:* see note on Ps 5:12. *Proclaim his deeds among the peoples:* see note on Ps 9:2.

105:3 *Hearts:* see note on Ps 4:8.

105:5 *Judgments:* see note on Ps 48:11.

⁶ You are the offspring of his servant Abraham,
   the children of Jacob, his chosen ones.*
⁷ He is the LORD, our God;
   his judgments prevail all over the earth.

⁸ He is mindful of his covenant* forever,
   the promise he laid down for a thousand
   generations,
⁹ the covenant he made with Abraham *j*
   and the oath he swore to Isaac.*

¹⁰ He established it as a decree for Jacob,*
   and as an everlasting covenant for Israel,
¹¹ saying, "To you I will give the land of Canaan
   as the portion of your heritage."*k*

¹² When they were few in number,*
   an insignificant group of strangers in it,*l*
¹³ they wandered from nation to nation,
   from one kingdom to another.

¹⁴ He permitted no one to oppress them,
   and in their regard he warned kings:*
¹⁵ "Do not touch my anointed ones;
   do no harm to my prophets."*

¹⁶ Then he invoked a famine on the land
   and destroyed their supply of bread.*m*

---

j Gen 15:1ff; 26:3; Lk 1:73; Gal 3:15-18.—k Gen 12:7; 15:18; Num 34:2.—
l 12-13: Deut 4:27; 26:5; Heb 11:9.—m Gen 41:54-57; Lev 26:26; Isa 3:1.

105:6 Here begin the allusions to Genesis (22:17; see Isa 51:2). *Children of Jacob, his chosen ones:* most manuscripts read instead: "Children of Jacob, his chosen one," which seems to fit better with the previous line.
105:8 *Covenant:* see Gen 15:9-21. This verse (and v. 9) are alluded to in Lk 1:72f.
105:9 *The oath he swore to Isaac:* another possible translation is "the oath concerning Isaac."
105:10-11 These verses recall the promise (see Gen 15:18) on which rest the hopes of Israel (see Pss 47:5; 72:8; Deut 4:31, 40).
105:12-41 The psalmist recapitulates God's saving acts for Israel from the making of the Covenant (see Gen 15:9-21) to its fulfillment (see Jos 21:43). In this connection, see the short summary of salvation prescribed to be said by the individual Israelite reaching the promised land (see Deut 26:1-11).
105:14 *He warned kings:* see Gen 12:11ff; 20:7; 26:7ff.
105:15 *My anointed ones . . . my prophets:* the patriarchs, Abraham, Isaac, and Jacob, who were in a sense "anointed," that is, consecrated to God, and the recipients of his revelations.

17 But he had sent a man ahead of them,
  Joseph, who had been sold as a slave.[n]

18 They shackled his feet with fetters
  and clamped an iron collar around his neck,[o]
19 until what he had prophesied was fulfilled
  and the word of the LORD proved him true.[p]

20 The king ordered that he be released;
  the ruler of the peoples set him free.[q]
21 He appointed him as master of his household
  and as ruler of all his possessions.[r]
22 He was to instruct his princes as he deemed fit
  and to impart wisdom to his elders.

23 Then Israel went down into Egypt;[s]
  Jacob lived as an alien in the land of Ham.*
24 God greatly increased the number of his people
  and made them too strong for their foes,[t]
25 whose hearts he then turned* to hate his people
  and to conspire against his servants.[u]

26 He sent his servant Moses,
  and Aaron whom he had chosen.[v]
27 They performed his signs among them
  and worked wonders in the land of Ham.[w]

28 He sent darkness that enveloped the land,*
  but they rebelled against his warnings.
29 He turned their waters into blood,
  and all their fish were destroyed.

30 Their land was saturated with frogs,
  even in the royal chambers.

---

n Gen 37:28, 36; 45:5; Acts 7:9.—o Gen 39:20; 40:15.—p Gen 40:20-22; 41:9-13.—q Gen 41:14.—r Gen 41:41-44.—s Ps 78:51; Gen 46:1—47:12; Acts 7:15.—t Ex 1:7-9; Acts 7:17.—u Ex 1:8-14; Acts 7:19.—v Ex 3:10; 4:27; Num 33:1.—w 27-36: Ps 78:43-51; Ex 7:8—12:51.

105:23 *Land of Ham:* i.e., Egypt.
105:25 *Whose hearts he then turned:* the ancients regarded every happening as coming from God, even evil (see Ex 4:21; 7:3; Jos 11:20; 2 Sam 24:1; Isa 10:5-7; 37:26f; Jer 34:22).
105:28-38 As in Ps 78:43-51, here also the plagues of Egypt are recalled with poetic license so that their order and number are different from Ex 7:14—12:30.

³¹ At his command there came hordes of flies
     and gnats throughout their country.

³² He sent them hail instead of rain,
     and flashes of lightning in all their land.
³³ He struck down their vines and their fig trees
     and demolished the trees of their country.

³⁴ At his word the locusts came,
     as well as grasshoppers beyond all count.ˣ
³⁵ They gobbled up every green plant in the land
     and devoured the produce of the soil.

³⁶ He struck down all the firstborn of the land,
     the firstfruits of their manhood.
³⁷ Then he led out his people with silver and gold,
     and there was not one among their tribes
     who stumbled.ʸ

³⁸ Egypt was glad when they departed,
     for dread of Israel had overwhelmed them.
³⁹ He spread a cloud over his people as a cover*
     and a fire to give light by night.ᶻ

⁴⁰ At their request he supplied them with quail,ᵃ
     and he filled them with bread from heaven.*
⁴¹ He split open a rock and water gushed forth,ᵇ
     flowing through the wilderness like a river.*

---

x Ex 10:1-20; Joel 1:4.—y Ex 3:21-22; 12:33-36.—z Ps 78:14; Ex 13:21-
22; Wis 18:3; 1 Cor 10:1.—a Ps 78:24-28; 114:8; Ex 16:13-15; Num
11:31ff; Deut 8:15; Wis 16:20; Isa 48:21; Jn 6:31.—b Ps 78:15-16; Ex 17:1-
7; Num 20:11; 1 Cor 10:4.

105:39 *As a cover:* the psalmist indicates that the cloud symbolizing God's
presence served as a protection for the people against the sun, somewhat like his
shading wings (see note on Ps 17:8). Other functions of the cloud given are: to
guide the people in the wilderness (see Ps 78:14; Ex 13:21; Num 9:17; Neh 9:12),
to protect the people from the Egyptians as a cover of darkness (see Ex 14:19f),
and to insulate them from the glorious manifestations of God's overwhelming
presence (see Ex 16:10; Num 11:25; Deut 31:15; 1 Ki 8:11).
   105:40 *Bread from heaven:* the psalmist names it thusly because it was the
immediate gift of the heavenly Father in contrast to the ordinary natural bread.
See also note on Ps 78:25 and Christ's use of this phrase in Jn 6:31.
   105:41 The psalmist concludes his account of God's saving deeds for Israel
with one of the most admired of them: creating a river of water from a rock in the
wilderness (see Ps 114:8; Isa 43:19f).

⁴² For he remembered the sacred promise
　　that he had made to Abraham, his servant.
⁴³ He led forth his people with rejoicing,
　　his chosen ones with exultation.*

⁴⁴ He gave them the lands of the nations,ᶜ
　　and they inherited the fruit of other people's
　　　toil,
⁴⁵ so that they might keep his decreesᵈ
　　and observe his laws.

　　Alleluia.

PSALM 106*

Israel's Confession of Sin and
God's Mercy

¹ Alleluia.

Give thanks* to the LORD, for he is good;
　　his kindness endures forever.ᵉ

---

c Deut 4:37-40; Jos 11:16-23.—d Ps 78:5-7; Deut 6:20-25; 7:8-11.—e Pss 100:5; 103:2; 107:1; 118:1, 29; 136:1-3; 1 Chr 16:34; Jer 33:11; Dan 3:89.

105:43 An allusion to the song of victory of Ex 15.

Ps 106 A beautiful acclamation opens this psalm, but from v. 6 onward the tone changes. We enter into a liturgy of grief and take part in a national confession. It is, especially after the Exile, a psalm for times of distress (see Isa 63:7—64:11; Neh 9:5-37). A repentant Israel evokes the sin of the ancestors, but only to confess its own sin. The people continue the long succession of infidelities of yesteryear. The meditation on Israel's history contrasts with the beautiful hymn of Psalm 105. Taking his inspiration from Num and Deut, the psalmist retains from the past only the concatenation of sins: the ancestors doubted God (v. 7; see Ex 14:12), murmured in the wilderness (v. 14; see Ex 15:24; 16:3; 17:2), adored the golden calf (v. 19; see Ex 32), balked at conquering the promised land (v. 24; see Num 14:3f), adopted pagan practices (vv. 28-35; see Num 25; Jdg 2:1-5), and sacrificed to idols (vv. 36-38; see 1 Ki 16:34).

Paul will later evoke how the flood of sin submerges humanity (see Rom 3:23). But the history of sin is opposed to that of the love of God; the Lord always pardons and delivers his people. On recalling such goodness, the community of his people gathered together acknowledges its sins and begs God to save it.

In praying this psalm, Christians recall that the wonders of God's mercy in favor of his chosen people were simple preludes to the works of mercy that he accomplishes in Christ on behalf of sinful but believing humankind (see Rom 5:20). Acknowledgment of sin opens the door to the experience of God's love.

106:1 *Give thanks:* a liturgical call to praise (see Pss 100:5; 103:2; 107:1; 118:1, 29; 136:1-3). *Kindness:* see note on Ps 6:5.

2 Who can possibly recount the mighty acts of
        the LORD
        and fully proclaim his praise?*
3 Blessed are those who do what is right
        and practice justice constantly.*f

4 Remember me, O LORD, out of the love you
        have for your people;g
        come to me with your salvation.*
5 Let me delight in the success of your chosen
        ones,
        share in the joy of your nation,
        and glory in your heritage.

6 Like our ancestors, we have sinned;*h
        we have gone astray and done evil.*
7 When our ancestors were in Egypt,
        they failed to be mindful of your wonders;
    they did not remember your many kindnesses
        and rebelled against the Most High at the
        Red Sea.

8 Yet he saved them for his name's sakei
        so that he might make known his mighty
        power.*
9 He rebuked the Red Sea, and it dried up;
        he led them through the depths as through
        a wilderness.j

f Ps 15:2; Isa 56:1-2; Hos 12:7.—g Ps 25:7; Neh 5:19; 13:14, 22, 31.—h
6-7: Ps 78:11-17; Ex 14:11; Lev 26:40; Jdg 3:7; 1 Ki 8:47; Neh 1:7; Bar
2:12; Dan 9:5.—i Pss 80:4; 107:13; Ex 9:16; Isa 25:9; Ezek 36:20-22.—j
Pss 18:16; 89:10; Ex 14:21-31; Isa 50:2; 63:11-14; Nah 1:4.

106:2 *His praise:* see note on Ps 9:2.
106:3 The Lord expects his people to persevere in righteousness and justice,
because they thus establish his kingdom (see Pss 15:1-5; 99:4; Isa 11:3-5;
33:15-17). *Blessed:* see note on Ps 1:1.
106:4 *With your salvation:* another translation is: "when you save them."
106:6-12 The psalmist sketches the people's lack of faith and their rebellion
at the Red Sea (see Ex 14—15).
106:6 This general theme (see Lev 26:40; 1 Ki 8:47; Dan 9:5) is reprised by the
Vulgate in Jud 7:29. *We:* the psalmist identifies himself with his sinful people.
106:8 A motive often ascribed to God by Ezekiel (see Ezek 20:9, 14; 36:21f;
39:25). *Name's sake:* see note on Ps 5:12.

¹⁰ He saved them from those who hated them;
    from the hand of the enemy he delivered
    them.

¹¹ The waters closed over their adversaries;
    not a single one of them survived.
¹² Then they believed his words
    and sang his praises.*ᵏ

¹³ But they soon forgot what he had done*
    and had no confidence in his plan.
¹⁴ In the wilderness they yielded to their crav-
    ings;
    in the wasteland they put God to the test.ˡ
¹⁵ He gave them everything they wanted
    but struck them with a consuming disease.ᵐ

¹⁶ In the camp they grew envious of Moses*
    and of Aaron, who was consecrated to the
    LORD.ⁿ
¹⁷ The earth parted and swallowed Dathan
    and closed over the company of Abiram.
¹⁸ Fire blazed all through them,
    and the wicked were consumed in flames.

¹⁹ They constructed a calf at Horeb*
    and worshiped this molten image.ᵒ
²⁰ They exchanged their Glory*
    for an image of a bull that eats grass.

---

k Ps 105:43; Ex 14:31; 15:1-21.—l Ps 78:18; Ex 15:24; 16:3; Num 11:1-6; 1 Cor 10:9.—m Ps 78:26-31; Ex 16:13; 17:2; Num 11:33.—n 16-18: Lev 10:2; Num 16:1-3; Deut 11:6; Isa 26:11.—o 19-20: Ex 32:1-9; Deut 9:8-21; Jer 2:11; Acts 7:41; Rom 1:23.

106:12 An allusion to Ex 15. Praise is the expression of faith in the divine word (see Pss 119:42, 65, 74, 81; 130:5).
106:13-15 The psalmist recalls the people's forgetfulness of the Lord in their craving for meat in the desert (see Num 11).
106:16-18 The psalmist recounts the challenge to Moses' authority in the camp by Korah, Dathan, and Abiram (see Num 16:1-35).
106:19-23 The psalmist recalls the people's worship of the golden calf at Sinai (see Ex 32; Deut 9:7-29; Hos 4:7; 9:10; 10:5).
106:20 *Glory:* none other than their Glorious one (see 1 Sam 15:29; Jer 2:11), their Savior-God (v. 21).

21 They forgot the God who had saved them,
    who had done great things in Egypt,*p*
22 wonders in the land of Ham,*
    and awesome deeds at the Red Sea.

23 He was contemplating their destruction,
    but Moses, his chosen one,
  stood in the breach* before him
    to keep his wrath from destroying them.*q*

24 * Then they derided the land of delights,*
    for they had no faith in his word.*r*
25 They grumbled in their tents
    and refused to obey the voice of the LORD.

26 Therefore, he swore with uplifted hand
    to strike them down in the wilderness
27 and disperse their descendants among the
    nations,
    scattering them in foreign lands.

28 They joined in worshiping the Baal of Peor*
    and ate food sacrificed to lifeless gods.*s*
29 They provoked the LORD to anger by their
    evil deeds,
    and a plague broke out among them.

30 Then Phinehas stood up and executed judgment,
    and the plague came to an end.
31 This was credited to him as righteousness*
    for all the generations to come.

---

p Pss 75:2; 78:42-58; Deut 32:18; Jer 2:32.—q Ex 32:11; Num 11:2; Deut 9:25; Ezek 22:30.—r 24-27: Lev 26:33; Num 13:25—14:37; Deut 1:25-36; Ezek 20:15, 23; Heb 3:18-19.—s 28-31: Ps 141:4; Num 25; Deut 26:14; Sir 45:23-24.

106:22 *Land of Ham:* see note on Ps 78:51.
106:23 *Stood in the breach:* see Ex 32:11-14, 31f.
106:24-27 The psalmist tells of the people's refusal to capture Canaan via the southern route and their punishment of not entering the promised land (see Num 13—14; Deut 1—2).
106:24 *Land of delights:* see the description given in Jer 3:19; 12:10; Zec 7:14.
106:28-31 The psalmist recalls the people's apostasy and rebellion in worshiping the Baal of Peor (see Num 25:1-10).
106:31 *Credited to him as righteousness:* reminiscent of Abraham's justification and that of the new People of God (see Gen 15:6; Rom 4:3, 23-25).

³² * At the waters of Meribah* they angered the
    LORD,ᵗ
        and Moses endured difficulties because of
        them.
³³ For they rebelled against the Spirit of God,
        and rash words issued from Moses' lips.*

³⁴ They did not exterminate the peoples*
        as the LORD had commanded them to do.ᵘ
³⁵ Rather, they mingled with the nations
        and adopted their practices.ᵛ

³⁶ They worshiped their idols,
        which became a snare to them.ʷ
³⁷ They sacrificed to false gods*
        their sons and their daughters.

³⁸ They shed innocent blood,
        the blood of their sons and daughters,
    whom they sacrificed to the idols of Canaan,
        polluting the land with their blood.
³⁹ Thus, they defiled themselves by their actions
        and prostituted themselves by their con-
        duct.*

---

t 32-33: Pss 95:8-9; 107:11; Ex 17:1-7; Num 20:1-13; Deut 6:16; 33:8;
Isa 63:10.—u Deut 7:1; Jos 9:15; Jdg 2:1-5.—v Lev 18:3; Jdg 1:27-35; 3:5;
Ezr 9:1-2.—w Deut 7:1; Jos 9:15; Jdg 2:1-5.—v Lev 18:3; Jdg 1:27-35; 3:5;
Ezr 9:1-2.—w Deut 7:1; Lev 18:21; Num 35:33; Deut 32:17; Jdg
2:11-13, 17, 19; 2 Ki 16:3; Bar 4:7; Ezek 16:20-21; 1 Cor 10:20.

106:32-33 The psalmist relives the people's quarreling with the Lord at
Meribah, which led Moses to sin (see Num 20:1-13).
106:32 *Meribah:* see note on Ps 95:8. *The LORD:* literally, "him." *Moses endured
difficulties:* he was not allowed to enter the promised land because of his rash
words (see Num 20:12). Deut 1:37 indicates that Moses was not allowed to do so
because of the people's sin, not his own.
106:33 *Spirit of God . . . Moses' lips:* literally, "his Spirit . . . his lips." The Old
Testament indicates that the Spirit of God was present and at work in the wilderness (see Ex 31:3; Num 11:17; 24:2; Neh 9:20; Isa 63:10-14).
106:34-39 The psalmist indicts the mingling of the people with the pagan nations and their evil practices (such as idolatry, infant sacrifices, and injustice of
all kinds) from the time of the Judges to the Babylonian Exile.
106:37 *False gods:* literally, "demons," i.e., pagan gods.
106:39 The people were made ritually unclean by the evils they practiced, and
the land was also defiled by their wickedness (see Num 35:33f; Isa 24:5; Jer
3:1f, 9).

⁴⁰ Then the anger of the LORD flared up against
    his people,*
    and he abhorred his own heritage.
⁴¹ He handed them over to the nations,
    and their foes became their rulers.ˣ

⁴² Their enemies oppressed them
    and kept them in subjection to their power.
⁴³ Time and again he came to their rescue,
    but they rebelled against his counsel
    and sank low because of their sin.ʸ

⁴⁴ Even so, he took pity on their distress
    when he heard their cries.
⁴⁵ He called to mind his covenant* with them,
    and he relented because of his great mercy.ᶻ
⁴⁶ He aroused compassion for them
    on the part of all their captors.

⁴⁷ Save us, O LORD, our God,
    and gather us from among the nations,
    so that we may give thanks to your holy name
    and glory in praising you.*ᵃ

⁴⁸ Blessed be the LORD, the God of Israel,
    from everlasting to everlasting.
    Let all the people say, "Amen."*

Alleluia.*ᵇ

---

x Jdg 2:14-23.—y Neh 9:28; Isa 63:7-9.—z Lev 26:42; Jer 42:10.—a Ps 28:9; 1 Chr 16:35.—b Pss 41:14; 72:18; 89:53; 1 Chr 16:36; Neh 9:5.

106:40-46 The psalmist recalls God's tempered judgment mingling chastisements and mercies.

106:45 *Called to mind his covenant:* see Pss 105:8, 42; Ex 2:24; Lev 26:42, 45. *Kindness:* see note on Ps 6:5.

106:47 The psalmist ends on a note of communal prayer for deliverance and restoration from dispersion. The triumph of the Lord results in thanksgiving and praise. *Praise:* see note on Ps 9:2.

106:48a-c This last verse does not belong to the psalm but is the doxology to Book IV (see note on Ps 41:14). The doxology declares the praise of the Lord as the God of Israel (see Lk 1:68). As his kindness endures forever (v. 1), so will his praise from his people be "from everlasting to everlasting." In hope of deliverance and prosperity (vv. 4-5, 47), the People of God respond with an "Amen" (see 1 Chr 16:35f).

106:48d *Alleluia:* i.e., "Hallelujah" or "Bless [or praise] the LORD," which very likely belongs to the next psalm (see note on Ps 104:35).

BOOK V—PSALMS 107–150*

PSALM 107*

God, Savior of Those in Distress

1 "Give thanks to the LORD, for he is good;
  his kindness endures forever."*c
2 Let this be the prayer of the redeemed of the
  LORD,
    those he redeemed from the hand of the
    foe d

---

c Pss 100:4-5; 106:1; 1 Chr 16:8; Jer 33:11.—d Ps 106:10; Isa 63:12.

Pss 107—150 Book V of the Psalter. Two collections are included in this final part: the pilgrimage chants or "Songs of Ascent" (Pss 120—134) and the Hallel or "Praise" psalms (113—118; 120—136; 146—150). In addition, we see a further group of psalms attributed to David (Pss 138—145). Jewish tradition also groups together Pss 113—118, known as the Egyptian Hallel, for use at the Passover. The "hymn" sung at the Last Supper (see Mk 14:26) was probably part of that Hallel.

Although cries of supplication still form part of the prayer of the psalmist, joy begins to radiate upon the face of the pilgrim who draws near to the Lord; the acclamation voiced in the presence of God will transform the conclusion of the Psalter into a prodigious symphony of happiness.

Ps 107 Even though this psalm is not part of Book IV, many believe that it was originally associated with Pss 105 and 106 and served as a kind of conclusion to the theme-related Pss 104—107. After the account of God's works in creation (see Ps 104:2-26) and his care for the animal world (see Ps 104:27-30) it recounts "the wonders [God] does for people" (Ps 107:8).

Ps 107 is a thanksgiving for "God's deliverances." Persons in distress have cried out to him and obtained help: wandering voyagers (vv. 4-9), prisoners (vv. 10-16), the sick (vv. 17-22), and the shipwrecked (vv. 23-32). The Lord reverses situations as he pleases (vv. 33-41), but only the believer can discern the divine action. Beneath the concrete life of the era, evoked at times with humor (vv. 26-27 remind us that the Israelites were not very seaworthy), we see the history of the chosen people: the journeys of the Exodus and the Exile, their temptations and their sins.

Visibly the author takes his inspiration from the Book of Consolation (see Isa 40—55) and the writings of the sages (see Job; Wis 16). Thanksgivings that are at first private ultimately express the gratitude of an entire people. For the believer, the events become signs: they invite him to discover in his life and that of the community of peoples a secret presence of God.

Christians pray this psalm to praise the Father for redeeming us in Christ. We have been saved by him from the hand of the infernal oppressor, gathered by him into the Church, and delivered by his love from the spiritual death to which we were doomed by the state in which Satan bound us and which was symbolized by the image of the wilderness, captivity, sickness, and the storm.

107:1 A conventional cry of praise in the liturgy of the temple often cited in the Old Testament (see Pss 106:1; 118:1; 136:1; 1 Chr 16:34; 1 Mac 4:24; Jer 33:11; Dan 3:89). *Kindness:* see note on Ps 6:5.

3 and gathered together from the lands,*e
    from east and west, north and south.

4 Some wandered in a barren wilderness,*
    unable to discover a path to an inhabited
    city.f
5 They were hungry and thirsty,
    and their life was wasting away.g

6 Then they cried out to the LORD in their an-
    guish,
    and he saved them from their distress.
7 He led them by a direct routeh
    to a city in which they could dwell.i

8 Let them give thanks to the LORD for his
    kindness
    and for the wonders he does for people.*
9 He has satisfied the thirsty
    and filled the hungry with good things.j

10 Some sat in darkness and the shadow of
    death,*
    bound in misery and in chains,*

---

e Neh 1:9; Isa 43:5-6; 49:12; Zec 8:7.—f Deut 8:15; 32:10; Jos 5:6.—g
Ex 16:3; Isa 49:10.—h Ezr 8:21; Isa 35:8; 40:3; 43:19.—i Deut 6:10; Jos
24:13.—j Ps 22:27; Isa 49:10; 55:1; 58:11; Mt 5:6; Lk 1:53.

107:3 *From the lands:* e.g., Assyria, Babylonia, Egypt, and Moab, into which
the catastrophe of 587 B.C. had dispersed the chosen people (see 2 Ki 17:6;
24:12-16; Isa 11:11f; 43:5f; Jer 52:28-30). *South:* literally, "[the] sea."
107:4-9 The psalmist evokes the Lord's deliverances of his people from the
wilderness in which they were lost, hungry, thirsty, and exhausted, especially during
the Exodus (see Jos 5:6), which prefigured the just completed return from the Exile
(see Neh 1:3). Jesus would later indicate that he delivered people from the same four
situations as the Way to the Father (see Jn 14:6), the Bread of Heaven (see Jn 6:41),
the Water of Life (see Jn 4:14), and the Giver of Rest (see Mt 11:28).
107:8 This refrain is repeated in vv. 15, 21, 31. *Kindness:* see note on Ps 6:5.
Wonders: see note on Ps 9:2 concerning God's "wonders."
107:10-16 The psalmist evokes God's deliverance of his people from foreign
bondage, especially in the return from the Exile (see Isa 43:5f; 49:12; Zec 8:7f).
In addition, guilt, darkness, grinding toil, and the constriction of chains, gates,
and bars are apt figures for the fallen state of human beings.
107:10 See Ps 105:18; 149:8; Isa 42:7; 49:9. The Exile was a chastisement
(see Lev 26:41ff; Job 33:19; 36:8ff; Prov 3:12), announced by the Prophets.
Shadow of death: see note on Ps 23:4.

11 because they had rebelled against the words of
God
and spurned the plan of the Most High.*k*
12 He humbled their hearts with hard labor;*
when they stumbled, no one was there to
offer help.*l*

13 Then they cried out to the LORD in their need,
and he rescued them from their distress.
14 He brought them forth from darkness and the
shadow of death
and tore their chains to pieces.*m*

15 Let them give thanks to the LORD for his
kindness
and for the wonders he does for people.
16 He has broken down gates of bronze
and cut through iron bars.

17 Some were made foolish by their wicked ways*
and were afflicted because of their iniquities.
18 All types of food became loathsome to them,*n*
and they were nearing the gates of death.*

19 Then they cried out to the LORD in their anguish,
and he rescued them from their distress.
20 He sent forth his word* and healed them,
saving them from the grave.*o*

---

k Ps 5:11; Job 36:8-9; Prov 1:25; Isa 42:7, 22.—l Ps 106:43; Lev 26:40-
41.—m Isa 42:7; 49:9; 51:14; Lk 1:79.—n Job 6:6-7; 17:16; 33:20.—o Ps
147:15; Deut 32:2; Wis 16:12; Isa 55:11; Mt 8:8; Lk 7:7; Jn 1:1.

107:12 *Humbled their hearts with hard labor:* i.e., a labor that broke their
spirit. Another translation is: "subjected them to bitter labor."
107:17-22 The psalmist evokes God's deliverance of his people from the chastisement of sickness unto death incurred because of sin.
107:18 *Gates of death:* metaphorical description for death (see Pss 9:14; 88:4)
in keeping with the ancient custom of picturing the realm of death as a city in
the netherworld with a series of gates that prevented return to the land of the
living (see Job 38:17; Mt 16:18).
107:20 The "word" is here personified as God's messenger of healing and deliverance from the "grave" (see Ps 147:15; Job 33:23ff; Wis 16:12; Isa 55:11; Mt
8:8; Jn 1:1).

21 Let them give thanks to the LORD for his
kindness
 and for the wonders he does for people.
22 Let them offer sacrifices in thanksgiving
 and recount his deeds with jubilation.

23 Some went down to the sea in ships*
 and engaged in commerce on the mighty
 waters.p
24 They beheld the works of the LORD*
 and his wonders in the deep.

25 He spoke and raised up a storm-wind
 that stirred up the waves of the sea.q
26 They were lifted up to the heavens, then cast
 down to the depths;
 their courage melted away in their plight.
27 They reeled and staggered like drunkards,
 and they were at their wits' end.r

28 They cried out to the LORD in their anguish,
 and he delivered them from their distress.
29 He reduced the storm to a whisper,
 and the waves of the sea were hushed.s
30 They rejoiced because of the calm,
 and he guided them to the port they
 sought.

31 Let them give thanks to the LORD for his
kindness
 and for the wonders he does for people.
32 Let them exalt him in the assembly of the
people
 and praise him in the council of the elders.*

---

p Ps 104:26; Sir 43:25; Isa 42:10.—q Ps 93:3; Jon 1:4.—r Isa 19:14;
29:9.—s Pss 65:8; 77:20; 89:10; Isa 43:2; Jon 1:15; Mt 8:26 par.

107:23-32 The psalmist evokes God's deliverance of his people from the perils
of the sea.

107:24-29 The merchants who cross the seas in search of wealth witness
God's wonderful deeds at sea (see Ps 104:24-26) and his ability to calm a storm
on the surging waters (see Pss 65:8; 77:20).

107:32 The merchants are urged to render worship to God by declaring, both in
communal worship and in places of leadership, what he has done for them.

33 He turns rivers into wasteland,*
     springs of water into parched ground,*ᵗ
34 and fertile land into a salt waste,ᵘ
     because of the wickedness of those who
     live there.*

35 He turns the wasteland into pools of water
     and the parched ground into bubbling
     springs.ᵛ

36 There he provides the hungry with a home,*
     and they build a city where they can settle.ʷ

37 They sow fields and plant vineyards
     that yield crops for the harvest.ˣ

38 He blesses them and they greatly increase in
     number,
     and he does not let their cattle decrease.ʸ

39 Eventually their numbers diminish and they
     are humbled
     because of oppression, adversity, and af-
     fliction;

40 he who pours forth his contempt on princes
     makes them wander in trackless wastes,ᶻ

41 while he raises the needy from their misery
     and increases their families like flocks.ᵃ

42 The upright see and exult,
     while the wicked* are reduced to silence.ᵇ

---

t Ps 74:15; Isa 35:7; 42:15; 50:2.—u Gen 13:10; 19:23-28; Deut 29:22;
Sir 39:23.—v Ps 114:8; 2 Ki 3:17; Isa 41:18.—w Ezek 36:35.—x 2 Ki 19:29;
Isa 65:21; Jer 31:5.—y Deut 7:13-14; Isa 49:21.—z Job 12:21, 23-25.—a Ps
113:7-9; Job 5:16.—b Pss 58:11; 63:12; Rom 3:19.

107:33-42 The psalmist evokes God's deliverance of his people by a "reversal
of fortune."
    107:33-35 Imagery like that found in Isa 35:6f; 41:18; 42:15; 43:19f; 50:2.
    107:34 Allusion to Sodom and Gomorrah (see Gen 13:10; 19; Deut 29:22; Sir
39:23). Salt was cast on cities that had been destroyed (see Jdg 9:45).
    107:36-41 These verses are written in general terms; however, scholars be-
lieve the psalmist is most likely referring here to the settlement and development
of the promised land (vv. 36ff), the hardships during the Assyrian and Babylonian invasions (v. 39), the humiliation and exile of the last kings of Judah (v. 40),
and the restoration of Zion after the Exile (v. 41).
    107:42 *Upright . . . wicked:* a comparison often made in the Old Testament
(see Prov 2:21f; 11:6f; 12:6; 14:11; 15:8; 21:18; 29:27).

⁴³ Let whoever is wise reflect on these things^c
   and understand the merciful love of the
   L<small>ORD</small>.*

PSALM 108*

Prayer for Divine Assistance
against Enemies

¹ A song. A psalm of David.

² My heart is steadfast, O God,*^d
   my heart is steadfast.
 I will sing and chant your praise;
   awake, my soul!*
³ Awake, lyre and harp!
   I will awaken the dawn.*^e

⁴ I will give thanks to you among the peoples,
   O L<small>ORD</small>;*
 I will sing your praises among the nations.^f
⁵ For your kindness extends above the heavens;
   your faithfulness, to the skies.^g

---

c Hos 14:9.—d 2-6: Ps 57:8-12.—e Job 21:12; 38:12.—f Pss 9:12; 18:50;
148:13.—g Pss 36:6; 71:19; Pss 106:45; 145:8; Ex 20:6; Num 14:18.

107:43 This conclusion transforms the hymn of thanksgiving and praise into a
wisdom psalm. The righteous will become wise by studying the Lord's deliverances of his people.
 Ps 108 Two fragments of psalms (with very slight modifications) have been used
to make up this song of praise (vv. 2-6 = Ps 57:8-12 and vv. 7-14 = Ps 60:7-14),
which Israel proclaims as it awaits liberation. We see the Lord already rallying all his
children and taking the lead of their combat, as in the past, to enable them to gain
redress against their enemies. This song of martial confidence will become a canticle of hope inculcating joy and praise, for the glory of God will fill all humankind.
 Christians can make use of this psalm to thank God for the redemption and
for the constant victories that he enables us to obtain over our spiritual enemies
by the aid of our Redeemer.
 108:2-6 The psalmist offers praise to God's kindness, which gives him steadfast hope.
 108:2 The psalmist is at peace because of his trust in the Lord. *Heart:* see
note on Ps 4:8. *O God:* after this phrase, some mss lack the words "my heart is
steadfast." *Awake my soul:* another possible translation is: "with all my soul."
 108:3 *Dawn:* personified as in Ps 139:9; Job 3:9; 38:12. The psalmist wishes to
awaken the dawn, for that is the usual time when deliverance comes from the
Lord (see notes on Pss 17:15 and 57:8).
 108:4-5 A vow to offer ritual praise to the Lord for his kindness (see note on Ps
7:18). *Kindness:* see note on Ps 6:5.

⁶ Be exalted, O God, above the heavens,
    and let your glory shine over all the earth.
⁷ With your right hand come to our aid*
    so that those you love may be delivered.

⁸ God has promised from his sanctuary,ʰ
    "In triumph I will apportion Shechem*
    and measure out the Valley of Succoth.
⁹ Gilead is mine, and Manasseh is mine;
    Ephraim is my helmet,*
    Judah is my scepter.
¹⁰ Moab is my washbasin;*
    upon Edom I will plant my sandal;
    over Philistia I will shout in triumph."ⁱ

¹¹ Who will lead me into the fortified city?*
    Who will guide me into Edom?
¹² Is it not you, O God, who have rejected us*
    and no longer go forth with our armies?ʲ

¹³ Grant us your help against our enemies,
    for any human assistance is worthless.
¹⁴ With God's help we will be victorious,
    for he will overwhelm our foes.

---

h 7-14: Ps 60:7-14.—i Ps 137:7; Gen 19:37; Ru 4:7-8.—j Ps 44:10; 60:12; 68:8; 89:39-52.

108:7-14 The psalmist prays for God's help against his enemies.

108:8-10 *Shechem* was west of the Jordan, and *Succoth* east of it; therefore, they indicate dominion over all Palestine. Next are named four Israelite tribes; hence, there are three regions in all that must be reduced to subjection.

108:9 *Helmet:* a symbol of the strength exhibited by the tribe of Ephraim (see Deut 33:17; Jdg 7:24—8:3). *Scepter:* a symbol of the King-Messiah who had been promised from Judah (see Gen 49:10).

108:10 *Moab is my washbasin:* i.e., its people will do menial work for the Israelites (see Gen 18:4). *Plant my sandal:* an Eastern way of signifying possession.

108:11 *Fortified city:* doubtless Bozrah in Idumea (see Isa 34:6; 63:1; Am 1:12). It was from this inaccessible refuge that the Edomites sent incursions into Judea.

108:12-14 The psalmist looks to the Lord rather than other human beings for an answer to the people's problems. He calls upon him to end his abandonment and lead his people to victory over their enemies. Indeed, he believes the Lord is still with them and will bring them through this trial with strength, joy, and success (see Pss 44:6; 118:15f).

PSALM 109*

Prayer for One Falsely Accused

1 For the director.* A psalm of David.

O God, whom I praise,*
  do not remain silent.*k*
2 Wicked and deceitful men
  have opened their mouths against me;*
  they have spoken against me with lying
    tongues.
3 They confront me with words of hatred
  and assail me without cause.

4 In return for my love they denounce me
  even as I offer up prayers for them.*
5 They give me back evil in exchange for good
  and hatred in place of my love.*l*

---

k Pss 35:22; 83:1; Ex 15:2; Job 34:29; Jer 17:14.—l Pss 35:12; 38:21; Gen 44:4; Prov 17:13; Jer 18:20.

Ps 109 The Psalter contains other cries of hatred or revenge (e.g., Pss 9; 35; 137; 139), but none is harsher than this one (vv. 6-19). It is ordinarily attributed to the psalmist who has been speaking from the beginning of the psalm. However, an attentive examination of the context leads some scholars to attribute these imprecations to another person—most likely, the leader of the psalmist's enemies.

It is a fact, of course, that in the East people enjoy exaggerated expressions, and it is also a fact that it was written before the Christian faith changed the harsh law of revenge or law of talion. But the Gospel itself contains curses (see Mt 23:13-26; Lk 6:24-26), and while it is true that Jesus and the apostles were able to forgive their enemies, they also saw the "ancient serpent" (Rev 12:9) at work, against God's will and for their destruction.

In taking up these imprecatory psalms, the Church invites Christians to commence an unceasing struggle against the spirit of evil (see Eph 6:12). Except for a few details, the formulas of this prayer were suitable for Jesus to express his own situation and sentiments and to describe the attitude and machinations of his enemies. In fact, the evangelists record that his enemies fulfilled certain passages to the letter (e.g., v. 25; see Mt 27:39; Mk 15:20).

109:1a *For the director:* these words are thought to be a musical or liturgical notation.

109:1b-5 This psalmist has never said and done anything other than good; will betrayal, hatred, and slander be his recompense? Bitter is the calumny that crushes the righteous.

109:2 *Opened their mouths against me:* see note on Ps 5:10.

109:4 *I offer up prayers for them:* the psalmist is not a man of evil and slander; he even prays for his foes (as in Ps 35:13f).

6 * They say:*
"Choose a wicked man to oppose him,
  an accuser to stand on his right.
7 At his judgment, let him be found guilty,
  with even his prayers deemed sinful.*

8 "May his remaining days be few,
  with someone else appointed to take his office.*[m]
9 May his children become fatherless
  and his wife become widowed.[n]

10 "May his children be vagrants and beggars,
  driven from the ruins they use for shelter.
11 May the creditor seize all he has,
  and strangers abscond with his life savings.

12 "May no one extend mercy to him*
  or take pity on his fatherless children.
13 May his posterity be doomed to extinction
  and his name be blotted out within a generation.[o]

14 "May the iniquity of his ancestors be remembered by the LORD,
  and the sin of his mother never be wiped out.[p]

---

m Job 15:32; Acts 1:20.—n Ex 22:23; Jer 18:21.—o Pss 9:6; 21:11; Num 14:12; Job 18:19; Prov 10:7.—p Ex 20:5; Isa 65:6-7; Jer 18:23.

109:6-15 Pitiless are the words of those who curse the innocent psalmist; he has taken them to heart and remembered every one. See note on Ps 5:11 concerning redress for wrongs.
109:6 *They say:* these words are lacking in the Hebrew, but they are called for by the context. *Wicked man:* or "the evil one." *Accuser:* i.e., a "satan" (see Job 1:6), a name later given to the devil (see 1 Chr 21:1). He stood as an advocate (v. 31) at the right of the accused (see Zec 3:1).
109:7 *With even his prayers deemed sinful:* another possible translation is: "with even his pleas being in vain."
109:8 *With someone else appointed . . . office:* applied to Judas in Acts 1:20.
109:12-13 The Law, the Prophets, and the Gospel all give warnings of what the sins of ancestors can bring down upon the children (see Ex 20:5; 1 Sam 2:31ff; Lk 19:41ff). *Name be blotted out:* see note on Ps 69:29.

15 May their guilt be continually before the LORD,[q]
and may he banish all remembrance of them from the earth.[r]

16 "For he never thought of showing mercy;*
rather, he hounded to death
the poor and the needy and the broken-hearted.
17 He loved to level curses* at others;
may they recoil on him.
He took no pleasure in blessing;
may no blessing be his.

18 "He clothed himself with cursing as his garment;
it seeped into his body like water
and into his bones like oil.
19 May it be like the robe that envelops him,
like the belt that encircles him every day."

20 May these evils my accusers wish for me
be inflicted upon them by the LORD.*
21 But you, O Lord, my God,*
treat me kindly for your name's sake;*
deliver me because of your overwhelming kindness.

q Ps 90:8; Hos 7:2.—r Ps 34:17; Ex 17:14; Deut 32:26.

109:16-20 No other place expresses with such vivid intensity the terrible logic of judgment whereby what humans choose they ultimately receive to the full.

109:17 *Curses:* see note on Ps 10:7.

109:20 *May these . . . by the LORD:* literally, "May this be the recompense of my accusers from the LORD / and of those who speak evil against me." Accordingly, the preceding curses may be understood as spoken either by the psalmist against his primary foe or by his enemies first and then willed by him to recoil against them. Another translation for the verse is also possible: "This is the work of those / who wish to call down harm upon me from the LORD." In that case, the only imprecations of the psalmist would be the mild ones in v. 29.

109:21-31 The poem seems to begin again at this point. The poor man once again invokes God, reveals his distress, asks for health, cries out his imprecations, and promises to give thanks. It is the rhythm of the prayer of a persecuted person. It testifies to a conviction: in the time of God's judgment, the evil one will return in defeat to the world of darkness where he willed to swallow up everything, but the righteous will obtain access to the glory of the Lord.

109:21 *For your name's sake:* see note on Ps 5:12. *Kindness:* see note on Ps 6:5.

²² For I am poor and needy,*
    and my heart is pierced within me.
²³ I am fading away* like an evening shadow;
    I am shaken off like a locust.

²⁴ My knees are weak from fasting;ˢ
    my flesh is wasting away.
²⁵ I have become an object of ridicule to my
      accusers;
    upon seeing me, they toss their heads.*

²⁶ Come to my aid, O LORD, my God;
    save me because of your kindness.*
²⁷ Let them know that your hand has done this,
    that you, O LORD, have accomplished it.

²⁸ When they curse, you will bless;
    when they attack, they will be put to
      shame,
    and your servant will rejoice.*
²⁹ My accusers will be clothed in disgrace,
    wrapped in their shame as in a cloak.

³⁰ I will thank the LORD with my lips,ᵗ
    and before all the people I will praise him.*
³¹ For he stands at the right hand of the poor
    to save him from his accusers who pass
      judgment on him.*

---

s 24-25: Pss 22:7-8; 35:13; 69:11-13.—t Pss 35:18; 71:22; 111:1.

109:22 *Poor and needy:* see note on Ps 22:27. *Heart:* see note on Ps 4:8.
109:23 *I am fading away:* the psalmist's illness draws the scorn of enemies (see note on Ps 5:10). *Like an evening shadow:* similar to Ps 102:12. *Shaken off like a locust:* allusion to the custom of brushing locusts off the plants in order to kill them on the ground. Another translation possible is: "swept away like a locust," an image similar to Job 30:22; in Palestine a strong wind sometimes ends a plague of locusts by blowing them out into the sea (see Ex 10:19; Joel 2:20).
109:25 His accusers seek the psalmist's downfall by casting scorn on him (see Pss 31:12; 79:4; 89:42) and by rejecting him ("[tossing] their heads": see Ps 22:8; Mt 27:39).
109:26 *Kindness:* see note on Ps 6:5.
109:28 This is a good prayer to turn the edge of an attack (see Rom 8:31ff).
109:30 A vow to praise the Lord for his deliverance (see note on Ps 7:18).
109:31 The final verse puts everything in perspective—replacing the figure of the "accuser," who stands at the right hand of his victim to accuse him, with the figure of God who "stands at the right hand of the poor" to save him.

PSALM 110*

The Messiah—King, Prophet, and Conqueror

^{1} A psalm of David.

The LORD says to my Lord:
  "Sit at my right hand
  until I have made your enemies a footstool
    for you."*^{u}

^{2} The LORD will stretch forth from Zion
  your scepter of power.*

---

u Jos 10:24; Mt 22:44; Mk 12:36; Lk 20:42f; Acts 2:34-35; 1 Cor 15:25; Heb 1:13; 8:1; 10:12-13; 12:2; 1 Pet 3:22.

Ps 110 These few surprising verses (which comprise essentially two oracles) became the supreme Messianic psalm in both the Jewish and the Christian traditions. It was so much used and adapted down the centuries before becoming part of the Psalter that it is difficult to reconstruct completely the original text. In its oldest version it certainly goes back to the earliest times of the monarchy.

The psalm was subsequently revised, perhaps on various occasions; the song no longer refers to the kings who are passing away but to the Messiah who is to come at the end of the earthly time and restore everything in the name of God. He will be of royal birth (see 2 Sam 7:16) and will be charged with judging the nations and ruling over the entire world. He will not be counted among the princes of the nations, who have their power from human beings, for God himself will invest him as everlasting King and Priest, as is shown by the parallel with the mysterious Melchizedek, priest and king of Salem, whose earthly ancestry no one knows (see Gen 14:18; Heb 7:3).

Jesus, who claims to be the Christ, that is, the Messiah, and Son of God, fulfills the promise given in this psalm, as he hints to the Pharisees (see Mt 22:42-45; 26:64); the apostles are inspired by this passage to proclaim the glory of the risen Christ, Lord of the universe (see Mk 16:19; Acts 2:33-35; Rom 8:34; 1 Cor 15:25-28; Eph 1:20; Col 3:1; Heb 10:12f; 1 Pet 3:22). The author of the Letter to the Hebrews finds in this psalm the proof that Christ is superior to the priests of the Old Testament and that he alone is the Savior of humankind (Heb 7).

110:1 The first oracle (vv. 1-3) establishes God's anointed as his regent over all (see Ps 2:7-12). *The LORD says to my Lord:* a polite form of address from an inferior to a superior (see 1 Sam 25:25; 2 Sam 1:10). By the word "Lord," the court singer is referring to the king. Jesus in interpreting this psalm takes the psalmist to be David, who was acknowledged by all to be referring to the Messiah. Hence, the Messiah must be David's superior and not merely his son or descendant (see Mt 22:41-46 par). *Right hand:* the place of honor beside a king (see Ps 45:10; 1 Ki 2:19), in this case making the Messiah second to God himself (see Mt 26:64; Mk 14:62; 16:19; Lk 22:69; Acts 2:33; 5:31; 7:55f; Rom 8:34; Eph 1:20; Col 3:1; Heb 1:3; 8:1; 10:12; 12:2). *Footstool for you:* see 1 Cor 15:25; Eph 1:22; Heb 10:12f.

110:2ab The Lord will expand the Messiah's reign to the extent that no foe will remain to oppose his rule (see Pss 2:6; 45:7; 72:8).

The LORD says:
  "Rule in the midst of your enemies!*
³ Yours is royal dignity in the day of your
    birth;
  in holy splendor, before the daystar,
  like the dew, I have begotten you."*ᵛ

⁴ The LORD has sworn,
    and he will not retract his oath:
  "You are a priest forever
    according to the order of Melchizedek."*ʷ

⁵ The LORD stands forth at your right hand;*
    he will crush kings on the day of his
    wrath.ˣ

---

v Pss 2:7; 89:28; Ex 15:11; Isa 49:1; Mic 5:7.—w Pss 89:36; 132:11; Gen
14:18; Num 23:19; Heb 5:6; 7:21.—x Pss 2:9; 16:8; Rev 2:27; 12:5; 19:15.

110:2cd The Messiah is the Lord's regent over his emerging kingdom.

110:3 *Yours is royal dignity . . . I have begotten you:* this is the usual Catholic
translation and comes from the revised Latin Vulgate, which is based on the ancient versions. The current Hebrew is obscure and seems to be corrupt. *Before the
daystar:* when the sun had not yet been created, i.e., from all eternity. *Like the
dew:* in a secret, mysterious manner. Hence, the Messiah and Son of God existed
before the dawn of creation in eternity.

The Hebrew is translated as follows: "Your people will volunteer freely / on your
day of battle. / In holy splendor, from the womb of the dawn / the dew of your
youth is yours." It refers to numerous royal troops at the Messiah's command. The
people come voluntarily on the day of battle, as in the days of Deborah (see Jdg
5:2, 9). They consecrate themselves, are fully prepared, and place themselves at
his service. They will be as abundant as the dew at dawn. The image is close to
those of Paul about "living sacrifices" (Rom 12:1) or a life poured out like a
"drink offering" (Phil 2:17). It should be noted that, even not considering the lin-
guistic difficulties that argue against this reading and the fact that the Septuagint of pre-Christian times already confirms the text of the Vulgate, the Hebrew
reading does not fit the great theme of the psalm as well as the Latin translation
does. Every connection with the central thought that speaks of the royal and
priestly dignity of Melchizedek is missing.

110:4 The prophet-psalmist pronounces a second divine oracle, guaranteed by
an oath. The Lord makes his king his chief priest for life, according to the order
and image of Melchizedek. There are three main points of resemblance between
Melchizedek and Christ. Both are kings as well as priests, both offer bread and
wine to God, and both have their priesthood directly from God (see Gen 14:18;
Heb 7). For a prophetic vision of the glorious union of the Messiah-Priest, see Zec
6:13; for the New Testament application, see Heb 5:6-10; 7:22. *Forever:* perhaps
alluded to in Jn 12:34.

110:5 *The LORD stands forth at your right hand:* when the king goes out to battle,
the Lord, as the Master of the universe, is right with him, and crushing the foes.

⁶ He* will judge the nations,
    filling their land with corpses
    and crushing rulers throughout the earth.
⁷ He will drink from the stream on his journey,
    and then he will lift up his head in triumph.*ʸ

PSALM 111*

Praise of God for His Wondrous Works

¹ Alleluia.

I will give thanks to the LORD with all my heart*
    in the council of the upright and in the as-
    sembly.ᶻ

² Great are the works of the LORD;*
    they are pondered by all who delight in
    them.

---

y Pss 3:4; 27:6.—z Pss 9:2; 27:6; 34:2; 138:1.

110:6 *He:* the Messiah-King. *Filling the land with corpses:* gory imagery symbolizing full victory (see Ps 2:9; Rev 19:11-21) when God's judgment comes to pass.
    110:7 Figurative language of uncertain meaning. Some see an allusion to a
rite of royal consecration at the spring of Gihon (see 1 Ki 1:33, 38). Others see an
image of the Messianic King bowing down in humility to drink of the waters of divine assistance before moving on to more victories (see Isa 8:6; Jer 2:13, 17f).
    Ps 111 In this acrostic psalm (see p. 23), a sage sets forth the essence of the
religion of Israel: the Lord has delivered his people in order to conclude a Covenant
with them and to reveal his will to them. The author contemplates the divine
"righteousness" (v. 3.), i.e., everything the Lord has done in favor of his chosen
ones, the wonders that in some way are renewed when they are recalled in the
liturgy (v. 4): the miracle of the manna and the quail (v. 5), the gift of the promised land (v. 6), and the stability of the laws of the world and the moral order (v.
7). The sages who pursue this meditation and observe the Law will be enabled to
understand who God is: holy and redoubtable, compassionate and tender, so that
they may render thanks to him.
    In praying this psalm, we should keep in mind that the wonders to which it al-
ludes are only a pale figure of the wonders that the Father has accomplished
through and in his Incarnate Son on behalf of his new people the Church (see Jn
5:20). After various physical cures and raisings from the dead, God works the glorious Resurrection of his Son and our own spiritual resurrection in him (see Eph 2:5f).
    111:1 *Heart:* see note on Ps 4:8. *Council of the upright:* probably a circle of friends
and advisors (as in Ps 107:32). *In the assembly:* in the temple (see Ps 149:1).
    111:2 *Works of the LORD:* sometimes his deeds, as in v. 6, but more often the
things he has made (e.g., the heavens, Pss 8:4; 19:2; 102:26; and the earth, Ps
104:24). Made "by . . . wisdom" (Ps 104:24), these lend themselves to meditation
and lead to delight.

3 His deeds* show forth majesty and splendor,
   and his righteousness endures forever.
4 He has won renown for his wonders;*
   gracious and compassionate is the LORD.*a*

5 He provides food for those who fear him*
   and is forever mindful of his covenant.
6 He has manifested the power of his works to
   his people
   by giving them the lands* of the nations.

7 The works of his hands are faithful and right,*
   and all his commandments are trustworthy.
8 They are established forever and ever
   to be observed in fidelity and truthfulness.

9 He has granted deliverance to his people
   and established his covenant forever;
   holy and awe-inspiring is his name.*

10 The fear of the LORD is the beginning of wisdom;*
   those who are guided by it will grow in understanding.
   His praise will last forever.*b*

---

a Pss 103:8; 112:4; Deut 4:31.—b Deut 4:6; Prov 1:7; 9:10; Sir 1:16.

111:3 *Deeds:* probably his providential acts as in Deut 32:4. We should keep in mind that, as Isa 45:9-13 indicates, God's Creation and Providence are of one piece. *Righteousness:* as embodied in his deeds.

111:4 *Won renown for his wonders:* by the celebration of annual feasts (see Ex 23:14), notably the Passover (for Christians, see 1 Cor 11:23-26). See also note on Ps 9:2. *Gracious and compassionate:* classic description of the meaning of God's name (see Ps 103:8; Ex 34:6f).

111:5 *Food for those who fear him:* probably a reference to the manna in the desert (see Ex 16:1ff), which in the New Testament is seen as a type of the Eucharist (see Jn 6:31-33, 49-51). The entire verse may also refer to God's giving of our daily bread (see Mt 6:11) and his daily forbearance. *His covenant:* see Ps 105:8-11.

111:6 *Lands:* literally, "inheritance, heritage."

111:7-8 There is complete harmony between what God does and what he says, between the "works of his hands" and "his commandments."

111:9 This verse recalls the miracles of the Exodus and the theophany at Sinai. *Name:* see note on Ps 5:12.

111:10 *The fear of the LORD is the beginning of wisdom:* the motto of the Wisdom writings (see Job 28:28; Prov 1:7; 9:10; Eccl 12:13; Sir 1:18, 24; 19:17). Here it refers to God especially as Creator, Redeemer, and Provider.

PSALM 112*

The Blessings of the Righteous

1 Alleluia.

Blessed is the man who fears the LORD,
who greatly delights in his precepts.*c
2 His descendants will be powerful upon the
earth;
the generation of the upright will be
blessed.*

3 His house will be filled with wealth and
riches,*
and his righteousness will endure forever.

---

c Pss 1:1-2; 13:6; 15:2-5; 103:11; 119:1-2, 14, 16, 47, 92; 128:1; Deut 18:13; Job 1:8; Mt 3:5ff.

Ps 112 This psalm provides the same literary characteristics as the preceding one and most likely stems from the same unknown author (see p. 23 for "acrostic" psalms). By their theme the two chants complete one another. The first celebrates the divine perfections and works, while the second sings of the virtues and deeds of the true righteous person and the happiness he attains.

The ancients believed that the man who faithfully observed the Law and was solicitous of his neighbor was assured prosperity, posterity, and renown. In this psalm a sage once again praises the righteous in these terms, but he adds another more mystical religious sentiment. In effect, applying to the righteous the qualities that the preceding psalm attributed to the Lord, he wishes to show that by dint of placing his delight in the will of the Lord, the righteous man ends up resembling him. Hence, the Law is not a burden imposed from without but a power that transforms the heart. To obey is to let oneself be invaded by the sentiments of God: mercy, tenderness, and righteousness. Is there any other source of happiness?

This psalm is also very suitable for describing the Christian ideal, the perfection we must achieve in the steps of the Master and the happiness we will find therein.

112:1 Blessed is the man who follows unswervingly God's will and call. *Blessed:* see note on Ps 1:1. *Fears the LORD:* see note on Ps 15:2-5.

112:2 The upright man is blessed in his children and brings blessings on them (see Pss 37:26; 127:3-5; 128:3).

112:3 *Wealth and riches:* see Pss 1:3; 128:2. *His righteousness:* i.e., his happiness, his successes, and his well-being. There is a tacit comparison of the upright person's righteousness to God's (they both "endure forever": see Ps 111:3b). Some scholars translate the word "righteousness" as "generosity," claiming that the original meaning of the Hebrew word in a later period of the language also acquired the meaning of "liberality, almsgiving" (see Sir 3:30; 7:10; Mt 6:1f).

⁴ He shines as a light for the upright in the
    darkness;*
    kindness, mercy, and justice are his hall-
    marks.*d*

⁵ The future bodes well* for him
    who is generous in helping those in need
    and who conducts his affairs with justice.

⁶ He will never be swayed;*
    the righteous man will be remembered for-
    ever.*e*

⁷ He has no fear of bad news,
    for his heart remains steadfast, trusting in
    the LORD.

⁸ Since his heart is tranquil, he will not be
    afraid,
    and he will witness the downfall of his ene-
    mies.

⁹ He bestows gifts lavishly on the poor;
    his righteousness will endure forever,
    and his horn will be exalted in glory.**f*

¹⁰ The wicked will be furious when he sees this,
    gnashing his teeth and pining away;
    the desires of the wicked will be fruitless.*

---

d Pss 18:29; 37:6; 97:11; Prov 13:9; Isa 58:10.—e Ps 15:5; Prov 10:7;
Wis 8:13.—f Pss 75:11; 86:17; Prov 22:9; Lk 19:8; Acts 9:36; 2 Cor 9:9.

112:4 The goodness of the righteous man overflows to others. He acts in the
same way as God does (see Ps 111:4b). This is brought out more clearly by the
older Catholic rendition: "He dawns through the darkness, a light for the upright;
/ he is gracious and compassionate and righteous."

112:5 *Future bodes well:* i.e., well-being and prosperity await him (see Ps
34:9-15). Good is also the quality of the righteous man. He is good in that he "is
generous" (see Pss 34:9-11; 37:21). Just as all the Lord's works are "faithful and
right" (see Ps 111:7), so the upright man "conducts his affairs with justice."

112:6-8 The righteous man observes the commandments of God that are "established forever and ever" (Ps 111:8); hence "he will never be swayed" (v. 6)
and "has no fear" (v. 7), for "his heart is tranquil" (v. 8). His trust is in the Lord
in spite of "bad news," reasons to "fear," or problems with others (vv. 7-8).

112:9 As God's name is held in holy awe (see Ps 111:9), so the righteous will be
held in honor. Paul uses this verse to support the principle that "if you sow generously, you will reap generously as well" (2 Cor 9:6, 9). *Horn:* here symbolizes dignity.

112:10 The only alternative way of life to that of the righteous is bitter, tran-
sient, and futile.

THE EGYPTIAN HALLEL—Ps 113–118*

PSALM 113*

Praise of the Lord for His Care of the Lowly

1 Alleluia.

Praise, you servants of the LORD,*
praise the name of the LORD.[g]

g Pss 22:23; 34:23; 99:3; 103:25; 134:1; 148:13.

Pss 113—118 The *Hallel* ("praise") psalms are found in three separate collections: the "Egyptian Hallel," also known as the "Little Hallel" (113—118), the "Great Hallel" (120—136), and the "Concluding Hallel" (146—150). The Egyptian Hallel and the Great Hallel (most of which are pilgrimage psalms: 120—134) were sung during the annual feasts (see Lev 23; Num 10:10). The Egyptian Hallel received a special place in the Passover liturgy; by custom 113—114 were recited or sung before the festive meal and 115—118 after it (see Mt 26:30; Mk 14:26). These were probably the last psalms Jesus sang before his Passion. Only the second (114) speaks directly of the Exodus, but the themes of the others make it an appropriate series to mark the salvation that began in Egypt and would spread to the nations. The concluding Hallel psalms (146—150) were incorporated into the daily prayers in the synagogue after the destruction of the temple in 70 A.D.

Ps 113 This psalm presents a surprising contrast in the praises of Israel: the acclamation of the glory of the Almighty One attains its summit, and certitude becomes even stronger that God is near to the lowly. His tenderness reaches those whom the powerful of the earth regard as nothing. The God of justice reverses established situations, as both the canticle of Hannah (see 1 Sam 2:4-8) and the Magnificat of Mary (see Lk 1:46-55) attest with equal intensity. In celebrating the salvation of the humiliated poor man and the abandoned woman, Israel keeps alive the hope of a wondrous renewal in the Messianic age (see Pss 76; 87; Isa 49:21; 54:1-8).

In praying this psalm, we are aware that the New Testament provides us with new motives for praising God the Father for the great condescension he manifests toward Zechariah, Mary, and those known as the poor of Yahweh. We can also chant this psalm in honor of the glorified Christ. Exalted by his Father above every earthly power and introduced by him into divine glory (Phil 2:9-11; Heb 2:7-9), Christ shows himself to be incomparable by uniting to his supreme transcendence an astonishing condescension. It was toward the poor and lowly that he stooped during his public ministry, eating and drinking with them (see Mk 2:16), offering them the kingdom of God (see Mt 5:3-12) with its mysteries (see Mk 4:11), and making them the princes of his new people (see Mk 3:13-19). It is on the poor and the weak in the eyes of the world that he continues to confer his spiritual riches and powers (see 1 Cor 1:26-28).

113:1 *Servants of the LORD:* the Lord's loyal people, together with the priests and the Levites, come together to worship the Lord. These are all those who know "the name of the LORD" (v. 3; see Ps 50:1; Zep 2:11; Mal 1:11). *Name:* see note on Ps 5:12.

2 Blessed be the name of the LORD*
    now and forevermore.
3 From the rising of the sun to its setting
    the name of the LORD is to be praised.

4 High is the LORD over all the nations,*
    and supreme over the heavens is his
    glory.*h*
5 Who is like the LORD, our God,*i*
    the one who is enthroned on high
and who stoops down to look
6   on the heavens and the earth?

7 He raises the poor from the dust*
    and lifts the needy from the rubbish heap,*j*
8 seating them with princes,
    with the princes of his people.
9 He settles the barren woman* in a home
    and makes her the joyful mother of
    children.*k*

Alleluia.

---

h Pss 99:2; 148:13.—i 5-6: Pss 11:4; 89:7-9.—j Pss 35:10; 68:11;
107:41; 140:13; 1 Sam 2:8.—k 1 Sam 2:5; Isa 54:1; Lk 1:25; Gal 4:27.

113:2-3 The name of the Lord is to be proclaimed so that every generation may remember what he has done and how he has revealed himself
(see Ex 3:16). This praise is to extend in time ("forevermore") and in space
("from the rising of the sun to its setting," i.e., from the east to the west; see Mal
1:11).
113:4-6 The psalmist calls attention to the contrast: the exalted rule of the
Lord and his accommodation to the needs of his people. *Over all the nations:* and
by implication over all their gods (see Pss 95:3; 96:4f; 97:9). *Over the heavens:*
i.e., above all creation.
113:7-9 The Lord does not ally himself with the high and mighty but takes
care of the poor and needy by transforming them from outcasts of society ("the
dust," see Isa 47:1, or "rubbish heap," see Lam 4:5) into those who have a position of prominence ("with the princes of his people," v. 8; see 1 Sam 2:8; Job
36:7). The afflicted man will be accorded recognition, and the oppressed woman
will be given honor.
113:9 *Barren woman:* a barren wife was considered cursed by God and a social outcast, a disappointment to her husband, to other women, and especially to
herself (see Gen 16:2; 20:18; 1 Sam 1:6; 2:5; Lk 1:25). The Lord blesses her with
children (see Ps 115:14; Isa 48:19; 54:1-3). *Alleluia:* i.e., "Hallelujah" or "Bless
[or praise] the LORD"; it probably was once the first line of Ps 114.

PSALM 114*

The Lord's Wonders at the Exodus

1 When Israel came out of Egypt,*
 the house of Jacob from a people of alien
 tongue,
2 Judah became God's sanctuary
 and Israel his domain.^{l}

3 The sea fled at the sight;*
 the Jordan turned back.^{m}
4 The mountains skipped like rams,
 the hills like lambs of the flock.^{n}

---

l Ps 78:68f; Ex 15:17; 19:6; Jer 2:3.—m Pss 66:6; 74:15; 77:17; Ex 14:21f; 15:8; Jos 3:14-16.—n Ps 29:6; Jdg 5:5; Wis 19:9.

Ps 114 By reason of its literary composition and poetic inspiration this poem constitutes a little masterpiece. Felicitously, the poet personifies herein the elements of nature led in a dance by God during the Exodus, to make them keen-eyed witnesses of the Lord's triumphal march at the head of his people. Israel belongs so strongly to God that it is like his sanctuary and his domain (v. 2). On an epic and triumphal tone, the people underline the time beyond compare when God established this destiny for them: it is the great adventure of their deliverance.

When the Lord passes by with his people, the sea and waters flee (see Ex 14:15-31; Jos 3:7-17), Sinai thunders and smokes (see Ex 19:16-18), the source springs forth in the desert rocks (see Ex 17:1-7; Num 20:1-13). These remembrances of the Exodus are like the prelude to the upheaval of the universe announcing the coming of God at the end of the earthly ages.

We can pray this psalm in union with the Church ceaselessly meditating on and celebrating the privileged hour of her beginnings: the Passover of Christ that opens up for humankind a destiny of salvation in a new Exodus. Nature bows down before the divine Pioneer of this Exodus. The waters become calm and peaceful in the Sea of Galilee at a word from him: "Be still!" (Mk 4:39), while the mountains tremble at the moment of his Death and Resurrection (Mt 27:51; 28:2) as well as at the moment of his great interventions in history (see Rev 11:19; 16:18).

114:1-2 The deliverance from a foreign country was only a preamble to the greater deeds: the election of the chosen people and the making of the Covenant on Sinai. Judah, the province of the tribe of that name, became the sanctuary of God and all Israel his kingdom; it was a theocracy, a priestly kingdom (see Ex 19:3-6; Jer 2:3). This was a grand event prefiguring the redemption to come and the birth of the Church.

114:3-4 The wonder of Israel's election as the People of God has its effect on the world of nature. The Red Sea and the Jordan River scurry around to make way for their Creator, and the mountains and hills are all animated and agog at his majestic coming (see Pss 18:8-16; 68:8ff; 77:17-20; Jdg 5:4f; Hab 3:3-10).

5 What causes you to flee, O sea?*
Why, O Jordan, do you turn back?
6 Why do you skip like rams, O mountains,
and like lambs of the flock, O hills?

7 Tremble, O earth, at the presence of the LORD,*
at the presence of the God of Jacob,[o]
8 who turns the rock into a pool of water,
and flint into a flowing spring.[p]

PSALM 115*

Hymn to the Lord, the One God

1 * Not to us, O LORD, not to us,*
but to your name give glory
because of your kindness and faithfulness.[q]

o Ps 68:9; 1 Chr 16:30.—p Ex 17:6; Num 20:11; Deut 8:15; 1 Cor 10:4.—q Ps 23:3; Ezek 36:22-23.

114:5-6 The psalmist calls upon the Red Sea, the Jordan, and the mountains to bear witness to the great event when God established his kingdom on earth.

114:7-8 The God of Israel ("Jacob") is none other than the Lord of the universe (see Ps 97:4-6; Rev 20:11). He is still providing streams of blessings for his people as he did at Kadesh, at the waters of Meribah (see Ps 107:35; Ex 17:6; Num 20:8; Deut 8:15; 1 Cor 10:4) and also at the return from the Exile, prefigured by the Exodus and Conquest (see Isa 41:15ff; 42:15; 43:20). On the symbolism of the waters, see Pss 46:2-7; 110:7.

Ps 115 This Psalm was probably used in the course of a celebration of the Covenant, with choir and soloists in turn voicing their confidence in the Lord. Ridiculing the jerry-built gods venerated by the pagans, the community professes its attachment to the one true God, from whom it hopes to receive prosperity. The formulas are brief and striking, with a captivating rhythm; the satire against idols has the flavor of a popular caricature. This simple prayer is at the service of a deep and demanding religious thought and turns into praise. After the Exile, such a clear credo was needed for the community of Jerusalem and for the communities of the dispersion who all coexisted with pagan civilizations that welcomed countless gods. Today, it is still necessary for us to depart from idols fashioned according to our tastes and desires and to turn to the one true God.

We can pray this psalm for the Church, the new Israel, who often experiences profound misfortunes, staggering oppressions, that seem to proclaim her inferiority and impotence before earthly powers and their satanic idol. We can beg Christ the Lord to intervene to restore the renown of the Church and especially his own in the world.

115:1-3 A song in praise of the living God who is faithful to his people and in derision of the pagan idols who are lifeless.

115:1 *Not to us:* God alone is responsible for Israel's Covenant blessings. *Name:* see note on Ps 5:12. *Kindness:* see note on Ps 6:5.

² Why should the nations ask,*ʳ*
   "Where is their God?"*

³ Our God is in heaven;
   he does whatever he pleases.**ˢ*
⁴ Their idols are merely silver and gold,*ᵗ*
   the work of human hands.**ᵘ*

⁵ They have mouths but they cannot speak;
   they have eyes but they cannot see.
⁶ They have ears but they cannot hear;
   they have noses but they cannot smell.

⁷ They have hands but they cannot feel;
   they have feet but they cannot walk;
   their throats can emit no sound.
⁸ Those who make them end up like them,
   as do all who place their trust in them.

⁹ The house of Israel trusts in the LORD;**ᵛ*
   he is their help and their shield.*ʷ*
¹⁰ The house of Aaron trusts in the LORD;
   he is their help and their shield.
¹¹ Those who fear the LORD trust in the LORD;
   he is their help and their shield.

---

r Pss 42:4; 79:10.—s Ps 135:6; Jud 9:5.—t 4-10: Pss 29:2; 135:15-20;
Wis 15:15-16; Isa 44:9f; Jer 10:1-5; Bar 6:3, 7ff.—u Isa 40:19; Rev 9:20.—v
Pss 118:2-4; 135:15-20.—w Pss 28:7; 33:20.

115:2 *Where is their God?:* implying that God does not help his people (see Pss
42:4, 11; 79:10; Joel 2:17; Mic 7:10).
115:3 The community expresses the belief that God is supreme and present;
everything that happens to Israel, good or bad, is his doing.
115:4 The theme of this verse is one that is often found in the Old Testament:
idols, unlike the God of Israel, do not speak, reveal, promise, or utter any spoken
word; ultimately, divine revelation is the difference between the religions made
by humans and the true religion of the Lord (see Ps 135:15-18; Deut 4:16; Isa
44:9ff; Jer 10:1ff; Bar 6:7ff).
115:9-11 In a litany the various classes of people express their confidence in
the Lord. The threefold division ("house of Israel," "house of Aaron," "those who
fear the LORD") occurs elsewhere (see Pss 118:2-4; 135:19f, with "Levi" instead
of "Aaron"). It is unclear whether the phrase "those who fear the LORD" is a synonym for "house of Israel" (see Ps 34:8, 10; 85:10) or all of Israel (laity as well as
priests) or whether it identifies a separate class from the house of Israel, namely
the "Godfearers" known as the proselytes in the Old Testament (see 1 Ki 8:41; Isa
56:6) and in the New (see Acts 13:16, 26; 16:14).

¹² The LORD will be mindful of us and bless us;*
     he will bless the house of Israel;
     he will bless the house of Aaron.
¹³ He will bless those who fear the LORD,
     the small no less than the great.*

¹⁴ May the LORD cause you to increase,*
     both you and your children.
¹⁵ May you be blessed by the LORD,
     the Maker of heaven and earth.

¹⁶ The heavens belong to the LORD,*
     but he has given the earth to humanity.ˣ
¹⁷ It is not the dead who praise the LORD,
     those who sink into silence.*ʸ
¹⁸ It is we who bless the LORD
     from this time forward and forevermore.*

     Alleluia.

---

x Pss 8:7-9; 89:12; Gen 1:28.—y Pss 6:6; 30:10; 88:11ff; 94:17; 115:17; Sir 17:22f; Isa 38:18.

115:12-15 Utilizing the same group of worshipers as in vv. 9-11, the thought moves forward from God's power to save to his power to enrich. The Lord does not discriminate among his people—all will be the recipients of his blessing. Although they may be put to the test by afflictions of various kinds, the Lord remembers those with whom he has made a Covenant (see Pss 98:3; 136:23; Isa 49:14f) and delivers them, bringing to fulfillment the promises he has made.

115:13 *The small no less than the great:* the outcasts and the powerful. All will be treated alike by the Lord (see Jer 6:13; 16:6; 31:34; Rev 19:5).

115:14-15 Through these words of blessing, the Lord renews his promise that Abraham's descendants will increase without end (see Ps 127:3-5; Deut 1:11; Isa 54:1-3; Zec 10:8-10).

115:16-18 The psalmist concludes with a short hymn of praise. In so doing he reminds his people that they have been given the earth to enjoy and care for, while praising the Lord.

115:17 The psalmist stresses that the dead cannot praise the Lord; for, according to the idea of the ancients, in the netherworld the souls of the dead had a kind of shadowy existence with no activity or lofty emotion and could not offer praise to God. *Silence:* a euphemism for the grave (see Ps 94:17; see also notes on Pss 6:6 and 30:2).

115:18 *Forevermore:* some view this as saying that those who serve the living God will themselves live on, unlike the worshipers of lifeless idols (v. 8). This would then add its witness to an afterlife to such passages as Pss 11:7; 16:8-11; 17:15; 23:6; 49:16; 73:23ff; 139:18). *Alleluia:* i.e., "Hallelujah" or "Bless (or praise) the LORD"; the Septuagint and Vulgate add this line as the opening of Ps 116.

PSALM 116*

Thanksgiving to God for Help Received

¹ I love the LORD because he has heard my voice
and listened to my cry for mercy,*
² because he has inclined his ear to me
on the day when I called out to him.*

³ The bonds of death* encompassed me;
the snares of the netherworld held me
tightly.
I was seized by distress and sorrow.ᶻ
⁴ Then I cried out in the name* of the LORD:
"O LORD, I entreat you to preserve my life."

⁵ Gracious is the LORD and righteous;
our God is merciful.ᵃ

---

z Ps 18:6-7; 2 Sam 22:6; Jon 2:3.—a Ps 86:15; Ex 34:6; Ezr 9:15.

Ps 116 Countless are the distresses of human beings and countless too are the deliverances worked by God. This psalm adapts itself to diverse situations; every believer knows the mortal dangers from which the Lord has extricated him in order to bring him to the joy of his presence. In a praying community, all can give thanks. In thanking the divinity it was the custom in the ancient East to pour a cup as a libation, i.e., the "cup of salvation" (that has been granted) (v. 13). The Jews certainly practiced a similar rite during the "fellowship [or: peace] offerings" (see Lev 7:11ff). By this act of thanksgiving the Israelites publicly bore witness that God had saved them; this is the loftiest expression of their religion.

It is also the loftiest expression of the Christian religion. It was certainly in this spirit that Jesus recited this psalm with his disciples after having instituted the Eucharist (see Mt 26:30). Who else could have fully relied on God even through the moment of his death? Once this psalm became the prayer of Jesus on the night in which he was betrayed, it proclaimed the hope of a life and a joy that are everlasting. The priest who mystically offers the divine victim anew still says: "We offer to you, God of glory and majesty . . . the cup of eternal salvation" (Eucharistic Prayer I) and "We offer you, Father, . . . this saving cup" (Eucharistic Prayer II).

In the Hebrew text this psalm is a single psalm, as the sense requires; in the Septuagint and Vulgate it is two distinct psalms, 114 (comprising vv. 1-9) and 115 (comprising vv. 10-19).

116:1 The psalmist expresses love for God who has heard his prayer. For a similar expression of God's care and people's love of him, see 1 Jn 4:19: "We love because [God] first loved us."

116:2 *On the day when I called out to him:* see Pss 4:4; 31:23; 34:5; 138:3. Another possible translation is: "I will call on him as long as I live."

116:3 *Bonds of death:* see note on Ps 18:6.

116:4 *Name:* see note on Ps 5:12.

⁶ The LORD watches over his little ones;*
    when I was brought low, he saved me.

⁷ Be at peace once again, O my soul,
    for the LORD has shown mercy to you.ᵇ
⁸ He has delivered my soul from death,
    my eyes from tears,
    and my feet from stumbling.*ᶜ

⁹ I will walk in the presence of the LORD
    in the land of the living.*ᵈ
¹⁰ I believed; therefore, I said,*
    "I am greatly afflicted."ᵉ
¹¹ In my dismay I cried out,
    "All men are liars."*ᶠ

¹² How can I repay the LORD
    for all the good he has done for me?
¹³ I will lift up the cup of salvation*
    and call on the name of the LORD.

¹⁴ I will fulfill my vows* to the LORD
    in the presence of his people.

---

b Pss 13:6; 62:2; Mt 11:29.—c Pss 56:14; 86:13; Isa 25:8; 35:10; Rev 7:17; 21:4.—d Pss 27:13; 56:14; Isa 38:11; Jer 11:19.—e Ps 9:19; 2 Cor 4:13.—f Pss 5:10f; 12:3; 35:11, 15; 109:2-4.

116:6 *Little ones:* just like the "poor," the "little ones" are those who depend on and trust only in the Lord (see Ps 34:7). They have a poverty of spirit, not simply of money. Just as the Spirit of God worked on the primeval darkness to produce all that exists, so the Lord works on his little ones to produce all that is good for them.

116:8 The psalmist here spells out salvation in terms of earthly well-being, but in words that are true at the deepest level (see, e.g., Rom 8:10f; 2 Cor 6:10; Jude 24). *Soul:* see note on Ps 6:4.

116:9 *The land of the living:* reference to this life or to the temple (see Pss 52:7; 116:9; Isa 38:11), where the God of life is present; the psalmist is speaking of the world of the living as opposed to the world of the dead.

116:10 *I believed; therefore, I said:* the psalmist kept faith even in the darkest times (see 2 Cor 4:13 where this text is cited).

116:11 *All men are liars:* the psalmist avers that his enemies are telling falsehoods about him (see Pss 5:10f; 35:11, 15; 109:2-4) because all people are liars. He could also be alluding to the fact that all people offer only a false hope of deliverance. These words are cited in Rom 3:4.

116:13 *The cup of salvation:* probably the libation of wine poured out in gratitude for one's deliverance (see Ex 25:29; Num 15:1-10). These words are used at Mass in Eucharistic Prayer I and II, as indicated in the introduction. *Name:* see note on Ps 5:12.

116:14 *Vows:* see note on Ps 7:18.

¹⁵ Precious in the eyes of the LORD
    is the death* of his faithful ones.ᵍ

¹⁶ O LORD, I am your servant.
    I am your servant, the child of your hand-
      maid;*ʰ
    you have loosed my bonds.
¹⁷ I will offer you a sacrifice of thanksgiving
    and call on the name of the LORD.ⁱ

¹⁸ I will fulfill my vows to the LORD
    in the presence of all his people,ʲ
¹⁹ in the courts of the house of the LORD,
    in your midst, O Jerusalem.

Alleluia.*

PSALM 117*

Universal Praise of God

¹ Glorify the LORD, all you nations;
    praise him, all you peoples.*ᵏ

---

g Ps 72:14; Num 23:10; Isa 43:4.—h Pss 86:16; 119:125; 143:12; Wis 9:5.—i Lev 7:12ff; Ezr 1:4.—j Jon 2:10.—k Ps 103:1; Rom 15:11.

116:15 *Precious . . . is the death:* the psalmist indicates that God consents to the death of his faithful only with difficulty (see Isa 43:4), for death was regarded as taking away their relationship with him (see Pss 6:6; 72:13; 115:17). The versions interpreted this passage according to the dogma of the resurrection: "the death of his faithful ones has worth in the eyes of God." See the analogous expression, "Their blood is precious in his sight" (Ps 72:14).

116:16 *Child of your handmaid:* see note on Ps 86:16.

116:19 *Alleluia:* i.e., "Hallelujah" or "Bless (or praise) the LORD"; the Septuagint and Vulgate add this line as the opening of Ps 117.

Ps 117 This psalm is a short invitatory earnestly exhorting all peoples to praise the Lord, the God of Israel, for the signal kindness and faithfulness that he manifests toward his people. His goodness toward Israel should inspire admiration and enthusiastic praise among foreigners, who are simply witnesses of his wonders (see Sir 36:1-4; Ezek 36).

Since God's kindness and faithfulness are manifested much more forcefully in the life of the Church than in the history of Israel, all people should on that account give more enthusiastic praise to the heavenly Father. Enabling his Son to vanquish his enemies (the devil and death), the Father fills him with divine riches (eternal life in glory, joy, peace, beatitude, royalty). And he has done the same for the Church and her members. Praise of God is to be unanimous (see Rom 15:11).

117:1 All nations and peoples are called to praise the Lord (see Pss 47:1; 67:4-6; 96:7; 98:4; 100:1-3; see also note on Ps 9:2). This verse is cited in Rom 15:11.

² For his kindness toward us is constant,
  and the faithfulness of the Lord will en-
    dure forever.*

Alleluia.

PSALM 118*

Thanksgiving for Salvation

¹ Give thanks to the Lord, for he is good;*
  his kindness endures forever.*ˡ

---

l Pss 100:5; 105—107; 136:1f; 1 Chr 16:8; 2 Chr 5:13; Ezr 3:11.

117:2 Universal praise is owed to the Lord because of his fidelity to his people. He has shown them constant kindness and faithfulness, that is, faithful love. Indeed, his love is not only great in depth and height (see Rom 5:20; 1 Tim 1:14) but also lasting (see Ps 89:29); see also note on Ps 6:5. In Christ the love of God has been even more powerfully shown both to Jews and to Gentiles so that all might praise him for it (see Rom 15:8ff). *Alleluia:* i.e., "Hallelujah" or "Bless (or praise) the Lord"; the Septuagint and Vulgate add this line to open Ps 118.

Ps 118 This psalm brings to a close the Egyptian Hallel. As the procession of pilgrims goes up to Jerusalem for the feast of Tabernacles (vv. 15, 27; see Lev 23:39-43), the celebrants and the crowd conduct a dialogue, the rhythm of which is determined by the stages of the journey. The procession starts out with a familiar refrain (vv. 1-4) and proceeds while singing a hymn of thanksgiving (vv. 5-18); it arrives at the gates of the temple that has been rebuilt (v. 19) and has become the sign of Israel's renewal after the Exile (vv. 22-24) where the priests respond to the acclamations of the people by blessing them (vv. 25-27). Finally, with palms in hand the procession reaches the sanctuary, whose courts are illumined, and the liturgy takes place with the most solemn thanksgiving (vv. 28-29).

Songs of thanksgiving such as this one called to mind the entire history of Israel, from past to present. Israel is ceaselessly put to the test, humbled, and then delivered, and in this very experience it discovers its calling to be a people that bears witness to God in the midst of the nations and to be the capstone of the world (v. 22).

Jesus makes this calling his own (see Mt 21:42), and the apostles speak of it in their preaching (see Acts 4:11; 1 Pet 2:4-7). For them this psalm expresses in advance the mystery of Christ who is rejected and then exalted and who is the foundation stone of the new People of God (see 1 Cor 3:11; Eph 2:20). This festal song soon became popular; we find the crowd spontaneously singing it on Palm Sunday to greet Jesus as the envoy promised by God (v. 26; see Mt 21:9; Jn 12:13). We find this same acclamation in the *Sanctus* of the Mass; in all the liturgical families the psalm has become an Easter song.

118:1-4 The liturgical call to praise that begins the procession. All Israel had benefited from God's goodness and kindness, i.e., the congregation of Israel, the priests ("house of Aaron"), and "those who fear the Lord" (see note on Ps 115:9-11). Now the people of God's kingdom (Ex 19:5-6; Ps 114:1) and the priests, the descendants of Aaron, are called to profess that the Lord is King and that he is good and kind in standing behind his Covenant.

118:1 A conventional call to praise (see Pss 105—107). *Kindness:* see note on Ps 6:5.

2 Let Israel say,*m*
  "His kindness endures forever."
3 Let the house of Aaron say,
  "His kindness endures forever."
4 Let those who fear the LORD* say,
  "His kindness endures forever."

5 In my distress I called out to the LORD;*
  he answered by setting me free.
6 With the LORD to protect me I am not afraid.
  What can mortals do to me?*n*
7 The LORD is at my side to offer me help;
  I will look down upon my enemies.

8 It is better to take refuge in the LORD*
  than to place your trust in mortals.*o*
9 It is better to take refuge in the LORD
  than to place your trust in princes.

10 All the nations surrounded me;*
  in the name of the LORD I overcame them.
11 They surrounded me on every side;
  in the name of the LORD I overcame them.
12 They swarmed around me like bees;
  they blazed like a fire in the midst of thorns;
  in the name of the LORD I overcame them.*p*

13 I was hard pressed and close to falling,
  but the LORD came to my aid.*q*

---

m 2-4: Pss 106:1; 115:9-11; 136:1-26.—n Pss 27:1; 56:12; Heb 13:6.—o 8-9: Ps 146:3; Isa 57:13.—p Ps 58:9; Deut 1:44.—q Pss 86:17; 129:1-4.

118:2-4 *Israel . . . house of Aaron . . . those who fear the LORD:* see note on Ps 115:9-11.

118:5-18 A song of thanksgiving for deliverance of the whole nation voiced by a single individual. Some believe the speaker is a king, others opt for Israel as a corporate body, and still others for a priest/Levite. In any case, the worshiper does a good job in reciting the deeds God worked in response to the prayers of his people in affliction.

118:8-9 All should be ever mindful of the motto learned through experience that it is better to have confidence in the Lord than to rely on flesh and blood (see Ps 33:16-19; see also Pss 62; 146).

118:10-13 The fury of the assault recalls the attacks experienced by Jesus at his trial (see Lk 22:63—23:25) and even during his Public Ministry (see Lk 11:53f). *Name:* see note on Ps 5:12.

14 The Lord is my strength and my song,ʳ
　　and he has become my salvation.*

15 Joyful shouts of triumph
　　　ring out in the tents of the righteous:
　　"The right hand of the Lᴏʀᴅ has done won-
　　　　drous deeds;
16　　the right hand of the Lᴏʀᴅ is exalted;
　　　the right hand of the Lᴏʀᴅ has done won-
　　　　drous deeds."

17 I shall not die; rather I shall live
　　and recount* the works of the Lᴏʀᴅ.
18 Even though the Lᴏʀᴅ punished me harshly,
　　he did not hand me over to death.

19 Open to me the gates of righteousness*
　　　so that I may enter them and praise the
　　　Lᴏʀᴅ.ˢ
20 This is the gate of the Lᴏʀᴅ
　　　through which the righteous enter.
21 I thank you for having answered me;
　　　you have become my salvation.

22 The stone that the builders rejected*
　　has become the cornerstone.ᵗ

---

r Ps 62:3; Ex 15:2; Isa 12:2.—s Ps 24:7; Isa 26:2.—t Isa 28:16; Zec 4:7;
Mt 21:42; Lk 20:17; Acts 4:11; Rom 9:33; 1 Cor 3:8; Eph 2:20; 1 Pet 2:7.

118:14 This verse is an exact quotation from the song of victory at the Red Sea
(see Ex 15:2) and is echoed in vv. 15 ("right hand") and 28 ("extol you"). Hence,
God's saving acts throughout history bear the stamp of the Exodus events (see 1
Cor 10:6) culminating in the work of Christ (see Lk 9:31: "his departure [literally,
'exodus'], which would come to pass in Jerusalem").
　118:17 *Live and recount:* see note on Ps 6:6.
　118:19-21 The procession has arrived at the gates of the rebuilt temple; all
the righteous may enter and give thanks.
　118:22-23 The community of the righteous join in with thanksgiving. They
praise the Lord because he has given prominence to his suffering servant Israel
like a "cornerstone." It was rejected by the worldly powers but has been made the
cornerstone for God's salvation of the world in the Messiah. These verses allude
to Isa 8:14; 28:16; Jer 51:26; Zec 3:9; 4:7, passages that are interpreted in a
Messianic sense. Israel is here a type of Christ, in whom these words have been
most eminently fulfilled (see Mt 21:42 par; Acts 4:11; Rom 9:33; 1 Cor 3:11; Eph
2:20; 1 Pet 2:7).

²³ This is the LORD's doing,
    and it is marvelous in our eyes.

²⁴ This is the day that the LORD has made;*
    let us exult and rejoice in it.
²⁵ O LORD, grant us salvation.*
    O LORD, grant us success.

²⁶ Blessed is he who comes in the name of the
        LORD.*ᵘ
    We bless you from the house of the LORD.
²⁷ The LORD is God,
    and he has given us light.
  Holding leafy branches, join in the festal pro-
        cession
    up to the horns of the altar.*

²⁸ You are my God, and I will offer thanks to
        you;*
    you are my God, and I will extol you.

²⁹ Give thanks to the LORD, for he is good;
    his kindness endures forever.

---

u Ps 129:8; Mt 21:9; 23:39; Mk 11:9; Lk 13:35; 19:38; Jn 12:13.

118:24 *This is the day that the LORD has made:* the day given by the Lord in which joy and jubilation are appropriate, the day of thanksgiving and rejoicing because of the wondrous deed of the Lord (vv. 22-23; see Ps 71:17; Jer 32:17, 27), the day of salvation. Used by the Liturgy as an antiphon for the Easter Season, this phrase identifies the "day" as that of Christ's Resurrection.

118:25 *O LORD, grant us salvation:* the Hebrew for this cry has come into English as "Hosanna." The crowd takes it up on Palm Sunday (see Mt 21:9; 23:39; Mk 11:9; Jn 12:13). It has become part of the *Sanctus* at Mass.

118:26 *Blessed is he who comes in the name of the LORD:* words used in the Gospels to welcome Jesus entering the temple on Palm Sunday (see Mk 11:9 par).

118:27 The people respond to the blessing by confessing that the Lord alone is God. He has made his light shine upon them, protecting them from the darkness of great trials (e.g., famine, war, and exile—see Ps 43:3). Accordingly, they are here renewing their commitment to the Lord in a formal liturgical celebration. *The horns of the altar:* the four corners of the altar of burnt offerings (see Ex 27:2; 38:2; Lev 4:25, 30, 34).

118:28-29 The psalm concludes with the community's affirmation that the Lord alone is God, similar to the confession of Moses (see Ex 15:2). *Kindness:* see note on Ps 6:5.

PSALM 119*

Praise of God's Law

Aleph

¹ Blessed are those whose way is blameless,*
    who walk in accord with the law of the
    LORD.*ᵛ
² Blessed are those who observe his statutes
    and seek him with their whole heart.*ʷ
³ They do nothing wrong;
    they walk in his ways.*

---

v Pss 1:1-2; 15:2; 112:1; Deut 18:13; Mt 5:3ff.—w Deut 4:29; 2 Chr 31:21.

Ps 119 This longest of the psalms is a monumental literary piece consisting of twenty-two strophes, each containing eight verses (sixteen lines) and each beginning with a letter of the Hebrew alphabet that is repeated at the beginning of each pair of verses. (See p. 23 for "acrostic" psalms.) Each strophe is a unit, but does not have a close connection with the strophe that precedes or follows. The whole is a free-flowing meditation, now sad, now joyous, now peaceful, now passionate. It is a reflection and a prayer in which the author, a sage and a mystic who draws his inspiration from the Prophets and Deuteronomy, converses with God and voices his deepest feelings: love of true wisdom, attachment and fidelity to the word of God in spite of weakness and obstacles; desire to better understand and live the truth; joy of outdoing oneself to follow the will of God manifested in the law.

In practically every verse, there is the word "law" or some equivalent. We can point to eight such terms—four with a more juridic nuance (statutes, precepts, decrees, commands or commandments) and four with a more religious nuance (law, promise, word, laws or judgments). These terms introduce us into the heart of the psalm, for they signify less an ensemble of laws to observe than the word of God, which sometimes ordains and judges and sometimes reveals and promises. It is a psalm of spiritual intimacy, of love for God (which means doing his will). In meditating on the law, believers contemplate above all the visage of God and let themselves be transformed in the very depths of their hearts. Such observance becomes liberty. Understood in this fashion, the law proclaims to us Jesus Christ, the living revelation of God, given to human beings to lead them to the Father: "I am the way, and the truth, and the life" (Jn 14:6).

119:1-3 Introduction to the entire psalm that stresses the theme: instruction in godly wisdom.

119:1 A beginning analogous to those of Pss 1:1-2 and 112:1 (see Ps 101:6; Mt 5:3ff). The word law and its synonyms are to be taken in the widest sense of revealed teaching, as transmitted by the Prophets. *Blessed:* see note on Ps 1:1.

119:2 This verse makes explicit what is implicit throughout the psalm: Scripture is revered because it consists in God's statutes; it is God that his servants seek and not the book for its own sake.

119:3 *Ways:* although the Hebrew for this word occurs infrequently in this psalm, it is found often in Deuteronomy and elsewhere. There it refers to the requirements of God's Covenant (see note on Ps 25:4-7).

⁴ You have ordained*
    that your commands be diligently observed.
⁵ May my ways be steadfast
    in the observance of your decrees.
⁶ Then I will never be put to shame
    when I take note of all your precepts.

⁷ I will praise you in sincerity of heart
    as I ponder your righteous judgments.
⁸ I will observe your decrees;
    do not forsake me completely.

Beth

⁹ How can a young man lead a spotless life?*
    By living according to your word.
¹⁰ I seek you with all my heart;
    do not let me stray from your precepts.*

¹¹ I treasure your word in my heart*
    for fear that I may sin against you.
¹² Blessed are you, O LORD;
    teach me your decrees.ˣ

¹³ With my lips I recite
    all the judgments you have announced.
¹⁴ I rejoice in following your statutes
    more than I would rejoice in endless riches.

¹⁵ I will meditate on your commands
    and respect your ways.
¹⁶ I find my delight in your decrees;
    I will never forget your word.

---

x Pss 25:4; 26:3; 27:11; 28:6; 86:11; 143:8, 10; Ex 18:20.

119:4-8 Those who obey God's law have a right to hope that he will come to their assistance.

119:9-16 The love for God's word is love for God, expressed in one's attitude of heart, in actions, and in words. With his entire being the godly person seeks God and delights in his will. Such a sublime teaching can lead "a young man" to keep his way pure.

119:10 The psalmist seeks the God of the law and the promises; he meditates on the latter only because they constitute God's word of life for him. *Heart:* see note on Ps 4:8.

119:11 *Treasure your word in my heart:* Prov 2:10-12 and Col 3:16 show that those whose hearts are steeped in the word of God are educated by God.

Gimel

¹⁷ * Be good to your servant
    so that I may live* and keep your word.
¹⁸ Open my eyes so that I may clearly see
    the wonders to be found in your law.

¹⁹ I am only a wayfarer on earth,ʸ
    but do not hide your precepts from me.*
²⁰ My soul is ever consumed
    with longing for your judgments.

²¹ You rebuke the arrogant,* the accursed,
    who stray from your precepts.
²² Set me free from scorn and contempt,
    for I have observed your statutes.

²³ Even though princes assemble and slander me,
    your servant meditates on your decrees.
²⁴ Your statutes are my delight,
    for they offer me counsel.

Daleth

²⁵ * My soul lies prostrate in the dust;*
    revive me in accordance with your word.ᶻ
²⁶ I proclaim my ways and you answer me;
    teach me your decrees.

---

y Ps 39:13; Gen 23:4; Heb 11:13.—z Pss 44:26; 119:50, 107; 143:11.

119:17-24 In difficulty and distress, the Lord and his word are a comfort to the godly. God's blessing comes to those who submit to his law, but his curse comes to those who stray deliberately from his revealed will.

119:17 *I may live:* here the psalmist is speaking of living in its fullest sense of happiness, security, prosperity—a frequent theme in Ezek (3:21; 18; 33; see Ps 133:3)—and, of course, fellowship with God (see Pss 16:11; 36:10; Deut 8:3).

119:19 Though the psalmist is a stranger (or wayfarer) on earth, he is the guest of God to whom the whole universe belongs; he will learn from the Lord how to conduct himself (see notes on Pss 39:13-14 and 39:13).

119:21 *The arrogant:* enemies of God and his faithful who act as though they are a law unto themselves (see notes on Pss 73:4-12 and 86:14; see also Isa 13:11; Mal 3:19). They are "cursed," i.e., ready for God's judgment.

119:25-32 Whether in distress or in prosperity, the psalmist is determined to remain close to God's law. In adversities, he becomes more teachable and his spirit is renewed in him, for the word of the Lord has the power to comfort. In prosperity, he enjoys a freedom from anxiety and care that enables him to focus on doing God's will.

119:25 *Lies prostrate in the dust:* see note on Ps 44:26.

27 Help me to understand the way of your com-
        mandments,
    and I will meditate on your wonders.
28 My soul is wasting away in sorrow;
        renew my strength in accordance with your
        word.

29 Keep me from the way of falsehood,
        and let me live according to your law.
30 I have chosen the way of faithfulness;*
    I have set your judgments before me.
31 I cling to your statutes, O LORD;
        do not allow me to be put to shame.
32 I run in the way of your precepts,
        for you have set my heart free.

He

33 Teach me, O LORD, the way of your decrees,*
        and I will follow it to the end.*a
34 Give me understanding, and I will observe
        your law
    and obey it with all my heart.*

35 Guide me in the way of your precepts,
        for in them is my delight.b
36 Dispose my heart to follow your statutes
        and to flee selfish gain.

37 Turn my eyes away from what is unimportant,
        and let me live in your way.

---

a Pss 19:12; 119:12.—b Pss 1:2; 25:4; 27:11; 86:11; 119:32; 143:8, 10.

119:30-32 Godliness is nicely summed up by the three opening verbs: choos-
ing (see Heb 11:25), clinging (see Acts 11:23), and running (see Phil 3:12-14).
Heart: see note on Ps 4:8.

119:33-40 Since God alone can interpret his revelation ("teach [it]," v. 33),
the psalmist prays that God will instruct him in his "law" (see Ps 25:4). He asks
the Lord to provide spiritual direction and motivation to direct his steps (see Prov
4:11-19) and incline his heart (see Ps 141:4) to do the divine will.

119:33 *And I will follow it to the end:* another possible translation is: "I will
keep it as a reward" (see Ps 19:12; Prov 22:4). In both translations the godly person finds his joy in doing the will of God.

119:34 The desire for understanding often voiced in this psalm conforms to
the ideal of the sages of Israel. *Heart:* see note on Ps 4:8.

³⁸ Fulfill your word to your servant,
　　so that you may be feared.*

³⁹ Let me escape the disgrace that I dread,
　　for your judgments are good.
⁴⁰ See, I long for your commandments;
　　in your righteousness preserve my life.

Waw

⁴¹ * Let your kindness* descend on me, O LORD,
　　your salvation in accord with your promise.
⁴² Then I will respond to those who insult me,*
　　because I trust in your word.

⁴³ Do not remove from my mouth the word of
　　truth,*
　　for I place my hope in your judgment.
⁴⁴ I will keep your law continually,
　　forever and ever.

⁴⁵ I will walk in complete freedom
　　because I have sought your commands.*
⁴⁶ I will speak of your statutes in the presence
　　of kings
　　and will not be ashamed.

⁴⁷ Your precepts fill me with delight
　　because I love them.

119:38 *That you may be feared:* as a result of the saving acts that the Lord does in accord with his promises, he is acknowledged as the one true God and feared (see Ps 130:5; 2 Sam 7:25f; 1 Ki 8:39f; Jer 33:8f). Another possible translation is: "Fulfill the word you have spoken / to the servant who fears you."

119:41-48 Here the psalmist, as it were, gives Christians what is needed for them to fulfill their desire to "proclaim [the Lord's] word with all boldness" (Acts 4:29). In order to be spoken, the word must first be appropriated (v. 41), trusted (vv. 42f), obeyed (v. 44), sought (v. 45), and loved (vv. 47f).

119:41 *Kindness:* see note on Ps 6:5.

119:43 *Do not remove from my mouth the word of truth:* for it will enable the psalmist to respond to the insults and calumnies to which he is subjected (see Pss 119:61, 85, 95, etc.).

119:45 *Sought your commands:* the psalmist strives to understand the meaning of the Scriptures and make them his rule of life (see Pss 119:94, 155; see also Ps 111:2; Ezr 7:10; Sir 51:23; Isa 34:16). Such a study is at the origin of the Midrashic literature.

⁴⁸ I lift up my hands* to your precepts, which I
       love,
   and I meditate on your decrees.

Zayin

⁴⁹ Remember the word you gave to your ser-
       vant*
   by which you have given me hope.
⁵⁰ This is my consolation in my distress:
   your word gives me life.

⁵¹ The arrogant* overwhelm me with scorn,
   but I refuse to turn away from your law.
⁵² I recall your judgments of old, O LORD,
   and I am greatly comforted.

⁵³ I am filled with fury against the wicked,
   those who forsake your law.
⁵⁴ Your decrees have become my songs
   wherever I make my dwelling.

⁵⁵ Even during the night I remember your name*
   and observe your teaching, O LORD.
⁵⁶ This is my practice:
   I obey your commandments.

Heth

⁵⁷ * My portion, I have said, O LORD,
   is to observe your words.*

119:48 *I lift up my hands:* as a sign of veneration and praise (see Pss 44:21; 63:5; 134:2; Neh 8:6).

119:49-56 The word of God provides hope and consolation even in suffering. The psalmist observes the commandments of the Lord because in them he finds life, restoration, and consolation.

119:51 *The arrogant:* see note on Ps 119:21.

119:55 *Name:* see note on Ps 5:12.

119:57-64 The Lord is the portion of the psalmist, and it is God's law that fills the earth with joy and security. Hence, far from regarding obedience as a crushing, disagreeable burden, the psalmist considers it a happy lot, a privileged destiny, and a signal favor.

119:57 *My portion . . . your words:* another possible translation is: "You are my portion, O LORD, / I promise to keep your words." A familiar formula of trust (see Pss 16:5; 73:26 and note; 142:5).

⁵⁸ With all my heart* I seek your favor;
      fulfill your word and be gracious to me.

⁵⁹ I have reflected on my ways
      and resolved to follow your statutes.
⁶⁰ I will make haste and not delay
      to observe your precepts.

⁶¹ Though the nets of the wicked entrap me,
      I do not forget your law.
⁶² At midnight I rise to offer praise to you
      for the righteousness of your judgments.

⁶³ I am a friend to all who fear you,
      all who observe your commands.
⁶⁴ The earth overflows with your kindness,* O
      LORD;
      teach me your decrees.ᶜ

Teth

⁶⁵ You have dealt kindly with your servant*
      in accord with your word, O LORD.
⁶⁶ Grant me good judgment and knowledge,
      for I place my trust in your precepts.

⁶⁷ Before I was afflicted* I went astray,
      but now I observe your word.
⁶⁸ You are good, and what you do is good;
      teach me your decrees.

⁶⁹ The arrogant* spread lies about me,
      but with all my heart I observe your com-
      mands.ᵈ

---

c Pss 33:5; 108:5; 119:12, 108.—d Pss 17:10; 73:8; 109:2; Job 13:4.

119:58 *Heart:* see note on Ps 4:8.
119:64 *The earth overflows with your kindness:* an exclamation of God's cosmic love; the world of creation witnesses to his love (see Pss 104:10-30; 136:1-9). For other glimpses of the world as God's handiwork and kingdom, see Pss 24:1; 33:5; Isa 6:3; Hab 2:14; 3:3.
119:65-72 The psalmist ascribes goodness to God in his past and present dealings, to the positive values of the trials God sent him, and to the ultimate value of God's law and divine teaching.
119:67 *Afflicted:* through God's doing (see note on Ps 119:25-32).
119:69 *The arrogant:* see note on Ps 119:21. *Heart:* see note on Ps 4:8.

⁷⁰ Their hearts are gross and insensitive,*
    but I find my delight in your law.

⁷¹ It was a blessing for me to be afflicted,
    so that I might learn your decrees.
⁷² The law from your mouth is more precious to
    me
    than thousands of gold and silver pieces.

Yodh

⁷³ * Your hands have created and formed me;*
    grant me understanding so that I may
    learn your precepts.
⁷⁴ Those who fear you will rejoice when they
    see me
    because I place my hope in your word.

⁷⁵ I know, O LORD, that your judgments are
    righteous
    and in your fidelity you have humbled me.
⁷⁶ May your kindness* bring consolation to me
    as you have promised your servant.

⁷⁷ Grant me your compassion so that I may live,
    for your law is my delight.
⁷⁸ May the arrogant* who oppress me without
    cause be put to shame;
    I will meditate on your commands.

⁷⁹ May those turn to me who fear you,
    those who understand your statutes.

119:70 *Gross and insensitive:* literally, "fat as grease," i.e., incapable of understanding divine things (see Pss 17:10; 73:7; Isa 6:10; Jer 5:28).
119:73-80 The psalmist declares his experiential knowledge of God, of his "kindness" and "compassion." He asks God to give the arrogant their just deserts and so enable the godly to be encouraged and rejoice at God's vindication.
119:73 *Your hands have created and formed me:* see Deut 32:6; Job 10:8; Zec 12:1. *Grant me understanding:* so that the psalmist can carry out what God willed in forming him.
119:76 *Kindness:* see note on Ps 6:5.
119:78 *The arrogant:* see note on Ps 119:21.

80 May my heart* be without blame toward your
    decrees
        so that I may not be put to shame.

Kaph

81 * My soul* pines for your salvation without
      ceasing;
        I place my hope in your word.*e*
82 My eyes fail,* looking for your word,
        and I cry out, "When will you comfort me?"*f*

83 I am shriveled like a smoke-filled wineskin,*
        but I do not forget your decrees.*g*
84 How long must your servant wait?*
        When will you pass judgment on my perse-
      cutors?

85 The arrogant* dig pits to entrap me,
        which is not in keeping with your law.
86 All of your precepts are true;
        come to my aid, for I am persecuted un-
      justly.

87 My enemies almost took away my life,
        but I have not forsaken your commands.
88 In your kindness* spare my life,
        and I will obey the statutes of your mouth.

---

e Pss 84:3; 119:20, 43, 123; 130:5.—f Pss 25:15; 119:41, 123; 123:1-2;
141:8; Lam 2:11.—g Ps 119:61; Job 30:30.

119:80 *Heart:* see note on Ps 4:8.
119:81-88 This last strophe of the first part of the psalm brings to a climax
the psalmist's need for God. In extreme distress, he looks to the Lord for his salvation as promised in his word, urgently calling upon him to come to his aid and
effect justice upon the arrogant who wrong him.
119:81 *Soul:* see note on Ps 6:4.
119:82 *My eyes fail:* see note on Ps 6:8.
119:83 *Like a smoke-filled wineskin:* the psalmist feels as brittle and useless
as tanned hides holding wine that are placed near the fireplace.
119:84 *How long . . . wait?:* literally, "How many are the days of your servant?"
i.e., the psalmist does not have too much time for God to delay in punishing his
persecutors. *Pass judgment on my persecutors:* see note on Ps 5:11.
119:85 *The arrogant:* see note on Ps 119:21.
119:88 *Kindness:* see note on Ps 6:5.

Lamedh

89 Your word, O LORD, is everlasting;*
   it is firmly fixed in the heavens.*h

90 Your faithfulness lasts through all generations;
   you established the earth, and it endures.

91 By your judgments all creatures continue to
      exist,
   for they are all your servants.

92 If your law had not been my delight,*
   I would have already perished in my misery.

93 Never will I forget your commands,
   for through them you have given me life.

94 I am yours; save me,
   for I seek your commandments.

95 The wicked lie in wait to destroy me,
   but I continue to ponder your decrees.

96 I have seen that every perfection is limited,
   but your precept is unlimited.*

Mem

97 I truly love your law.*
   It is my meditation throughout the day.

---

h Isa 40:8; 51:6; Mt 5:18; 1 Pet 1:25.

119:89-91 Like the first three verses of the first half of the psalm, these first three verses of the second half teach a general truth: there is constancy and order in all of creation, reflecting the "faithfulness" of the Lord (see Pss 89:3; 104; 147:7-9). Nature serves and abides by the word and the laws of the Lord (see note on Ps 93:5).

119:89 This verse is an echo of Prov 8:22ff where divine wisdom is presented as a living being existing from all eternity (see Wis 7:22—8:1; Isa 40:8).

119:92-96 The psalmist confesses that if through God's law he had not found meaning in the experience of his affliction, he would have perished. Therefore, no matter what his persecutors do, he will not forget God's precepts because they give order and preservation of life. For he knows that just as there are laws for the order in nature, so also are there laws for human conduct.

119:96 Everything on earth is limited; perfection belongs only to God and his commands.

119:97-104 God's law is heavenly wisdom, which is far greater than earthly wisdom. Meditation on it is a form of devotion to the Lord himself, and hence the psalmist regularly cultivates its practice. God's words, likened to honey, are sweet only when God's instruction is received and leads to understanding as well as an obedient life style.

⁹⁸ Your precept has given me greater wisdom
      than my enemies,*
  for it is mine forever.

⁹⁹ I am wiser than all my teachers
  because I meditate on your commands.

¹⁰⁰ I have greater insight than the elders,*
  because I keep your commandments.ⁱ

¹⁰¹ I point my feet away from evil paths
  so that I might observe your word.

¹⁰² I refuse to ignore your judgments,
  for it is you yourself who have taught me.

¹⁰³ Your words are sweet to my palate,
  even sweeter to my tongue than honey.*ʲ

¹⁰⁴ Through your commandments I achieve wisdom;
  therefore, I hate every way that is false.

Nun

¹⁰⁵ * Your word is a lamp for my feet*
  and a light to my path.ᵏ

¹⁰⁶ With a solemn vow I have sworn*
  to obey the judgments of your righteousness.

¹⁰⁷ I have been afflicted beyond measure;
  O Lᴏʀᴅ, let me live in accord with your word.

---

i Deut 6:17; Job 32:6; Wis 4:8-9.—j Ps 19:11; Jer 15:16.—k Ps 18:29; Prov 6:23; 2 Pet 1:19.

119:98-100 These verses are illuminated by the New Testament, which shows that heavenly wisdom is a gift to "little children," hidden from the worldly wise (see Lk 10:21; 1 Cor 1:18ff; 2:6-10).

119:100 The psalmist speaks in the same vein as Elihu (see Job 32:6ff; Wis 4:9). *Elders:* the aged, taught by experience.

119:103 *Your words are . . . sweeter to my tongue than honey:* see Ps 19:11; Job 23:12; Jer 15:16; Jn 4:32, 34.

119:105-112 The word of the Lord enlightens the psalmist's path of life; therefore, he has accepted the Covenant and obeys the Lord. Even in affliction, the psalmist has learned to give God willing praise, for his joy and determination to please the Lord are far greater than the affliction that is constantly with him.

119:105 *Your word is a lamp for my feet:* the word of the Lord is a guide and life-sustaining source (see Pss 18:29; 97:11; 112:4; Prov 6:23; Jn 8:12).

119:106 *With a solemn vow I have sworn:* the psalmist has made a pact to follow God's laws (see Neh 10:29).

108 Receive, O LORD, the homage my lips offer you,
   and instruct me about your judgments.*l*

109 Even though I continually take my life in my hands,*
   I do not neglect your law.
110 The wicked seek to entrap me,
   but I have not strayed from your commands.

111 Your statutes are my everlasting heritage;
   they are the very joy of my heart.*
112 I have set my heart on keeping your decrees,
   even to the end.

Samekh

113 * I detest those who are hypocritical,*
   but I love your law.
114 You are my refuge and my shield;
   I put my hope in your word.

115 Depart from my presence, you evildoers,
   so that I may observe the precepts of my God.*m*
116 Sustain me according to your promise, and I will live;
   do not delude me in my hope.

117 Uphold me, and I will be saved
   and will remain completely focused on your decrees.

---

l Pss 50:14, 23; 51:17; Heb 13:15.—m Pss 6:9; 139:19; Job 21:14.

119:109 *I continually take my life in my hands:* i.e., my life is constantly exposed to danger, for I am ready to risk it for God (see Jdg 12:3; 1 Sam 19:5; Est C:15=4:17¹; Job 13:14).
119:111-112 *Heart:* see note on Ps 4:8.
119:113-120 The ways of the righteous and the wicked are completely divergent. The psalmist dissociates himself from the wicked; he hates the double-minded but loves the law of the Lord. He draws near to God, his refuge and his shield. For, unlike the wicked whom the Lord will discard, the godly have hope in and veneration for the Lord.
119:113 *Hypocritical:* those who hesitate between fidelity and infidelity to God (see 1 Ki 18:21); they are "inconsistent in everything [they do]" (Jas 1:8).

118 You cast away all those who swerve from
    your decrees;
  their cunning is futile.

119 You discard all the wicked of the earth like
    dross;*
  therefore, I love your teachings.

120 My flesh trembles* before you in terror;
  your judgments fill me with awe.

Ayin

121 Since my conduct has been just and upright,*
  do not abandon me to those who oppress me.

122 Guarantee the well-being of your servant;
  do not allow the arrogant to oppress me.*

123 My eyes fail* as I long for your salvation
  and for the promise of your justice.

124 Deal with your servant in accordance with
    your kindness,*
  and teach me your decrees.

125 I am your servant; grant me discernment
  so that I may understand your statutes.

126 It is time, O LORD, for you to take action;
  your law has been broken.

127 That is why I love your precepts
  more than gold, even the purest gold.*

119:119 *You discard . . . like dross:* the Lord discards evildoers like "dross," i.e., the scum that forms in refining precious metals and is discarded (see Jer 6:28-30).

119:120 *My flesh trembles:* a reminiscence of Job 4:15; 23:15 (see Ps 88:16). It denotes the dread of the sacred, the fear of the awesome God.

119:121-128 The psalmist has entrusted himself to God's care and done what is just and upright; now he expects the Lord to keep his promise according to which the godly will be relieved of all adversities. He prays to receive understanding and, while affirming his devotion to the Lord and his commands, calls for God to deal justly with the ungodly, who have broken his law.

119:122 This is the only verse in the psalm that lacks either a direct or an indirect reference to the law of God; some have suggested replacing "servant" by "word" as a remedy. *The arrogant:* see note on Ps 119:21.

119:123 *My eyes fail:* see note on Ps 6:8.

119:124 *Kindness:* see note on Ps 6:5.

119:127 The psalmist compares the Lord's commands favorably with pure gold (see Job 22:25; 28:15f; Prov 3:14; 8:10, 19; 16:16).

¹²⁸ That is why I regard all your command-
ments as right
and despise every way that is false.

Pe

¹²⁹ Wonderful are your statutes;*
therefore, I willingly observe them.
¹³⁰ The explanation of your words gives light
and imparts understanding to the simple.*
¹³¹ I open wide my mouth and sigh,*
longing eagerly for your precepts.
¹³² Turn and have mercy on me,*
as you always do to those who love your
name.*ⁿ

¹³³ Guide my steps in accord with your word
and never let evil triumph over me.
¹³⁴ Rescue me from the oppression of men
so that I may observe your commandments.

¹³⁵ Allow your face to shine* upon your servant
and teach me your decrees.
¹³⁶ Streams of tears flow from my eyes
because your law is disregarded.*

---

n Pss 6:5; 9:14; 25:16; 86:16; 91:14; 2 Sam 24:14.

119:129-136 God's word illumines so that even those not experienced in the realities of life (the "simple"; see Ps 116; Prov 1:4) may gain wisdom (see Ps 19:8). The psalmist longs to receive, understand, and put it into practice. So great is his zeal for God's law that he weeps over the continuance of rebellion and transgression on the part of evildoers.

119:130 The law is a luminous sanctuary that fills souls with its clarity (see Ps 73:16f) when it is explained to them. *Explanation:* literally, "opening."

119:131 *Open wide my mouth and sigh:* same image as in Job 29:23.

119:132-136 The psalmist asks for the Lord's blessing (see Num 6:24-26), which brings down God's grace to enable him to direct his steps in accord with the divine law and away from sin and adversity (vv. 133-134). He also asks for the Lord's face to shine on him (v. 135), i.e., to bring him nothing but good in all circumstances of his life; for when God's face shines on people it brings deliverance and blessings.

119:132 See Pss 5:12; 25:16; 91:15. *Name:* see note on Ps 5:12.

119:135 *Allow your face to shine:* the psalmist asks God to smile on him with favor (see note on Ps 13:2; see also Pss 67:2; 80:4; Num 6:25).

119:136 The godly are saddened in the face of evil (see Ezr 9:3ff; Job 16:20; Ezek 9:4).

Sadhe

137 You are righteous, O Lord,*
    and your judgments are right.o
138 You have set down your statutes as righteous
    and as completely faithful.

139 Zeal has consumed me
    because my adversaries ignore your words.
140 Your word has been tested through and
        through,*
    and your servant cherishes it.

141 Although I am despised and unimportant,
    I do not forget your commands.
142 Your righteousness is everlasting,
    and your law is forever true.

143 I am afflicted by anguish and distress,
    but your precepts are my delight.
144 Your statutes are forever righteous;
    grant me understanding and I will live.

Qoph

145 I call out to you with my whole heart;*
    answer me, O Lord, so that I may observe
        your decrees.
146 I cry out to you;
    save me so that I may obey your statutes.

147 I arise before dawn and cry out for help;
    I place my hope in your word.

---

o Ex 9:27; Ezr 9:15; Neh 9:13; Tob 3:2.

119:137-144 The troubles and disgraces of his holy ones reflect upon the Lord and his word. Hence, the psalmist points out his sad state and prays that the Lord will establish righteousness in his world. Though he is still immersed in troubles, he knows the Lord is faithful and so he wholeheartedly puts his trust in him.

119:140 *Tested through and through:* literally, "refined." God's word is fire-tried; it is genuine and reliable.

119:145-152 The psalmist urgently presents his lament before the Lord to be delivered from adversity. So intense is his longing for this salvation that he prays through the night watches. Even though his foes hunt him down, the Lord is near and will rescue him, for the psalmist keeps the law.

148 My eyes are awake before each watch of the night*
so that I may meditate on your word.[p]

149 In accordance with your kindness* hear my voice, O LORD;
grant me life in accordance with your judgments.
150 Those who plot wickedness draw near me,
but they are far from your law.*

151 Yet you, O LORD, are near,
and all your precepts are true.
152 Long have I known your decrees
and that you have established them forever.

Resh

153 See my suffering and deliver me,*
for I have not forgotten your law.
154 Defend my cause and redeem me;*[q]
let me live in accord with your word.

155 Salvation is far from the wicked
because they do not consider your decrees.*
156 Great is your compassion, O LORD;
let me live in accord with your judgments.

157 My persecutors and my enemies are many,
but I do not cast aside your statutes.

---

p Pss 63:7; 77:7.—q Pss 35:1; 43:1; 119:25, 41; Jer 50:34; Mic 7:9.

119:148 *Each watch of the night:* see note on Ps 63:7.

119:149 *Kindness:* see note on Ps 6:5.

119:150-152 Although the wicked are closing in on the psalmist, he remains serene, for the Lord is also near to protect him (see Pss 69:19; 73:28). The wicked will get nowhere, for they break the statutes of the Lord (v. 150: "are far from your law"), which were meant to last forever.

119:153-160 The lament becomes more intense as the psalmist prays for deliverance, mercy, and life. By protesting his innocence, bringing up his affliction, and mentioning the perfidy of the wicked, he seeks to move God to act, for he alone can preserve the psalmist's full enjoyment of Covenant life. The fidelity and righteousness of God's word sustain the psalmist in his belief of total vindication.

119:154 *Redeem me:* or "Be my redeemer" (see Pss 19:15; 69:19; 72:13f).

119:155 The godless haunt the psalmist, for they flaunt the commandments of the Lord. *The wicked:* see note on Ps 119:21 ("the arrogant").

158 I regard the faithless with indignation*
    because they do not observe your word.*r*

159 Consider how I love your precepts, O LORD;
    let me live in accord with your kindness.*
160 Every word you utter is true,
    and all your righteous judgments are ever-
        lasting.*

Shin

161 The powerful persecute me without cause,*
    but it is your word that awes my heart.*
162 I rejoice in your word
    like one who discovers a great treasure.

163 Falsehood I abhor and detest,
    but I love your law.
164 Seven times* a day I praise you
    for your righteous judgments.

165 Those who love your law have great peace;*
    they encounter no stumbling blocks.**s*
166 I await your salvation, O LORD,
    and I carry out your precepts.

---

r Pss 119:104, 136; 139:22; Ex 32:19.—s Pss 37:11; 72:7; Isa 57:19; 1
Jn 2:10.

119:158 *I regard the faithless with indignation:* i.e., they are people who have
broken the Covenant relationship and whose words and acts are unreliable (see
Ps 25:3; Isa 48:8; Jer 5:11; Mal 2:10f).
   119:159 *Kindness:* see note on Ps 6:5.
   119:160 The word ("word . . . righteous judgments") of the Lord is a source of
life that never languishes because it is fed by infinite truth that continues forever. Therefore, it can never be exhausted no matter how many drink from this
life-giving fountain.
   119:161-168 Despite the continuation of his adversity, the psalmist rejoices in
the promise of the Lord, praising him many times a day for his righteous laws.
The godly have peace, for they know that the Lord in his righteousness will vindicate them. While waiting for the great day of salvation, the psalmist keeps his
hope alive and follows God's commands.
   119:161 *Heart:* see note on Ps 4:8.
   119:164 *Seven times:* a Hebrew idiom for "many times" (see Ps 12:7; Gen
4:24; Prov 24:16; Mt 18:21f; Lk 17:4).
   119:165 The godly have peace, for, even surrounded by adversity, they are
confident of God's loving care and his promise that they will not stumble (see
Prov 4:12; 1 Jn 2:10). *Great peace:* i.e., complete security and well-being (see Ps
37:11; Isa 26:3, 12; 32:17; 54:13; 57:19).

¹⁶⁷ I obey your statutes,
　　　for I love them dearly.
¹⁶⁸ I obey your commands and your statutes;
　　　indeed, all my ways are known to you.*

Taw

¹⁶⁹ May my cry come before you, O LORD;*
　　　grant me understanding according to your
　　　　word.*t
¹⁷⁰ May my supplication come before you;
　　　deliver me according to your word.

¹⁷¹ May my lips proclaim your praise
　　　because you teach me your decrees.
¹⁷² May my tongue sing of your word,
　　　for all of your precepts are upright.
¹⁷³ May your hand* be ready to help me,
　　　for I have chosen your commandments.

¹⁷⁴ I long for your salvation, O LORD,*
　　　and your law is my delight.
¹⁷⁵ Give life to my soul that I may praise you,
　　　and let your judgments sustain me.
¹⁷⁶ I have wandered away like a lost sheep;*
　　　seek out your servant,
　　　　for I have not forgotten your precepts.u

---

t Ps 88:2; Job 16:18.—u Isa 53:6; Jer 50:6; Ezek 34:1ff; Lk 15:1-7.

119:168 *All my ways are known to you:* for a similar thought, see Prov 5:21.

119:169-173 In this last strophe, the psalmist offers a prayer for the Lord's salvation. Although his problems have not yet been resolved, he raises the spirit of expectation in those who love God's word. He prays for complete deliverance so that he may praise his faithful God.

119:169-173 The psalmist comes before the Lord with a broken spirit, asking for understanding and deliverance. Looking forward to the moment of redemption, he dwells on the joyful expressions of his thanksgiving.

119:173 *Your hand:* a metaphor for God's powerful deliverance (see Deut 32:39).

119:174-176 These final three verses form the conclusion to the whole. They succinctly restate and summarize the main themes.

119:176 *Lost sheep:* the Prophets' theme of lost sheep is here applied to an individual (see Isa 53:6; Jer 50:6; Ezek 34:16; Zec 11:16; Mt 10:6; Lk 15:4; 1 Pet 2:25). *For I have not forgotten your precepts:* this final line sums up the inner state of the psalmist, who is zealous for the knowledge and practice of the divine law.

THE SONGS OF ASCENTS AND GREAT HALLEL—Pss 120–136*

PSALM 120*

A Complaint against Treacherous Tongues

¹ A song of ascents.

Whenever I am in distress,
   I cry out to the LORD and he answers me.ᵛ
² Deliver me, O LORD, from lying lips
   and from deceitful tongues.*ʷ

³ What will he* inflict upon you,
   and what more will he add to it,
   O deceitful tongue?

---

v Ps 18:7; 2 Sam 22:7; Jon 2:2.—w Pss 12:2-4; 31:19; 52:3-5; Sir 51:3.

Ps 120—136 Human beings are born to be pilgrims in search of the Absolute, on a journey to God. We advance by way of stages, from the difficulties of life to the certitudes of hope, from the dispersion of cares to the joyous encounter with God, from daily diversions to inner recollection. The "Songs of Ascents" (Pss 120—134) are prayers for the path we travel as human beings.

This group of psalms, which forms a major part of the Great Hallel (Pss 120—136: see introduction to Ps 113—118), served as a kind of handbook for pilgrims as they went up to the holy city for the great annual feasts (see Ex 23:17; Deut 16:16; 1 Ki 12:28; Mt 20:17; Lk 2:41f). Two other explanations are offered but are regarded as less likely: namely, that they were sung by the returning exiles when they "went up" to Jerusalem from Babylon (see Ezr 7:9), or that they were sung by the Levites on the fifteen steps by which they ascended from the Court of the Women to the Court of the Israelites in the temple. The latter would account for the name "Gradual Psalms" or "Psalms of the Steps" by which they also are known. The name "gradual" may also be assigned to them because of their rhythm, in which every other verse continues the thought of the preceding verse.

Ps 120 Ill at ease in a hostile environment, often detested and calumniated because his faith and his Law place him apart—such is the pious Jew situated far from Palestine. Sometimes he gets the feeling of living among the savage peoples of the Caucuses and the Syrian desert (v. 5: Meshech and Kedar). We can appreciate his desire to return to Jerusalem, the city of his God.

We Christians have the same kind of feeling of nostalgia to be with God (see 2 Cor 5). Without belonging to the world from which Christ's call has taken us (see Jn 15:19), we are sent by him into the world. It is in this hostile environment that we must live while continually journeying toward the Father (see Jn 17:15, 18, 24). Thus, we can in all truth make this psalm our prayer when suffering distress caused by the continuous hostile pressure of this world.

120:2 *Lying lips . . . deceitful tongues:* see note on Ps 5:10.

120:3 *He:* i.e., the Lord. *What more will he add to it:* the full curse formula was: "May the LORD do such and such to you *and add still more to it*" (see Ru 1:17; 1 Sam 3:17; 14:44; 25:22; 2 Sam 3:35; 1 Ki 2:23).

⁴ He has prepared a warrior's sharp arrows
   and red-hot coals* of the broom tree.ˣ

⁵ Why have I been doomed as an exile in
      Meschech
      and forced to dwell among the tents of
      Kedar?*

⁶ Far too long have I lived
   among people who despise peace.

⁷ When I proclaim peace,ʸ
   they shout for war.*

PSALM 121*

God, Guardian of His People

¹ A song of ascents.

I lift up my eyes to the mountains;*
   from where will I receive help?ᶻ

---

x Pss 11:6; 57:5; 140:11; Deut 32:23; Prov 16:27; 25:18; Jas 3:6.—y Pss 35:20; 140:3-4.—z Pss 87:1; 125:2; Jer 3:23.

120:4 *Sharp arrows . . . red-hot coals:* the evil tongue is like a sharp arrow (see Pss 57:4; 64:3; Prov 25:18; Jer 9:8) and a scorching fire (see Prov 16:27; Jas 3:6); but the enemies of the psalmist will be destroyed by the far more potent shafts of God's arrows of truth (see Ps 64:8) and coals of judgment (see Ps 140:11). *Broom tree:* apparently its roots burn well and yield coal that produces intense heat.

120:5 *Meshech . . . Kedar:* Meshech is located to the far north in Asia Minor by the Black Sea (see Gen 10:2; Ezek 38:2). Kedar stands for the Arab tribesmen of the south in the Arabian Desert (see Isa 21:16f; Jer 2:10; 49:28; Ezek 27:21). The psalmist feels that he is dwelling among a barbarian and ungodly people.

120:7 The godly have nothing in common with the wicked. The godly speak of peace, but the wicked sow discord and adversity (see Gal 5:19-21; Jas 3:14f). God alone can be of help in this situation.

Ps 121 The ground of Palestine is rough, and journeys meant discomforts: rocks, cold, nights in the open; but the pilgrim took courage, for the Lord protects each of his own.

This psalm is a prayer for Christians in a time of uncertainty. We find ourselves engaged, like the patriarchs, in the adventure that will lead us to the "rest" of the promised land, across the difficulties and dangers of the wilderness of this world (see Heb 11). We can ask ourselves with distress whence help will come to us that will enable us to complete our pilgrimage. We can be reassured. Sending us into the world on mission and pilgrimage, Jesus guarantees us his almighty assistance together with that of his Father (see Mt 28:19f; Jn 17:15-17). To enable us to overcome the world, its seductions, and its snares, Christ sends us the Holy Spirit, who continues the safeguarding solicitude of the Master toward us (see Jn 14:16f; 16:8).

121:1 *Mountains:* the ridge on which Mount Zion with its temple was situated (see Pss 87:1; 125:2).

² My help comes from the L<small>ORD</small>,
    the Maker of heaven and earth.*ᵃ

³ He will not permit your foot to stumble;ᵇ
    he who guards you will not fall asleep.*
⁴ Indeed, the one who guards Israel
    never slumbers, never sleeps.*

⁵ The L<small>ORD</small> serves as your guardian*
    he is at your right hand to serve as your
      shade.ᶜ
⁶ The sun will not strike you during the day,ᵈ
    nor the moon during the night.

⁷ The L<small>ORD</small> will protect you against all evil;*
    he will watch over your life.ᵉ
⁸ The L<small>ORD</small> will watch over your coming and
    your going
    both now and forevermore.ᶠ

---

a Pss 104:5; 124:8; 146:6; Gen 1:1; Hos 13:9.—b Pss 66:9; 91:12; Deut 32:10; 1 Sam 2:9; Prov 3:23.—c Pss 1:6; 16:8; 73:23; Isa 25:4.—d Wis 18:3; Isa 49:10.—e Pss 9:10; 97:10.—f Gen 28:15; Deut 28:6; Job 5:17f.

121:2 *Maker of heaven and earth:* the psalmist makes what amounts to a credal statement, which has been incorporated into the Apostles' Creed. It affirms the Lord's sovereignty over the whole universe—heaven and earth—and demolishes all claims of sovereignty made for the pagan gods. The source of help can come only from the Lord, whose power is unlimited (see Pss 115:3; 124:8; 134:3; 146:6; Jer 10:11f).

121:3 The pagan gods were said to sleep (as well as eat and drink), but the psalmist points out that the Lord never sleeps. Therefore, he can protect his devoted servants at all times and in all circumstances.

121:4 The Lord also watches over Israel without sleeping. He is a guard who never falls asleep at his post, never goes off duty. He is always watching over his people to protect them from their enemies.

121:5-6 The Lord maintains himself at his faithful's "right hand," the side of favor and trust, to "shade" them from the fierce heat of the sun and the malevolent influence of the moon. The ancients feared the evil spiritual effects of the moon (see Mt 17:15) as well as the bad physical effects of the sun (see Jud 8:3; Isa 49:10). The antiphon used with this psalm during the Easter Season in the Liturgy of the Hours, "The Lord watches over his people, and protects them as the apple of his eye," reminds us that in Christ's Passion and Resurrection no physical or spiritual force can ever separate us from the love of God that is in Christ Jesus (see Rom 8:31-39).

121:7-8 The Lord is present to deliver his faithful both now and forever. *Your coming and your going:* an idiom signifying all ordinary human activity (see Deut 28:6; 31:2; Jos 14:11; 2 Sam 3:25).

PSALM 122*

The Pilgrim's Greeting to the Holy City

¹ A song of ascents. Of David.

I rejoiced when they said to me,*
  "Let us go to the house of the LORD."*g*
² And finally our feet are standing
  at your gates, O Jerusalem.

³ Jerusalem is built as a city
  that is firmly bound together in unity.**h*
⁴ There the tribes go up,
  the tribes of the LORD,
as it was decreed for Israel
  to celebrate the name of the LORD.**i*

---

g Pss 42:4; 43:3-4; 84:2-5; Isa 2:3; Mic 4:2; Zech 8:2.—h Ps 48:13-14; 2 Sam 5:9; Eph 2:19-22.—i Ex 23:17; Deut 16:16.

Ps 122 The pilgrims arrive where they can see Jerusalem, and their faces light up with joy, a joy that formed part of the Messianic Hope. They come to a halt to admire the holy city restored by Nehemiah, and their remembrances sing in their heart: those of the gathering of the tribes at the Tent of Meeting (see Num 2:2) and of the happy era when David and Solomon ruled in their capital. The latter appeared to them as the symbol of unity and peace—"Shalom" signifies peace. In their desire for happiness, they already dream of the gathering together at some future time (see Isa 33:20; Zec 9:9ff).

One day Paul will speak of Christ present in his Church to reestablish the links of the human family (see Eph 2:19-22), and the visionary of Patmos will celebrate the definitively rediscovered unity in his marvelous description of a heavenly Jerusalem (see Rev 21:2—22:5). Hence, in praying this psalm, we as Christians must go beyond the original sense since we find ourselves drawn along by Christ in a spiritual pilgrimage that causes us to leave the world and enter ever further into the Church and ultimately leads us from earth to heaven, the heavenly Jerusalem.

122:1-2 The trials of an expatriate (see Ps 120) and the hazards of travel (see Ps 121) are overshadowed now by the joy that had drawn the pilgrim to his journey. The doxology in Jude 24 is the Christian equivalent of this progress and arrival: "To him who is able to keep you from falling [see Ps 121] and to bring you safely to his glorious presence unblemished and rejoicing [see Ps 122]." *The house of the LORD:* the temple (see 2 Sam 7:5, 13; 1 Ki 5:17, 19).

122:3 *That is firmly bound together:* Jerusalem is the symbol of the unity of the chosen people and the figure of the unity of the Church (see Eph 2:20ff). The versions have translated this as: "where its community is one."

122:4 This verse presupposes the Deuteronomic law concerning unity of sanctuary (see Deut 12; 16:16; 1 Ki 12:27). *To celebrate the name of the LORD:* because of God's saving acts and blessings for his people.

⁵ For there the thrones of judgment were estab-
    lished,
  the thrones of the house of David.*

⁶ Pray for the peace* of Jerusalem:
  "May those who love you rest secure.
⁷ May there be peace within your walls
  and security in your palaces."ʲ

⁸ Out of love for my relatives and friends,*
  I will say, "May peace be within you."
⁹ Out of love for the house of the LORD, our God,
  I will pray for your well-being.

PSALM 123*

Prayer in Time of Spiritual Need

¹ A song of ascents.

  I lift up my eyes to you,ᵏ
  to you who are enthroned in heaven.*

---

j Ps 128:5f; Est 10:3; Song 4:4.—k Pss 25:15; 119:82; 121:1; 141:8; Isa 6:1.

122:5 Jerusalem was both the religious center, symbolized by the "house of the LORD" (v. 1), and the political center, symbolized by "the thrones of judgment." The kings of Judah ruled by God's will and upheld his kingship to the extent that they dispensed justice, which was a feature of the Messianic Age (see Isa 9:7; 11:3-5).

122:6ff *Peace:* the customary greeting in Hebrew, *shalom,* which also includes the idea of happiness and prosperity.

122:8-9 Jerusalem is transferred into an ideal, an eschatological expression of what God had planned for his people, and the psalmist prays for the fulfillment of God's plan. What Jerusalem was to the Israelite, the Church is to the Christian.

Ps 123 Upon returning from the Exile, Israel experienced prolonged and harsh humiliations: vexations from nearby nations and from the Persian administration and persecution later on. The pilgrims do not feel the need to recite at length the list of their misfortunes, for these are too well known. The prayer is expressed in a simple attitude: eyes humbly and perseveringly fixed toward the Lord await a sign of hope. Can people be more true before God?

This psalm can serve to show the right attitude we should have toward Christ. John (10:28f) amply indicates that the inner and outer life of the Church and Christians is sovereignly regulated by the risen Christ together with his Father. Our faith assures us that the almighty hand of Christ will save us when we call for help against our inner and outer enemies. We should keep our eyes fixed continuously on him in the never-ending battle we must wage in this world (see Heb 12:2).

123:1 The psalmist indicates the awesome power of God, the Ruler of the universe enthroned "in heaven," who "does whatever he pleases" (Ps 115:3), and whose love and wisdom are beyond our calculation (see Ps 36:5; Isa 55:9).

2 Behold, as the eyes of servants
      are on the hand of their master,
   or as the eyes of a maid
      focus on the hand of her mistress,
   so our eyes are on the LORD, our God,
      as we wait for him to show us his mercy.*

3 Show us your mercy, O LORD, show us your
         mercy,
      for we have suffered more than our share
         of contempt.*[l]
4 We have had to suffer far too long
      the insults of the haughty
      and the contempt of the arrogant.*

---

l Pss 44:14-15; 123:3-4; Neh 4:4; Job 12:4; 30:1; Dan 9:16.

123:2 The fate of male or female slaves was entirely in the hands of their masters or mistresses. Their welfare or their woe depended completely on the will of their overseers, whose hands could bestow benefits or punishments. Hence, the psalmist pictures the slaves as keeping their eyes fixed on their masters and mistresses. In like manner, God's people fix their eyes on their Lord with utter dependence; like "servants" and a "maid," they look to their Master—for acts of kindness and mercy.

For the Lord rules sovereignly. He is on the throne (see Pss 2:4; 11:4; 102:13; 115:3) even when the arrogant assail his people. No matter how exalted this God of Israel may be, he is still the Lord ("Yahweh"), the God who is faithful to the Covenant he has made with his people and is ever ready to help them in any adversity.

123:3 The psalmist prays for God's favor (see Pss 6:3; 57:2; 86:3) to right the injustice done to God's children, who have unjustly endured great contempt (see Ps 119:22) and ridicule (see Ps 44:13; Neh 2:19; 4:1). It is interesting to recall that in the Sermon on the Mount contempt ("You fool") ranks as more grievous than anger (see Mt 5:22). Yet, from the Christian point of view, to endure suffering (including contempt) for Christ is a necessity (see Lk 9:23; Col 1:24), as well as an honor (see Acts 5:41), for all his followers as they make their way to glory (see 1 Pet 4:13f).

123:4 As is the case in our day, the People of God are mocked by the haughty and the arrogant (see Pss 52:3; 73:2ff), who rely on and seek only themselves, giving little thought to God. Although it is entirely permissible to pray to be delivered from this ridicule, another approach is to accept it in union with the suffering Christ. Even the Old Testament has passages recommending the acceptance of such suffering: "Let him offer his cheek to one who would smite him, and let him be sated with disgrace. For men are not cast off by the Lord forever. Though he causes grief, he will show compassion, in accord with his great kindness. For he does not enjoy bringing affliction or grief to the children of men" (Lam 3:30-33).

PSALM 124*

Thanksgiving for the Lord's Help

1 A song of ascents. Of David.

If the LORD had not been on our side—*
    let Israel now proclaim—*m
2 if the LORD had not been on our side
    when our enemies attacked* us,
3 then they would have swallowed us alive*
    as their wrath was kindled against us.n
4 The waters would have washed us away,*
    the torrent would have swept over us,o

---

m Pss 118:25ff; 129:1.—n Prov 1:12; Jer 51:34.—o Pss 18:5; 69:2f; 88:18.

Ps 124 This psalm is the thankful cry of the chosen people that God saves because he has made a Covenant with them. It contains four classic images—the monster (v. 3: "swallowed"), the water (v. 4: "waters" and "torrent"; v. 5: "waters"), the bull (v. 6: "prey to their teeth"), and the trapped bird (v. 7: "from the snare of the fowlers")—that evoke the trials undergone by Israel as well as the sudden and extreme danger in which each person can find himself.

Christians can pray this psalm with the sentiments suggested by Paul in a similar situation (see 2 Cor 1:8-10). We can direct it to the Father and Christ, through whom God saves the Church. Without Christ, who will be with us till the consummation of the world (see Mt 28:20), the Church and her members could not hold out against the gates of the netherworld (see Mt 16:18). As the Good Shepherd, Christ gives his life to save his flock from the ravenous wolf who never ceases prowling around her, ready to devour her (see Jn 10:11-15; 1 Pet 5:8). Christ masters the storm that is on the verge of swallowing up the already sinking boat with his disciples (see Mk 4:35-41); he breaks the snare that holds his imprisoned apostles, among others Peter and Paul (see Acts 5:17-19; 12:1-11; 16:19-26). Truly, we can say with assurance: "Our help is in the name of the LORD, the Maker of heaven and earth" (v. 8).

124:1-2 Because the Lord has been with his people, they have not perished (see Pss 94:17; 119:92) and have hope instead (see Neh 4:14). The ancients had a grateful awareness of God's presence among them.

124:1 *Let Israel now proclaim:* the people are invited to repeat the first phrase like a refrain (see Pss 118:2; 129:1).

124:2 *Enemies attacked:* i.e., the arrogant (see Ps 123:4).

124:3-5 The trials undergone by Israel are described in traditional images (monsters, wild beasts, drowning, and snares) to indicate the totality of the disaster that loomed so near. *Swallowed:* in addition to indicating death at the hands of some beast, it also functions as a metaphor for death itself, which is often portrayed by "the netherworld" that devours its victims (see Ps 55:16; Prov 1:12).

124:4-5 The metaphor of water as a destructive force is common in the Old Testament (see Pss 18:17 and note; 32:6; 42:8; 69:2f, 16; Isa 8:7f; Lam 3:54) because of the destructive torrential rains common to that part of the world (see Jdg 5:21; Mt 7:27).

San Cristoforo
Martire

Gli scritti antichi narrano che Reprobo, vero nome di Cristoforo, si mise al servizio del Signore perché più grande e più forte di tutti. Per servire degnamente Gesù, egli, anima semplice ma dal fisico portentoso, divenne traghettatore senza zattera e senza barca usando solo la forza delle sue gambe e delle sue braccia. Mentre attendeva al suo servizio, un giorno un bambino gli chiese di attraversare il fiume; Reprobo si caricò il bimbo sulle spalle e si diresse a guado verso l'altra riva. Ma ad ogni passo che faceva il peso diventava più grave e la corrente più forte. Giunto infine a destinazione, il bambino si rivelò essere Gesù. Reprobo divenne così Cristoforo, *Christum ferens*, colui che porta Cristo, e dedicò il resto della sua vita a confortare i condannati cristiani. Fu per questo imprigionato, torturato e decapitato da Dagno, re della Licia.

⁵ and we would have drowned
   in the raging waters.

⁶ Blessed be the LORD,
   who did not give us as prey to their teeth.
⁷ We have escaped like a bird
   from the snare of the fowlers;
   the snare was broken,
      and we escaped.*
⁸ Our help is in the name of the LORD,
   the Maker of heaven and earth.*ᵖ

PSALM 125*

God, Protector of His People

¹ A song of ascents.

Those who put their trust in the LORD are like
   Mount Zion,
      which cannot be shaken but stands fast
         forever.*q

---

p Pss 115:15; 121:2; 134:3; 146:6; Gen 1:1; 2 Sam 17:45. —q Pss 46:5f; 48:3-6; Prov 10:25; Isa 33:20.

124:7 A triumphant note underlies this verse: "we escaped" by the Lord's doing; therefore, he is to be praised.

124:8 The psalm culminates in the great confession (see note on Ps 121:2).

Ps 125 In place of the grandeur and freedom to which it aspired during the Exile, Israel after the return experiences nothing but difficulties, miseries, and foreign oppressions. Under the weight of this cruel disillusionment, its courage fails and its faith in the Lord wavers. Fortunately, men of strong character like Zephaniah, Ezra, Nehemiah, and the aged prophet Haggai providentially appear to restore its confidence in the Lord's faithfulness.

The present psalm may date from this period of restoration. It sings of the perfect stability and security assured to his faithful by the Lord, who surrounds them as the mountains surround Jerusalem making it well-nigh impregnable. However, despite threats and against all appearances, God is the only certain power in human existence.

We can pray this psalm mindful of the help the Father granted to Israel of old but above all of the far superior aid he accords to the Church, to her Head as well as to each of her members. It is this same aid that we are to praise with Christ.

125:1 God's people ("those who put their trust in the LORD") are like Mount Zion, which symbolizes God's help (see Pss 121:1f; 124:8), his presence in helping and protecting his people (see Pss 76:7-10; 132:13-16), and the privileges of the Covenant relationship, and which cannot be shaken but endures forever (see Pss 16:8; 46:6; 112:6f; Isa 28:16; 54:10).

2 As the mountains surround Jerusalem,[r]
   so the LORD surrounds his people
   both now and forevermore.*

3 The scepter of the wicked will not prevail
   over the land allotted to the righteous,
so that the righteous will not be tempted
   to turn their hands to evil.*

4 Do good, O LORD, to those who are good,*
   to those who are upright of heart.*[s]
5 But the LORD will assign to the ranks of the
   evildoers
   those who turn their hearts to wickedness.*[t]

May peace be granted to Israel.[u]

---

r Ps 32:10; Deut 32:11; Mt 28:20.—s Pss 18:26ff; 119:65.—t Ps 92:10;
Prov 3:32.—u Pss 128:6; 130:7f.

125:2 In the mountain range around Jerusalem, Mount Zion is surrounded by
higher peaks: to the east lies the Mount of Olives, to the north Mount Scopus, to
the west and south other hills. So Mount Zion was regarded as secure because of
its natural defensibility. God is around and present to his people (see Ps 34:8;
Zec 2:7), both now and forevermore (see Pss 113:2; 115:18; 121:8).
125:3 Over the years the enemies of Israel have invaded and occupied the
land of Canaan and even annexed all or part of Israel and Judah (see Ps 124:2-
5). However, the psalmist declares that the Lord will never allow such a situation
to endure. For foreign rulers often attempted to introduce the worship of their
gods to the local population. Such foreign rule (symbolized by the term
"scepter"—see Isa 14:5) imposed on Israel cannot coexist with the Lord's protecting presence. For it might be an occasion for some of the godly to be tempted,
to lose heart, and to fall away. *Land allotted to the righteous:* i.e., the promised
land (see Ps 78:55).
125:4-5 Though confident in the Lord's protection, the people pray for his help.
For the Lord deals with everyone as that person is and does. In times of trouble,
God gives his grace more abundantly; at the same time, he never permits his
faithful to be tested beyond their strength. However, he wishes us to pray for that
grace. The psalm therefore closes with a petition for grace and judgment. One's
own weakness and the malice of the enemy conceal many dangers. May God not
refuse his assistance to those who are of goodwill and try to walk the path of
virtue, and at the same time may he banish those who follow the path of evil.
125:4 *Heart:* see note on Ps 4:8.
125:5 The "evildoers" are apostates who have turned to "wickedness," i.e.,
paths that twist away from the main road (see Jdg 5:6). The psalmist invokes the
law of talion against them (see Ps 18:27ff). *Peace be granted to Israel:* perhaps a
short form of the priestly blessing (see Num 6:24-26), with Israel designating the
group of the poor of the Lord (see Pss 73:1; 102:2; 128:6; 130:7f).

PSALM 126*

God, Our Joy and Our Hope

¹ A song of ascents.

When the LORD brought home the captives to
    Zion,*ᵛ
  we seemed to be dreaming.*
² Our mouths were filled with laughter
    and our tongues with songs of joy.ʷ

Then it was said among the nations,
  "The LORD has done great things for them."*

---

v Pss 14:7; 85:2; Ezr 1:1-3; Hos 6:11.—w Ps 65:9; Job 8:21; Lk 1:49.

Ps 126 The Jewish community takes pains to be reestablished. But joy fills the
people's hearts. They still resound with the gladness and hope of the caravans returning from the Exile, and every pilgrimage unfolds like a new Exodus (vv. 1-3; see
Isa 48:21), a return from the Exile. It is also faith in an even more wondrous future,
the gathering together of all by the side of the Messiah. Such happiness is prepared for in the suffering of the present just as the harvest grows out of the grain
sown into the earth where it dies (see Jn 12:24; Rom 8:8-25; 1 Cor 15:35-49).

In praying this psalm, we can also be mindful of the wondrous spiritual salvation of sinners worked by Christ in accord with the will of the Father. This salvation constitutes a spiritual Exodus from the sinful world to the divine dwelling of
the earthly Church and then of the heavenly Church, a transferral from satanic
tyranny to the gentle yoke of Christ and then of the heavenly Father, a conversion
from infidelity to fidelity toward Christ and his Father. Such are the wonders that
God has worked radically for all in causing Christ to pass from the grave to
heaven, from death to glorious life (see Eph 4:8), and that he works effectively for
every believer who shares in this mystery through faith (see Jn 5:24).

126:1-3 The edict of the Persian King Cyrus the Great in 538 B.C. that permitted the exiles to return home was totally unexpected despite the oracles issued by
Isaiah and Jeremiah. The long period of the captivity had caused many to give up
hope. Hence, the joy of their deliverance was indescribable. The Gentiles, too,
were impressed by this event; for many nations in the ancient Near East had vanished owing to conquest and exile, and the conventional wisdom was that little
Israel would suffer the same fate. When this proved not to be the case, the People
of God acknowledged that it was the Lord who had done great things for them.

126:1 The restoration of the captives to Zion took place in 538 B.C., in fulfillment of the prophetic word (see Isa 14:1f; 44:24—45:25; 48:20f; Jer 29:14; 30:3;
33:7, 10f; Am 9:14). However, when the actual moment came, it felt like a mi-
rage. *When the LORD . . . dreaming:* another translation is: "When the LORD restored the fortunes of Zion, / we were like men restored to health."

126:2 So great was the act of restoration and the joy of the people that the nations heard about it too (see Ps 98:2; Isa 52:10; Ezek 36:36) and praised the Lord
(see note on Ps 46:10).

³ The LORD has indeed done great deeds for us,
   and we are overflowing with joy.*

⁴ Once again restore our fortunes, O LORD,*
   as you did for the streams in the Negeb.*

⁵ Those who sow in tears
   will reap with songs of joy.*ˣ
⁶ Those who go forth weeping,
   carrying the seeds to be sown,
 will return with shouts of joy,
   carrying their sheaves.*

---

x Pss 6:7; 16:11; 20:5; 23:6; 80:6; Isa 35:10; 51:11; 65:19; Jer 50:4; Bar 4:23; Gal 6:9; Rev 21:4.

126:3 The psalmist affirms that the Lord has done great things for the people, and they are filled with joy. We Christians can use this verse in our own right to declare the manifold blessings bestowed on us in Christ, especially his Resurrection, which turned the disciples' sorrow into joy and brought salvation to the world that had previously been in bondage to the devil.

126:4-6 The reality of life in Canaan soon tempered the joy of the repatriates, for they had to eke out an existence in the land that had remained untended for years. So the people cry out to God for a continuation of the restoration: restoration of their well-being in the land ("fortunes"; see Ps 14:7). And they are assured of God's continued fidelity to his promise.

126:4 The repatriates, disappointed by the limited fulfillment of the prophetic word, turn to the Lord. They beg him to grant them a complete restoration and give them a brighter future even if to do so he has to perform a miracle like creating streams in the Negeb. *Restore our fortunes:* another possible translation is: "Bring back our people from captivity." No matter what the text, the prayer is one for a better future. *Streams in the Negeb:* the wadis of southern Palestine, almost always dry, are suddenly filled by the winter rains and fertilize the earth (see 2 Ki 3:20; Isa 41:18), representing proverbially the sudden coming of God's blessing.

126:5 God will be true to his promise, but the people must also do their part—they must sow the seed in order to have a harvest. God will turn the people's "tears" into "songs of joy" by blessing them in their various endeavors and rewarding their laborious toil.

126:6 The psalm concludes on the expectation of another miracle to take place; the people will return with "shouts of joy" because of the plentiful harvest. The time of exile was like a sowing of tears; it was a time of penance. The time of the harvest has not yet come. But as certainly as in nature the harvest follows upon seeding, so certain is it that a time of joy will follow for God's people. Thus, the psalm attests to the certainty of the Lord's promise. *Seeds to be sown:* "Previously the seed had not sprouted, and the vine and the fig tree, the pomegranate and the olive tree, had borne no fruit. From this day forward I intend to bless you" (Hag 2:19).

PSALM 127*

Need of Divine Assistance

¹ A song of ascents. Of Solomon.

If the LORD does not build the house,*
   those who construct it labor in vain.
If the LORD does not guard the city,
   those who keep watch over it do so in vain.*

² It is useless for you to rise earlier
   and delay taking your rest at night,
   toiling relentlessly for the bread you eat;
for while those he loves sleep,
   he provides all of this for them.*ʸ

³ Behold, children are a gift from the LORD,*
   a reward of the fruit of the womb.ᶻ

---

y Gen 3:17; Num 6:26; Job 11:18; Eccl 2:24-25; Mt 6:11.—z Pss 115:14;
128:3; Gen 1:28; Deut 28:11; Prov 17:6.

Ps 127 Without God, human undertakings are doomed to fail. It is God who is responsible for all of life's blessings (see Deut 28:1-14). There is no need for us to become overly anxious. His providence takes care of us (see Mt 6:25-34; Jn 15:5). This is the constant teaching of the Old and New Testament. Nowadays we know that natural laws follow a determined course that can be put to use in invention, technology, and the human sciences. But what do we expect to achieve? And if our endless affairs take away from us our time and taste for true joys, e.g., that of breaking bread together and of the fraternal home—what then?

We can and should recite this beautiful psalm in its original sense to praise the Lord who fills us with earthly goods and gifts. We can also transpose it to the spiritual plane to express our radical impotence in this sphere and to proclaim that all success and supernatural fecundity suppose the concurrence of Christ Jesus, acting in the name of the Father, in the holy Spirit (see Jn 15:4f).

127:1-2 The psalmist wishes to have the people become more God-centered in their everyday lives, for it is the Lord who provides shelter, security, and food.

127:1 The building of a "house" may refer to the construction of a house within the protective walls of the city or to the raising of a "family," for in the Old Testament it is usual to speak of a family as a house in much the same way as we speak of a prominent family as a dynasty (see Gen 16:2; 30:3; Ex 1:21; Ru 4:11; 1 Sam 2:35; 2 Sam 7:27). Even the best watchmen (see 2 Sam 13:34; 18:24-27; Song 3:3; 5:7) are not enough to protect the city against attack unless the Lord is guarding it (see Pss 121:4; 132).

127:2 The higher way of life is to trust the Lord in one's work. A good harvest results from God's blessing, not endless toil (see Prov 10:22; Mt 6:25-34; 1 Pet 5:7).

127:3-5 It is the Lord too who as a sign of his favor gives sons who ensure the perpetuity of the family that is faithful to him and provide protection for the family members.

⁴ Like arrows in the hands of a warrior
        are the children born in one's youth.*

⁵ Blessed is the man
        who has filled his quiver with them.
He will never be forced to retreat
        when he is confronted by his enemies at
        the city gate.*

PSALM 128*

Happy Home of the Righteous

¹ A song of ascents.

Blessed are all those who fear the LORD*
        and walk in his ways.*ᵃ

---

a Pss 1:1-2; 37:3-5; 112:1; 119:1-2; 128:1.

127:4 Children, especially sons, also provide a sense of security and protection for the family—especially if they are born early in the parents' life (see Prov 17:6; Lam 3:13). As the arrows protect the warrior, so do sons guard the godly man.

127:5 A house full of children is a protection against loneliness and abandonment in society. They will speak on behalf of their aging parents, especially at the city gate, where court was held (see Ps 69:13; Deut 17:5; 21:19; 22:15, 24; Prov 31:23; Am 5:12).

Ps 128 A prosperous home, such is the happiness reserved by God for the righteous—so thought the sages of Israel (see Prov 3:33). Although the people soon realized that God's reward is more mysterious, the joy and intimacy of the hearth, delicately invoked in this psalm, and the gathering of all in a Jerusalem radiant with peace remain the most suggestive images of the happiness that God will bestow on the righteous. The psalmist is encouraging the individual to contribute to the building up of the kingdom of God by living a godly life. Through him his family will be built up and God's blessing will be extended to all the People of God.

In praying this psalm, we can apply it above all to the spiritual goods that God reserves for Christian families. However, we know that the heavenly Father does not fail to add to his supernatural benefits such natural ones as the blessings and happiness promised by the psalmist: prosperity, professional success, fecundity, longevity, and peace.

128:1-4 The psalmist delineates the blessings of a God-fearing family: the right relationship with God, obedience to his words, fruitful labor, compatible loving parents, godly children, and domestic harmony.

128:1 The wise man was especially concerned with walking in the ways of the Lord (see Pss 1:1; 25:9f; Prov 14:2), ways of love, fidelity, and uprightness. *Blessed:* see note on Ps 1:1. *Fear the LORD:* see note on Ps 15:2-5. *His ways:* i.e., his commandments (see Pss 27:11; 86:11; 143:8).

2 You will eat the fruit of your labors;
    you will enjoy both blessings and prosper-
        ity.*b
3 Your wife will be like a fruitful vine
    within your house;
  your sons will be like shoots of an olive tree
    around your table.*c
4 Such are the blessings that will be bestowed
    on the man who fears the LORD.

5 May the LORD bless you from Zion*
    all the days of your life.d
  May you rejoice in the prosperity of Jerusalem*
6   and live to see your children's children.*e

Peace be upon Israel.f

---

b Pss 58:12; 112:3; Isa 3:10.—c Pss 52:10; 144:12; Job 29:5; Jer 11:16;
Hos 14:6.—d Pss 20:3; 122:9; 134:3; 135:21.—e Gen 50:23; Job 42:16;
Prov 17:6.—f Ps 125:5.

128:2 In godly living, the judgment of God on humans (see Gen 3:17-19) is al-
leviated, for labor is truly blessed by God.

128:3 The imagery of vine and olive shoots recalls the times of David and
Solomon (see 1 Ki 4:25) and the blessing associated with the Messianic Age (see
Mic 4:4; Zec 3:10). To sit under one's vine and fig tree symbolized tranquillity,
peace, and prosperity. The metaphor of the vine indicates that the wife will be
not only fruitful but also everything that a wife should be for the good of the family (see Prov 31:10-31). The children ("shoots of an olive tree") will be strong and
later on continue the father's work (see Ps 52:10; Jer 11:16; Hos 14:6).

128:5-6 The psalmist further summarizes the blessedness of the righteous—
unbroken prosperity, true relationship with God, secure national defense, and
long life. In doing so, he implicitly calls upon and encourages each one of the
faithful to contribute to the building up of the kingdom of God by leading an upright life in the presence of God.

128:5 The presence of God extends to his faithful servant wherever he may
live. For the new People of God, it signifies the blessing of God on all who have
the Spirit dwelling in them. *From Zion:* see Pss 9:11 and note; 20:3; 135:21.

128:6 *May you . . . live to see your children's children:* this prayer for the righteous corresponds to the phrase found in v. 5: "all the days of your life." It calls
down upon them God's blessing of longevity, which was one of the greatest favors to be sought in a time when an idea of the afterlife had not yet been fully attained. *Peace be upon Israel:* see note on Ps 125:5. By these words, the psalmist
applies God's blessing on the individual to the whole People of God, requesting
well-being and prosperity for all. Paul may be echoing this phrase in Gal 6:16:
"May *peace* and mercy be given to all who follow this rule, and *to the Israel of
God.*" It sums up Paul's concern that God's people should show themselves true
citizens of "the Jerusalem that is above" (Gal 4:26).

PSALM 129*

Prayer in Time of Persecution

¹ A song of ascents.

* They have greatly oppressed me from my
    youth—*
    let Israel say—*g*
² they have greatly oppressed me from my
    youth,
    but never have my enemies prevailed
    against me.*h*

³ The plowers plowed upon my back,*
    making deep furrows.*i*
⁴ However, the LORD is righteous,
    freeing me from the bonds of the wicked.

---

g Pss 88:16; 124:1-2.—h Ps 118:13; Mt 16:18; Jn 16:33.—i Isa 51:23.

Ps 129 The present psalm repeats the theme of Ps 124, concerning the past endurance of Israel, joining to it a prayer for the prompt defeat and eviction of its enemies. Recalling past oppressions and attacked on all sides, the pilgrims besought the Lord to overthrow the postexilic dominations. From the time of their Egyptian bondage, the chosen people have suffered oppression (vv. 1-2), but the Lord has always delivered them from their enemies. The poet expresses his theme by utilizing felicitous rural images. He leaves us a prayer of recourse to God—not of resignation—when we are haunted by the memory of fear or too much distress.

Christians can pray this psalm while evoking the continuous assaults that the Church has suffered from her birth and the future triumph that God will assure her over her enemies. The entire Book of Revelation illustrates this theme.

129:1-4 The enemies of Israel, who are at the same time enemies of the Lord, have much stomped on, oppressed, and tried to snuff out the chosen people from their youth in Egypt and during the Exodus. But they have been unable to do so because the Lord has broken their yoke in time. The psalmist may be thinking of the nomads making incursions at the time of the Judges; the Philistines dangerously invading at the time of Saul and David; the Assyrians conquering and destroying Samaria; and the Babylonians conquering and destroying Jerusalem.

129:1 *From my youth:* from the sojourn in Egypt and the entrance into the promised land (see Ps 89:46; Ezek 23:3; Hos 2:15).

129:3 *The plowers plowed upon my back:* in Ps 124 the enemies are likened to destructive floods and to a hunter; here they are likened to a farmer who plows the field with long furrows. The plowers are the warriors, the long furrows are the wounds and adversities, and the field is the back of Israel—a metaphor of Israel's history of suffering (see Isa 21:10; 41:15; Jer 51:33; Am 1:3; Mic 4:13; Hab 3:12).

⁵ May all those who hate Zion*
    be thrown back in shame and confusion.*
⁶ May they be like grass on the rooftops*
    that withers before it can be plucked, *ʲ*
⁷ so that it can never fill the hands of the reapers
    or the arms of the binders of sheaves.
⁸ May those who pass by never cry out,
    "The blessing of the LORD be upon you!
    We bless you in the name of the LORD."*ᵏ*

PSALM 130*

Prayer for Pardon and Peace

¹ A song of ascents.

Out of the depths* I cry to you, O LORD;
²   O Lord, hear my voice.*ˡ*

---

j Ps 102:12; 2 Ki 19:26; Isa 37:27.—k Ps 118:26; Ru 2:4.—l 1-2: Pss 5:2-3; 55:2-3; 86:6; 142:6f; 2 Chr 6:40; Neh 1:6; Lam 3:55-56; Jon 2:2.

129:5-8 The psalmist prays that God may humiliate pagan powers to whom Israel remains subject after the Exile (see note on Ps 5:11 and introduction to Ps 35).

129:5 Those who hate Zion disregard God and include not only the wicked of the world but also the Israelites who do not fear the Lord (see Ps 125:5).

129:6-8 May God make the wicked suffer the same fate as the grass that sprouts in the protective coating of clay covering roofs (see 2 Ki 19:26; Isa 37:27), which the dry and burning desert wind brutally withers up or men hastily root out. Just as this grass is taken up neither by the reaper nor by the sower, so may God cause the enemies of Israel, once beaten, to find no one to gather them or lift them up, no ally or reaper to whom others would wish success in his task with the cry, "The blessing of the LORD be upon you," traditionally addressed by passers-by to the harvesters who in turn would respond in kind: "We bless you in the name of the LORD" (see Ru 2:4). May they thus be a wasted growth.

Ps 130 This is the sixth of the seven Penitential Psalms (see Ps 6) and perhaps the psalm that has been most often recited down the centuries since the time when it became an invocation on behalf of the dead. It is both a prayer of sorrow and a hymn of hope. No other psalm reveals in so marvelous a way the mystery of God who forgives, reconciles, and redeems even those who abandon him. While wonderfully suitable for the deceased, it also befits anyone in the depths of sadness (e.g., Israel), for it makes hope rise for them like the dawn.

Because of the lofty plane on which it moves, this psalm does not need a transformation but only a greater profundity to become a Christian prayer. The parable of the Prodigal Son illustrates this perfectly (Lk 15).

130:1 *Depths:* a metaphor of adversity (see Ps 69:2f, 15; Isa 51:10; Ezek 27:34), connoting alienation from God (see Jon 2:2-5) and approaching death.

Let your ears be attentive
　　to my cries of supplication.*

3 If you, O LORD, kept a record of our sins,
　　O Lord, who could stand upright?*ᵐ
4 But with you there is forgiveness
　　so that you may be revered.*

5 I wait for the LORD in anxious expectation;
　　I place my hope in his word.*ⁿ
6 My soul waits for the Lord
　　more than watchmen wait for the dawn.º

More than watchmen wait for the dawn*
7 　　let Israel wait for the LORD.

---

m Ps 143:2; 1 Sam 6:20; Job 9:2; Ezr 9:15; Nah 1:6; Rev 6:17.—n Pss 5:4; 27:14; 40:1; 119:74, 81; Isa 8:17; 26:8; 30:18; 49:23.—o Ps 63:7; 2 Sam 23:4; Isa 21:11; 26:9.

130:2 In his extremity, the psalmist appeals to the Lord, calling him by his proper name and so obliging him to answer his prayers and intervene. Although the reason for the distress is not indicated here, the petition implies that it is related to sin, and the next verse makes this point explicit.

130:3 The unfortunate psalmist is well aware that the nature of his trouble is different from the depression of illness, homesickness, or persecution seen in some other psalms (e.g., Pss 6; 42; 69). It is guilt for sin, an evil that can cease only if God puts an end to the sins that cause the evil. Unless God granted pardon, no one could "stand," i.e., pass through his judgment (see Ps 1:5) or enjoy the benefits of his presence (see Ps 24:3).

130:4 God is full of forgiveness (see Dan 9:9; see also Pss 86:5; 103:3; Ex 34:7; 1 Jn 2:1f). And he is feared not only because of his great judgment and chastisement but also because of his great love in forgiving. The righteous respond with love and holy fear (see Deut 5:29; 1 Pet 1:17) as well as the desire not to offend him in the future (see Rom 2:4).

130:5 After noting that God liberally dispenses pardon, the psalmist expresses in splendid phrases his desire (indeed his certitude) of seeing God come close to him soon to grant him pardon. The words "I wait for the LORD" indicate that the psalmist ardently desires God and seeks to draw near to him with all his might. In patient waiting, faith looks up to the Lord to grant his grace (see Lam 3:25f). *In anxious expectation:* literally, "My soul waits": see note on Ps 6:4. *His word:* especially his Covenant promises (see Pss 119:25, 28, 37, 42, 49, 65, 74, 81, 107, 114, 147) and his word of pardon.

130:6 The psalmist waits for the Lord with much greater anticipation and certitude than watchmen wait for the dawn when they will be relieved of duty after guarding the city from night attacks (see Ps 127:1). *More than watchmen . . . wait for the dawn:* by this twofold repetition after a fourfold expression of "hope" in the Lord, the psalmist succeeds in inculcating a true sense of longing, dependence, and assurance.

For with the LORD there is kindness,
   as well as plenteous redemption.*p
8 He alone will redeem Israel
   from all its sins.q

PSALM 131*

Childlike Trust in God

1 A song of ascents. Of David.

O LORD, my heart is not proud,
   nor are my eyes raised too high.
I do not concern myself with great affairs
   or with things too sublime for me.*r

---

p Pss 25:5; 71:14; 86:15; 100:5; 103:8; 111:9; 1 Chr 21:13; Isa 30:18; Rom 3:24.—q Ps 25:22; Ex 34:7; Mt 1:21; Lk 1:68; Tit 2:14.—r Pss 101:5; 139:6; Job 5:9; Isa 2:12; Jer 45:5; Mic 6:8; Rom 12:16.

130:7-8 Like the psalmist, crushed by miseries, Israel must also hope and wait for the Lord. Rich in grace (compassionate and saving love) and redemption (pardon), God will redeem Israel from all temporal and spiritual miseries; he will deliver the people from all their misfortunes and sins as he delivered them from Egypt once before. The word "redemption," at first applied to the deliverance from slavery in Egypt (see Ex 12:27), later designates every type of liberation, every form of salvation (see Pss 25:20; 31:5; 44:27; Isa 43:14); here it signifies the profound liberation effected by the forgiveness of sins. The New Testament uses the word in the same sense—the redemption wrought by Christ (see Lk 2:38; Rom 3:24; Eph 1:7; Col 1:14; Rev 5:9). *Kindness:* see note on Ps 6:5.

Ps 131 Certainly the Prophets dared to state that God was like a mother for his people (see Isa 66:12f; Hos 11:4). But here is a man who has not fled from the experience of life; he lays bare the depth of his heart: the soul of a child before God. This psalm strikes us with great freshness and simplicity, and it is the most moving and evangelical of the psalms. A believer of the Old Testament has discovered the voice of spiritual childhood: "Unless you change and become like little children, you will never enter the kingdom of heaven" (Mt 18:3).

We can pray this psalm with the awareness that after practicing abandonment to God's hands, Jesus offers it as an ideal for us also, for like him we are children of the heavenly Father: "Learn from me, for I am meek and humble of heart" (Mt 11:29). We must flee from all desire to go beyond God and his help (see Mt 23:11; Jas 4:6f; 1 Pet 5:5f). The Father alone can make our labors fruitful through Christ (see Jn 15:1-17; 1 Cor 3:5-8); without Christ we can do nothing (see Jn 15:5).

131:1 The psalmist has completely submitted himself to God in all humility (see Mic 6:8). He is not like the proud who rely only on themselves (see note on Ps 31:24). He knows that true holiness begins in a heart bereft of pride (see Prov 18:12), with eyes that do not envy (see Pss 18:28; 101:5; Prov 16:5), and a manner of life that is not presumptuous, not preoccupied with great things (see Jer 45:5) and achievements that are "too sublime," i.e., too difficult or arduous, beyond one's powers (see Deut 17:8; 30:11). *Heart:* see note on Ps 4:8.

² Rather, I have stilled and calmed my soul,
    hushed it like a weaned child.
Like a weaned child held in its mother's arms,
    so is my soul within me.*ˢ

³ O Israel, put your hope in the LORD
    both now and forevermore.*

PSALM 132*

The Divine Promises Made to David

¹ A song of ascents.

Remember, O LORD, for David's sake,
    all the difficulties he endured.*

---

s Isa 30:15; 66:12-13; Mt 18:3.

131:2 The psalmist keeps a guard over his desires. He is like a "weaned child," who no longer frets for what it used to find indispensable and walks trustingly by its mother or lies peacefully in its mother's arms. *Soul:* see note on Ps 6:4.

131:3 Likewise all Israel, all God's people, must hope only in the Lord. Weaned away from insubstantial ambitions, we must hanker for the sole solid fare: "My food is to do the will of him who sent me, and to finish his work" (Jn 4:34).

Ps 132 By means of this psalm, the pilgrims, assembled for the procession, sing the glory of Zion, the dwelling place of God and the residence of his anointed, i.e., the king descended from David and like him consecrated with holy oil. Doubtless, this is a celebration of the anniversary of the bringing of the Ark of the Covenant to Jerusalem at the time of King David (see 2 Sam 6; 1 Chr 13—16). This hymn provides a splendid occasion to remind God of the commitment he made in favor of his people: David had sworn to build a dwelling in which to house the Ark, sign of the divine presence, and it was the Lord who promised him that he would ensure his lineage on the royal throne (see oracle of Nathan, 2 Sam 7 and 1 Chr 17) at Jerusalem, where the king had projected to build God's residence.

Each new reign gave birth to a new hope, for every one of David's descendants is "anointed," that is, "Messiah" in Hebrew and "Christ" in Greek. When the fallibility of the monarchy became flagrant, the hope subsisted with more intensity. All Israel awaits a last descendant of David, a true Messiah, who will permanently restore God's reign and his worship forever. It will be the time of God's glory and salvation; it will be the coming of Jesus Christ, son of David, whom Luke (1:69) presents to us by citing v. 17 of this psalm. Verses 8-10 and 16 are cited by the Chronicler at the end of the prayer of Solomon (see 2 Chr 6:41f).

Therefore, as we pray this psalm, we can remind God of the merits of David as well as those of Christ, asking him to fulfill the oaths made to David as supplementary motives for fulfilling those made to Christ. We can urge him to enthrone his Son fully in the heavenly Zion and establish therein his perfect kingship for the benefit of his faithful and the eternal confusion of his enemies.

132:1 *All the difficulties he endured:* in the conquest of Jerusalem (see 2 Sam 5:6-12) and in bringing the Ark to Jerusalem (2 Sam 6:1-23). Some translate: "and all his anxious care," i.e., to build the temple (see 2 Sam 7:1-17; 1 Ki 8:17).

² He swore an oath to the LORD*
   and vowed to the Mighty One of Jacob:

³ "I will not enter the house I live in
   or lie down on the bed where I sleep,ᵗ
⁴ neither will I allow myself to fall asleep
   or even to close my eyes,
⁵ until I find a home for the LORD,
   a dwelling for the Mighty One of Jacob."

⁶ We heard of it in Ephrathah;
   we came upon it* in the fields of Jaar.
⁷ Let us enter his dwelling place,*
   let us worship at his footstool.ᵘ

⁸ Arise, O LORD, and go up to your resting place,ᵛ
   you and the ark of your might.
⁹ Let your priests clothe themselves with righ-
      teousness,*
   and let your saints shout for joy.

---

t 2 Sam 7:1-2, 27; 1 Chr 28:2.—u Pss 5:8; 99:5; 122:1; 2 Sam 15:25; 1 Chr 28:2.—v 8-10: Pss 2:2; 68:2; 89:21; 95:11; Num 10:35; 2 Chr 6:41-42; Job 27:6; Sir 24:7; Isa 61:3, 10; Mal 3:3; Eph 6:14.

132:2-5 Although the oath and vow of David have not been recorded in the Bible, it is clear that when David heard that God had blessed Obededom, the guardian of the Ark (see 2 Sam 6:12), he immediately made efforts to bring the Ark to Jerusalem. *Mighty One of Jacob:* a title used by Jacob in Gen 49:24 and by Isaiah (49:26; 60:16) that emphasizes God's action in saving and redeeming his people. *Jacob:* a synonym for Israel (see Gen 32:28f).

132:6 *It . . . it:* often regarded as referring to the Ark, but more likely it refers to the call to worship that follows. *Ephrathah:* David's hometown near Bethlehem (see Ru 4:11; Mic 5:1). *Fields of Jaar:* i.e., Kiriath-jearim, where the Ark remained for a few generations (see 1 Sam 7:1f; 2 Sam 6:2; 1 Chr 13:5f).

132:7-8 Together with David and his men, the people wished to worship the Lord in Jerusalem. The Ark had been transported by the priests until it was placed in the tabernacle at Shiloh (see 1 Sam 4:3). With the capture of the Ark by the Philistines it was taken from city to city (see 1 Sam 4—6) until David brought it to Jerusalem and inaugurated a new era in God's rule over Israel: the Davidic era. The Ark was the footstool of the Lord's throne (see Ps 99:5) and symbolized God's earthly rule (see Ps 99:1f; Num 10:35f; 2 Chr 6:41f). *Arise, O LORD:* the invocation whenever the Ark set out in the days of Moses (see Num 10:35).

132:9 *Righteousness:* here synonymous with salvation (see 2 Chr 6:41), signifying victory, blessing, and deliverance (see Pss 4:2; 22:32; 24:5). *Saints:* the People of God who should be faithful to him (see note on Ps 34:10)

¹⁰ For the sake of your servant David,
  do not reject your anointed one.*

¹¹ The LORD swore this oath* to David,ʷ
  an oath that he will not renounce:ˣ
"One of your own descendants
  I will place on your throne.
¹² If your sons keep my covenant
  and the statutes that I will teach them,
their sons will also rule
  on your throne from age to age."*

¹³ For the LORD has chosen Zion;
  he has designated it for his home:
¹⁴ "This will be my resting place forever;
  here I will reside, for such is my wish.

¹⁵ "I will bless it with abundant provisions*
  and satisfy its poor with their fill of bread.
¹⁶ I will clothe its priests with salvation,
  and its saints will shout for joy.ʸ

¹⁷ "There I will raise up a horn for David*
  and prepare a lamp for my anointed one.ᶻ

---

w Pss 89:4f, 36; 110:4; 2 Sam 7:12; 1 Chr 17:11-14; Mt 1:1; Lk 3:3.—x
11-14: Ps 68:17; 2 Sam 5:9f; 1 Ki 8:13; Sir 24:7.—y Ps 149:5; 2 Chr 6:41;
Job 8:21; Isa 61:10; Jer 31:14.—z Pss 18:29; 84:10; 92:11; 1 Sam 2:10; 1
Ki 11:36; Isa 11:1; Jer 33:15; Ezek 29:21; Zec 3:8; Lk 1:69.

132:10 The Messiah or Christ is the "anointed one" of the Lord (see Ps 2:2; 1
Sam 10:1), the descendant of David awaited by Israel.

132:11 *Swore this oath:* no oath is mentioned in 2 Sam 7. However, elsewhere
God's promise to David is called a Covenant (see Pss 89:4, 29, 35, 40; 2 Sam
23:5; Isa 55:3), and Covenants were made with an oath.

132:12 God's sovereignty decrees that the dynasty of David will rule, but God's
holiness and justice stipulate that such will hold only if David and his descendants are loyal to his Covenant statutes.

132:15-16 The Lord will bless his people abundantly in his royal presence (see
Deut 15:4-6); the poor and the priests will share in this new age.

132:17 *I will raise up a horn for David:* a line close to Ezek 29:21; it has a
Messianic sense (see Isa 11:1; Jer 33:15; Zec 3:8). The word "horn" here designates a powerful descendence (see Ps 75:6); God will strengthen the Davidic race
from which the Messiah will arise (see Lk 1:69). *Prepare a lamp for my anointed
one:* promise recorded in the Books of Kings (see 1 Ki 11:36; see 2 Ki 8:19). The
house in which light no longer dawns is uninhabited (see Job 18:5; Jer 25:10).
The Messiah will be the light of the Gentiles (see Isa 42:6; 49:6; Lk 2:32).

¹⁸ I will clothe his enemies with shame,
　　　but on his head there will be a resplendent
　　　crown."*

PSALM 133*

The Blessings of Brotherly Accord

¹ A song of ascents. Of David.*

How wonderful and delightful it is
　　　for brothers to live together in unity.*
² It is like fragrant ointment poured on the head,
　　　running down upon the beard,
　　running down upon the beard of Aaron,ᵃ
　　　and flowing on the collar of his robes.*

---

a Ex 29:7; 30:25, 30; Job 8:22; 2 Sam 12:30.

132:18 This word of promise contains the Christian hope in the majesty, rule, and dominion of the Lord Jesus, who will put down all God's enemies (see 1 Cor 15:25-28; Rev 19:17-21).

Ps 133 The fragrant oil of anointing and the beneficial dew—such images speak for themselves for a Palestinian; for the poet they evoke the charm of a living community gathered together around the priests and Levites in the holy city on the occasion of a pilgrimage. The holy city (v. 3), the priesthood (v. 2), and the communion of brothers—all is newness of grace at this moment.

This psalm easily finds an appropriate place on our lips to proclaim the advantages of concord among Christians in the bosom of the House of God, the Church. John the apostle reveals the evils of discord. The person who hates another is a murderer and remains in sin and death. Such a person is not loved by God and can receive no gift from him (see 1 Jn 3:15-17). Fraternal love constitutes the sign of true faith and with it the key to all the divine goods (see Mt 22:34-40; Jn 13:34f; 15:12-17). Only this love manifests that we are true children of God, born of him, and at the same time true disciples of Christ (see Jn 13:35; 1 Jn 4:7).

133:1a *Of David:* these words, omitted from some mss, refer to the reunion of the tribes of Israel at David's anointing in Hebron (see 2 Sam 5:1ff).

133:1bc The psalmist pronounces a blessing on those who live together in unity, as, for example, those on pilgrimage who included people from many different walks of life, regions, and tribes, coming together for one purpose—to worship the Lord in Jerusalem.

133:2 Brotherly accord is compared with the copious oil running down the head, beard, and robes of the priests who were anointed. Just as the holy oil poured on the priests consecrated them to the Lord's service, so brotherly unity sanctifies God's people. Thus, the fellowship of God's people on earth is an expression of the priesthood of all believers (see Ex 19:6), promised to Israel and renewed for the Church in Christ (see 1 Pet 2:9f).

³ It is like the dew of Hermon
     falling upon the mountains of Zion.*ᵇ
For there the LORD has bestowed his blessing,
     life forevermore.ᶜ

PSALM 134*

Invitation to Night Prayer

¹ A song of ascents.

Come forth to bless the LORD,
     all you servants of the Lord,
who minister throughout the night
     in the house of the LORD.*ᵈ
² Lift up your hands toward the sanctuary
     and bless the LORD.*ᵉ

---

b Job 29:19; Isa 26:19; 45:8; Hos 14:6.—c Ps 36:10; Deut 28:8; 30:20.—
d Ps 135:1-2; 1 Chr 9:33; Rev 19:5.—e Pss 28:2; 63:4; 141:2.

133:3 *Dew of Hermon . . . mountains of Zion:* because of its height (nearly ten thousand feet above sea level) and the rain, snow, and dew that fell atop it, Mount Hermon was famous for its rich foliage even during the dry summer months (see Ps 89:13; Deut 33:28; Song 5:2; Hos 14:6). Thus, the dew of Mount Hermon would make the mountains of Zion just as fruitful (see Gen 27:28; Hag 1:10; Zec 8:12). The psalmist indicates that no matter how harsh the conditions of the pilgrimage might be, the fellowship of God's people was refreshing. *For there . . . life forevermore:* the divine blessing almost personified (see Lev 25:21; Deut 28:8) will procure happiness and salvation (see Pss 28:9; 36:11) in a definitive manner (see Pss 61:5; 73:26; Deut 30:16, 20).

Ps 134 As the pilgrims leave the temple and invite the priests to keep up their praise during the night, the latter direct to them a blessing that brings to a close the Songs of Ascents, the Pilgrim's Psalter, just as Ps 117 concludes the collection of Alleluia (or Hallelujah) psalms (Pss 111—117).

This psalm should remind us that Jesus spent whole nights in prayer (see Lk 6:12) and that he urged the disciples to pray always and not lose heart (see Lk 18:1), a point reiterated by Paul in his first Letter: "Pray continually. Give thanks in all circumstances" (1 Thes 5:17f). Hence, this dialogued hymn can be exchanged between Christians on earth: those who are often taken away from divine praise by their earthly duties should ask those who are better prepared for this (priests and religious) to assure in their name the work of praise that is so necessary.

134:1 The psalmist calls upon the priests and Levites to lead the people in worship. These are the "servants of the LORD" who "minister" (literally, "stand") in the house of the Lord. The priestly and Levitical ministry is often designated by the verb "stand" (see Ps 135:2; Deut 10:8), and they offered up musical praise to the Lord both day and night (see 1 Chr 9:33; 23:26, 30).

134:2 The priests and Levites also prayed with hands lifted up (see Ps 28:2; 1 Tim 2:8) "toward" the sanctuary (see 1 Ki 8:30).

³ May the LORD, the Maker of heaven and
earth,
   bless you from Zion.*^f

PSALM 135*

Praise of God, Benefactor of His People

¹ Alleluia.

Praise the name of the LORD;*
   offer him praise, you servants of the
   LORD,*^g
² you who minister in the house of the LORD,
   in the courts of the house of our God.*^h

---

f Pss 20:3; 118:26; 124:8; 128:5; Lev 25:21; Num 6:24.—g Pss 113:1;
134:1; Neh 7:72.—h Pss 116:19; 134:1; 1 Chr 15:2; Lk 2:37.

134:3 The words of this verse recall the words spoken by the priests when
blessing (see Num 6:24f). The blessing follows the people wherever they may go
or live, because it comes from the Maker of heaven and earth, i.e., the Great King
of the universe (see Ps 121:2). Yet, like God's commandments, the blessing is not
"beyond reach," not "in heaven" nor "beyond the sea" but "very near" (see Deut
30:11-14; Rom 10:6ff)—"from Zion." And it is the true Mount Zion, the heavenly
Jerusalem, where Jesus the "mediator of a new covenant" reigns in the midst of
his people (see Heb 12:22-24).

Ps 135 Composed of fragments taken from other psalms (Pss 113; 115; 134;
136), this hymn sings the praises of the true God. The psalmist acclaims the one
who holds the whole universe in his hands; he glorifies the one who chose the people of Israel and guided them to their destiny from the liberation from Egypt up to
their establishment in Canaan. The entire people—priests, Levites, faithful, and
God-fearers (vv. 19-20)—is convoked to this praise, which celebrates the Creator
of the world and the Redeemer of Israel. In the face of such solid faith, all mention
of false gods becomes a caricature. Are our hymns to God true enough to cast
scorn on all the new idols that we ceaselessly create for ourselves?

We can use this psalm to praise the heavenly Father for his wonders in favor
of Israel (with whom we are spiritually united) and in favor of his Son Jesus, King
of Israel. We can also use it to praise the Lord Jesus, Master of nature for the service of the new Israel, Savior of his Church, the only true God in the unity of the
Father and the Holy Spirit.

135:1-4 An exhortation to praise God, who is good and who has love for his
own.

135:1 Taken from Ps 113:1; see Jud 4:14. The praise of God included a recitation of his wonders in creation (vv. 5-7) and in redemptive history (vv. 8-12). *Servants of the LORD:* although the identity of the "servants" is debated, the general
consensus, based on the text itself, is that the word denotes the priests and
Levites, who praised the Lord day and night (see 1 Chr 9:33; 23:26, 30).

135:2 Taken from Ps 134:1; see Ps 92:14.

3 Praise the LORD, for the LORD is good;
     sing to honor his name, for he is gracious.*
4 For the LORD has chosen Jacob for himself,
     Israel as his treasured possession.*i

5 I know that the LORD is great,*j
     that our LORD is superior to all gods.*
6 The LORD does whatever he pleases
     in heaven and on earth,
     in the seas and in all their depths.*k
7 He causes clouds to rise
     from the ends of the earth;
   he sends lightning with the rain
     and brings forth the wind from his store-
       houses.*l

8 * He struck down the firstborn of Egypt,*
     those of humans as well as of animals.m
9 He sent signs and portents into your midst, O
     Egypt,*
     against Pharaoh and all his servants.

---

i Pss 33:12; 144:15; Ex 19:6; Deut 7:6; Mal 3:17.—j Pss 95:3; 145:3; Ex 18:11.—k Ps 115:3; Mt 6:10.—l Pss 68:9, 11; 148:8; Job 37:9; Isa 30:23; Jer 10:13; 51:16; Joel 2:23; Am 4:13; Zec 10:11.—m 8-9: Pss 78:51; 105:27, 36; 136:10; Ex 4:23; 7:9; 12:29.

135:3 Praise is due because the Lord himself is good and gracious (or beautiful; see Ps 27:4). The second part of the verse is close to Ps 147:1. *He is gracious:* another possible translation is: "it is pleasant."

135:4 Although all the nations are the Lord's, he has chosen Israel as his own in a special way. *Treasured possession:* this phrase is found in Ex 19:5; Deut 7:6; 14:2; 26:18; see also Ps 33:12.

135:5-7 The psalmist spells out the greatness of the Creator, who rules over all creation and is above all gods.

135:5 *Our LORD is superior to all gods:* taken from Ex 18:11; see Ps 95:3.

135:6 The Lord does whatever he pleases (see Ps 115:3) in his acts in heaven, on the earth, in the seas, and in the subterranean waters ("all their depths").

135:7 The Lord's greatness extends to the elements and powers of nature: rain (see Ps 29), lightning (see Ps 148:8), wind (see Ps 104:4), and the storehouses from which any of the elements could be brought forth (see Pss 33:7; 65:10f).

135:8-14 The psalmist indicates the greatness of the Lord's redemption of Israel through the Exodus and the Conquest by using climactic strokes. Most of the phrases in these verses reappear in Pss 136:10, 18-22.

135:8 *Struck . . . of Egypt:* the tenth plague (see Pss 78:51; 105:36; Ex 12:29).

135:9 *Into your midst, O Egypt:* similar in form to Ps 116:19, this phrase recalls Ps 136:11 (see Ps 78:43).

10 He struck down many nations[n]
   and slew mighty kings:
11 Sihon, king of the Amorites,
   Og, king of Bashan,
   and all the kings of Canaan.*
12 He then gave their lands as a heritage,
   a heritage to his people Israel.*

13 Your name, O LORD, endures forever,
   your renown, O LORD, lasts throughout the
      ages.*[o]
14 For the LORD will vindicate his people
   and show compassion to his servants.*[p]

15 The idols of the nations are silver and gold,*
   the work of human hands.[q]
16 They have mouths but they cannot speak;
   they have eyes but they cannot see.
17 They have ears but they cannot hear,
   and there is no breath in their mouths.
18 Those who make them end up like them,
   as do all who place their trust in them.

19 O house of Israel, bless the LORD!*
   O house of Aaron, bless the LORD![r]
20 O house of Levi, bless the LORD!
   You who fear the LORD, bless the Lord!

n 10-12: Pss 44:3; 136:17-22; Num 21:21-35; Deut 2:24—3:17; Jos 24:8-11.—o Ps 102:13; Ex 3:15; Isa 63:12.—p Deut 32:36; Heb 10:30.—q 15-18: Pss 96:5; 115:4-6, 8.—r 19-20: Pss 115:9-11; 118:2-4.

135:11 *Sihon . . . Og . . . and all the kings of Canaan:* see Ps 136:19f; Num 21:21-26, 33-35; Deut 2:30-33; 3:1-6; Jos 12:2-24).
135:12 Recalls Ps 136:17-22.
135:13 Extract from Ex 3:15; see Ps 102:12; Isa 63:12. The name God revealed to Moses was to increase in significance as the Lord increased his activities in redemptive history.
135:14 *Show compassion to his servants:* taken from Deut 32:36.
135:15-18 The psalmist reproduces Ps 115:4-6, 8 almost exactly. His point is that idols, unlike the God of Israel, do not speak, reveal, promise, or utter any spoken word. Ultimately divine revelation is the difference between the religions made by humans and the true religion of the Lord (see Ps 115:4-8; Deut 4:16; Isa 44:9ff; Jer 10:1ff; Bar 6:7ff).
135:19-21 Employing the language of Pss 115:9-11 and 118:2-4 (with the addition of "O house of Levi"), the psalmist calls upon all to praise the Lord present in Zion.

²¹ Blessed from Zion be the Lord,
    he who dwells in Jerusalem.

Alleluia.*

PSALM 136*

Thanksgiving for the Creation
and Redemption

¹ Give thanks to the LORD, for he is good,*
    for his love endures forever.ˢ
² Give thanks to the God of gods,
    for his love endures forever.
³ Give thanks to the LORD of lords,
    for his love endures forever.

⁴ He alone works great wonders,ᵗ
    for his love endures forever.

---

s Pss 100:5; 105:1; 106:1; 118:1; 145:9; 2 Chr 5:13; Ezr 3:11; Jer 33:11; Nah 1:7.—t Ps 72:18; Ex 15:11; Deut 10:17.

135:21 *Alleluia:* i.e., "Hallelujah" or "Bless [or praise] the LORD"; some regard this line as belonging to the beginning of Ps 136.

Ps 136 This psalm was for Israel the last of the "Great Hallel" psalms or, according to some Jewish authorities, the only Hallel psalm, the supreme song of praise. Associated with the great annual feasts, especially with the Feast of Passover, it is made up of exclamations of gratitude to God (accompanying a list of his wonders) and of enthusiastic assents from the crowd. In this list there are three great wonders that are never separated in Israel. First the creation and life of the world (vv. 5-9). Next the deliverances worked by God for Israel: the Exodus from Egypt (vv. 10-12), the passage through the Red Sea (vv. 13-15), the sojourn and victories in the wilderness (vv. 16-20), and the Conquest of the promised land (vv. 21-24). Finally, God's solicitude for every living being, the grace of the bread for each day (v. 25). As it goes through this list of favors, Israel sings of God's merciful love.

Such a psalm could not fail to become a favorite of the Church for the Easter Vigil. By his Passion and Resurrection, Christ has given life to a new world; human beings are snatched from slavery to sin and advance in their earthly pilgrimage to become the people reunited around God in the new promised land, the kingdom of heaven. In the accents of the Great Hallel, Christians thus sing of the Passover of the world.

136:1-4 The words "give thanks" here mean "confess" or "acknowledge" (see Lev 5:5; Prov 28:13) and therefore call us to grateful worship indicating what we know of God's glory and his deeds. Since he is "the God of gods" and "the LORD of lords" (see Deut 10:17), he alone is to be thanked for all the acts in creation and redemption (see Ps 72:18; Ex 15:11).

5 In his wisdom he made the heavens,*u
   for his love endures forever.
6 He spread out the earth upon the waters,*v
   for his love endures forever.

7 He made the great lights,w
   for his love endures forever.
8 He made the sun to rule over the day,
   for his love endures forever.
9 He made the moon and stars to rule the night,
   for his love endures forever.

10 He struck down the firstborn of Egypt,*x
   for his love endures forever.
11 He led forth Israel from among them,
   for his love endures forever.
12 He did so with a strong hand and outstretched
   arm,y
   for his love endures forever.

13 He divided the Red Sea in two,*
   for his love endures forever.
14 Then he led Israel through its midst,
   for his love endures forever.
15 But he swept Pharaoh and his army into the
   Red Sea,z
   for his love endures forever.

---

u Gen 1:9-19; Prov 3:19; 8:1, 22-31; Jer 51:15.—v Ps 24:2; Gen 1:6; Isa 42:5; Jer 10:12; 33:2.—w 7-9: Gen 1:16; Jer 31:35.—x 10-16: Pss 78:51-52; 105:43; 135:8; Ex 4:23; 12:12, 29, 51; 14:22, 27; 15:22.—y Ex 3:20; 6:1, 6; Deut 4:34.—z Ex 14:21f; 40:38; Num 9:15-22; Deut 1:33; Neh 9:19; Wis 10:17.

136:5-9 The psalmist here brings together two Old Testament treatments of the creation theme: that of Proverbs, which speaks of the understanding and "wisdom" (v. 5) presupposed by creation (see Prov 3:19f; 8:1, 22-31; see also Ps 104:24; Jer 10:12), and that of Genesis, which gives the account of it (vv. 6-9: see Gen 1:9f, 16-18).

136:6 *Upon the waters:* see Ps 24:2.

136:10-12 Of the many wonders during the Exodus from Egypt, the psalmist mentions the tenth plague (see Pss 78:51; 105:36; 135:8) and the Lord's mighty hand and outstretched arm, a metaphor for God's great and personal strength in favor of his people (see Ex 6:1, 6; Deut 4:34).

136:13-15 At the Red Sea, the Lord discredited Pharaoh and his forces by judging them (see Ex 14:27), while he rescued his people (see Ps 106:7ff; Ex 4:23).

16 Then he led his people through the wilderness,*ᵃ
    for his love endures forever.

17 He struck down great kings,ᵇ
    for his love endures forever.
18 He slew powerful kings,
    for his love endures forever.
19 Sihon, king of the Amorites,
    for his love endures forever.
20 Og, king of Bashan,
    for his love endures forever.

21 He gave their land as a heritage,*
    for his love endures forever.
22 The heritage was for his servant Israel,
    for his love endures forever.

23 The LORD remembered us in our wretched
    state,
    for his love endures forever.
24 He rescued us from our enemies,
    for his love endures forever.
25 He provides food to every creature,*
    for his love endures forever.

26 Give thanks to the God of heaven,
    for his love endures forever.

---

a Ps 78:52; Ex 13:18.—b 17-22: Ps 135:10-12; Ex 14:27; Num 21:23-25, 33-35; Deut 29:6ff; Jos 12:1ff; 24:8-11.

136:16-20 The Lord guided his people through the wilderness(see Deut 8:15; Jer 2:6; Am 2:10) and won victories for them. He struck down the great and mighty kings like Sihon and Og (see Ps 135:11; Deut 2:30ff; 3:1), who are representative of a long number of Canaanite kings. Verses 17-22 are practically identical with Ps 135:10-12.

136:21-24 God was with "his people Israel" during the Conquest of the promised land, which became their heritage (see Ps 135:12), as well as from that time till the present. The Lord's remembrance is based on the Covenant and is intended to effectively bring out the complete redemption of his afflicted people (see Ex 6:5).

136:25-26 Finally it is the Lord who provides daily bread for all his creatures; therefore, all should praise him. *God of heaven:* an expression current during the Persian epoch (see Ezr 1:2; 5:11; 6:9; Neh 1:5; 2:4) that became classic (see Jud 5:8; Dan 2:18).

PSALM 137*

The Exiles' Remembrance of Zion

¹ By the rivers* of Babylon
    we sat down and wept
    when we remembered Zion.ᶜ
² There on the poplars*
    we hung up our harps.ᵈ

³ For it was there that our captors
    asked us to sing them a song,
    and, tormenting us, demanded a joyful song:
    "Sing us one of the songs of Zion."ᵉ

---

c Neh 1:4; Lam 3:48; Ezek 3:15.—d Lev 23:40; Job 30:31; Isa 24:8; Jer 25:10; Lam 5:14; Ezek 26:13.—e Pss 79:1-4; 80:6; Jer 51:50; Ezek 16:57.

Ps 137 Let us imagine the setting in which this psalm was sung for the first time. Some Levites, after returning from the Exile, have gathered for a penitential liturgy. They are unable to suppress the memory of the humiliations they suffered on the banks of the Euphrates, where, to heighten their sadness, they were compelled not to sing the songs they loved, since it would have been a profanation to make these known in a foreign land for the amusement of idolaters. Now their cry of attachment to Jerusalem becomes vehement and their song leads to an outburst of vengeful anger that, though in keeping with the custom of the time, seems to us cruel beyond description (see note on Ps 5:11 and introduction to Ps 35).

Events now in the distant past become symbols; the psalm speaks of Edom, but the singers think of all the forces united to destroy the People of God and the righteous; the psalm mentions Babylon, but this suggests the most hateful wickedness. This same wickedness the Book of Revelation will later image forth in the monstrous figure of "Babylon the great," mother of blasphemers (see Rev 17:5).

We can pray this psalm as citizens of heaven (see Phil 3:20) living in exile on earth (see 2 Cor 5:6f). Strangers to a world that does not acknowledge us as its own, we are hated and persecuted by it for this reason (see Jn 15:18f; 17:14-18). We are cognizant that our exile deprives us of our true home and our Father and dooms us to divers physical and moral miseries including death, and we "groan inwardly as we wait for . . . the redemption of our bodies" (Rom 8:23).

137:1 *Rivers:* the Euphrates and Tigris, as well as the numerous irrigation-canals that branched off from them (see Ezr 8:21; Ezek 1:1; 3:15). *Sat:* the posture of mourning (see Job 2:8, 13; Lam 2:10); it could also refer to the idea of being settled in accord with the word of the prophet Jeremiah who urged the exiles to work for a living, to multiply, and to seek the peace and prosperity of the land (see Jer 29:4-9). *Wept:* see Isa 24:8; Jer 25:10; Lam 3:48; 5:14.

137:2-3 The exiles were tauntingly requested to sing "the songs of Zion" on their harps. The taunts were tantamount to the question "Where is your God?" (Pss 42:4, 11; 79:10; 115:2), and might have been concerned the "songs of Zion" that celebrated the Lord's majesty and protection (see Pss 46; 48; 76; 84; 87; 122).

4 But how could we sing songs of the LORD
    while living in a foreign land?*

5 If I forget you, O Jerusalem,*
    may my right hand fail me.
6 May my tongue stick to the roof of my mouth
    if I do not remember you,
  if I do not regard Jerusalem
    as the greatest of my joys.

7 Remember, O LORD, the cruelty of the Edom-
     ites*
    on the day when Jerusalem fell,*
  how they shouted, "Tear it down!
    Tear it down to its very foundations!"*f*

8 O Daughter* of Babylon, you destroyer,
    happy will he be who repays you
    for the suffering you inflicted upon us!*g*
9 Happy will he be who seizes your babies
    and smashes them against a rock!**h*

---

f Jer 49:7; Lam 4:21-22; Ezek 25:12-14; Ob 1:11.—g Isa 14:22; 47:1-3;
Jer 50—51; Rev 18:6.—h Hos 14:1; Lk 19:44.

137:4 The exiles could not bring themselves to sing any of the holy songs while
they rested on foreign, unclean soil; that would be a profanation (see Hos 9:3; Am
7:17).

137:5-6 The exiles could not forget Jerusalem and what it symbolized: Covenant, temple, God's presence and kingship, atonement, forgiveness, and reconciliation. They vowed to wait for the redemption promised by God.

137:7-9 See note on Ps 5:11 and introduction to Ps 35.

137:7 *On the day when Jerusalem fell:* literally, "the day of Jerusalem" or "that
day at Jerusalem." The "day" in question is either the ninth day of the fourth month
(June-July 587 B.C.) when the Babylonians broke through the walls of Jerusalem (see
Jer 39:2; 52:7) or the tenth day of the fifth month (July-August 587 B.C.) when the
temple was set afire (see Jer 52:12; Zec 7:5; 8:19). The *Edomites* collaborated with
the besiegers and did everything they could to disgrace Judah and keep the people
from escaping (see Lam 4:21f; Ezek 25:12; 35:12; Ob 11), and their name became a
symbol of Israel's enemies as well as an object of the Lord's judgments (see Isa
63:1-4; Jer 49:7-22; Ezek 25:8, 12-14; 35; Ob 1-21).

137:8 *Daughter:* a personification of Babylon, on whom the Lord had passed
judgment (see Isa 13; 21:1-10; 47; Jer 50—51; Hab 2:4-20).

137:9 *Happy will he be who seizes . . . :* in accord with the ruthless practice of
ancient warfare, this scene was often played out during the sacking of a city
after its fall (see 2 Ki 8:12; 15:16; Isa 13:16, 18; Hos 10:14; 14:1; Am 1:13; Nah
3:10). A beatitude is here transformed into a terrible curse.

PSALM 138*

Thanksgiving for God's Favor

[1] Of David.

I offer you thanks, O LORD, with all my heart;
  before the "gods" I sing your praise.*[i]
[2] I bow down toward your holy temple
    and I praise your name*
  for your kindness and your faithfulness,
for you have exalted above all things
    your name and your word.
[3] On the day I cried out, you answered me
    and granted strength to my spirit.

[4] All the kings of the earth will praise you, O
    LORD,*
  when they hear the words of your mouth.
[5] They will sing of the ways of the LORD:
  "How great is the LORD's glory!"

---

i Pss 9:2; 27:6; 95:3; 96:4; 106:2.

Ps 138 This psalm begins a collection of eight Davidic psalms (Pss 138—145). The believer, representing the people of Israel, knows from experience the God who saves the human race from its distress. He does not want to keep this conviction for himself but to share it with all peoples, all human beings. A deep faith in a universal plan of the Lord illumines this beautiful thanksgiving prayer.

We can pray this psalm keeping in mind the various victories that God empowers his Church to achieve against her material and spiritual enemies. These enable us to bless our Savior and to indicate the praise offered to him by earthly powers who witness and suffer under these victories.

138:1 The psalmist stresses that praise belongs to the Lord alone and not to the gods of the nations, whose kings will have to submit to the Lord. After the word "heart" the Greek adds another line: "for you have heard the words of my mouth," which is not in the Hebrew; it seems to have been a variant of v. 4b accidently inserted here. *Heart:* see note on Ps 4:8. *Gods:* the Hebrew is *"elohim,"* which is the word for "God," "gods," and sometimes "godlike beings," such as the angels. The Septuagint and Vulgate have "angels" (see Ps 8:6); other versions, "kings" or "judges."

138:2 *Name:* see note on Ps 5:12. *Kindness:* see note on Ps 6:5. *Your word:* i.e., God's promise. By his faithfulness to his promise, God has made his name renowned.

138:4-5 The psalmist prays that the nations together with their gods and kings will also pay homage to the Lord (see note on Ps 9:2). For the "words" and "ways" of the Lord reveal how great is his "glory" (see Ps 57:6; Isa 40:5; 60:1).

6 For though the LORD is exalted, he cares for
the lowly,
but he remains far distant from the proud.*[j]

7 Although I walk in the midst of hostility,
you preserve my life.
You stretch out your hand against the wrath
of my enemies,
and with your right hand you deliver me.*

8 The LORD will fulfill his plan for me.
Your kindness, O LORD, endures forever;
do not forsake the work of your hands.*

PSALM 139*

God's Infinite Knowledge and Universal Power

1 For the director.* A psalm of David.

O LORD, you have examined me*
and you know me.

---

j Pss 40:5; 113:7-9; Isa 57:15; Mt 23:12; Lk 1:51-52.

138:6 The Lord lifts up the lowly (see note on Ps 113:7-9; Lk 1:48, 52) and puts down the proud (see notes on Pss 31:24 and 131:1; see also Ps 101:5).

138:7 The psalmist describes the Lord extending his hand to offer help while passing judgment on those who cause his adversity (see Ps 144:7; Ex 3:20; 9:15). *Right hand:* symbol of strength (see Pss 60:7; 139:10).

138:8 The Lord has loving concern for his people and creation (see Pss 90:16; 92:6; 143:5; Isa 60:21; 64:8) and has a purpose for them (see note on Ps 57:3).

Ps 139 This psalm is one of the pearls of the Psalter in its literary beauty and profound doctrine: the complete knowledge that God has about each person. The human heart is transparent to God's look; he knows the most secret and most unknown movements of our souls. Feeling the hand of God on himself provoked sadness and anxiety in Job (see Job 23—24; Jer 15:6f), but in the psalmist it instills serenity and abandonment. He no longer asks God to turn away his face but to lead him on the path of fidelity. The psalmist awakens to God; the one whom he thought he had to seek out is already there, present in him as his source of life, more present to him than he is to himself.

We can pray this psalm to remind ourselves of the complete knowledge that Jesus has of us (see Jn 10:14f). For he is our Creator and Savior (see Col 1:16f; Heb 1:1f), who restores the supernatural world and re-creates each of his disciples, making new creatures of them to his own image (see Eph 2:10; Col 3:11).

139:1a *For the director:* these words are thought to be a musical or liturgical notation.

139:1b-6 God is all-seeing and all-knowing. His knowledge is not sterile but personal and active, discriminating in favor of those who are faithful to the Lord.

2 You know when I sit and when I stand;*
     you perceive my thoughts from a distance.*k*

3 You mark when I go out and when I lie down;
     all my ways are open to you.
4 A word is not even on my tongue
     and you, O LORD, are completely aware of it.

5 You enfold me from in front and from behind,
     and you place your hand upon me.*
6 Your knowledge is beyond my comprehension,
     far too sublime for me to attain.*l*

7 Where can I go to hide from your spirit?*
     Where can I flee from your presence?*
8 If I ascend to the heavens, you are there;
     if I take my rest in the netherworld, you
          are also there.*m*

9 If I rise on the wings of the dawn*
     and settle at the farthest limits of the sea,
10 even there your hand will guide me,
     and your right hand will hold me fast.

11 If I say, "Surely the darkness will conceal me*
     and the day around me will turn to night,"
12 even the darkness is not dark to you;
     the night is as bright as the day,
          for to you darkness and light are the same.

---

k Ps 44:22; 2 Ki 19:27; Job 12:13; Heb 4:13.—l Ps 131:1; Rom 11:33.—
m Job 23:8-9; Jer 23:23-24; Am 9:2-3.

139:2 *You know when I sit and when I stand:* a Hebrew idiom that, when combined with the parallel "go out and lie down" (or "go out and come in": see Isa 37:28), signifies: "in all that I do."
139:5 *Place your hand upon me:* a gesture performed by the judge or the witness (see Job 9:33). It expresses God's absolute mastery over human beings (see Ex 33:22; Rev 1:17).
139:7-12 God is all-present; he is everywhere to protect his children. He perceives all things in all places and there is no escaping him.
139:7-8 The same images and teaching are found in Am 9:2f. See also Job 11:8; 23:8f; Prov 15:11; Isa 7:11; Jer 23:24; Jon 1:3.
139:9 *Rise on the wings of the dawn:* go to the most distant extremities of the east. *Settle at the farthest limits of the sea:* the uttermost bounds of the west.
139:11-12 There is only light with God, and his light brightens up the darkness. *For to you darkness and light are the same:* some consider this line to be a gloss.

13 You created my inmost being;*[n]
    you knit me together in my mother's womb.[o]
14 I praise you because I am wonderfully made;
    awesome are your works,
    as I know very well.

15 My body was not hidden from you
    when I was being made in secret.
When I was woven together in the depths of
    the earth,
    you saw me in the womb.*
16 The sum total of my days*
    were all recorded in your book.*
My life was fashioned
    before it had come into being.[p]

17 How precious to me are your designs, O God!
    How vast in number they are!
18 If I were to attempt to count them,
    they would outnumber the grains of sand.[q]
When I awake,*
    I am still with you.

19 If only you would slay the wicked, O God,*
    and the bloodthirsty would leave me!*[r]

---

n Ps 119:73; Job 10:11; Dan 2:22.—o Job 1:21; 10:8; Eccl 11:5; Wis 7:1; Jer 1:5.—p Pss 69:29; 90:12; Mal 3:16.—q Ps 40:6; Job 11:7; 29:18; Rom 11:33.—r Pss 5:7; 119:115; Job 21:14; Isa 11:4.

139:13-18 God not only sees all and penetrates the inaccessible, but he is completely operative there, creating people and providing a purpose for all.

139:15 God knows all human beings intimately.

139:16-18 The text of these verses is obscure in several places.

139:16 *[They] were all recorded in your book:* an image familiar to the Prophets (see Neh 13:14; Dan 7:10; Mal 3:16) as well as the psalmists (see Pss 69:29; 109:13), which was reprised in the *Dies Irae* (the Sequence formerly used at Masses for the Dead): *Liber scriptus proferetur, in quo totum continetur:* "Lo, the book exactly worded, in which all has been recorded." See note on Ps 56:9.

139:18 *When I awake:* in this context, these words may express a glimpse of the resurrection on the part of the psalmist, as in Ps 17:15 (see note there).

139:19-24 God is all-holy and opposes the wicked, whom he punishes for their wrongdoing. He leads the psalmist and the righteous in the way of God ("the way to eternity": see Pss 1:6; 5:9; 73:18; 143:10; and note on Ps 16:9-11) and not in the way of idolaters (the "offensive way": see Ps 16:4; Isa 48:5).

139:19-22 See note on Ps 5:11 and introduction to Ps 35.

20 They blaspheme your name
   and treacherously rise up against you.*

21 Do I not hate those who hate you, O LORD,
   and loathe those who rise up against you?*s*

22 My hatred for them is unlimited;
   I regard them as my personal enemies.

23 Examine me, O God, and know my heart;*
   test me and understand my thoughts.*t*

24 See if I follow an evil way,
   and guide me on the way to eternity.

PSALM 140*

Prayer for Deliverance from the Snares
of the Wicked

1 For the director.* A psalm of David.

2 Deliver me, O LORD, from evildoers;*
   protect me from those who are violent,*u*

3 who plan evil schemes in their hearts*
   and stir up strife continually.

---

s Pss 26:5; 119:158; 2 Chr 19:2.—t Pss 17:3; 26:2; 1 Sam 16:7; Prov 17:3.—u Pss 17:13; 25:20; 59:2f; 71:4; 142:7.

139:20 *And . . . against you:* the Hebrew is uncertain here.
139:23 *Heart:* see note on Ps 4:8.
Ps 140 More than once already we have heard the voice of a suffering righteous person; he is the persecuted victim of the wicked, thieves, and calumniators. He calls down the vengeance of God on his enemies, while retaining his trust in the Lord. The state of the righteous and the harshness of the wicked are expressed in images often used. The opposition that Biblical prayer places between poverty and violence, humility and arrogance, simplicity and falsehood is inescapable. To recite this psalm is to bear human misfortune, to become poor.
   We can pray this psalm in the name of the Church who is continuously assailed by treacherous adversaries, both material and spiritual. Knowing the futility of earthly help, the Church takes her heavenly Spouse, Christ, as her sole refuge. He provides spiritual armor that is efficacious against the attacks of the enemy (see Eph 6:13-17; 1 Thes 5:8).
140:1 *For the director:* these words are thought to be a musical or liturgical notation.
140:2-6 The psalmist prays for deliverance from evildoers who sow discord with their speech and devise evil schemes, leading to anarchy and continuous agitation. Instead of following God's way, they have chosen the alternative way of the "father of lies" who was "a murderer from the beginning" (Jn 8:44).
140:3 *Hearts:* see note on Ps 4:8.

⁴ Their tongues* are as sharp as those of a serpent,ᵛ
    while the venom of vipers is on their lips.
                                        Selah

⁵ Guard me, O LORD, from the hands of the wicked;
    protect me from those who are violent,
    who are determined to cause my downfall.ʷ
⁶ The arrogant have set a hidden trap for me;
    they have spread out cords as a net,
    laying snares for me along the way.*
                                        Selah

⁷ I say to the LORD, "You are my God.*
    Listen, O LORD, to the voice of my suppli-
    cations."ˣ
⁸ O LORD, my God, my strong deliverer,
    you shield my head on the day of battle.
⁹ Do not grant the desires of the wicked, O LORD;
    do not permit their evil plots to succeed,
    or they will become proud.   *Selah*

¹⁰ Those who surround me raise up their heads;*
    let them be overwhelmed by the malice
    they threaten.
¹¹ May burning coals rain down on them;
    may they be flung down into the miry
    depths,
    never again to rise.*ʸ

---

v Pss 57:5; 58:5; 64:3; Rom 3:13; Jas 3:8.—w 5-6: Pss 28:2, 6; 36:12;
56:7; 57:7; Sir 12:16; Jer 18:22.—x Pss 16:2; 31:15.—y Pss 11:6; 21:10;
120:4; Gen 19:24; Num 16:31; Mt 3:10; Lk 12:49; Rev 20:15.

140:4 *Tongues:* see note on Ps 10:8.
140:6 The wicked seek to entrap the righteous as a fowler catches animals
with a snare, net, or trap (see Pss 31:5; 119:110; 141:10; 142:4; Mt 22:15; Lk
11:54). *Arrogant:* see note on Ps 31:24.
140:7-9 The psalmist seeks protection from the Lord of the Covenant, for he
alone is God and the Master of the world.
140:10-12 The psalmist's plea now becomes an imprecatory prayer, which is
an expression for God's just rule. Using metaphors for the divine judgment (burning coals and miry depths), he asks for redress (see note on Ps 5:11 and introduction to Ps 35).
140:11 Allusion to Sodom (see Gen 19) and Dathan (see Num 16). See also Pss
11:6; 36:13; 55:24; 141:10.

¹² Do not permit slanderers to find rest in the
    land;

    may evil hunt the violent to their death.

¹³ I know that the LORD secures justice for the
    poor*

    and upholds the cause of the needy.

¹⁴ Then the upright will give thanks to your name,

    and the righteous will dwell in your pres-
    ence.^z

PSALM 141*

Prayer for Protection against Evildoers

¹ A psalm of David.

O LORD, I call to you; come quickly to my aid;*
    listen to my plea when I call out to you.

² May my prayer be like incense* before you,
    the lifting up of my hands like the evening
    sacrifice.^a

---

z Pss 11:7; 16:11; 17:15; 138:2.—a Pss 28:2; 63:5; 134:2; Ex 30:8; Lev
2:2; Num 28:4; Lk 1:9; 1 Tim 2:8; Rev 5:8; 8:3.

140:13-14 The psalmist is confident that the Lord, the just Judge (see Pss
7:9f; 9:5), will vindicate the righteous poor (see notes on Pss 22:27 and 34:7),
who will then praise his name (see note on Ps 7:18) and live in his presence (see
notes on Pss 23:5-6 and 27:4).

Ps 141 Surrounded by the wicked who persecute him in order to drag him with
them into impiety, the psalmist offers up an evening prayer, matching the morning prayer referred to in Ps 5:4. The poet begs God to protect him against every
defection, to help him refuse all connivance with the wicked, and to enable him
ultimately to escape their plots against him.

  This psalm is a reminder to us that, impelled by the devil, our greatest enemy,
the world hates us because we are not of the world (see Jn 15:19; 17:14). By
every available means, it strives to snatch us away from Christ to serve the devil.
Aware of our weakness, we should "pray so that [we] may not enter into temptation" (Mk 14:38), reciting this psalm when necessary.

141:1-2 The psalmist is in a precarious position, so he hopes his prayer for
help will be like a pleasing offering before the Lord.

141:2 *Incense:* literally, "smoke," i.e., the fragrant fumes that wafted from the
altar at the daily burning of sacrificial animals or aromatic spices. *The lifting up
of my hands:* a symbol of dependence on and praise of the Lord (see Pss 28:2;
63:5; 1 Tim 2:8).

3 Set a guard over my mouth, O LORD;*
  keep watch over the door of my lips.[b]
4 Do not permit my heart to be drawn to evil,
  or to the pursuit of wicked deeds
 in the company of those who do evil;
  let me not share in their corruption.

5 If a righteous man strikes me, I regard it as
    kindness;*
  if he rebukes me, it is oil on my head.*[c]
 But never let the oil of the wicked anoint my
    head,
  for my prayer is always opposed to their
    evil deeds.

6 When their leaders are flung down in stony
    places,*
  they will learn that my prayers were heard.
7 As the soil is shattered when the ground is
    plowed,
  so our bones are scattered at the mouth of
    the netherworld.

8 But my eyes are turned to you, O Lord GOD;*
  in you I seek refuge;
  do not take my life away.[d]

---

b Pss 12:3; 34:14; Sir 22:27; Jas 1:26; 3:8.—c Ps 23:5; Ex 29:7; Prov 9:8; 19:25; 25:12; Eccl 7:5.—d Pss 2:12; 11:1; 25:15; 123:1-2.

141:3-4 The psalmist, like the sages, carefully watches over his heart so as not to give in to sins of speech or action, for he knows that the wicked use their tongues for destruction (see Ps 140:4) while the righteous express love and fidelity (see Ps 15:2f). He begs the Lord to keep his heart from sin and temptation so that he may do God's will (see Pss 119:10, 36, 133). *Let me not share in their corruption:* literally, "let me not eat of their delicacies."
141:5-7 The psalmist delineates the fate of evil rulers at God's hands, and hopes that the shock may bring their followers to their senses.
141:5 Oil was poured on the head in a gesture of welcome and hospitality (see Lk 7:46).
141:6-7 The text of these verses is obscure and their meaning uncertain. As it stands here, the meaning of v. 7 may be: As a farmer breaks up the soil and brings up the rocks, so the bones of the wicked will be scattered without a decent burial (see Ps 79:2-3).
141:8-10 The psalmist prays for deliverance and for vindication, for he remains with eyes of faith fixed on the Lord (see Ps 25:15).

⁹ Keep me safe from the traps they have laid for
me,
    from the snares of evildoers.*e*
¹⁰ Let the wicked tumble into their own nets all
together
    while I pass by unharmed.*

PSALM 142*

Prayer in Time of Abandonment

¹ A *maskil** of David. When he was in the cave. A prayer.

² I cry out to the LORD with my plea;*
    I entreat the LORD to grant me mercy.
³ Before him I pour out my complaint
    and tell my troubles in his presence.
⁴ No matter how faint my spirit is within me,*
    you are there to guide my steps.*f*

---

e Pss 38:13; 64:6; 140:5; 142:4.—f Pss 6:3; 77:4; 84:3; 88:5; 143:4, 7; Jer 8:18; Lam 1:22.

141:10 God's vindication comes in the form of retribution; the schemes of the wicked will recoil upon them (see note on Ps 5:11 and introduction to Ps 35).

Ps 142 The psalmist issues a prayer for deliverance from powerful enemies. Whether he is King David (see 1 Sam 22:10) or someone unknown, he has been trodden upon by everyone and is undergoing the agony and passion of so many others. He is also an image of Christ, isolated and suffering without protest.

Often we too find ourselves exhausted on our journey through life, strewn as it is with many snares. For some, it is social or political oppression that prevents us from leading a fully human and Christian existence. For others, religious persecution itself intervenes to restrain or destroy our goods and freedom. Upon each one, our spiritual enemies (the world and the devil) impose a continuous struggle, both fierce and treacherous, that each must wage practically without human help. In these struggles, we can make use of this psalm to direct to God an ardent and confident appeal.

142:1 *Maskil:* see introduction to Ps 32; for the words *When he was in the cave,* see Ps 57:1; 1 Sam 22:10; 24:1f.

142:2-3 The psalmist uses the formal third person (customary when addressing kings) to pour out his troubles to God.

142:4-5 The psalmist is at the point of spiritual exhaustion (see Pss 76:13; 77:3; 143:4; Jon 2:8), and only God can help for he knows the faithful's destiny, his present and future life (see Ps 139:24). Yet the Lord is not present to help him along this path of his enemies, which is filled with snares. *My right:* i.e., the place where one's witness or legal counsel stood (see Pss 16:8; 109:31; 110:5; 121:5).

Along the path on which I travel*[g]
   they have hidden a trap for me.[h]
5 I look to my right,
   but there is no friend who knows me.
There is no refuge available to me;
   no one cares whether I live or perish.*[i]

6 I cry out to you, O LORD;*
   I say, "You are my refuge,[j]
   my portion in the land of the living."*[k]
7 Listen to my plea for help,
   for I am in desperate straits.

Rescue me from those who seek to persecute
   me,
   for they are too strong for me.*[l]
8 Set me free from my prison,*
   so that I may praise your name.
Then the righteous will assemble around me
   because of your great generosity to me.

---

g Ps 139:24.—h Ps 141:9.—i Pss 16:8; 73:23; 121:5; Jer 30:17.—j Pss
46:2; 91:2, 9.—k Pss 16:5; 27:13; 116:9; Deut 32:9; Isa 38:11.—l Pss 17:1;
25:20; 79:8; Jer 31:11.

142:4c *Along the path on which I travel:* the present path on which the
psalmist is traveling, i.e., the path of his opponents, which is covered with such
snares as to fill him with dread, in contrast to the path of the Lord, which leads
to such salvation as to fill him with hope (vv. 7-8).

142:5 *No one cares whether I live or perish:* the psalmist is like an outcast for
whom no one cares and whom no one comes forward to protect. He is alone and
extremely vulnerable.

142:6-8 The psalmist reiterates his distress and his plea for deliverance, confessing that the Lord is his refuge (see Ps 91:2; Jer 17:17) and his hope ("my portion in the land of the living": see Pss 16:5; 73:26; 119:57; Lam 3:24). In turn, he
will give thanks for his deliverance (see note on Ps 7:18), and the righteous will
rejoice in the Lord with him (see Pss 22:25; 34:3; 64:10; 107:42).

142:6 Hence, the psalmist cries out to the Lord for help. The Lord is his Covenant God; he most of all should be solicitous for his servant. *In the land of the
living:* i.e., here below, during his earthly life (see Ps 27:13).

142:7 The enemies of the psalmist are too strong for him. Unless the Lord
comes to his aid, the afflicted man is lost. There is no one else who can save him.

142:8 *Prison:* a word that may denote actual imprisonment or may be a
metaphor for the psalmist's desperate plight characterized by adversity and isolation (see Ps 107:10; Isa 42:7). *Assemble around me:* the Greek and Syriac
translate this phrase as "hope [or wait] around me" (see Job 36:2). All the
friends of God are united in praise and joy (see Pss 22:26; 34:4; 64:11; 107:42).

PSALM 143*

Prayer of a Penitent in Distress

[1] A psalm of David.

O Lord, hear my prayer,*
    incline your ear to my supplications.
In your faithfulness respond to me
    with your righteousness.
[2] Do not subject your servant to your judgment,[m]
    for no one living is righteous before you.*

[3] An enemy has stalked me unrelentingly*
    and crushed me into the ground;[n]
he has left me to live in darkness
    like those long dead.*[o]
[4] My spirit is faint within me,
    and my heart* has succumbed to fear.[p]

---

m Ps 14:3; Job 4:17; Eccl 7:20; Rom 3:20.—n Ps 7:6; 130:3; Job 9:2; 14:3f; 15:14; Eccl 7:20.—o Ps 107:10; Lam 3:6; Mic 7:8.—p Pss 30:8; 142:4; Job 17:1.

Ps 143 This is the seventh and last of the Penitential Psalms (Pss 6; 32; 38; 51; 102; 130; 143), probably because of v. 2, with its admission of universal guilt, the only reference to sin and forgiveness in it. Throughout the Psalter, amid praise and joy, there is the lament of the poor person who is dependent on God for everything. Here is the last pressing supplication of the sufferer who cannot despair of God, of his love and his righteousness. The true Israel, the community of the poor of the Lord, understood it even unto suffering. As Paul indicates (Rom 3:20ff), no one merits to be delivered from evil, not even the person who observes the Law; one can only rely on the Lord's unfailing love for human beings. Those who truly pray will experience the Lord's deliverance.

There are many occasions on which we too can pray this simple and ardent psalm to implore divine aid. The demons and all those whom they incite never cease to threaten us, either in our material sustenance or in our physical and spiritual life.

143:1-2 The psalmist cries out to God to have mercy because of his faithfulness and righteousness, for he knows that God's judgment could find him guilty of sin and condemn him to remain afflicted (see Ps 130:3).

143:2 *For no one living is righteous before you:* this text is used in Rom 3:20 (see Pss 51:7; 130:3; Job 9:2; 14:3f; 15:14; Eccl 7:20).

143:3-6 The psalmist sketches the distress he suffers and is encouraged by the memory of God's past acts of deliverance.

143:3 The same images are found in Ps 7:6; Lam 3:6; Mic 7:8. *Darkness:* see note on Ps 27:1.

143:4 *Heart:* see note on Ps 4:8.

5 I remember the days of old,
    reflecting on all your actions[q]
    and meditating on the works of your hands.*
6 I stretch out my hands* to you;
    my soul thirsts for you like a parched land.[r]
                      Selah

7 Answer me quickly, O LORD,*
    for my spirit grows faint.
Do not hide your face from me
    or I will be like those who go down to the
      pit.*[s]

8 At dawn* let me experience your kindness,
    for in you I place my trust.
Show me the path I must walk,
    for to you I lift up my soul.[t]

9 Deliver me from my enemies, O LORD,
    for in you I seek refuge.
10 Teach me to do your will,
    for you are my God.*
Let your gracious Spirit lead me
    along a level path.

11 For your name's sake,* O LORD, preserve my
      life;
    in your righteousness deliver me from dis-
      tress.

---

q Ps 77:6, 12f; Gen 24:63.—r Pss 42:3; 63:2; Ex 9:29.—s Pss 27:9; 28:1;
30:4; 88:5; Prov 1:12.—t Pss 6:4; 17:15; 25:4; 27:11; 86:11; 119:12, 35.

143:5 See Pss 42:5; 77:6, 12f.
143:6 *Stretch out my hands:* in supplication (see Pss 44:21; 88:10; Ex 9:29).
Soul: see note on Ps 6:4. *Thirsts for you:* see Ps 63:2.
143:7-12 The psalmist here appends a mosaic of prayers for deliverance,
guidance, and commitment to the Lord.
143:7 See similar phrases in Pss 10:1; 28:1; 69:18; 84:3; 88:5; 102:3; 141:1.
143:8 *At dawn:* see introduction to Ps 57 and note on Ps 57:9; see also Pss
17:15; 90:14; 101:8; 108:3. *Kindness:* see note on Ps 6:5. *I lift up my soul:* see
Pss 25:1; 27:8; 32:6; 33:22; 86:4.
143:10 *Teach me . . . my God:* see Pss 25:4f; 118:28. *Spirit:* the divine Spirit
was regarded as a force and not yet as a person (see Ps 51:13; Neh 9:20; Ezek
36:27). *Lead . . . path:* see note on Ps 26:12 (see also Pss 27:11; 139:24).
143:11 *For your name's sake:* see Ps 25:11. *Deliver me from distress:* see Pss
31:5; 119:25, 88; 142:8.

¹² In your kindness, destroy my enemies,
       and annihilate all those who oppress me,
       for I am your servant.*ᵘ

PSALM 144*

Prayer for Victory and Peace

¹ Of David.

* Blessed be the LORD,* my Rock,
       who trains my hands for war
       and my fingers for battle.
² You are my safeguard and my fortress,
       my stronghold and my deliverer,
   my shield in whom I take refuge,
       the one who subdues nations under me.*

³ O LORD, what is man that you care for him,ᵛ
       or the son of man that you think of him?*

---

u Pss 8:3; 54:7; 116:16.—v Ps 8:5; Job 7:17; Heb 2:6.

143:12 The psalmist calls upon the Lord to deal righteously with his adversaries, reflecting a hope that is expressed in the imprecatory psalms (see note on Ps 5:11 and introduction to Ps 35; see also Ps 54:5). *Kindness:* see note on Ps 6:5.

Ps 144 This psalm combines two compositions that are quite different in rhythm and tone. The first is suited to a royal liturgy and is drawn largely from Ps 18, a canticle of the king's victories. The second part was originally a kind of fine painting to illustrate a time of prosperity. By the time of the final redaction of the psalm, the monarchy had disappeared, and the two compositions were combined into a hymn of the Messianic Hope.

   A new David will come, the true Messiah upon whom will rest the blessing of God for the benefit of the whole community. He will inaugurate an era of happiness and peace. The ancient images are nothing more than starting points, giving color and life to this prayer of expectation. The essential point is to preserve the hope of a humanity finally filled with the joy of God. It is in this vein that we can pray it with Christ in mind.

144:1-4 In jubilant language the psalmist praises God as the Redeemer-King who cares for him and watches over him, because he has the inherent weakness of all humans and is in need of help.

144:1 *Blessed be the LORD:* the psalm begins with the prayer of David in 1 Chr 29:10 and the prayers in Tob 3:11; 8:5, 15; 13:1 (see Dan 3:26; Lk 1:68; Eph 1:3). *My Rock . . . for battle:* see Ps 18:47, 35.

144:2 This verse reflects Ps 18:3, 48. *My safeguard:* literally, "my unfailing kindness" (see note on Ps 6:5).

144:3 This verse reflects Ps 8:5.

4 Man is nothing more than a breath;
  his days are like a fleeting shadow.*w

5 Part the heavens, O LORD, and descend;*
  touch the mountains so that they smoke.*x

6 Flash forth lightning bolts and scatter my foes;
  rout them with your arrows.*

7 Reach forth your hand from on high;
  deliver me and rescue me
from the mighty waters
  and from the power of foreign foes*

8 whose mouths utter lies*
  and whose right hands are raised to swear
    to untruths.

9 I will sing a new song to you, my God;*
  on a ten-stringed lyre I will play music for
    you.*y

10 You grant victory to kings
  and deliverance to your servant David
    from the cruel sword.*z

---

w Pss 39:6-7; 62:10; 90:9-10; Job 7:16; 14:2; Eccl 6:12; Wis 2:5.—x Ps 18:10; Isa 64:1.—y Pss 33:2-3; 92:4; 144:9.—z Ps 18:51; 2 Sam 8:14.

144:4 This verse is close to Ps 39:6-7 (see also Job 14:2).

144:5-8 The psalmist calls upon God to become involved and deliver him, to come as the Divine Warrior as he did at Sinai. There he came accompanied by volcanic eruption, thunder, and lightning to save his people (see Ex 19:11, 18f).

144:5 This verse takes up Ps 18:10 and Ps 104:32. It also reveals the anxious expectation of Israel, the prey of persecutors and haunted by the hope of a divine intervention.

144:6 See Ps 18:15. *Arrows:* i.e., the Lord's lightning that serves to rout the enemies and take away their power.

144:7 See Ps 18:17, 46. *Hand:* symbolic of the Lord's power (see Ps 18:17), which is capable of rescuing the psalmist out of the "mighty waters" into which he is sinking, i.e., out of the clutches of foreigners. For the Lord, who has subdued the stormy seas (see Ps 65:8; Gen 1:2), can certainly overpower stormy "foreign foes" (see Isa 56:6; 61:5).

144:8 The enemies are completely opposed to the law of God and filled with lies, deceit, and wickedness. *Mouths utter lies:* see note on Ps 5:10. *Right hands are raised to swear to untruths:* see Ezr 10:19; see also Ps 106:26; Ex 6:8; Deut 32:40).

144:9-10 The psalmist makes a vow to praise the Lord for the expected victory.

144:9 This verse is close to Ps 33:2f (see Pss 40:4; 98:1; 149:1).

144:10 This verse takes up the conclusion of Ps 18. "My servant David" became a Messianic title (see Jer 33:21; Ezek 34:23ff; 37:24); it is found again in Pss 78:70; 89:4, 21).

11 Deliver me and rescue me
    from the hands of foreign foes
  whose mouths utter lies
    and whose right hands are raised to swear
      to untruths.*

12 May our sons in their youth*
    be like carefully nurtured plants,
  and may our daughters be like pillars
    designed to adorn a palace.*a
13 May our barns be filled
    with every kind of crop.

  May our sheep increase by thousands,
    by tens of thousands in our fields,*
14   and may our cattle be well fed.*
  May there be no breach in our walls,
    no going into exile,
    no cries of distress in our streets.b

15 Blessed are the people for whom this is true;
    blessed are the people whose God is the
      LORD.*c

---

a Pss 12:3; 36:4; 106:26; 128:3; Job 42:14-15.—b Lev 26:6; Prov 14:4; Isa 24:11; 65:19; Jer 14:2-3.—c Pss 29:11; 33:12; Deut 28:3.

144:11 The psalmist repeats the prayer in vv. 7-8, probably as an introduction to vv. 12-15.

144:12-15 The psalmist prays for the people, asking the Lord to bless their children, their lives, and their livelihoods. When the enemies are defeated, the rule of the Lord will reach its height and the Messianic blessings will pour in upon his people and upon the land. The blessings are described in terms that are understandable to a people whose main occupation was agriculture and cattle raising. Even the fortified cities will receive a Messianic blessing, that of invincibility.

144:12 The Hebrew text of this verse is obscure and its meaning uncertain. It may refer to the great strength of the sons and the physical beauty of the daughters.

144:13 Material abundance is a gift of God (see Lev 26:5; Deut 7:13).

144:14 *May our cattle be well fed:* other possible translations are: "may our oxen be heavy with flesh" or "may our oxen be heavy with young" or "may our chieftains be firmly established."

144:15 Blessed are the people who experience the Lord's ability to save, protect, and bless. *Blessed:* see note on Ps 1:1.

PSALM 145*

Praise of the Divine Majesty

1 Praise. Of David.

I will extol you, my God and King;*
    I will bless your name forever and ever.*
2 Every day I will bless you[d]
    and praise your name forever and ever.*

3 Great is the LORD and worthy of the highest
        praise;*
    no one can even begin to comprehend his
        greatness.*[e]
4 Each generation will praise your works to the
        next[f]
    and proclaim your mighty deeds.*

---

d Pss 34:1; 68:19; 71:8; Isa 25:1; 26:8.—e Pss 48:2; 95:3; 96:4; 2 Sam 22:4; Job 5:9; 36:26.—f Pss 22:31-32; 48:14-15; 71:18; 78:4; Ex 10:2; Deut 4:9; 11:19.

Ps 145 This "acrostic" psalm (see p. 23) is a hymn to God the Great King. It is not original, for the psalmist strings together his verses in the order of the alphabet and takes the passages from several other psalms. The cantors of Israel were not reluctant to dip into the common treasury of sacred chant to celebrate God's praise with the same words and the same phrases. But the repetition or the acclamation of certain terms also enables one to express the ardor of a conviction, which is the case here. By means of the words *kingdom, power, majesty, name, works, mighty deeds, righteousness, faithfulness, compassion, love,* and *truth,* the psalm exalts above all the God of the Covenant. It then proclaims his benevolence that is manifested in the help, subsistence, and salvation accorded in some manner to all who invoke him. Thus, the cantor acknowledges God's presence in the world, in history, and in life.
    We can pray this psalm to bless, praise, and extol the heavenly Father in his perfections and prodigious works. But we can also recite it in honor of Christ, who shares fully in the perfections (see Col 1:15, 19; Heb 1:3) and works of his Father (see Jn 5:19).
    145:1-2 The psalmist calls for praise of God the Great King. This praise is to be given unceasingly and forever.
    145:1 See Pss 30:2; 44:5; 71:14. *Praise your name:* see note on Ps 5:12.
    145:2 See Pss 34:2; 68:20; 71:14; 146:2. This verse has been incorporated into the *Te Deum,* the great prayer of Christian praise to the Trinity.
    145:3-7 The psalmist specifies the reason for praising God: his mighty deeds, which reveal his greatness and goodness. The same two themes are combined in Pss 86:10, 17; 135:3, 5.
    145:3 See Pss 48:2; 96:3f; Job 36:26.
    145:4 See Pss 71:17; 78:4; Isa 38:19. Salvation history is transmitted from generation to generation by the proclamation of God's mighty deeds and wonderful works (see Ps 22:31f). *Your works:* of creation, providence, and redemption.

⁵ People will proclaim the glorious splendor of
   your majesty,
   and I will meditate on your wonderful
   works.*g*

⁶ They will speak of the power of your awesome deeds,
   and I will relate your greatness.*h*

⁷ They will celebrate your abundant goodness
   and sing joyfully of your saving justice.

⁸ The LORD is gracious and merciful,*
   slow to anger and abounding in kindness.**i*

⁹ The LORD is good to all,
   showing compassion to every creature.*j*

¹⁰ All your creatures praise you,* O LORD,
   and all your saints bless you.*k*

¹¹ They relate the glory of your kingdom
   and tell of all your power.*

¹² They make known to all people your mighty
   deeds
   and the glorious majesty of your kingdom.*l*

¹³ Your kingdom will last forever,
   and your dominion will endure throughout
   all generations.*

---

g Pss 96:3; 105:2; 148:13.—h Pss 66:3; 78:4.—i Pss 86:5, 15; 103:8; Ex
34:6f; Num 14:18; Wis 1:13f; Sir 2:11; Isa 63:7.—j Ps 103:13; Wis 1:13-14;
11:24; Mt 19:17.—k Ps 8:7; Dan 3:57.—l Pss 10:16; 102:13; 146:10; Deut
7:9; Tob 13:6ff; Lam 5:19; Dan 3:100; 1 Tim 1:17; Rev 11:15.

145:8-13b Now the psalmist moves to praise God because of his divine attributes, e.g., compassion and love. These attributes lead all his works, including
the "saints," to give him thanks for the expressions of his "glory," "power," and
"kingdom."

145:8 See Pss 86:15; 103:8, 13; Ex 34:6f; Num 14:18; Wis 1:13f; Isa 63:7.

145:10 *All your creatures praise you:* see note on Ps 65:14. *Saints:* see notes
on Pss 4:4 and 34:10.

145:11 See Ps 93:1; 1 Chr 29:11.

145:13 Text cited in Dan 3:100; 4:31, and applied to Christ the King. See Ps
102:13; Tob 13:6ff; Dan 7:14; 1 Tim 1:17; Rev 11:15.

The LORD is faithful in all his promises*
    and kind* in all his deeds.
14 The Lord supports all those who are falling
    and raises up all who are bowed down.*[m]

15 The eyes of all look hopefully to you,
        and you give them their food at the right
        time.[n]
16 You open your hand
        and satisfy the needs of every living crea-
        ture.*

17 The LORD is righteous in all his ways*
    and merciful in everything he does.*[o]
18 The LORD is near to all who call out to him,
    to all who call out to him sincerely.*[p]

19 He satisfies the desires of all who fear him;
    he hears their cry and saves them.*[q]
20 The LORD watches over all who love him,
        but he will completely destroy all the
        wicked.*[r]

21 May my mouth declare the praise of the LORD,
        and may every creature* bless his holy
        name
    forever and ever.[s]

---

m Pss 37:17; 94:18; 146:8.—n Pss 104:27-28; 136:25; Gen 1:30; Mt 6:25-34.—o Deut 32:4; Ezr 9:15.—p Deut 4:7; Isa 55:6; 58:9; Jer 29:13.—q Pss 20:4; 34:18; 85:10.—r Pss 1:6; 34:18; 91:4; 105:35; 139:19; Jdg 5:31.—s Ps 71:8; Sir 39:35.

145:13c-16 The psalmist calls for praise of God because of the Lord's faithfulness to the Covenant. The first two lines (v. 13c) are not in the Hebrew; they are in the Dead Sea Scrolls and the Septuagint.
145:13d *Kind:* see note on Ps 6:5.
145:14 See Pss 94:18; 146:8.
145:16 See Ps 104:27f; Mt 6:25-34.
145:17-21 The psalmist calls upon all creatures to praise God for his righteous acts—acts of restoration, redemption, and vindication.
145:17 See Deut 32:4.
145:18 See Deut 4:7; Isa 55:6; 58:9; Jer 29:13.
145:19 See Pss 20:4; 34:18; 85:10.
145:20 See Pss 34:18; 91:14; 104:35; 139:19; Jdg 5:31.
145:21 *Every creature:* literally, "all flesh."

THE CONCLUDING HALLEL—Ps 146–150*

PSALM 146*

Trust in God, Creator and Redeemer

¹ Alleluia.*

Praise the LORD, O my soul.*
² 　I will praise the LORD as long as I live;*t*
　　I will sing praise to my God throughout my
　　　　life.*

³ Do not place your trust in princes,
　　in mortal men who have no power to save.*u*
⁴ When the spirit departs, they return to the
　　　earth;
　　on that very day all their plans come to
　　　naught.*v*

---

t Pss 7:18; 63:5; 103:1; 104:33; 105:2.—u Pss 60:13; 108:13; 118:8-9;
Isa 2:22.—v Pss 90:3; 104:29; Gen 3:19; 1 Mac 2:63; Job 34:14-15; Eccl
3:20; Sir 40:11; Isa 2:22; 1 Cor 2:6.

Pss 146—150 The Concluding Hallel (see introduction to Pss 113—118).
After all the prayers and praises of the Psalter, we are now at the end; all the instruments of creation and all the voices of human beings enter into a great cho-
rus, a symphony destined never to end. The Psalms are a foretaste of and prelude
to the acclamations of eternity.

Ps 146 The long procession of the unhappy and the persecuted has wound its
way through the Psalter, endlessly repeating their supplications. This time, their
prayer takes the form of a hymn of happiness and security. How uncertain is the
help of the mighty! God alone truly frees us of every anxiety.

Inaugurating the third Hallel and composed of reminiscences, this hymn sings of
what the Prophets promised (see Isa 29:18f; 49:9; 61:1), promises whose fulfillment
Jesus proclaims (see Lk 4:16-21). "The blind receive their sight, the lame walk,
those who have leprosy are cured, the deaf hear, the dead are raised to life, and the
poor have the good news proclaimed to them" (Mt 11:5)—such is the kingdom that
comes; it inaugurates a new time, that of peace. Accordingly, like the next four
psalms, it is framed with "Alleluia" or "Hallelujah" ("Praise [or bless] the LORD").

We can pray this psalm in honor of the heavenly Father but also in honor of
Christ "[whom] God exalted . . . at his right hand as leader and Savior so that he
might grant repentance and forgiveness of sins to Israel" (Acts 5:31).

146:1-4 The psalmist calls upon his people to praise and trust the Lord, for
human beings are unable to provide salvation owing to their mortality.

146:1 The Septuagint and Vulgate attribute this psalm to the prophets Haggai
and Zechariah. *Soul:* see note on Ps 6:4.

146:2 Life is for the purpose of praising the Lord (see Pss 103:1; 104:33).

146:4 See Pss 90:3; 104:29; Eccl 9:5; 12:7; Isa 2:22.

5 Blessed is he whose help is the God of
    Jacob,*
  whose hope is in the LORD, his God,*
6 the Maker of heaven and earth,
    the sea, and everything in them—
    the one who keeps faith forever.*w
7 He grants justice to the oppressed*x
    and gives bread to the hungry.

The LORD releases prisoners y
8   and opens the eyes of those who cannot see.*
The LORD lifts up those who are bowed down;
    the LORD loves the righteous.z
9 The LORD watches over the stranger
    and sustains the fatherless and the widow,*
    but he blocks the way of the wicked.a

10 The LORD will reign forever,*
    your God, O Zion, for all generations.b

Alleluia.

---

w Pss 115:15; 121:2; 124:8; Ex 20:11; Deut 7:9; Jer 32:17; Acts 14:15;
Rev 14:7.—x Ps 103:6.—y Pss 68:7; 107:9; 145:15; Isa 49:9; 61:1.—z Ps
145:14; Prov 20:12.—a Ps 68:6; Ex 22:22; Deut 10:18.—b Ps 145:13; Ex
15:18; Lam 5:19; Rev 11:15.

146:5-10 The psalmist identifies this Lord as the "God of Jacob," the Covenant
God who is Creator and Lord over all, Sustainer and Provider, the Righteous One
who dispenses justice to both the godly and the wicked, and the Great King who
reigns forever.
  146:5 See Ps 2:12; Deut 33:29; Jer 17:7. *God of Jacob:* the God of Zion (see v.
10 below), whose kingship is established (see Ps 47:8; 48:2), and who blesses
those who trust in him (see Ps 84:13).
  146:6 The Lord is faithful, using his power to control creation, including the
unruly sea, and to bless his creatures (see Ps 107:8f) with his kindness (see note
on Ps 6:5). *Maker of heaven and earth:* see Pss 121:2 and note; 124:8; Ex 20:11;
Jer 32:17; Acts 14:15.
  146:7 *He grants justice to the oppressed:* see Ps 103:6; Deut 7:9. *The LORD releases prisoners:* see Ps 68:7; Isa 49:9; 61:1.
  146:8 *Opens the eyes of those who cannot see:* see Isa 35:5; Bar 6:36; Mt 9:30;
Jn 9:1ff; Acts 26:18. *Lifts up those . . . bowed down:* see Ps 145:14; Lk 13:12.
  146:9 *Watches over the stranger . . . the fatherless and the widow:* see Ps
68:6; Ex 22:21. *Blocks the way of the wicked:* see Pss 11:6; 147:6; Job 5:12.
  146:10 The Lord is the Great King who has promised to dwell with his people
and to deliver them (see Pss 29:10; 132:13-15; Ex 15:17). *The LORD will reign forever:* see Ps 145:13; Ex 15:18.

PSALM 147*

Hymn to the City of God

[1] Alleluia.

How good it is to sing praises to our God;*c
    how pleasant it is to give him fitting praise.*

[2] The LORD restores Jerusalem
    and gathers together the dispersed people
      of Israel.*d
[3] He heals the brokenhearted
    and bandages their wounds.*e

[4] He fixes the number of the stars
    and assigns a name to each.*f

---

c Pss 33:1; 92:2; 135:3.—d Ps 51:20; 106:47; Isa 11:12; 56:8; Jer 31:10.—e Ps 34:18; Num 12:13; Job 5:18; Isa 30:26; 61:1; Jer 33:6; Ezek 34:16.—f Gen 15:5; Isa 40:26; Bar 3:34f.

Ps 147 Three times the psalmist sounds the invitation to praise, and three times he acclaims the almighty God. Immense is his power deployed throughout the universe, and without measure is his benevolence for his people. He rebuilds Jerusalem, leads captives back to freedom, and reveals his Law. Yet the author of wonders in nature and the liberator of his people is a God who takes pleasure in the lowly. "He will wipe every tear from their eyes" (Rev 21:4)—such will be the grace of the Almighty in the new Jerusalem (see Isa chs. 60 and 62).

In the Septuagint and Vulgate this psalm is divided into two (147:1-11 = Ps 146; 147:12-20 = Ps 147) and attributed to the prophets Haggai and Zechariah. It contains many reminiscences of Isaiah, Job, and Psalms.

We can pray this psalm while keeping in mind that the restoration of Jerusalem and Israel after the disaster of 587 and the Babylonian Captivity constitutes a wonderful work of God. However, it is only a pale image of a more beautiful work of restoration that the heavenly Father accomplishes through Christ in building his Church.

147:1-6 The psalmist enumerates the reasons why it is good to praise the Lord: the restoration that he has worked for his people in accord with his word by rebuilding Jerusalem and bringing back the exiles; his concern for all creation; and his redemption, i.e., the vindication of his people.

147:1 See Ps 92:2 and note on Ps 135:3.

147:2 See Deut 30:3f; Isa 11:12; 56:8; Jer 31:10; Dan 9:25.

147:3 See Job 5:18; Isa 30:26; 61:1; Jer 33:6; Ezek 34:16. *Brokenhearted*: e.g., those in exile (see Ps 137) and those who returned from exile and attempted to rebuild the walls of Jerusalem (see Neh 2:17-20; 4:1-23).

147:4 See Gen 15:5; Isa 40:26; Bar 3:34f. In this connection, scholars cite the Wisdom of Ahiqar (VIII, 116): "Numerous are the stars of heaven, and no one knows their names."

5 Great is our LORD and awesome in power;
  his wisdom is without limit.*g

6 The LORD sustains the poor
  but humbles the wicked in the dust.*h

7 Offer songs of thanksgiving to the LORD;*
  play the lyre in honor of our God.i

8 He veils the heavens with clouds,
  supplies the earth with rain,
  and makes the hills sprout with grass.*j

9 He provides food for the animals
  and for the young ravens when they call.*k

10 He takes no pleasure in the strength of the
    horse,*
  or delight in the fleetness of a runner.l

11 The LORD takes pleasure in those who fear him,
  those who place their hope in his kindness.

12 Praise the Lord, O Jerusalem!*
  Glorify your God, O Zion!

13 For he strengthens the bars of your gates
  and blesses your children within you.*m

14 He brings peace to your borders
  and fills you with the finest of wheat.*n

---

g Ps 48:2; Jud 16:13; Isa 40:28; Jer 51:15.—h Pss 37:9-10; 146:9; 1 Sam 2:7-8.—i Pss 30:5; 71:22.—j Ps 104:13f; Deut 11:14f; 2 Sam 1:21; Job 5:10; Jer 14:22; Joel 2:23.—k Ps 104:27-28; Job 38:41; Mt 6:26.—l Pss 20:8f; 33:16-18.—m Pss 48:14; 128:5.—n Ps 81:17; Lev 26:6.

147:5 See Ps 48:2; Job 36:22, 26; Isa 40:28; Jer 51:15.
147:6 See Pss 37:9-10; 145:20; 146:9; 1 Sam 2:7f; Job 5:11; Lk 1:52.
147:7-11 God is owed praise because he is the Great King over his creation, sustaining all that he has made, both the creatures in the heavens and the creatures on earth. He wants people to trust in him rather than in themselves.
147:8 See Pss 104:10-14, 27f; Job 5:9f; Jer 14:22; Joel 2:23.
147:9 See Job 38:41; Mt 6:26. *When they call:* the Lord feeds the birds, especially the ravens, whose cawing resembles a call for food (see Mt 6:26-30).
147:10-11 Arrogant reliance on one's own natural ability is both futile (see Am 2:14f) and displeasing to God, who comes to the aid of those who trust only in him (see Pss 20:8f; 33:16-18; Eccl 9:11; Mal 3:16f). *Kindness:* see note on Ps 6:5.
147:12-18 The psalmist stresses that God is to be praised because he has brought about restoration, security, peace, and prosperity, for he alone commands the forces of nature.
147:13 See Pss 48:14; 128:5; Isa 65:18f; Jer 33:10f.
147:14 See Ps 81:17 and note; Lev 26:6.

15 He sends a command to the earth;
his word runs with utmost speed.[o]
16 He gives the snow like wool
and scatters the frost like ashes.*[p]
17 He hurls down his hail like crumbs;
who can withstand his cold?*
18 He sends his word, and the ice melts;
he stirs up his breezes, and the waters flow.
19 He has revealed his word to Jacob,*[q]
his decrees and his judgments to Israel.
20 He has not done this for the other nations;
they are not aware of his judgments.

Alleluia.

PSALM 148*

Song of the Universe

1 Alleluia.

Praise the LORD from the heavens;*
offer praise to him in the heights!

---

o Pss 33:9; 107:20; 148:5; Isa 55:10-11.—p 16-17: Ps 148:8; Job 6:16; 37:10; 38:22.—q 19-20: Ps 78:5; Deut 4:7-8; 33:3-4; Jos 1:8; 2 Ki 22:8; Bar 3:37; Mal 3:23; Rom 3:2; 9:4.

147:16 See Job 37:6, 10.

147:17 See Job 6:16; 37:10; 38:22.

147:19-20 Finally, God is to be praised because he has given his people his word of revelation, making known his saving plan (see Ps 50:16f; Deut 33:3f; Neh 8; Eph 3:10f), which he has done for no other people (see Deut 4:7f; Acts 14:16).

Ps 148 The exiles have returned home, the temple has been rebuilt, and its precincts have been restored. God has reestablished the people he loves. What a testament to his glory (vv. 13-14). Joy invades all hearts and expands to worldwide dimensions. The whole universe and all earthly creatures are invited to praise the Lord, the Creator and Redeemer. This theme also permeates the next two psalms, forming the conclusion and the synthesis of the Psalter.

We can pray this psalm to exhort all creation, both animate and inanimate, to praise the Triune God not only as the Creator but also as the Savior and Sanctifier. For although all creation is presently subject to vanity, it hopes to be freed from corruption so as to enter into the freedom of God's children, when God will transform the universe with a new heaven and a new earth (see Rom 8:19-22; Rev 21:1-5). May the angels and saints of heaven do likewise.

148:1-6 The psalmist calls upon all creatures in the heavens to praise the Lord because of his creative and redeeming acts.

2 Praise him, all his angels;
    offer praise to him, all his hosts!*r

3 Praise him, sun and moon;
    offer praise to him, all you shining stars!*
4 Praise him, you highest heavens,
    and you waters above the heavens.*

5 Let them praise the name* of the LORD,
    for it was at his command that they were
        created.s
6 He established them in place forever and ever;
    he issued a law that will never pass away.*

7 Praise the LORD from the earth,*
    you sea monsters and ocean depths,t
8 fire and hail, snow and clouds,
    storm winds that carry out his word,*
9 all mountains and hills,
    all fruit trees and cedars,u
10 wild animals and all cattle,
    creeping creatures and flying birds,*v
11 kings of the earth and all nations,
    princes and all rulers on the earth,
12 young men and women,
    the elderly as well as children.*

---

r Ps 103:20f; Job 38:7; Dan 3:58-63.—s Ps 33:9; Gen 1:3f; Jud 16:14; Jn
1:3, 10.—t 7-8: Pss 74:13-14; 103:20; 135:6; 147:15-18; Gen 1:21; Ex
9:18; Deut 33:13; Jos 10:11; Job 37:11f.—u Isa 44:23; 49:13; 55:12.—v Gen
1:21, 24f; Isa 43:20.

148:2 See Ps 103:20f; Job 38:7.
148:3 See note on Ps 65:13.
148:4 See Gen 1:6f; 1 Ki 8:27; 2 Cor 12:2; Eph 4:10. *Highest heavens:* literally,
"the heavens of the heavens," i.e., the space above the "expanse," which separated the "waters above" from the "waters below" (see Ps 104:3, 13; Gen 1:6f).
148:5 *Name:* see note on Ps 5:12.
148:6 See Jer 31:35f.
148:7-12 The psalmist now calls upon all creatures on earth to praise the
Lord: sea creatures, depths, the powers of nature, mountains and hills, fruit trees
and the cedars, animals and birds, and finally all human beings, including the
powerful as well as the young and old.
148:8 *Carry out his word:* i.e., "do his bidding" (see Ps 147:15).
148:10 See Gen 1:21, 24f; Isa 43:20.
148:12 See Jer 31:13.

¹³ Let them all praise the name of the LORD,*
　　for his name alone is exalted;
　　his majesty is above the earth and the
　　　heavens.*^w
¹⁴ He has raised high a horn* for his people,
　　to the glory of all his saints,
　　for the people of Israel who are close to
　　　him.

Alleluia.

PSALM 149*

Glorification of God, Lord and Creator

¹ Alleluia.

Sing* to the LORD a new song,*
　　his praise in the assembly of the saints.^x

---

w Pss 8:2; 30:5; 36:6; 71:19; 108:5; 113:2-4; 138:4; 145:5; 148:13; Deut 4:7.—x Pss 22:23; 26:12; 28:7; 35:18; 40:11; 96:1; 103:1; Jud 16:1; Rev 5:9.

148:13-14 The psalmist gives the reasons behind the praise: God is the exalted Ruler, who is not subject to the limitations of the earth or the heavens, and he has unique concern for his people, i.e., those devoted to him, his saints.
148:13 See Ps 108:5; 113:2-4.
148:14 *Horn:* i.e., the Lord's anointed (see note on Ps 18:3; see also Ps 2:2); it may also refer to the strength and power of God's people (see Ps 92:11; 1 Sam 2:1; Jer 48:25; Lam 2:17). *Saints:* see notes on Pss 4:3 and 34:10.
Ps 149 The spiritual elite of God's people rebuilt the walls of Jerusalem, weapons at the ready (see Neh 4:11); they put up an unyielding resistance to the persecution of Antiochus IV Epiphanes (see 1 Mac; 2 Mac). They were conscious of defending the rights of God and the right to worship him. This was their glory: Israel was the sword of God against the advance of blasphemous and wicked forces (see Zec 9:13-16). But the images of war foretell victories, those of God's elect over the forces of evil at the time of the Messiah. The seer of the Book of Revelation will also describe great battles in heaven (see Rev 11:14).
We can pray this psalm for the Church, the new People of God, enduring in this world an ever-difficult existence, an ever-renascent war. She scores blows and gains victories against her spiritual enemies, but never decisive ones. Happily, it is Christ who leads her and animates her in battle in order to ensure victory for her and renew her fervor (see Mt 16:18; 28:20).
149:1-5 The psalmist calls on the people to sing a new song in view of the restoration and the eschatological expectation of the Lord's complete victory over evil (see Isa 61:2ff; Rev 14:3). The object of praise is the Maker and King of his people, and the devout among them are the beneficiaries of his mighty acts.
149:1 *New song:* see note on Ps 33:3. *Saints:* see notes on Pss 4:3 and 34:10.

2 Let Israel rejoice in its Maker;
    let the children of Zion rejoice in their
        king.
3 Let them praise his name* with dancing
    and make music to him with tambourine
        and lyre.ʸ

4 For the LORD takes delight in his people,
    and he crowns the humble with salvation.*
5 Let the saints exult in their glory
    and sing for joy on their beds.*

6 May the praises of God be on their lips*
    and a double-edged sword in their hands*ᶻ
7 to wreak vengeance* on the nations
    and punishment on the peoples,ᵃ
8 to shackle their kings with chains
    and their nobles with iron fetters,
9 to execute the judgments decreed against
        them:*
    such is the glory for all his saints.

Alleluia.

---

y Pss 68:26; 81:2-3; 87:7; 150:3-4; Ex 15:20; 2 Sam 6:14; Jer 31:4.—z
Ps 66:17; Neh 4:10-12; 2 Mac 15:27.—a Num 31:3; Wis 3:8; Zec 9:13-16.

149:3 *Name:* see note on Ps 5:12. *Dancing:* which formed part of the liturgy (see Pss 87:7; 150:4; Ex 15:20; Jer 31:4).
149:4 See Ps 73:1; 1 Sam 2:8; Isa 49:13; 61:9; 62:4f.
149:5 *Beds:* the beds, which had before been soaked with tears, share in the Lord's deliverance (see Pss 4:5; 6:7; 63:7; Hos 7:14). Some take "beds" as "couches" used in worship or at banquets.
149:6-9 The psalmist envisages the eschatological future (see Isa 61:2ff) and presents God's people as the instruments of the divine vindication (see Zec 9:13-16). The Lord will grant victory to his people, as he did to Nehemiah and his men (see Neh 4:10-12), which will be their glory.
149:6 The godly will become the sword of the Lord (see Jdg 3:16; Prov 5:4; Zec 9:13). Some interpret this verse as saying that the praise of God is a fearsome but peaceful weapon in the hands of the godly (see 2 Chr 20:17ff).
149:7 *Vengeance:* see note on Ps 5:11 and introduction to Ps 35. The new People of God depends on the "sword of the Spirit" to combat the powers of evil (see 2 Cor 6:7; 10:4; Eph 6:12, 17; Heb 4:12) and will obtain complete victory only at the Last Judgment (see 1 Cor 6:2f).
149:9 Allusion to the prophecies against the nations, announcing their final defeat by Israel (see Ps 139:16 and note; Ezek 25:14; 39:10; Joel 4:2; Mic 4:13; Zec 10:5; 12:6; 14:3, 12ff).

PSALM 150*

Harmonious Praise of God

¹ Alleluia.

Praise God in his sanctuary;
    praise him in the firmament of his power.*ᵇ
² Praise him for his awesome acts,
    praise him for his immeasurable greatness.*ᶜ

³ Praise him with the sound of the trumpet,*
    praise him with the harp and lyre.ᵈ
⁴ Praise him with tambourines and dancing,
    praise him with strings and flutes.ᵉ

---

b Ps 102:20; Dan 3:53.—c Ex 15:7; Deut 3:24.—d 3ff: Pss 57:9; 81:3-4; 149:3; 2 Sam 6:5; 1 Chr 13:8; 16:5, 42; 2 Chr 5:12-13; 7:6.—e Ps 68:26; Ex 15:20.

Ps 150 In the same manner in which our "Glory be to the Father" concludes the recitation of our psalms, this doxological psalm concludes the Psalter on an urgent invitation to praise (see the conclusions to the first four books: Pss 41:14; 72:18f; 89:53; 106:48). May every living creature praise the Lord everywhere, on the part of everyone, and by every means. The word "Alleluia" or "Hallelujah" (translated as "Praise [or bless] the LORD" or "Praise [or bless] him") echoes thirteen times in this psalm. The Psalter could not end on a richer or more powerful note. Everything leads to the immensity of God's glory (see Rev 15:3-4; 19:4-8). "Then I heard every creature in heaven and on earth and under the earth and in the sea, and all that is in them, singing: 'To the One seated on the throne and to the Lamb be blessing and honor and glory and might forever and ever!'. . . Amen!" (Rev 5:13f).

We should heed this recommendation and carry it out, for we Christians are more aware than the psalmist of the work of God and Christ in the world and in us. Christ is enthroned in the highest heavens, his own sanctuary, but he is present and active in the heart of every creature, giving to each existence, motion, and life, as the case may be. He is in the heart of the whole world, directing its march in the material, living, human, and spiritual spheres and realizing his greatest victory in the last—the construction of the Church, his Body, his spiritual Spouse.

150:1 God is to be praised in his sanctuary on earth and his sanctuary in heaven (see Ps 8:3). The Church of the New Covenant has the mission to glorify God in the world, and her members must gather in the house of God in order to carry out this mission. *Firmament of his power:* this is also translated as "mighty heavens," which ensures the well-being of those on earth.

150:2 God is to be praised because of his creating and redeeming "awesome acts" (see Pss 106:2; 145:4, 12), which reveal his greatness (see Pss 145:3; 147:5; 1 Chr 29:11).

150:3-5 God is to be praised with a full orchestra (with trumpet, harp, lyre, and tambourine) and with dance in a liturgy of praise that will reach as high as the heavens.

⁵ Praise him with clanging cymbals,
   praise him with crashing cymbals.

⁶ Let everything that breathes
   offer praise to the LORD.*f*

Alleluia.*

---

f Ps 103:22; Rev 5:13.

150:6 God is to be praised by everyone and everything endowed with life by the Creator (see Pss 103:22; 148:7-12; Rev 5:13). By doing so, Christians will be following the "way" of the Lord, with which the Psalter began (see Ps 1:2), a way that leads to eternal life.

APPENDIX

INDEX OF SUNDAY RESPONSORIAL PSALMS

Year A

Year B

Year C

Major Feasts of the Year

TABLE OF PSALMS IN FOUR-WEEK PSALTER FOR MORNING AND EVENING PRAYER